STUDIES IN INDIAN THOUGHT

Studies in Indian Thought

Collected Papers of Prof. T.R.V. Murti

EDITED BY
Harold G. Coward

MOTILAL BANARSIDASS PUBLISHERS
PRIVATE LIMITED • DELHI

First Edition: Delhi, 1983
Reprint: Delhi, 1996

ISBN: 81-208-1310-3

Also available at:

MOTILAL BANARSIDASS
41 U.A. Bungalow Road, Jawahar Nagar, Delhi 110 007
8, Mahalaxmi Chamber, Warden Road, Mumbai 400 026
120 Royapettah High Road, Mylapore, Madras 600 004
Sanas Plaza, Subhash Nagar, Pune 411 002
16 St. Mark's Road, Bangalore 560 001
8 Camac Street, Calcutta 700 017
Ashok Rajpath, Patna 800 004
Chowk, Varanasi 221 001

PRINTED IN INDIA

BY JAINENDRA PRAKASH JAIN AT SHRI JAINENDRA PRESS,
A-45 NARAINA, PHASE I, NEW DELHI 110 028
AND PUBLISHED BY NARENDRA PRAKASH JAIN FOR
MOTILAL BANARSIDASS PUBLISHERS PRIVATE LIMITED,
BUNGALOW ROAD, DELHI 110 007

To My Revered Elder Brother

ŚRI T. R. GOVINDA RĀJA ŚARMĀ

CONTENTS

PREFACE

Professor T. R. V. Murti is best known to the English speaking world as a scholar of Buddhism. Indeed, his *The Central Philosophy of Buddhism* (George Allen and Unwin, 1960 & 1974) has become a classic in the field. But Professor Murti's scholarly contributions have also been significant in other areas such as Advaita Vedānta, Grammar and Contemporary Western Philosophy. Many of these articles are not widely known because they were originally published in Indian Journals which afterwards folded. The purpose of this book is to make available the best of these articles to a new generation of students of Indian thought. The articles included were selected by the editor in consultation with Professor Murti. An attempt was made to choose from the large number of Professor Murti's papers those which would best represent the range of his scholarship, and be of interest to today's students. Thanks are due to Mr. J. P. Jain of Motilal Banarsidass for his efforts in bringing out this volume, and to the University of Calgary for a grant which made the editing and preparation of these papers possible. The publication of the collected papers of Professor Murti is a fitting conclusion to his distinguished career as a dedicated teacher and a leading scholar in the field of Indian thought.

There is some amount of repetition in the articles on Buddhism, especially in *Radhakrishnan and Buddhism* and *The Metaphysical Schools of Buddhism.* As they occur in different orientation, these have been allowed to remain. Grateful thanks are due to Dr. Harsh Kumar of St. Stephens College, University of Delhi, and to Dr. G. P. Bhatt for reading the proofs and suggesting many emendations.

HAROLD COWARD
University of Calgary

ACADEMIC BIOGRAPHY OF PROF. T. R. V. MURTI*

by

Harold G. Coward

Tiruppattur Rameseshayyar Venkatachala Murti was born on the 15th of June, 1902, in a South Indian middle class Brāhmaṇa family. He was educated first at Tiruppattur and later at Tiruchhirapalli where early undergraduate study was undertaken at the then Bishop Heber College (Formerly S. P. G. College). His college studies were interrupted when at a young age he joined the nationalist movement started by Mahatma Gandhi. Part of the independence movement requirement was a boycott of colleges, courts and other public offices, as these were conducted under British auspices. Leaving college, he and his brother walked some one thousand and five hundred miles to North India, where Murti entered the second stage of his educational career. His one year stay at the Nationalist educational centre of Gurukul Kangri at Haridwar can be described as a period of apprenticeship for his subsequent Sanskritic studies.

After a gap of several years spent in the cause of Gandhi's Nationalist Movement (which included, among other things, being jailed for five months), Murti, in 1925, joined the Banaras Hindu University, the all-India Nationalist Movement University started by Pandit Madan Mohan Malaviya, one of the foremost Hindu nationalist leaders of the times. Banaras was the renowned seat of Hindu classical learning, providing a forum for top ranking scholars and teachers in fields of Sanskritic Studies and Sanskrit Grammar. This was especially true of the Banaras Sanskrit College. Banaras Hindu University, however, even though begun as a part of thc Nationalist Movement against the British, followed the traditional British style of university education with English as the medium of higher learning and research. The presence of both the Sanskrit College and the

*Reprinted from *Revelation in Indian Thought : a Festschrift in Honour of Professor T. R. V. Murti*, edited by Harold Coward and Krishna Sivaraman. Emeryville: Dharma Publishing, 1977.

Hindu University side by side in Banaras allowed Murti the unique and for him formative experience of simultaneously pursuing classical Sanskrit training and Western style University study—a pattern which he has continued to follow. In 1927 Murti received a B.A. with honours in Sanskrit and Philosophy from the Banaras Hindu University, and in 1929 an M.A., mainly in Western Philosophy. Also in 1929, from the Sanskrit College where he studied under such teachers as Balakrishna Misra, Kaliprasad Misra and Devanarayan Tiwari, Murti was awarded *Śāstri* (the classical Sanskrit equivalent to a B.A.) with specialization in Vedānta; in 1941 he was awarded *Āchārya* (the classical Sanskrit equivalent to an M.A.) with specialization in Vyākaraṇa or Grammar. All of the above degrees were achieved with 1st class standing. In 1948 the D.Litt. degree (the highest degree of Banaras Hindu University) was awarded to Professor Murti for his thesis entitled "The Mādhyamika Dialectic."

A unique aspect of the above survey of Murti's academic training is its dual character. Murti mastered the classical punditic system involving the studying of Sanskrit texts line by line—until great depths of understanding were reached—and then committing these texts—every inflection and every syllable—to memory. Not only were the basic texts thus learned, but also the important commentaries. Murti demonstrated equal excellence in the modern, Western system of education with its impulse toward critical examination and free exploration. Both these influences have been continuously present in Murti as a teacher and research scholar. His ability to achieve distinction in both Classical Indian and Modern Western scholarship, and his ability to bring these two traditions into academic dialogue, has helped to establish a model for a new generation of Indian scholarship. This dual background also qualified Professor Murti for important service on the "Sanskrit Commission" which was constituted during the period 1956-57 by the Indian Government to review the scope and future of Sanskrit *vis-a-vis* higher education in India.

Another landmark in Murti's career—of formative significance toward his role as the 'thinker' of Indian Philosophy—was his seven year stay, from 1929-36, at the Institute of Philosophy at Amalner, near Bombay. He was initially a Fellow and subsequently a member of the Faculty. The Institute was the only institution of its kind founded with the express object of promoting creative philosophical thinking in keeping with the spirit of Vedānta. The *Philosophical Quarterly* was its official organ; it was the only journal of its kind during the Thirties, Forties and the Fifties of this century which embodied original Indian philosophical writing. Many of Murti's writings appeared first in this journal. Murti has himself acknowledged the debt he owes to the Institute for furnishing him a good basic training for his vocation as a scholar. Contemporary Indian philosophers such as G. R. Malkani, Rashvihari Das, D. M. Datta and N. V. Banerjee were also associated with the Institute during Murti's stay. However, he was principally influenced by the original and profound Indian philosopher K. C. Bhattacharya. Murti has consistently acknowledged that K. C. Bhattacharya was the teacher who influenced him most, especially in the creative relating of classical German philosophy to the key issues of Advaita Vedānta. Murti's own later philosophical writings, quickened as they are by his first-hand acquaintance with Mahāyāna Buddhism, depart considerably from Bhattacharya's perspectives; yet, one can see continuity between the two especially in their interpretation of Advaita Vedānta, Sāṅkhya and Jaina systems of thought.

In 1936 Murti was appointed Assistant Professor of Philosophy in the Banaras Hindu University at the special initiative of its founder Paṇḍit Madan Mohan Malaviya, who saw in Murti the requisite potential for a regeneration of Indian Philosophy in keeping with both the Classical Sanskrit tradition and the stringent expectations of modern academia. Evidence that Murti lived up to this expectation is in the fact that he became the first Professor of Philosophy who was also completely at home in Sanskrit. Radhakrishnan, the great Indian philosopher and statesman, was then Vice-Chancellor of the University, and Murti had close intellectual contacts with him. Radhakrishnan continued to be his well-wisher and always extended his full support to Murti. It was Radhakrishnan's discovery of Murti as a major talent that was responsible for his introduction to the international audience. Murti deputized for Radhakrishnan as the Spalding Professor of Eastern Religions and Ethics at Oxford in 1949-50.

In 1949 Murti was invited to be the first Professor of Philosophy at the University of Ceylon. He had by then achieved recognition for his excellent scholarship in the area of Buddhism, and his three year stay at the University of Ceylon resulted in the inauguration of a full-fledged Department of Philosophy oriented towards Indian Philosophy and Buddhism.

At the special invitation of the then Vice-Chancellor of Banaras Hindu University, Murti returned to Banaras in 1953 and occupied the very prestigious Sayaji Rao Gaekwad chair as Professor of Indian Civilization and Culture, succeeding Radhakrishnan. During his eventful life as Professor at Banaras, he also held the following visiting appointments: Lecturer at the Hebrew University, Jerusalem, in 1958; Professor of Philosophy, Stanford and Yale Universities, 1960-61; and Professor of World Religions, Center for the Study of World Religions, Harvard University, 1963. In 1964 he attended, as a Panel Member, the 4th East-West Philosophers' Conference held at Honolulu, and in 1965 participated in the 11th Congress of the International Association for the History of Religions held at Claremont, California. In due recognition of his special expertise and international reputation, in 1962 Murti was appointed Vice-Chancellor of the Sanskrit University, Banaras.

Centers of Advanced Study in Philosophy were created in three University centers in India thanks to the happy circumstance that the President of India was the philosopher statesman Radhakrishnan. Murti was made Director of the Center at Banaras. In addition to this recognition from within academia, Murti was selected by the Government of India to receive the *Padma Bhushan* (award of Distinction).

The sincere concern to communicate the teachings of Indian Philosophy to the West, evident throughout Murti's career, reasserted itself following his retirement from Banaras Hindu University. In 1968 he was appointed Professor at both Brock and McMaster Universities in Canada. From 1969-72 he continued as Professor at McMaster University, Hamilton, Ontario.

With regard to scholarly publication, Murti has a distinguished record. His study of the Mādhyamika System entitled *The Central Philosophy of Buddhism*, first published in 1955 with a second edition in 1960, has achieved world-wide recognition as a standard and authoritative work on the subject. As Edward Conze put it in his review of the book, "The rare combination of philological accuracy with philosophical profundity and spiritual zest makes this one of the most outstanding publications on Buddhism which we have seen for some time."[1] Conze's assessment of Murti's book is not an isolated opinion but one which has been repeated by the leading Buddhist scholars from 1955 right up to the present. The *Central Philosophy of Buddhism* is certainly one of the most important philosophical books to come out of India in this century. In addition to this major book, Murti was joint author of another entitled *Ajñāna* on the theory of ignorance in Vedānta. He has also published some fortyfive articles in leading journals of philosophy throughout the world.

In more recent years Murti's interest has turned from Mādhyamika Buddhism and Vedānta to the topic of language in Indian philosophy. His article entitled "Some Thoughts on the Philosophy of Language in the Indian Context," first given as his Presidential Address at the 37th Session of the Indian Philosophical Congress in 1963, and recently published in the *Journal of Indian Philosophy*, has sparked a scholarly reassessment of the place of language in Indian thought—as evidenced in the essays by Sivaraman and Coward included in this volume. Murti's other area of important scholarly research is that of Advaita Vedānta. Perhaps his most important article in this regard is the paper entitled "Taṭastha and Svarūpa Lakṣaṇa of Brahman in Advaita" written for the K. C. Bhattacharya Memorial volume.

In addition to his own writing Murti has made significant editorial contributions. He was General Editor for the Darśana (Philosophy) Research Series and responsible for publishing some six volumes. In his capacity as Director of the Center of Advanced Study in Philosophy at Banaras, Murti inaugurated publication of the All-India Seminar Proceedings, which related to different themes of Indian Philosophy. In this regard he conducted systematic textual seminars analyzing difficult and often intractable Advaita Vedānta texts like *Vivaraṇa*, *Citsukhi* and *Advaita Siddhi*. He also continued to lead in the study of Bhartṛhari's writings and Kashmir Śaiva texts. As many as forty-five doctoral dissertations were written during this period under his immediate supervision; among them are

1. Edward Conze, "A Review of the Central Philosophy of Buddhism by T. R. V. Murti" in the *Journal of the Royal Asiatic Society*, April 1956.

many which have been acclaimed as major publications in Indian Philosophy. Many of his students are now professors of philosophy or religious studies in Indian and Western universities.

Those who were privileged to hear or study with Professor Murti know him to be a rare and gifted teacher. He can make archaic Sanskrit texts come alive from the musty corridors of time in which they are framed. Through his explanation and insight, the issues that these old texts grapple with are 'lifted' out of the past to speak powerfully to the problems of today. Through him one gains a respect for and understanding of tradition, not as static authoritative doctrine, but as the source from which flows a continuous stream of thought and culture. From him one also learns to be open to all philosophical viewpoints, and to make every effort to understand each position in its own terms.

Murti's relationship with his students was challenging, demanding and yet forgiving, loving, and supporting in a most intimate and indescribable way. He communicated an unspoken criterion of excellence which drove one never to be satisfied with anything less than the very best effort—and even then to realize the weakness and inadequacy in what was being presented. But this high requirement for academic excellence was never directed toward any shallow or surface intellectual achievement, its goal was always the student's own spiritual awakening and self-understanding. The student who came into contact with Professor Murti could have the rare experience of perceiving that such a forbidding challenge could also become a most exciting opportunity.

1. RISE OF THE PHILOSOPHICAL SCHOOLS*

THE PRINCIPAL TRADITIONS IN INDIAN PHILOSOPHY

The schools of Indian philosophy have sprung from two or rather three original sources or traditions. The Brāhmaṇical systems based on the Ātman doctrine of the Upaniṣads and the Buddhist schools on the *nairātmya* doctrine of Buddha conceive reality on two distinct and exclusive patterns. The Upaniṣads and the systems drawing their inspiration from them conceive reality on the pattern of an inner core or soul (*ātman*), immutable and identical amidst an outer region of impermanence and change to which it is unrelated or but loosely related. This may be termed the substance view of reality (*ātmavāda*). In its radical form, as in the Advaita Vedānta, it denies the reality of the apparent, the impermanent, and the many, and equates them with the false. The Sāṁkhya does not go so far; still it inclines more towards the substantial, the permanent, and the universal. The Nyāya with its empirical and pluralistic bias accords equal status to both substance and modes. Not only do these systems accept the *ātman*, but what is more, they conceive all other things too on the substance pattern. The *ātman* is the very pivot of their metaphysics, epistemology, and ethics. In epistemology, substance makes for unity and integration of experience; it explains perception, memory, and personal identity better than other assumptions. Bondage is ignorance of the self or the wrong identification of the self with the non-self (*ātmanyanātmādhyāsa*). Freedom is the discrimination between the two.

The other tradition is represented by the Buddhist denial of substance (*ātman*) and all that it implies. There is no inner and immutable core in things; everything is in flux. Existence for the Buddhist is momentary (*kṣaṇika*), unique (*svalakṣaṇa*), and unitary (*dharmamātra*). It is discontinuous, discrete, and devoid of complexity. Substance (the universal and identical)

*Reprinted from the *Cultural Heritage of India*, Vol. 3, Calcutta: Ramakrishna Mission, 1953.

is rejected as illusory; it is but a thought-construction made under the influence of wrong belief (*avidyā*). This may be taken as the modal view of reality. The Buddhists brought their epistemology and ethics into full accord with their *nairātmya* metaphysics. Their peculiar conception of perception and inference and the complementary doctrine of mental construction (*vikalpa*) are necessary consequences of their denial of substance. Heroic attempts have been made to fit in this theory with the doctrine of Karma and rebirth. *Avidyā*, which is the root-cause of pain, is the wrong belief in the *ātman* (*satkāya-dṛṣṭiprabhavāḥ sarve kleśāḥ*); and *prajñā* (wisdom) is the eradication of this belief and its attendant evils.

The terminology employed above is after the best Jaina epistemological treatises. Philosophical views, they say, are principally two—the *dravyārthika-naya* (substance view) and *paryāyārthika-naya* (modal view).[1] Each view, carried to the extreme, denies the reality of the other. One emphasizes the universal and the continuous to the exclusion of the changing and the different, and the other holds the opposite view. The Vedānta is cited as the exponent of the extreme form of the substance view;[2] and Buddhism (*tathāgatamata*) represents the exclusive modal view.[3]

The Jaina system ostensibly reconciles these two opposed views by according equal reality to substance and its modes. There is no substance without modes, nor are there modes without substance.[4] Reality is manifold (*anekāntātmaka*); it is not of one nature; it is unity and difference, universal and particular, and permanent and changing. The Jaina philosophy shaped its epistemology on this pattern and formulated the logic of the disjunction of the real (*syādvāda*). This view may be said to constitute the third stream of Indian philosophy, lying midway between the two extremes of the *ātmavāda* and the *anātmavāda*. Seemingly partaking of the nature of both, it was essentially

1. *Pramāṇa-naya-tattvāloka*, VII.5. 'Samāsatastu dvibhedo dravyārthikaḥ paryāyārthikaśca.' See also *Sammati-tarka*, *Gāthā*, 3.

2. *Pramāṇa-naya-tattvāloka*, VII.17-18.

3. *Ibid.*, VII.28, 30-31.

4. *Sammati-tarka*, Gāthā, 1. 'Dravyaṁ paryāyaviyuktaṁ paryāyā dravyavarjitāḥ; kva kadā kena kiṁrūpā dṛṣṭā mānena kena vā.' Cf. also the Jaina dictum, dravyaparyāyātmakaṁ vastu prameyam.

un-Brāhmaṇical and un-Buddhistic. It was un-Brāhmaṇical in that it accepted a *changing* Ātman and even ascribed different sizes to it; no Brāhmaṇical system could ever accept that. It was un-Buddhistic in that it accepted a permanent entity, *ātman*, besides change. As a result, the Jaina found favour with neither. The synthesis of two views is a third view, and is no substitute for either. The Jaina system had comparatively little influence on the course of Indian philosophy, and was little affected by other systems. Jainism has remained practically stationary down the ages.

Indian philosophy must therefore be interpreted as the flow of two vital streams—one having its source in the Ātman doctrine of the Upaniṣads and the other in the *anātmavāda* of Buddha. Each branched off into several sub-streams. There were lively sallies and skirmishes, but no commingling of the two streams. Throughout the course of their development they have remained true to their original inspirations. The Brāhmaṇical systems are wedded to Being, Buddhism to Becoming; the former espouse the existential and static view of reality, the latter the sequential and dynamic; for the one space, for the other time is the archetype. The Brāhmaṇical systems are relatively more categorical and positive in their attitude (*vidhimukhena*), while the Buddhists are more negative (*niṣedhamukhena*). Again, the former are more dogmatic and speculative, the latter empirical and critical. Subjectively minded, Buddhism is little interested in cosmological speculations and constructive explanations of the universe. The Brāhmaṇical systems are bound to an original tradition; they all accept the authoritarian character of the Vedas. Buddhism derives its inspiration from a criticism of experience itself. The tempo of development is quicker and intenser in Buddhism than in the Upaniṣadic tradition.

An opposite view has been advocated by a not inconsiderable section of the schools of Indian thought. They interpret Indian philosophy as having developed out of one tradition, the Upanisadic. Buddhism and Jainism are treated as deviations, rather than radical departures, from the *ātmavāda* of the Upaniṣads. This, however, ignores the sharp differences and exclusive attitudes inherent in these systems. Similarly it overlooks the internal differences within the fold of Buddhism, and considers it one unitary system instead of a matrix of many systems.

Nairātmyavāda is the genus of which the different Buddhist systems—the Vaibhāṣika, the Sautrāntika, the Mādhyamika, and the Yogācāra—are the species; they are the various attempts to express the same denial of substance.

The entire course of the development of Indian philosophy is proof of our contention. No Buddhist system did ever accept the reality of the Ātman, the permanent and the unchanging. No non-Buddhist system except the Cārvāka, on the contrary, could ever reject it as unreal.

It may be said that this state of affairs is true of the later scholastic phase of Buddhism, and not of the original teachings of its Master. Reliance may be placed on certain texts affirming the Ātman. But we have to consider, as against this, more numerous passages which deny the self in unmistakable terms. It will not do therefore to select those texts that favour a preconceived interpretation and to ignore the others. A systematic exegesis of the texts and a synthesis of the doctrines can alone prove fruitful. Such syntheses have been made by the Buddhist systems from time to time, notably by the Ābhidharmika, the Mādhyamika, and the Vijñānavāda systems. The modern exponent has to take these into account, as *prima facie* they claim to embody and express the origina l teachings In the case of Buddhism too, we must accept the law of evolution that the later phases are potentially contained in the earlier. The theory of a primitive soul-affirming Buddhism followed by a soul-denying scholasticism does not solve any problem; it adds one more. 'In the attempt of bridging the difference between the Upaniṣads and Buddha we would have immeasurably increased the distance between Buddha and Buddhism. Nor can we find any adequate reason for such a gross misunderstanding of Buddha by his followers.'

It may be said that the denial of the self is beset with such insuperable difficulties that it could not have been seriously maintained by any philosopher. The answer is that the doctrine of an entity, immutable and impervious to change (*ātmavāda*), is also beset with equally insuperable difficulties, though of an opposite kind. The Buddhist schools have made very consistent and commendable efforts to explain phenomena on their own hypothesis, as the Brāhmaṇical systems have on theirs, though in the opposite direction. The deep opposition between these radical standpoints stimulated the systems on either side; they gained in depth and maturity. It also helped the emergence of the dialectical consciousness, which we find in a systematic form in the Mādhyamika philosophy. Dialectic is the consciousness of the total and interminable conflict of the ideas of reason, of philosophical views. It presses towards their resolution in the Absolute which is the negation of the opposites (*advaita*, *advaya*). The Advaitic turn in the Buddhistic and Brāhmanical systems is a necessary outcome of this.

THE CLASSIFICATION OF THE SCHOOLS

It is customary to speak of the six orthodox and six heretical systems.[1] The Sāṁkhya, the Yoga, the Nyāya, the Vaiśeṣika, the Pūrva Mīmāṁsā, and the Vedānta (also called the Uttara Mīmāṁsā) constitute the former; the four classical schools of Buddhism (the Vaibhāṣika, the Sautrāntika, the Vijñānavāda, and the Mādhyamika), Jainism, and the Cārvāka make up the latter. This traditional enumeration errs by being at once too narrow and too wide; too narrow, as it does not include many other schools—the non-Advaitic schools of the Vedānta, the various Śaiva systems, the philosophy of language, etc. which are not mentioned at all. If the intention is to include the basic systems only, then it is too wide. For there are only three basic systems (the Sāṁkhya, the Nyāya-Vaiśeṣika, and the Advaita Vedānta) on the Brāhmaṇical side, and three (the Ābhidharmika, the Mādhyamika, and the Yogācāra) belonging to Buddhism. The Jaina may be taken as different from both these groups.

The Nyāya-Vaiśeṣika is a rigorous realism and pluralism. It advocates a mechanistic theory of causation, and is committed to the logic of difference rather than of identity between

1. Haribhadra's *Ṣaḍdarśana-samuccaya* deals with the Buddhist, Nyāya, Sāṁkhya, Jaina, Vaiśeṣika, and the Jaiminīya systems; it adds, however, that where Nyāya and Vaiśeṣika are treated as one system, Lokāyata is to be regarded as the sixth. *Sarva-darśana-saṅgraha* is a much fuller compendium. Besides the above, it expounds the Cārvāka, Rāmānuja, Mādhva, Nakuliśa-Pāśupata, Śaiva, Pratyabhijñā, Raseśvara, Pāṇinīya, and Pātañjala systems and ends with the statement that the author had already treated of Śaṅkara's system elsewhere. The *Sarva-darśana-kaumudī* and the *Sarva-siddhānta-sāra-saṅgraha* (ascribed to Śaṅkarācārya) are other short compendia.

substance and attribute, whole and parts, and so on. The Sāṁkhya-Yoga is a dualism, as it recognizes the ultimacy and exclusiveness of two realities—spirit and matter Emphasizing identity and continuity of cause and effect, it does not, however, rule out all difference and emergence. It may be said to advocate the logic of identity-in-difference or the organic conception of things. Though realistic, the Sāṁkhya is not rank realism comparable to the Nyāya. The Advaita Vedānta denies duality: spirit is the sole reality, and matter (*jaḍa*) is unreal. The Advaita conception of the transcendence of substance (*ātman*) is really the logic of pure identity; difference and change are illusory.

The Mīmāṁsā, as a school of realism, agrees with the Nyāya in its ontology; it has, however, some important differences in its epistemology. The Śaiva and the Vaiṣṇava schools very largely adopt the Sāṁkhya and in some cases, the Vaiśeṣika categories within a theistic framework; they are a blend of religion and philosophy.

Though all Buddhist schools rejected the reality of substance (*pudgala-nairātmya*) and were thus subjective and critically minded, in the earliest realistic phase this was interpreted in such a way as to retain the reality of the separate elements (*dharmas*). The Theravāda and the Sarvāstivāda (the Vaibhāṣika) are the chief exponents of this dogmatic pluralistic phase. The Sautrāntika is a critical edition of this realism. The Mādhyamika philosophy (*c.* second century A.D.) represents the central and second phase of Buddhism. It denied the reality of the separate elements too (*dharma-nairātmya*), and established a critical absolutism through the dialectic. The Yogācāra is absolutist idealism; criticizing the Mādhyamika, it identifies the Absolute with Consciousness (*vijñāna*) and rejects the reality of the object.

This division of Buddhist thought into the realistic, the absolutistic, and the idealistic schools and phases is in full accord not only with its logical and chronological development, but also with the testimony of the historians[1] of Buddhism.

As an eclecticism or synthesis of all view-points, the Jaina system may not be treated as a basic philosophy. But a combi-

1. Buston's *History of Buddhism* (trans. by Obermiller), II, pp. 52-54.

nation of views introduces a new pattern and implies a different view which is distinct from the components taken singly. Reality for the Jaina is not merely many, but manifold (*anekānta*); the formulation of it in thought is therefore manifold (Syādvāda, *sapta-bhaṅgi-naya*). The Jaina cannot therefore subscribe to the logic of either pure identity or difference, but accepts a disjunction of all modes.

STAGES IN THE FORMATION OF THE SCHOOLS

Every system of Indian philosophy has passed through three or four well-defined stages of development. A seer or a great man of insight gives utterance to his intimate vision of Reality. This is the *mūla mantra*, the original inspiration, which initiates a new path and is the basis of a new philosophy. The second stage consists in defining and systematizing the suggestions in aphoristic (*sūtra* or *kārikā*) form; a philosophical system is thus formulated. Then there is further elaboration—drawing implications, application of experience to details, removing discrepancies, etc. A further stage is reached when the systems indulge in the criticism and refutation of other systems to strengthen their own position. Doctrinally, the stages are suggestive, systematic, and scholastic; from the literary point of view, they are canonical, *sūtra* (*śāstra*), and *ṭikā* stages.

Centuries of gestation and fermentation must have preceded the systematization of the doctrines of a school in the *sūtra* form. The very ease with which the doctrines are formulated leads to this conclusion. We have direct evidence of a succession of teachers in the case of the Vedānta, the Mīmāṁsā, and the Sāṁkhya. The classical schools of Buddhism attained their present form as a result of the agelong disputation and discussion among the numerous Buddhist sects and schools.

The *sūtras* are mnemonic aids, and could never have been meant to be taken by themselves; some sort of oral exegesis must have always accompanied them. This points to the propagation of the doctrines among specific circles and also to a continuity of tradition. The *sūtrakāras* are in most cases the final redactors rather than the authors of the systems.

Two aspects of the exegesis (*bhāṣya*) may be discerned; discussion on points of issue (*vārttika*) and explanation or elaboration (*bhāṣya* proper). Some of the *bhāṣyas* (e.g. the *Nyāya-*

bhāṣya) still retain traces of this. The commentaries on each *sūtra* which have come down to us must be taken as the crystallization, in their final form, of these agelong discussions and elaborations so essential to make up a complete and coherent system. The *ṭikās* (sub-commentary or gloss) pay attention to minute details and revel in subtlety. Theoretically, there is no conceivable end to this process, and *tikās* on the various *bhāṣyas* still continue to be written.

Polemic (*parapakṣanirākaraṇa*) is also an integral part of each system. It is evidence of the maturity not merely of one system, but of several contemporary ones from which it is differentiated. In spite of the heroic language used, polemic does not mean that rival systems are refuted out of existence; they are only differentiated from each other. Confusion of standpoints is warded off, and clarity results. Very often, criticism is employed against sub-schools and undesirable trends within a system in order to stabilize a standard view. All these aspects are exemplified in each system. Philosophical schools have attained their fullness because of criticism and opposition.

THE AGE OF THE DARŚANAS

The dates of the systems are still very largely conjectural. The problem is complicated by the fact that the *sūtras*, which form the basis of a system of philosophy, are not unitary works. With regard to many of them,[1] e.g. the *Brahma-Sūtra*, the *Nyāya-Sūtra*, and the *Yoga-Sūtra*, it has been shown with some plausibility that they are of multiple authorship and therefore belong to different periods of time. No one date can therefore be assigned to the origin of a system. Regarding the reputed originators of the systems, the traditional account is scanty and legendary. Kapila, the founder of the Sāṁkhya, is quite a mythical figure; Patañjali's identification with the author of the *Mahābhāṣya* is not generally accepted; Kaṇāda and Akṣapāda are nicknames; Gautama and Bādarāyaṇa are family appellations; and we know next to nothing of Jaimini. With regard

1. See Belvalkar, 'The Multiple Authorship of the *Vedānta-Sūtras*', *The Indian Philosophical Review*, II.2, pp. 141-154; see also his *Sreegopal Basu Mullick Fellowship Lectures*, Lecture IV. Vidyabhushan, *History of Indian Logic*, pp. 49-50. Dasgupta, *A History of Indian Philosophy*, I, p. 230.

to the Buddhist systems we are by no means in a better position. Max Walleser observes about Nāgārjuna thus: 'It has to be agreed that even today, an exact fixing of Nāgārjuna's lifetime must remain entirely doubtful having regard to the contradictory sources of the tradition, always supposing that a writer of this name existed at all.'[1] The historicity of Maitreyanātha,[2] the founder of the Yogācāra school, is just beginning to be accepted.

This is hardly the place to discuss the particular problems regarding the date and life of the founders of the schools. What can be attempted with regard to the rise of the philosophical schools in general is mainly this. It is possible to fix with a reasonable measure of certainty the higher and the lower time-limit of the age of the *darśanas* and to determine an order of priority among them.

The *terminus a quo* is supplied by the references to what might be construed as the beginnings of the classical schools in some of the older dialogues of Buddha (sixth-fifth century B.C.) and the Jaina canons (especially the *Sūtrakṛtāṅga* and *Bhagavatī-Sūtra*). In the *Brahmajāla-Sutta, Sāmaññaphala-Sutta,* and elsewhere we find again and again short and stereotyped sketches of the six *tithiyas* (heretics) We find in them the beginnings[3] of the Cārvāka (Ajita Keśakambala), the Sāṁkhya (Pūraṇa Kassapa), the Vaiśeṣika (Pakudha Kaccāyana), the Jaina (Niganṭha Nātaputta), the Ājīvaka (Makkhali Gosāla), and dialectical scepticism (Sañjaya Belaṭṭhiputta). As in both the Buddhist and the Jaina canons the interest is in moral consciousness, they characterize the other systems as species of *akriyāvāda* (inaction). We have meagre information about their metaphysical tenets. It is, however, certain that the Brāhmaṇical systems, including the Sāṁkhya, were just beginning to get into shape.

The *terminus ad quem* is provided by the pointed references to well-known Buddhist doctrines and schools in the *Brahma-Sūtra*, the *Nyāya-Sūtra*, etc. Allowing about two or three centuries

1. *Life of Nāgārjuna*, p. 6.

2. See G. Tucci, *On Some Aspects of the Doctrines of Maitreya* [*nātha*] *and Asaṅga*, pp. 2ff.

3. For a very suggestive and full exposition of these philosophers, see Dr. Barua's *Pre-Buddhistic Indian Philosophy*.

for the evolution of thought, we cannot be grossly wrong if we put the emergence of the systems, in almost their present form, in the second century B.C.; the process must be deemed to have been complete by the end of the third century A.D. if not a little earlier.

Jacobi, who has made a special study of the subject, says: 'The results of our researches into the age of the philosophical *Sūtras* may be summarized as follows: *Nyāya-Darśana* and *Brahma-Sūtra* were composed between A.D. 200 and 450. During that period lived the old commentators: Vātsyāyana, Upavarṣa, the Vārttikakāra (Bodhāyana), and probably Śabara Svāmin. The *Vaiśeṣika-Darśana* and the *Mīmāṁsā-Sūtra* are about as old, or rather somewhat older than the *Nyāya-Darśana* and the *Brahma-Sūtra*. The *Yoga-Sūtra* is later than A.D. 450, and the *Sāṁkhya-Sūtra* is a modern composition.'[1] Jacobi bases his argument on the contention that the references to Buddhist doctrines in the *Nyāya-Sūtra* and the *Brahma-Sūtra* are to the Śūnyavāda and not to the Vijñānavāda. Hence, they are posterior to Nāgārjuna (A.D. 150), but prior to Asaṅga (A.D. 350) The argument is not very conclusive, because Nāgārjuna's date[2] itself is not fixed with absolute certainty. The Śūnyavāda is much older than Nāgārjuna, and hence reference to it does not necessarily mean posteriority to him. In his *Vigrahavyāvartanī*, Nāgārjuna makes distinct references to the Nyāya objections.[3]

It must never be forgotten with regard to the Indian systems that they have all along been developing side by side, and cross references are quite natural. The argument is also inconclusive, because of the possibility of multiple authorship and stratification in the case of the basic *sūtras*.

The consensus of opinion among scholars now is in favour of accepting a somewhat earlier date for the *darśanas*. We may assign them to the period covering a century and a half before

1. *Journal of the American Oriental Society*, XXXI, p. 29, 'The Dates of the Philosophical *Sūtras* of the Brāhmaṇs'.

2. 'It is a good working hypothesis, though nothing more, that he lived in the latter half of the second century A.D.' Winternitz, *History of Indian Literature*, II, p. 342.

3. *Vigrahavyāvartanī*, I.1-6 and 20. The Yogācāra view is attacked in the *Brahma-Sūtra*, II.2.27-29 (Rāmānuja) or II.2.28-31 (Śaṅkara) and the Mādhyamika in II.2.30 (Rāmānuja) or II.2.31 (Śaṅkara).

and roughly two centuries after the Christian era. It is not possible, in the present state of our knowledge, to assign a more exact date.

The above discussion should also help us to fix the relative priority of the systems. The Sāṁkhya is admitted on all hands to be the oldest system; it is even pre-Buddhistic in its origin, if not in its final form. This is the dominant philosophy of the epic period. That all other systems, including the Buddhistic schools, have arisen as a criticism of the Sāṁkhya, and that the Sāṁkhya itself does not show the influence of other systems, is sufficient proof of its early formulation. The *Vaiśeṣika-Sūtra* is next to the Sāṁkhya only. Buddhist doctrines are not directly referred to in this. Its theory of knowledge, especially the doctrine of *anumāna* (inference), is less developed than that of the Nyāya; its language and terminology also clearly point to an older period. All these considerations apply to the *Mīmāṁsā-Sūtra* also. Next in order come the *Nyāya-Darśana* and the *Brahma-Sūtra*, and last of all the *Yoga-Sūtra*.

THE DEVELOPMENT OF THE SYSTEMS

The ideological development of the philosophical systems is of greater interest than their chronological sequence. A general outline of this development may be indicated.

The Sāṁkhya grew as the first synthesis, on a rationalistic basis, of the Upaniṣads. There are two chief tenets of the Upaniṣads: the immutability and purity of the self (Ātman), and the creation of the world from the self which was taken as the sole reality. To the Sāṁkhya, it appeared axiomatic that what changes cannot be conscious, and what is conscious cannot change. It therefore tried to remove the apparent contradiction in the Upaniṣads by sacrificing the sole reality of *ātman*, and by bifurcating the real into two—the real as changing (*pariṇāmi-nitya*) and the real as unchanging (*kūṭastha-nitya*). Nothing is common to both of them; they thoroughly exclude each other. In calling them both real we are, however, using a common measure. Causation for the Sāṁkhya is self-becoming and is a continuous movement. And though it emphasizes the identity aspect of things, it does not rule out difference. In a rigorous formulation of the real, this has to be eschewed. The real cannot be heterogeneous or composite.

Prakṛti is independently real, as real as Puruṣa, and in that sense, it can be called a 'self' existing by itself. Prakṛti exists and acts by itself but is not *for* itself; the value of its existence is for another (*saṅghāta-parārthatvāt*). The Sāṁkhya would not go to the extent of asserting that Prakṛti would exist even if there were no Puruṣa. The *raison d'être* of Prakṛti's existence and activity is the satisfaction of the needs of Puruṣa. Not only is the real bifurcated into two, but even in Prakṛti's nature there is the bifurcation of existence and value.

The Sāṁkhya position is inherently unstable. In it there are elements which are mutually conflicting. This arises because of the adoption of two patterns of the real (*puruṣa* and *prakṛti*). And this in turn necessitates the sundering of existence and value and the admission of identity and difference as equally real. Criticism, as the drive towards rigour and consistency, can take either of the two directions. If change and impermanence are the sole pattern of reality, then *puruṣa* (self) must be replaced by the states of the *buddhi* (mind), and change itself must be construed as the momentary flashing of things into existence and their subsidence. For, the acceptance of an *abiding* entity (*prakṛti*) which *changes*, introduces heterogeneity into the structure of the real; it partakes of the substance and modal views at once. If change is to be accepted as real, the permanent element must be discarded as unreal. This is exactly what Buddhism does when it explains all things on one single pattern of impermanence and non-substantiality.

The other direction in which the Sāṁkhya could be given consistency is to deny change and impermanence; it is to take Puruṣa (spirit) as the norm of the real. This would tend to monism, and in its rigorous form, to the absolutism of the Vedānta, by the rejection of difference and change as illusory. An intermediate standpoint is that of the Vaiśeṣika which accepts the changing and the permanent, and not the changing permanent, as real. The Sāṁkhya holds that the permanent (*prakṛti*) itself changes; for the Vaiśeṣika, the permanent, viz. the atoms (the ultimate parts of things) and the other substances like *ātman*, *kāla*, *diś*, and *ākāśa*, do not change at all, but a new thing is produced *in* them when they are brought together. The same mechanical conception underlies the Vaiśeṣika notions of substance and attribute, whole and parts, etc.

In the Sāṁkhya there are idealistic and realistic trends in an ununified state. *Prakṛti* exists only for the *puruṣa,* though it does not owe its existence and activity to the latter. It rightly holds that empirical existence is conditioned by the wrong identification of spirit and object; but it has not much justification for holding that *prakṛti* will not be affected if this wrong identification ceases on the attainment of knowledge. Consistency would demand that one or the other should be made exclusively real: either spirit is all and the object is an appearance, or everything is object, the spirit itself being conceived as an object (*jaḍa*). The first is the position of the Advaita Vedānta, and the second is that of the Nyāya-Vaiśeṣika realism, which objectifies everything (*viṣaya*) and converts the Sāṁkhya dualism into pluralism.

There were several stages in the attainment of the final form in the Vedānta. From the Sāṁkhya dualism we have first the establishment of the monism of the older Vedānta and then of the Advaitism of Śaṅkara. The older Vedānta of the *sūtrakāra* Bādarāyaṇa and his pre-Śaṅkara commentators criticized the dualism of the Sāṁkhya, but generally accepted the modification (*pariṇāma*)[1] of Brahman. They did not perceive any contradiction in conceiving Brahman as both unity and difference.

It was left to Gauḍapāda and his illustrious successor Śaṅkara to revolutionize the Vedānta by introducing the theory of *vivarta* (appearance), by a searching criticism of the earlier *brahma-pariṇāmavāda* and asserting Advaitism as the true teaching of the Upaniṣads. This development, which was a turning point in the history of Indian philosophy, was brought about by two sets of influences; one, the drive towards self-consistency which was at work in the older Vedānta too, and the other, the adoption of the technique (dialectical method) already perfected by the Mādhyamika and also used by the Vijñānavāda. We have definite evidence of this influence in Gauḍapāda, though in Śaṅkara the traces are almost obliterated. There was, however, an adoption of the technique of the Mādhyamika dialectic, and not the borrowing of its tenets. Influence is not necessarily

1. The fact that the *Brahma-Sūtra* finds it necessary to controvert, at several places, the Sāṁkhya interpretation of the Upaniṣadic doctrines means that it was a rival in the field of the Upaniṣadic exegesis.

acceptance or borrowing of doctrines. That too is influence which stimulates the systems to modify, revise, or even reaffirm their doctrines. Influence may be expressed through opposition as well as by acceptance. In this sense alone have the Brāhmaṇical systems, the Vedānta and the Nyāya, been influenced by Buddhism.

The Nyāya-Vaiśeṣika system, as it emerged at the end of its long-sustained duel with the Buddhist systems, very rigorously established the objectivity of relation (*samavāya*), of the whole (*avayavin*), of the universal (*sāmānya*), and even of non-existence (*abhāva*). It minimized and even denied the work of thought. It objectified and externalized all thought-forms, and put them up as categories of the object. In order to realize the truth of this, one has to look into the polemic found in the works of Vātsyāyana, Uddyotakara, Vācaspati Miśra, Jayanta, Udayana, Śrīdhara, and a host of others. The Nyāya brought its ontology and epistemology into full accord with its basic principle or assumption by resisting the subjectivistic and critical attitude of the Buddhist schools all along the line.

An almost analogous and parallel development obtained within the Anātma tradition (Buddhism). Like the Sāṁkhya on the Upaniṣadic side, the first attempt to synthesize the teachings of Buddha was the Ābhidharmika system. We may comprise under this the Theravāda as well as the Sarvāstivāda. Internal evidence within the Mahāyāna systems and historical evidence unmistakably point to the Sarvāstivāda as the matrix from which the Buddhist systems developed as departures and deviations. The Ābhidharmika system is analogous to the Sāṁkhya in a more vital sense We may consider its *dharmas* (the Skandhavāda) as the Buddhistic version of the Sāṁkhya conception of *prakṛti* and *puruṣa*. The inadequacy and inconsistency of the Ābhidharma system—the theory of elements—led to the Mādhyamika dialectic.

The tempo of development was intenser and quicker in the Anātma tradition. Schools and sub-schools multiplied rapidly, and in the welter of ideas Mahāyāna was born. It was a revolution in Buddhism, but was in a sense the reaffirming of the oldest and central teaching of Buddha. Here too two influences may be seen at work. The one is the passion for consistency; the very dynamism of the *nairātmyavāda* must have made the realist phase (the theory of the elements) seem just a step. Then there was the Sāṁkhya and probably the other systems which conceived reality from a totally different standpoint. The difficulties in each standpoint with regard to philosophical problems were there as ever. This must have led an acute and sensitive mind to reflect that the fault lay not in this or that system; there was something fundamentally wrong about the constitution of reason itself. Kant was led, in similar circumstances, when faced with the impasse created by rationalism and empiricism, to examine the claims of reason in his *Critique of Pure Reason*. We have reason to think that the opposition in philosophy created by the Sāṁkhya and the Vedānta on the one hand and the Ābhidharmika philosophy on the other was much more total and basic than that between rationalism and empiricism. Reflective criticism was inevitable. The Mādhyamika dialectic is the expression of this.

'The basic ideas of the Mādhyamika system—the Absolute as devoid of empirical determinations, the falsity of appearance, and the distinction between the ultimate and phenomena—were accepted. There was, however, a reaction against what appeared to some as its extreme and unqualified rejection of phenomena. The idealism of the Yogācāra (Vijñānavāda) school is to be understood as a significant modification of the Mādhyamika negativism (*śūnyavāda*). It contends that the sole reality of consciousness cannot be denied, while the duality of subject and object with which it is apparently infected must be considered non-existent (*śūnya*); the duality is unreal; but *that*, where the negation of duality (*dvaya-śūnyatā*) obtains, *does exist*; it is not nothing (*śūnya*).'

The critical philosophy of Kant led to the idealistic systems of Fichte, Schelling, and Hegel in the West; here, too, the Yogācāra idealism follows as a direct outcome of the Mādhyamika. This is the third great phase of Buddhism.'

Tāntricism (Vajrayāna, Mantrayāna, etc.) supervened on the Vijñānavāda. Tāntricism is a unique combination of *mantra*, ritual, and worship on an absolutistic basis; it is both religion and philosophy. It was especially this phase of Buddhism that was propagated in Tibet when it disappeared from India.'[1]

1. Quoted from the writer's article on the 'Schools of Buddhism' in *Philosophy—Eastern and Western*.

There was a corresponding Tāntric phase on the Brāhmaṇic side too. The necessary ingredients of the Tantra—*mantra*, ritual, and worship—are already present in the *Ṛk-* and the *Atharva-Saṁhitās* and the Brāhmanas. What it needed was a philosophic basis. And when absolutism and the theory of emanation (*śaktivāda*) were developed, Tāntricism was established. It is found either by itself or as a complementary part of the absolutist and non-absolutist systems, especially of the Śaiva schools. There is, however, no doubt that this phase was the outcome of the Buddhist influence.[1]

A word may be said about the religio-philosophical schools which were systematized in the post-Śaṅkara period. These fall under two main groups; the Śaiva (including the Śākta) and the Vaiṣṇava schools. We have definite evidence regarding their great antiquity and widespread character; though systematized later than the classical-schools of philosophy, they have been cultivated as cults and groups for centuries. They derive their inspiration from the religious strain found not only in the *Ṛg-Veda*, the Upaniṣads, and the *Bhagavad-Gītā*, but also from the canonical sources, variously called the *āgamas* (Śaiva) and the *saṁhitās* (Vaiṣṇava). The lives and inspired utterances of the saints (Śaiva Nāyanārs and Vaiṣṇava Āḷvārs) have impressed these systems with a religious stamp. They emphasize devotion and self-surrender to God as necessary means to salvation; they are thus, implicitly or otherwise, opposed to the doctrine of knowledge as the sole means to liberation (*mukti*) All of them formulate their systems as a vehement protest against absolutism—the impersonality of the Highest; they all affirm the reality and individuality of the finite selves (*jivas*). Though these systems incorporate philosophical elements, their main interest is religious. As such, they may rightly be regarded as schools of theology rather than of philosophy.

1. See Dr. B. Bhattacharya's *Esoteric Buddhism*, p. 163: 'It is thus amply proved that the Buddhist Tantras greatly influenced the Hindu Tāntric Literature.'

2.1 KNOWING, FEELING AND WILLING AS FUNCTIONS OF CONSCIOUSNESS*

An attempt is made in this paper[1] to lay the foundations of an *a priori* or transcendental psychology—to use a more ambitious title. Our task is to fix the precise meaning of the terms Knowledge, Feeling and Will and their sub-forms, and also to show the sense in which every mental state can be said to involve all the three forms.

There may be some thinkers who might consider excursions into psychology as of no value or at least as having no relevance to epistemology or metaphysics; because such enquiries are not calculated to determine the ultimate nature of things. This is clearly a mistake. For, when we employ such concepts and terms as perception, memory, judgment, feeling, willing, etc. we would then be uncritically accepting what certain psychologists have said about them. But such a use of these terms may not be in accord with our metaphysics. In fact, just as an uncritical and realistic view of our knowledge of objects is unacceptable, so we should discount an account of our mental functions that is not explicitly epistemological. There is thus the need for bringing our psychology into accord with our epistemology. Rather, the contention is that psychology, if it is to be of any significance for philosophy and not merely be of literary value, has to be merged into epistemology; it should not be, as it is at present, a superficial description of what appears to untutored introspection. As such, our enquiry sets itself against the commonly received notion about the infallibility of psychological introspection or the deliverances of the inner sense. We have just to appeal to introspection to determine the nature of our states, it may be said; and being a direct and immediate awareness, there can be no illusion. One can easily have illusions about external objects; but the possibility of their occurrence with regard to mental states is hardly conceivable.

*Reprinted from the *Philosophical Quarterly*, January, 1934.

1. I am deeply indebted to Professor K. C. Bhattacharyya for his lectures on the subject-matter of this paper delivered at the Institute.

Our contention, however, is that the deliverances of the inner sense are as much fallible and misleading as those of the outer senses; no special privilege can be claimed for them. It is only our habitual attitude of distraction that prevents us from realising this fact. Some grounds for this contention will be adduced later on. To distinguish our psychology from the one that relies too much and too readily on introspection, and from all forms of "behaviourism," which denies introspection only to reduce conscious functions to certain "reflexes" and their compounds, we call it *a priori* or transcendental.

I

Beginning with an *a priori* scheme we shall try to justify it by an appeal to experience. We start with two entities—consciousness and content. Content can be understood as the object in any sense, the presented something. We need not, at this stage, enter into the discussion whether it is a physical object or merely a thought-content, or even an image. It is something basic to all—a presentation. Nor should any question about the reality or unreality of the object be allowed to engage us at present. The object may thus be understood; but what is consciousness in general which is not knowing, feeling or willing, it might be asked. We can however take it as attention which is basic to all the three; attention is the factor which distinguishes conscious from unconscious existence. Knowing, Feeling and Willing may be conceived, *prima facie*, as modes of attending to the object, as modes of relation of attention to object. The relation itself is to be conceived as one of determination. In this scheme, 'determination of one entity by the other or by both' is taken as the fundamental meaning and type of relation between two entities For, relation of one entity with another actualises or limits the capabilities of either, at least their possible relationships. The one may be said to be defined or determined by the other and *vice versa*.

There can be three sets of relat on between consciousness and content : one in which the content determines the mode of attention; attention is, as it were, entirely lost in the object, and not *vice versa*; or second in which consciousness determines the content and not *vice versa*; or that in which the determination is either way. If the third alternative is not to be a mere repetition of the former two, it must mean that attention and consciousness mutually determine each other, *i.e.*, their determination is not separately distinguishable; the whole thing is indeterminate. Fourthly, it might be thought that neither determines the other; the two things are separate and unconnected. But this is clearly tantamount to denying all relation; the two things fall asunder, and we cannot even speak of them as two. This is pure agnosticism. Our *a priori* scheme has thus really yielded only three modes of relation between consciousness and content. And these can be identified with Knowing, Willing and Feeling respectively.

II

The notions of truth and falsity imply that knowledge is a mode of consciousness which is, or should be, determined solely by the object.[1] Consciousness or the subject must merely reveal or discover the object neither adding anything to it nor distorting it. To be discovered, the object of knowledge should exist prior to and independent of the knowing; it must be an accomplished fact—a *siddha vastu*—, one that is not brought into being through the knowing. If it were simultaneous with knowledge or were created by it, how can any knowledge be true or false? The perception of the "rope-snake" would not be an illusion and would not be recognised as such any time, if the rope were not conceived as existing both during and before the illusion; it must be something absolutely independent of our knowing of it. Once this is granted that the object of knowledge should exist prior to it, we cannot also assign any period or limit to its priority. For, to do any such thing, we have to reach a stage when consciousness alone existed and the object was ushered into being later on, presumably by the former. It is evident that such a consciousness is not knowledge; it is will. However far back we may trace our knowledge, it will always presuppose the object as something prior to it. This priority is not primarily temporal, but only signifies the accomplished character of the object.

1. cf. "jñānaṁ tu pramāṇajanyaṁ, pramāṇaṁ ca yathābhūtavastuviṣayam ato jñānaṁ kartum akartum anyathā vā kartum aśakyaṁ *kevalaṁ vastutantram eva tat*, na codanātantraṁ nāpi puruṣatantram." *Śaṅkara's Bhāṣya* on the *Br. Sūtr.* 1, i. 4, "na vastu yāthātmya-jñānaṁ puruṣabuddhyapekṣaṁ, kiṁ tarhi, *vastutantram eva tat*", *Ibid.*, 1, i. 2.

Similar considerations require that the object of knowledge should not be subject to the accidental conditions of the percipient. To take the example of perspectives. If a certain object were to be known from a certain position at a certain time and by a certain person only, we cannot call that object real, nor that knowledge true. For, we have absolutely no means of deciding whether the object is not our creation or a joint product of the conditions of the percipient and those of the object. Thus the object of knowledge cannot be particular; it must be universal, free from all conditions. And if this were pushed further, it would mean that strictly speaking only pure Being can be said to be the object *par excellence*.

Not only is the object to be independent of knowledge, but we have also to regard the object as not requiring its being known by any consciousness not even the possibility of such in the last resort. When we know an object we need not at once be conscious of this very knowing. For, the object, which alone should determine the nature of consciousness in knowledge, says nothing about its present knownness or past unknownness. A self-conscious knowing is possible, as will be shown later, through its complication with will.

The above contentions about the ideal of knowledge run counter to the commonly received principle of idealism that the object is mind-dependent in some way or the other. But all arguments of idealism, *e.g.* those of Berkeley and Hegel, rely upon feeling and will and misapply them to knowledge. The knowledge-absolutist agrees with the realist and with Kant, as against the idealist, that the object of knowledge is, or should be, independent of the knowing consciousness. There is profound disagreement, however, with realism in another respect; the realist uncritically believes that what is ordinarily given is knowledge. The *a priori* psychology adumbrated here holds with Kant, that knowledge as we generally understand is invariably mixed up with other functions; much of what passes off as knowledge is feeling and imagination (will) especially. There is thus a call to purify the given to arrive at what is really known. This comes to mean that what passes for knowledge is illusory, phenomenal. Knowledge-illusion is possible through the complication, in varying degrees, of knowledge with feeling and will; the latter are mistaken for knowledge. And it is the peculiar feature of transcendental psychology to justify this contention by showing the complication and the resolution of the functions.

III

We take the second kind of relation between consciousness and content, namely that in which the former determines the latter. This can be identified with willing. Willing is to be defined as the consciousness of a content that is brought into being *through* the willing; the content is consciously felt to have had no being apart from the willing of it; it is *as* we will it, neither before nor after the willing. The content is conditioned and determined wholly by consciousness. This definition of will is satisfied with regard to our activity in the physical and psychic spheres. When we will any action, *e.g.* a certain changed position of our limbs, we are at once conscious that the object of our will is not an existent fact, which we could have come across in the natural course of things—that would precisely be Knowing—but as one about which there is the consciousness of our *freedom* in bringing it about, alter or even abandon it.[1] The same attitude is illustrated in pure imagination or conscious dreaming. Pure imagination is to be distinguished from reproductive imagination or memory and from hypothesis—all of which is in the service of knowledge. In these, we recur to a fact already known, accomplished. Pure imagination creates and shapes its object. The difference between the two is analogous to the difference between history and story. Construction or imagination may be necessary in history too, but such imagination is strictly subordinated to the accomplished facts.

In contradistinction to knowing which is surrender to the object, willing is just the reverse. If truth be the ideal of knowledge, freedom is the ideal of will. There is also another difference. When we know an object there is not at once the knowledge that we know it, or even that we were not knowing it before, for we have, in knowledge, to confine ourselves strictly to the deliverances of the object. Not so in willing. Self-consciousness, self-assertion, seems to be inseparable from willing. When we

1. cf. "kriyā hi nāma sā yatra vastusvarūpanirapekṣaiva codyate, puruṣacittavyāpārādhīnā ca." *Śaṅkara's Bhāṣya* on *Br. Sūtr.* 1, i. 4. "kartum akartum anyathā vā kartuṁ śakyam laukikaṁ vaidikaṁ ca karma", *Ibid.*, 1, i. 2.

are willing, we cannot be self-forgetful. The self-conscious or reflective character of the functions is thus due to the presence of will. Reflection in all cases means an arrest of functioning. The functioning itself acquires an interest, which may be either in the service of further and efficient functioning, as when we examine an instrument to improve its efficiency, or purely to understand the function itself without any ulterior motive. The former attitude is that of science; the latter is that of philosophy.

We have to controvert the position that willing can be reduced to either knowledge or feeling and that it is itself known. In knowing, our consciousness is that we are merely discovering an existent being; in willing it is just the reverse; the willed being what is formed *through* the willing. Nor is will known; for an object of knowledge on our definition, is an accomplished fact, and willing is not a piece of thing that you can find lying about somewhere; it is precisely the activity itself and is not to be had before or after the willing. How then do we speak *about* will, if it were not known? Precisely the same question might be asked about knowing. Speaking seems common to all the functions. It might be thought that before we can will anything, we must know what to will, and only then can we desire to bring it about through our willing. This seems so axiomatic and unquestionable that no further argument seems necessary. So knowledge precedes willing, it is concluded. But things might be put the other way round. Before we could know an object, our consciousness must reach up to it, and this reaching itself cannot be actuated by a knowledge of the thing to be known. This difficulty is obviated, one may urge, because we already know the thing. In that case, however, we cannot assert we know anything; for how could we say 'we know', if we have been knowing an entity always, invariably? There must therefore have been a time when it was unknown, unreacted to. Some self-alienation or factual gap is pre-supposed in the assertion 'we know it'. And for this gap to be transcended, a pure activity is needed. Willing is thus a mode of consciousness co-ordinate with knowledge.

Illusion in willing happens when what is really knowledge or feeling is mistaken for will. For instance, in most of our volitions we are actuated by feelings, by desires and passions, the apparent exercise of freedom notwithstanding. That we should incline towards one course of action out of several equally possible alternatives can never be explained on the basis of pure will alone. Will has no content, no material pattern by which it could prefer one and reject others. To say that we choose what is rationally higher or the good and that therefore we are free agents is to beg the question. For with regard to the next question what is good or is in the interests of the true self etc. our only appeal would be to feelings, to what we feel as pleasurable. Thus in any exercise of volition, which ends in commitment to a positive course of action, it is not pure will that is functioning. Something else, some content which has become a mode of the subject, is getting things done through us. Illusory or wrong willing is no willing at all.

IV

To take up the third and last kind of relation that can obtain between content and consciousness, that in which the determination of the one or the other is not emphasised. Knowing involves the distinction of the object from consciousness; the object is something accomplished and independent. In willing, consciousness is distinguished from the content, which is immediately felt as having a being only through the former. In both of these, a distinction between content and consciousness seems necessary and can be validated by experience. Now if we could prove that there is a mode of consciousness in which the distinction between consciousness and content is either not made or only very imperfectly made, we could have evidenced feeling. Feeling is the contact or identification of consciousness with object. It is the nature of feeling that it is a unity which militates against any aloofness or emphasis of one side against the other. It is not contended that feeling is possible without object but only that it is a state in which consciousness and content are not distinguishable; and this very fact of non-distinction becomes evident only when we pass over from the unreflective to the reflective stage.

It might be contended that feeling is of the nature of pleasure or pain, there being no feeling which is neither of these, and that it is always known. But, being opposed to each other, pleasure and pain cannot both be considered feeling; it should be either the one or the other. That both are considered feeling implies that there is something common and more basic to them. And this can only be the contact of the subject with the object; if the contact is favourable, the feeling is one of pleasure; if otherwise pain is the feeling. It will be shown that pleasure and pain involve willing, reflection. Pain is the consciousness of the unavailing efforts to get away from contact with some undesired object, while pleasure is the consciousness of the success of effort.

Is feeling known? By knowing we should always take the apprehension of a content which is an accomplished fact and independent of the apprehending consciousness; the object is distinguished from the knowing of it. Feeling is not known, and this for two reasons. Feeling is not an object existing by itself, an accomplished fact, which we only view calmly and dispassionately. There cannot be feeling, if such a detachment or distinction is made between consciousness and content. Secondly, the difference between feeling, if it were objectified, and knowledge would not be a functional or co-ordinate difference, for feeling would be a species of object as red or the table and not a mode of relation between consciousness and content. The difference between feeling and the table would be sought to be made on the ground that the latter is an outer object while the former is an inner one. But this very distinction of the 'inner' and the 'outer' would involve feeling; we call that 'inner' with which we are identified intimately and perhaps inseparably.

Hitherto we have essayed to show that feeling is a mode of consciousness that is different from either knowing or willing, something more basic and primitive to them. It might be thought that feeling as such is unreflective and that there is no reflective, or reflection into, feeling. In one sense it must be admitted that each feeling is particular and unique; the very same feeling cannot be resurrected; and this because of some obvious considerations. Even if we had the identical feeling once again, we would still have to account for the consciousness of *two* occurrences of the *same* feeling; the second and later occurrence is thus an individual feeling different from the previous one, though it might have a feeling reference to that. The essence of feeling is not its unreflective character which may be its limiting case, but the comparative non-distinction between consciousness and content. This is available in a reflective state too. A reflective feeling can be defined as that state in which to feel and at once to be aware of it as feeling are not distinct, distinguishable.

An explicit case of such a reflective feeling is present in recognition. In recognition there is the feeling of familiarity, of encountering the same object. Recognition can be roughly taken as the collation of two percepts. How are we to account for the feeling of familiarity without having recourse to a reflective feeling? It is obvious that the object, in its first or second encounter, does not carry with it any mark that it is the same object encountered before. It might be said that the identity of the object on the two occasions accounts for the feeling of familiarity. But the question is how is the identity of the object on two or more occasions ascertainable at all without bringing in two experiences, without feeling the two experiences to be the same. If this is accepted, we must also guard against the error that the first experience is somehow made the object of the second and so on, as some realists hold. For this would raise precisely the same difficulty about the identity of the first experience with what is objectified in the second one. Nor is the one experience an identical repetition of the other, for then there would not even be the notion of *two* experiences; the two are not numerically one. So our ordinary notions of identity based on the object of knowledge are inapplicable: the identity here is compatible with difference: there are two numerically distinct experiences but still the later experience is direct and self-conscious. We have thus to grant that in recognition the feeling of familiarity is to be accounted for by the supposition that the two experiences without losing their uniqueness as two are in some sense indistinguishable from each other. Therefore we cannot say that the first experience is the *object* of the second; if it were so, it would amount to knowledge, not feeling. Because the two experiences are imperfectly distinguished, we should call the state feeling, and as there is a distinct reference by the one to the other, it is reflective. The whole thing is felt as feeling without the mediation of any other state. How precisely is the one experience included in the other is more than what we can say. Possibly, there is a re-enactment of the first feeling in an attenuated form in the later stage.

What is true of recognition or reperceiving the same object is true of any determinate cognition, reflective thought. We have to show that determinate cognition is really re-cognition. Reflection is, for our purposes, the consciousness of a content *as* to a consciousness. That is, we are attending more intensely to that object which we were attending to unreflectively; we are merely making things more definite, determinate. Thus the identity of the object presented to us in the two stages is necessary for reflection. But has not the very attempt to make things more determinate constituted a break in our experience, made one reflective and the other unreflective in contrast? Now the identity of the object, *i.e.*, the identity of the substantive, is necessary; otherwise our judgment will be a mere fancy; it must refer to the 'that' or the given. How is this identity of the substantive accounted for? Not as the realistic view as exemplified in the Nyāya, would have it that the indeterminate cognition (*nirvikalpa*) is made the object of a subsequent determinate cognition; for we still have to account for the identity of the first indeterminate cognition with the object of the subsequent cognition. The only feasible solution is that the identity of the substantive is felt, not known : the reflective is at once directly aware of the unreflective not as an object distinctly presented before it but as one with itself, indistinguishable from, though not completely merged with itself. What is true of the reflective and unreflective consciousness, *i.e.* of the adjective and the substantive, is true of all relations as well. The being of a relation is really a mode of feeling, though ordinarily relation is taken as an accomplished object of knowledge.

Pain and pleasure are also feelings on the reflective level. They are reflective in the sense that to feel pleasure or pain and to be aware of feeling it are one and the same thing. This is not to be construed, as already shown, that pleasure and pain are presented as objects of knowledge. Cancellation of an illusory feeling is also of the nature of reflective feeling; for cancellation has a reference to the prior illusion and to itself as a correction, both rolled into one.

V

These three modes of consciousness—Knowing, Willing and Feeling—thus represent three different and complementary ways of attending to the object. All mental life is compounded of these. Any particular indeterminate element or any related whole is to be traced to feeling; self-consciousness, reflection and the transition from one state to another are due to will; determinateness—describability and universality—is to be attributed to knowledge.

Though not reducible to one another, each is expressible negatively in terms of others, as all are speakable. Willing, in terms of knowledge, is conscious absence of knowledge, which amounts to no knowing at all. When will is complete, as in absolute negation, there is no object left; knowing is eliminated. Feeling, with reference to knowledge, is something unknown, vague—one that is mere datum requiring determination. It can be said to be known as unknown. Knowing, in terms of willing, is dependence, a surrender to something non-existent, and if knowing were complete, as in pure contemplation, there is an end to will. Consciousness is absorbed and lost in the object. Feeling, with regard to will, serves as a basis for its exercise. Knowledge in terms of feeling, is what is unfelt, indifferent, something lacking on the subjective side. Will, in relation to feeling, is intense desire, something lacking on the objective side. It might be seen that feeling is more primitive and basic than the other two; it is 'thicker.'

VI

Such is our *a priori* scheme. It is to be seen whether it can be useful in interpreting our mental states. We have a two-fold thesis to maintain. One is that each state—not the pure abstractions we have been considering—is compounded of all the three, and we have to find the precise meaning of the involution in one mode of the others. Secondly, we must, by emphasising one of the modes to the exclusion of others, arrive at an absolute and pure form in each case, as Pure knowledge, Pure willing and Pure feeling. These are incapable of entering into any further combination and are, what may be called, 'incommensurable absolutes.'

To elucidate the first thesis. Any text-book on psychology acquaints us with the notion that every mental state is not expressible in less than three attitudes towards a presentation. We know a certain thing, feel towards it, *i.e.* affected by it in a certain way, and there is conation. But the way in which these modes are present in a mental state is left vague. It is evident that the modes are not precipitated together either simultaneously or together. For both will militate against the unity and continuity of mental life; there will be no sense in one involving the other attitudes; they would be merely juxtaposed, and the utmost that can be said is that they are close to each other. A more plausible view is that one mode *appears* unitary and single, but it implicitly contains others; greater attention is required to bring out the complication. This hypothesis has at least the merit of explaining how, for introspection, the states appear entire and unitary and also make provision for critical analysis. Each state is thus an illusion, only waiting to be resolved into its components by analysis, which thereby constitutes its cancellation.

It might be urged that there are no subjective illusions; for introspection—which is the only evidence available here—is not liable to error, being a direct and immediate awareness. Our hypothesis, however, questions the infallibility of introspection. The very impossibility of having any objective illusion without confusion of subjective functions is an argument in our favour. Take, for instance, the 'rope-snake' illusion—"This is a snake." The 'this' before me is apprehended as the snake. Analysis here shows that I am in actual contact with the 'this'—whatever that may be; it is not determinate; we merely feel it, perceive it unreflectively. Simultaneously, there is the knowledge of the 'snake', which is a universal in the sense that it is a character which has no habitation, and has certainly nothing to do with the 'this' before me. There are thus two distinct functions—feeling and knowing, and because of a confusion of these two there is illusion; the 'snake' confronts us as the 'this'. Cancellation merely analyses the apparently unitary nature of illusion into the different functions, and at the same time evidences that the different functions were present at the time of illusion but as confused, not carefully attended to as they should have been. The 'this' which was indeterminate, feeling, becomes more determinate as the rope; the 'snake' which though a universal, was tied up with the presentation 'this', is contemplated, after cancellation, as a pure universal. All this comes to mean that the confusion of the subjective functions of knowing and feeling ceases. To take another instance. Intense brooding or even dreaming, when beguiled by feeling, results in the apparent confronting by us of an accomplished object out there. The willed or imagined character of the content is lost sight of; it appears as an object of knowledge, accomplished and independent. There is illusion because the two functions are not kept separate, and cancellation, when it follows, brings out the purely willed character of the content.

The second thesis is that the contention about these functions being confused usually requires their being available in a pure form. As a matter of fact, if the functions were not analysable and available separately, the first contention itself could not have been made. It is because after the cancellation of an illusion the components can be had without confusion of the one with the other are we able to say that in illusion there was no such discrimination, that anything appeared unitary and simple. The thesis can be put in more general terms: any distinction demands the experience of the distincts in a pure form. Distinction cannot be precipitated all at once in one stage of consciousness; it presupposes a prior non-distinctive stage and points out to a subsequent one of distincts in a pure experience. For instance, if the judgment were a distinction of the 'what' from the 'that' or as the bringing of a percept under a concept, our thesis demands a state wherein these distinctions are not made, *e.g.*, the perceptive or non-reflective consciousness, and another wherein the 'what' is contemplated. We should be able to point to a stage prior to the judgment and one supervening it.

Both these theses will be illustrated if we began with the less developed states and by proper arrangement reached up to the pure forms. This will at once show that ordinary forms of Knowing, Feeling and Willing are really compounded of all the three, and that the functions are available in their pure form only as absolutes. We can but indicate the general trend of such an arrangement leaving, for a future occasion, the detailed working out of such a series in each of these functions.

VII

Taking the judgment as on the reflective level of consciousness, wh ch may be knowing, will or feeling as already shown, we should be able to posit an experience prior to the judgment and another beyond it. The judgment stands midway between the unreflective and supra-reflective or transcendental consciousness.

Any genuine judgment is of the form--'This is A,' involving belief in the existence of a fact; a given something is judged. Judgment may thus be said to work upon a percept. The content of a judgment is thus necessarily differentiated into the 'that' and the 'what'; the whole judgment however is but very imperfectly distinguished from the judging consciousness. Our first contention is that the 'that' refers to a fact, a percept and is a unique particular, while the 'what' is a concept, universal. As Bradley says, Reality must fall outside the judgment, so that it can be predicated of that. Slightly changing this, we might say that the 'that' must refer to an actual perception; otherwise the entire judgment would be a fiction, surreptitiously put in the form of a judgment; moreover, if all judgments were such creations implying no reference to a reality outside the judgment, the distinction of the 'what' from the 'that' would not itself be made.

Ordinarily, there is much reason to regard the unreflective or the perceptival stage as feeling, as it is indeterminate. But it can be interpreted on the knowledge-side too, if the subsequent reflective consciousness is informative and not affective or conative. The transition from perception to judgment is coincident with greater determination, universalisation and idealisation, of the content. To discriminate is to disengage; the 'what' is disengaged from the 'that'. The transition is engendered by recognition and judgments of quantity. Recognition, as the collation of two percepts helps to free certain characters common to both, helps in the disengaging of the adjective from the substantive.

In a judgment the 'what' is no doubt distinguished from the 'that'; but it still seems to be tied up with, or to belong to, the 'that'. There is a demand to completely free and contemplate it as a pure universal. The transition from the judgment to the contemplative stage is engendered through the disjunctive and the hypothetical and culminates in the negative judgment. Now the disjunctive and the hypothetical fall short of the judgment-ideal which is an affirmation or ascription; the 'or' and the 'if' do not amount to any information but suggest the possibility of the freedom of the 'what' from the 'that'; and as such they point to a stage of no-judgment or negation. Negation presents itself as correction or cancellation of illusions. The ultimate import of negation may be viewed in two different ways : one in the service of knowledge and the other in that of will. What all can we negate is wrong ascription, all relation in the last resort; the essential speakable character of an entity cannot be denied; for to deny is to speak it and evidence it as an essence. What all can we deny of the rope-snake ? Only its relatedness to other entities; to the 'this' etc. and its temporal and spatial position, bringing out thereby its essential indescribable character. The 'snake' will still be an object of contemplation. Interpreted on the will-side, negation would mean the utter nothingness of the negated; it would not even be a speakable. For, it may be urged about the 'snake' etc. that when all its relatedness is denied, nothing is left over; the 'snake' never appeared except in the related way; it has no provable existence apart from the relation.[1]

We now reach a stage in which the objects of knowledge are universals or essences; there is no relation, reference or implication; everything appears entire; there is nothing dark or confused about the essences. This is the stage of contemplation. Even here some stages may be imagined. First, the sense of transition from one universal to another has to be eschewed, for this smacks of distraction of attention. Likewise the feeling of one's subjective act (the 'I') contemplating such forms has also to be transcended. In the last resort the subject must merge, as it were in the object—Pure Being. This would mark the culmination of knowledge-series; the absolute of knowledge, Pure Being, is reached. Thus we could indicate three stages—the unreflective (perceptual), reflective (judgment) and the contemplative stages. *Mutatis mutandis*, these stages exemplify those of Feeling and Will.

Some general and baffling questions arise here. One is the question whether the Absolutes of Knowledge, Feeling and Will are really incommensurable. Is not there a very deep and inexpressible identity of all the three, the differences being

1. These two ways of interpreting negation correspond roughly to the two theories of illusion—*anirvacanīya-khyāti* and *asat-khyāti*, advocated by the Vedāntin and the Śūnyavādin (Mādhyamika), respectively.

due to the different modes of approach and not to any essential diversity? The second question is about the necessity of a spiritual discipline, in each of these functions, for reaching the absolute, how much do they have in common and what are their specific features.

2.2 ILLUSION AS CONFUSION OF SUBJECTIVE FUNCTIONS*

The paper attempts to explicate and to extend the thesis elaborated in Professor K. C. Bhattacharyya's paper, "The False and the Subjective."[1] Therein the Professor proves the twin theses that the consciousness of the false is the consciousness of the subjective and *vice versa*. His main contention is that the consciousness of the false is the consciousness of a content that is not speakable except as the content of a belief, which again is apprehended only as it is rejected or disbelieved; the consciousness of the subjective too implies belief. Our present endeavour is to see whether this contention can be extended to all subjective forms. The attempt is to define and enumerate all the subjective forms and not merely to prove the subjective in general. Instead of starting with an *a priori* and hypothetical formulation of the possible modes of relation between consciousness and content and then identify the abstract modes with knowing, feeling and willing, which may have an air of architectonic neatness about it, we ask to be told how we arrived at the notion of functions or subjective forms at all in the first place and then their exhaustive formulation. We claim that illusion, the realisation of anything as illusory, is impossible without implying a consciousness of the functions. Any ordinary mode of consciousness, as veridical perception etc. would equally involve them; but the preference for illusion is that nothing shows up the inner working of a mechanism as disorder; when it is well-attuned and smooth-working we seldom appreciate the precise functions of the several parts. Our starting-point may thus be justified *prima facie*.

The thesis elaborated in this paper is two-fold : the possibility of illusion depends on the confusion of functions and secondly wherever there are functions there is illusion. The second thesis may seem a mere verbal converse of the first. It would however become evident that it is more in the nature of a demand that

*Reprinted from the *Philosophical Quarterly*, April 1935.

1. *Calcutta Review*, Oct. 1932.

something be realised *as* illusory than that it is so actually. The whole paper can also be taken as an essay on matter and form.

Illusion, in contrast to a thinking error, involves an original belief; it is a perceptual fact, to all intents. The belief is so complete that we are not conscious of meaning its negation, the possibility of its being otherwise. A thought, even an affirmative judgment, is always conscious of its possible negation. Again, it refers to, or seeks, a percept; it involves belief only in a very general sense, bearing general applicability to fact or percept. It is however to be sharply distinguished from figments of imagination, which are avowedly felt to have no such reference at all. When we become aware of an error in thinking, as in fallacious reasoning or miscalculation of a happening, we only realise what we apprehended even initially, namely the possibility of its negation. Hence the correcting thought does not intrude upon us as a shock like the cancellation of illusion. Nor is the correcting thought capable of negating, in entirety, the reference of the previous thought to fact; for, like any other thought, it carries the possibility of its own negation.

*2. To take up the first thesis that illusion is not possible without confusion of functions, or that a consciousness of anything as illusory is at once to be reflectively aware of the operation of subjective functions. The thesis may be denied in two ways : first, by contending that illusion and cancellation can be explained without reference to the subjective, i.e., purely in objective terms; second, that even if the subjective were necessary, it is to be conceived as unitary in function and determinate, i.e., there is no confusion of subjective forms. We have to develop our thesis by refuting both these contentions.

The first view is the mainstay of all forms of realism in diverse sorts and degrees. They would take illusion as objective confusion or non-distinction of several objective entities. We have, for instance, a radical and uncompromising type in the bold statement of Holt that contradictions and confusions are as much objective facts as any others. We have the Prābhākara who interprets illusion as the non-distinction of objects with a parallel non-distinction of the respective cognitions. A more modified type would have the confusion only in the relation of the terms. Objective confusion or non-distinction is unintelligible. For, each entity being definite and distinct from all others, how could there be confusion among them? It is not that their natures are lost in each other. Obviously, the confusion has reference to our powers of discrimination only and is not a fact of nature without reference to a subject. Suppose we grant an objective confusion, which gets clarified later on. But at the time of confusion it was a real state of things, and when they are clarified later on it would be another real state of the now existing situation. But our notion of illusion is that even at the very time things were not what they seemed to be. To put it in a slightly different form, the transition from illusion to cancellation is not an objective change, a becoming in nature; it is something subjective. It is in the interest of realism to deny illusion in the last resort. But the very denial is paradoxical; for it means correction of illusion.

To avoid all these predicaments suppose we took illusion to be a subjective affair, a sort of *representation* of facts in thought, and being but a representation it is quite intelligible that it is sometimes false. The falsity of the first subjective fact is evidenced by a subsequent one. It may be that the second state may, for aught, turn out to be false in the long run; but for the time being this is not so patent and hence cancels or replaces the first. This view of illusion and cancellation as both subjective facts one following the other seems to take the subjective as unitary and determinate. It has of course the merit of being simple and readily appealing. We have to bring home, from a correcter interpretation of illusion and cancellation, that more than one subjective function is involved.

Any view of cancellation must make provision for two evident characteristics about the cancelling consciousness. That unlike illusion, cancellation is at once aware of itself *as cancelling*; it is reflective. And even if we hold that illusion and cancellation are subjective states equally, we must make a vital distinction between the two. We are necessarily conscious of illusion only later on. Second, cancellation is not a state that merely supervenes on the first; the cancellation is hardly temporal. We have got to find out its corrective force. If it were merely an other state which succeeded the first, then any two states in the order of prior and later would be illusion and cancellation respectively. We shall see that the two questions are intimately connected.

On the theory that illusion and cancellation are two unitary subjective states, we shall be told that illusion has for its object, mistaken it may be, an external or physical fact. The reflective nature of cancellation is accounted for by its having as object a previous subjective fact; or that the inner sense is operative in cognising the prior subjective state. Both these grounds of accounting for reflection are untenable. For the structure is the same whether we have an internal object or employ a different sense; the inner sense may acquaint us with a presentation not accessible to the outer senses; it cannot make known anything *as* object. This predicament is unavoidable : either every state is self-conscious, illusion included, or none is. Nor is the peculiar corrective character of cancellation explained on the notion that illusion and cancellation have two different objects—an external fact and an internal one, the illusion itself, respectively. Referring to different contents, there is no opposition between them at all, and hence no correction. And if to have an object is to believe in it, the cancelling consciousness will usher in another belief—belief in the illusion as a subjective fact. But our idea of cancellation is that it is disbelief or withdrawal of belief and not a new belief.

We maintain that illusion has no object presented *to* it; there is no awareness of an object *as* to a consciousness, as it *appears to it only*; for this is precisely the state of affairs in cancellation. There is thus no distinction of subject from object or *vice versa* in illusion. It is not proper then to speak of illusion as having an object or content which it grasps. Instead, we should say that illusion is the content of cancellation; for only the latter knows it *as* illusion, *as* object; cancellation has no other content. There being no diversity of content, correction is intelligible as withdrawal of belief from the content or appearance, and as we withdraw, the distinction between content and belief emerges. This also evidences that such a distinction was not made in illusion. *Prima facie*, there is thus a case for conceiving cancellation as the analysis or distinction, and illusion as the confusion of functions.

* 3. To determine the nature and number of functions involved in illusion, let us take an example, the stock one of "rope-snake," which might be expressed as 'That is a snake.' Now we are considering illusion from the standpoint of cancellation. We are conscious of the rope or the 'substratum' as having

been there at the time of illusion, though not perceived; we credit it with a being or existence of its own. If the rope came to have a being *as* it is known as rope, the "snake" could have hardly appeared as *that* snake, an existent; illusion would have been impossible. Our attitude towards the rope is that it need not appear to have being; it is self-evident and self-existent. This attitude may well be called knowing, being determined entirely by the object; all knowledge is, or should be, of some being independent of our subjective act of knowing.

In contrast to the consciousness of the "is" or being, there is the appearance—"the snake"—which gives a character to the illusion. The "snake" may be said to be all surface and no depth; its being is exhausted in consciousness; its existence is one with knownness. We call the "snake" illusory precisely because it has no being of its own like the rope; it is not an "is". Is it nothing then ? It appears as something standing. No distinction however can be made between *it* and consciousness. Any apparent distinction would be due to its history, as *that* snake which appeared *to* consciousness, a history that is realised as untenable in correction. We may call this attitude feeling, for want of a better term. There is a felt and inherent lack of separation between content and consciousness characteristic of all feeling.

The above two functions alone are not enough to engender illusion; the "is" and the "snake" would have remained separate then; the snake would not have been taken as an "is", nor the "is" identified with the "snake". Cancellation evidences the *withdrawal* of belief from the "snake", of the "is" from the appearance. Belief really pertains to the "is". No belief is created; it is only transferred to the appearance, and cancellation is *dis*belief or dissociation of belief from the content. Unlike the other two functions, the transference or withdrawal is not intelligible as something in itself, not a being, nor an appearance; it is not speakable without reference to the negating activity of consciousness. This is willing, to all intents.

These three functions—attitudes as we have called them—we consciously become aware of only in cancellation, which at once evidences that they were present before too. Otherwise, we would be considering that illusion and cancellation have two different contents or that illusion is a unitary fact—a view that has been already refuted. Cancellation, without adding any new factor, merely analyses and clarifies the previous situation. The distinctive nature or self of each subjective function shines out. In contrast, illusion has to be conceived as the confusion or self-alienation of each form. This is object or matter *par excellence.* An epistemological definition of matter would be what is indeterminate, confused, and form is what is determinate, with a self as it were. The difference between the two is directly felt as in the transition from illusion to cancellation. Any other definition of matter, as what is external, dead, inert, etc. is open to objection as lacking experiential support. On our view, matter is the confusion or self-alienation of forms, not an independent, or self-sufficient entity, the confusion itself not another form. If it were so, there is nothing to prevent it from persisting in the full light of discrimination; to discriminate is to dispel confusion. Primordial illusion or matter is the utter lack of all determination, a glimpse of which we have in deep sleep. Empirical illusions are determinate in varying degrees. In the order of discovery, matter is prior to form, as in consciousness the sequence is from the indeterminate to the determinate; there is no obligation or need to pass from the definite to the indefinite; it is all just the other way about. In terms of reality, however, matter is nothing at all; it lacks self-hood. It thrives by not being the forms, so long as they are not realised as distinct.

The implications of the view presented here are many : 1. Without a plurality of subjective functions illusion or confusion is not possible. 2. Illusion and objectivity are coincident; object is the primitive denial or alienation of form or self; we know anything *as* object only in cancellation. 3. Any reflective consciousness is, *ipso facto*, a cancelling or analysing consciousness. 4. And reflection is the analysis into distincts or the return to the self-hood of each form. Cancellation is self-conscious because of this inwardising or denial of self-alienation. Illusion is not an analytic or inwardising consciousness, but just the opposite; so it is unreflective, indeterminate and false.

*4. So far our view contends that each subjective function is a self-sufficient, distinct form owing nothing to others, although to engender illusion each should be confused with others. It might be pointed out that the distinction of the subjective into three forms is itself illusory. We have however to ask for the evidence of the cancelling consciousness. But this, if our contentions are cogent, leads us into a vicious circle; for any cancelling consciousness is an analysing consciousness; we would still be left with the functions. No illusion is possible without plurality of functions. Attempts may however be made to show how some of the functions are derivative. We showed that belief in a being not depending for its existence on its knownness, in the substratum like the rope, was essential for illusion, for the "snake" to be perceived as there. Now it might be pointed out that this belief is a pure creation along with the "snake": not only is the "snake" created but at once the belief in its existence. But can belief be manufactured at all? I can easily build castles in the air; but it is not so obvious that I believe them to have a being apart from my imagination. If I do, as it sometimes happens, it is through self-forgetfulness, through a lapse from pure imagining. Anyway, the belief in the independence of the castle is not part of the building of it. A pure sport cannot be consciously degraded into a grim alien reality opposing us. All this is to say that we can start with illusion; but cannot consciously arrive or aim at it. There is no demand to pass from the determinate to the indeterminate.

Likewise, the attempt to derive appearance from being is futile; for being does not need to appear; its intelligibility is complete without the appearance; this is really our attitude towards the rope or the substratum. That it seems to require to be known is to be realised as false in the last resort. Nor can appearance put forth being; the "rope-snake" does not demand that it is to be realised as an existent being; rather it requires to be realised as appearance *only*. It is evident that we have three independent self-sufficient attitudes.

The argument used is that as each attitude is complete, the complication of some other factor in any one attitude is not intelligible from that attitude; it has to be referred to some other co-ordinate function. The argument is on a par with the following one. What is not perceived cannot be imagined to be perceived; and only that can be perceived which is actually sensed, i.e., in the last resort we have to refer to some actual sensing, as the sensa are qualitatively distinct. Take for example a case of sense-complication, the *cold look* of a slab of ice. Coldness, though appearing one with the look, is really a tactual sensum.

It is of course not realised separately in that context; for that would hardly make for complication. The eye cannot give the tactual sensum as well; it is a new quality altogether; and the function of the eye is complete with the colour sensum. So too with regard to each of the subjective functions. As each is self-sufficient and determinate, the complication of other forms with it introduces an element of indeterminateness or matter. They are to be regarded, from the standpoint of each function, as accidental accretions which may well be rejected; they are its free adjectives as it were.

It thus follows from our analysis of illusion, as the confusion of subjective forms each being complete in itself, that it is capable of *alternative* interpretations. By this we mean that each is a comprehensive explanation and includes all, though the place assigned to each function would necessarily be different in each interpretation. An attempt at such an explanation is here made. We have in each case to take something as basic and indubitable, the ground of illusion as it were. We may consider the being of the rope as the most indubitable fact which makes illusion, the illusion of the "snake," possible. Its being is so deep and intrinsic that it need not appear at all. The "snake" is its *free* appearance then. How and why being puts forth the appearance is not intelligible at all. It is its degradation in a sense; for it engenders the semblance that existence belongs to the "snake," or at least that it requires to be known to be. That is we say that the "*snake*" *is*, whereas, if we had a proper view of things, it should be that the "snake" *belongs* to the "is," the *belonging* itself being peculiar. There is thus a duality of the "snake" and the "is," a duality made possible through the self-alienation of the "is"; for the "is" becomes, in illusion, a mode of the appearance; it appears as object. Cancellation would mean the negation of the self-alienation—the reinstatement of the "is" in its pristine eminence, by the elimination of all "knownness," knownness being illusory on this view. This would be the Vedântic interpretation of illusion.

Instead of belittling the appearance, we may consider that alone as the one thing which is immediate and patent; the belief in the "this" is made possible *through* it. It is not false or nothing; for the utmost that we can retract from it is its relationship to the "this" or externality, not its intrinsic character of appearance.

True, we cannot say that it "is," but that we can say anything at all is *through* it. It may be taken therefore as the ground or the basis of illusion; the illusion here being its externality, its appearing as *that* snake divorced and set against consciousness, engendering thereby the false duality or abstraction of subject and object. The formula for feeling is not that A and B constitute C, but A and B are false abstractions of C which is their necessary basis. The "thatness" of the "snake" is a free accretion taken by it, the matter or indefiniteness which it sheds off in cancellation. The true character of the "snake" as an immediate presentation is felt only by denying thatness, its self-alienation or objectivity. If it still seems to be distinct from the subject, it is because of its past history.[1]

In the above two interpretations we took our stand respectively on being and the appearance; we may now hold as our ground something more immediate—the negating or cancelling activity itself. For in that alone is the illusion apprehended as such, as object. The activity is pure and something in itself; we negate illusion, not because we believe in something else but because the very fitness of things demands it. And the negation applies to both the "is," and the appearance. Take away the "that" or the "is," and the "snake" also collapses; its distinctness is bound up with the "is," and what is the "that" except the snake ? It is not that the "is" and the appearance are the necessary creations or completions of the conscious activity; for as we have pointed out, though we can negate the given we cannot pass from the negative activity to the given, i.e., from the determinate to the indeterminate.[2]

It is however to be admitted that not all classes of illusion are explainable with equal plausibility in all the three alternatives, the reason being that empirical illusions are already determinate, to a certain extent, one way or the other. Where the sense of objectivity is predominant, as in external perception, the knowledge-interpretation would be more natural. Hallucinations, where subjective projection counts for much with little or no objective basis, are best explained on the will-interpretation. The cancelling consciousness denies the self-

1. This interpretation of illusion approximates to the *ātmakhyāti* of the Vijñānavādin.

2. This interpretation broadly corresponds to the *śūnyakhyāti* of the Mādhyamikas.

forgetfulness of the projective activity. Dreams are best interpreted as feeling-illusions; cancellation just denies the externality of the dream-pictures, leaving intact their aesthetic appearance. The case of what may be called permanent illusions or real appearances presents some peculiarity. Such are, e.g., the elliptical shape of the coin, the bent stick in water, the small size of the moon, etc. Here though we are reasonably persuaded that the elliptical shape cannot belong to the coin, it continues to appear all the same. There is a curious alternation of attitudes: Either we reduce, siding with the idealists, all, the thing-hood included, to the status of the aesthetic appearance, or, with the realists, we take all the appearances as *in* the thing irrespective of the percipient. The illusion persists and gives rise to alternation because the percipient is embodied and is not able to effect a separation between the intellectual and affective elements of his composite nature.

*5. In the previous section we spoke of the alternative interpretation of illusion and of the complication of forms, one form being the substantive or the ground and the others its free adjectives. The complication, inspite of the distinction of forms, introduces an element of indeterminateness or matter. This indeterminateness is to be contrasted with that of illusion or confusion, where there is not even the distinction of functions. Illusion is purely indeterminate; we may call it *primary* matter and the other *secondary* matter. There is another vital distinction between the two kinds of matter : primary matter can never be realised as form; it is matter *par excellence*, realisable only in the transition from illusion to cancellation; secondary matter however is some other form or forms in complication; it is intelligible from some other standpoint. It is thus something positive, while primary matter is negative, being the self-alienation of *all* the forms and not of one only.

*6. We now take up the second thesis, namely that the presence of several forms spells for illusion. What is the need for this proposition, it might legitimately be asked. In proving the first proposition that illusion is possible through the confusion of functions, we could rely upon an actual cancellation, upon the consciousness of something as illusory. But it is conceivable that there may be cases in which such a consciousness is either lacking or impossible to attain on the reflective level.

In such a situation this proposition may be of value as voicing forth a demand and providing a warning that the work of cancellation is not complete.

Cancellation we took to be a reflective consciousness; reflective in the sense that there is an inwardising of the subjective attitudes; the denial of self-negation. That landed us with the several functions; and as each form is complete and distinct in itself, we attempted the alternative interpretation of illusion by taking one function as the self or the sole ground of intelligibility putting others as *its* matter. Unintelligibility or matter still lurks; there is a necessary demand to realise each form as absolute, complete in itself without any complication with other forms, a demand to get rid of, what we have termed as, secondary matter. It might be even stated that it is a necessary implication of illusion and cancellation that each of the forms should be available without complication whatsoever, that the complication is an accidental affair. In fact, any relation would demand the existence of at least one of its terms without the relation; otherwise, if the nature and existence of the terms were exhausted within the relation, no distinction of terms even within the relation is possible—the very impossibility of any relation. It is not enough to realise the distinctness of the appearance and the substratum, the rope, but to free the latter from all semblance of relation with the "snake" and *vice versa*.

So far the second proposition may set to voice a demand. But the demand is not to be satisfied in reflection. A reflective cancellation, will be, as we have seen, an analysis of the given, the illusion, into the several functions by denying their self-alienation, by distinguishing them from one another. This would lead us, at best, to some other forms more ultimate, it might be. Still there would be plurality and indistinctness but no realisation of the absolute character of each function. Suppose we held, to avoid this predicament, that there is no distinction of functions, then there would be nothing to distinguish cancellation, i.e., reflection, from illusion. So we conclude that reflective cancellation points to a higher stage of consciousness, without itself giving it. It hardly falls within the scope of the paper to deal with the modes of realising the Absolute in each case. But one thing seems implied on our view : we can realise the Absolute in *one* of these modes only.

2.3 THE UNIVERSAL AND THE PARTICULAR*

I. We shall start with the readily acceptable notion of the particular as the unique or the unrepeatable, and of the universal as the repeatable. The latter is so, as it is a determinate character, a content that can be fixed upon by thought. Conversely what is determinate in thought is universal. Not being a thinkable character, the particular is not repeatable.

Three views can be held with regard to the nature of the particular and the universal. Some philosophers—the empiricists and the nominalists—hold that the particular alone is what is given in knowledge, the universal being but an ideal and generalised entity, more often a mere name. There are others who think that both the universal and the particular are given, there being no thought without these. Against both the above, we have to maintain that the universal alone is given. On each theory, the relation between the universal and the particular is a problem, though it takes a different form in each case.

The difficulties of the empiricist theory are insuperable. How is the object of thought made intelligible at all without determinate and distinguishable characters? If they are present, for even to deny them they should be fixed upon by thought, the universals are *ipso facto* given. It is not that we start with the particular, but through some mysterious leap we generalise it through induction, and that generalisation is not strictly valid. This view labours under the misconception that universality is distributedness, extensity and that the universal is an ensemble of particulars, thought supplying the needed glue that binds them. We should, however, conceive the universal more intrinsically as a thinkable character, e.g., colour, sound, pain, pleasure, etc.

The second view does lip-service to the self-intelligible character of the universal; it is insisted that the universal too, if it were not to be abstract, must somehow depend upon the particular. Are the two precipitated simultaneously in one thought or successively? If the first, it is hard to see how the universal

*Reprinted from the *Philosophical Quarterly*, December 1932.

mediates the other, or that it is *through* that the particular is made intelligible, or vice versa. The distinction between the two will not, in that case, arise. If successively given, it is evident that either of them does not depend upon the other for its intelligibility; the universal does not need the particular.

It is more reasonable to hold that only universals, thinkable characters are given. Being intelligible in themselves, they do not stand in need of being defined, but all definition is possible through them. The universal is certainly not reached through a process of generalisation. The problem on this view is : how does the universal get particularised; how does the colour of the rose come to stand for a unique unrepeatable fact? The particular is the universal caught in a net of external relations. Only *position*, a fixed place in a series, is particular. The universal does not contain any principle of particularity. It might be thought that "This tree before me" is particular. But its meaning "A tree that the speaker has before him" is still universal; for a number of such situations are possible.

Our contention involves two things : that only in order or position can particularity be found, and that position cannot be given in thought but must be posited. Take for instance, the two combinations that are different, though their constituents are identical—5F, F5, and 'But' and 'Tub'. Position is neither in one of the constituents—5, nor in the other—F, nor in both taken as a whole; for this would be a unit itself, and can have position only with regard to entities outside the group. Position has somehow to be understood. Number, Language, causal chain, etc. are examples of order. But there is no order which does not involve Space and Time; they are the greatest individualisers. For, a togetherness of entities having a certain dimension or spread-out-ness is indispensable to any position. And without succession the position of entities is not sustainable. But spatial or temporal position is impossible without entities which sustain the relative positions; ciphers cannot engender position.

Mere spread-out-ness and succession do not suffice to make anything particular; we are still in the realm of the ideal. The play of *Hamlet* has certainly spatial distinctions and succession of events; still it has no assignable position. To have one, an entity must sustain relationships not only with certain entities, but with all and sundry. Herein consists the superiority of the world of action. My speaking can be particularised beyond any chance of repetition, if it is related with the room I am in, and that with other places, they in turn with others and so on, until all conceivable entities are related or thought to be related. So too in the case of time, my speaking shall have to be fixed in position with regard to other happenings, and these to others and so on. An historical event can sustain such relations to any extent, and, therefore, is a real particular. An ideal event, e.g. the death of Hamlet can have relationships only with other events in the play i.e. in a very limited sphere; it is, hence, not a particular. A particular is what it is in virtue of its position i.e. infinite relationships with other particulars. It is evident that when one entity is known all its relationships are not known, as this would mean the apprehension of the entire universe when a tiny drop of water is seen. Position is believed in, and is posited in action. It is not a thinkable. What is thought being wholly within the apprehending consciousness, it cannot sustain any relation to things outside it, and without this there is no position. The particular belongs eminently to the field of action, and the universal to contemplation.

2. Several considerations of importance follow from this conception of the particular and the universal :

(i) The totality of spatial and temporal positions--the cosmos for instance—is not a particular, though entities within it are particulars with regard to other entities equally within. For, it cannot be fixed in position, moored to anything, there being nothing, by our definition of cosmos, external to it. It is a universal, and is repeatable indefinitely. In keeping with this view is the Hindu conception of cycles of creation intelligible.

(ii) This leads us to another point—the confusion between universality and necessity. Kant, as is well-known, speaks in terms which would imply that universality and necessity are identical, or that they are invariably connected. The necessary is that which is inexorably fixed; this is unthinkable if an entity were considered in itself; then it is absolutely free. Necessity is nothing if not a position, a relation to other entities. The absolutely necessary is thus that which is inexorably related to all things; it is the particular par excellence. The absolutely free, on the other hand, is the unrelated, for, if there were anything external to it, it could be related to that.

(iii) It might be thought that the universal is related to its particulars, in ways variously conceived by philosophers both in the west and the east. But the universal is not related in any way even to the particular. For, both of them never appear on the same plane to get related. To the universal the particular never appears in that light, for we have seen that the particular owes its particularity to its relation to, or position in the midst of, other particulars. The universal itself is not a specific position; if it were so, the difference between it and any one particular will not be shared in common by others equally; particulars as such will not be different from it. This is to say that they will not be comparable even on one plane of existence. Therefore, the difference between the particular and the universal belongs to a plane different from that of the difference among particulars themselves. From the side of the universal there is no particular, and hence there is no relation.

(iv) There cannot be one particular at any time; the very notion of particularity, as due to position, militates against it. Obviously, no position is possible with one entity. It would be indistinguishable from the universal and from thought. The particular is essentially and inherently many. It would thus appear that the particular is doubly conditioned; it depends on the universal, for it is just the universal caught in the midst of external relations. The contribution of other particulars to its nature is very evident. The dependence of particulars upon one another is reciprocal, while its dependence on the universal is not so. The being of the particular is a standing contradiction. For A, a particular, is what it is owing to the being of other particulars which in turn depend upon A—an unavoidable vicious circle. No such contradiction is to be found in the being of the universals.

3. Hitherto we have been considering the universal and the particular without any reference to their relation with knowledge. It may at once be pointed out that all statements about the universal are valid in their entirety of knowledge. It is intelligible in itself and does not need to be defined in terms of others. It is never coincident with the object, which is essentially many and limited. If it were one, the object would be indistinguishable from knowledge. The object can, therefore, be taken as particular. Knowledge must extend before and after

the object to know it as an object. The difference between knowledge and object is not on a par with the differences among objects. Not being presentable in one plane of being, the relation between knowledge and object, like the supposed relation between universal and particular, is not tenable.

It is in keeping with this view of knowledge as universal, that Pure Being—Brahman—the highest Universal and Consciousness—Caitanya—are conceived as absolutely identical in Vedānta. From the standpoint of Consciousness—Pure Being—the world of particulars does not exist, or even appear as such. Spirit or Pure Consciousness cannot know any particular; to do so it shall have to take a station in the midst of particulars, identifying itself thereby with one specific position and viewing other particulars from that privileged and prejudiced position. Spirit has to become the ego; consciousness has to become discursive thinking. Even the Ego, limited as it is, is still more universal than the objects it encounters. This particularisation of Spirit is inexplicable, but it has a *de facto validity*.

4. Can there be many universals? *Prima facie* there seems to be no objection to their plurality; there are colours, sounds, pains and pleasures of various kinds. The pertinent question, however, is to ask whether the plurality of the universal is in conformity with its self-intelligible character. When I see a colour, its being one among many universals is not an immediate datum to me as the colour is. Its plurality is a character acquired in relation to others, and hence the universal has *ipso facto* lost its self-intelligent character. But a universal must rigorously avoid all reference to things not immediately given, just as it does not countenance the particulars. Pure Being, therefore, is the only true universal; other universals are particulars with regard to that. It alone is in itself, being self-intelligent. It is absolutely free, for its universality precludes its relationship with anything inside or outside it. It has no position. The essential character of the universal is not repeatability, but its self-intelligent and immanent nature.

2.4. THE CONCEPTION OF BODY*

Almost all the difficulties of the relation of the body and the self are due to the faulty and non-epistemological conception of the body. The paper proposes to enquire into the nature of the body and its possible relation to the self. I believe the conception presented here represents in the main the Absolutist position, especially of the Vedānta and possibly of the Sāṅkhya as well. But I have tried freely to reconstruct the theme, and I alone am responsible for the details and the consequent shortcomings of the conception.

I

The usual conception of the body is that of an object, as what is perceived as external to the self. The Cartesian conception is a well-known example. There are two insuperable difficulties which beset this conception. One is how an entity totally indifferent to the self can function as our body at all. Secondly, even if it could, we cannot resist the claims of each and every object to be equally the body of the self. The position may be sought to be improved by saying that not all objects are body, but only some with a determinate content. And we may possibly pitch upon some physiological characteristics as defining the body. This however serves to distinguish one object from another, but cannot impart that uniqueness and preference which we associate with our body. Nor can we, on purely objective grounds, explain the appropriation of the body by the self.

A more fruitful conception is to take the body as an instrument or activity which reaches you to something, the means by which we attain a desired end. It is not however necessary that I should *know* the body *as a means* before I can use it as a means. Rather the fact is otherwise. If I were to consciously appreciate anything as a means before I can utilise it to reach other things, I must first acquire it. It is yet *to be* reached. And I must use something else as the means to reach it. But if that in turn were to be consciously appreciated and reached, it would

*Reprinted from *The Philosophical Quarterly*, April, 1939.

require another means and so on *ad infinitum*. The sword before it can be wielded as an instrument must be reached at and grasped by the hand. In that state it is not an instrument, but a mere object. But the hand itself is not so reached; it is already one with us. The real body therefore is not reached at consciously, but it is already one with the self, when it acts as the body in reaching an end.

We now arrive at the notion that the body is not itself reached, when it helps us to other things. Unless it were initially one with the self, it cannot function as the body at all. This is at least true of the most primary body, one through which we acquire other bodies. A direct consequence of this is that it is not a true statement of affairs that we have the self and the body as separate and unrelated entities at first, and that afterwards they get somehow related. The mind and the body may, for eternity, be existing alongside of each other, and yet they would not get related unless a *deus ex machina* were invoked. It must therefore be taken as already one with the self.

If it were one with the self, how then do we know it *as body* or even that it is or has been one with the self? This is to say that the distinction between the self and its body could never have arisen. For, if two things are always coincident both in extent and duration and neither of them could be had apart from the other, we cannot even assert their duality. We are left with no ground of distinction. Therefore, if anything is known as body—and the very discussion of the body-problem implies at least this—it must be known as an object, as having a determinate and presentable character. A distinction between two entities, one of which at least does not possess any determinate character, cannot be made. If one has this character, the other can be distinguished from it by the lack of the said character.

There are two ways which facilitate the emergence of the distinction between the body and the self: want of consonance in our pursuit and the emergence of other bodies. No one is ordinarily conscious of one's seeing *through* the eye so long as the eye does not give one any trouble. But the moment it begins to pain or distort our perception resulting in a check to our usual pursuit, we begin to realise that *we have been* using the eye as an instrument of perception.

Again, suppose after seeing a coloured surface, I attend to sounds. When seeing the colour, I was not conscious of seeing it through the eye; I just see the object. But when I hear sounds subsequently, I am led to this sort of reflection. Now is one kind of sensation, now another; I am of course the same. There must have been some factor, not present now, which was responsible for the colour-sensum. Differences in the objective lead to the distinction of the self from the differents.

From the foregoing analysis, it follows that the body while it is actually functioning as a body, is not, and cannot be, known as body. Only when it ceases to function, it is known as body. Our consciousness of it is invariably retrospective: it is always apprehended as what *was* the body and *not as what is*. The reason for this is obvious. The body is so intimately identified with the self that it cannot be *known*, perceived as object. And only as it gets dissociated from the self do we know it at all. Without bringing in the identification with the self and the subsequent dissociation from it, the body cannot be defined as something in itself. Its essence consists in this spiritual history, its relation with the self.

II

Identification is mistaken identity: one entity is taken for, and appears as, another. An analogous case is that of illusion, e.g., the "rope-snake". While we are actually in illusion, we are not conscious of the illusion. Cancellation, which effects a dissociation of the "snake" from the rope for which it is mistaken, is at once the awareness of the previous state as illusion. Likewise, the body is known as body when we dissociate it from the self, when we annul its identification with the latter.

It might be thought that the body is at least an object, something in its own right apart from the self, though initially it is mistaken for the self. A more correct analysis of the identification-relation would show that only the unreal can be identified with another, the real. Two reals cannot simply be mistaken for each other; they cannot even be related. Two entities, real and independent, do not contain any ground of unity which would bind them together. They have to be related by a *tertium puid*, which somehow unifies them. Two substances, the chair and the table, can be related because of the space which underlies them. Two or more qualities can be related because of the substance which underlies them. It is not the cluster of the qualities which make the substance; but qualities cluster because of substance. By bringing in the *tertium quid* the problem is not solved but shifted. How is this *tertium quid* related to the body and the self? If the latter are independent of that too, we would be requiring a fourth to unite these, and so on *ad infinitum*.

The Cartesian conception of mind and matter as independent realities leads necessarily to their dependence on God as the ground of their unity—a position made explicit in Occasionalism, which rightly denies interaction. A logical outcome of this is the pantheism of Spinoza—the denial of the independence and reality of the modes, mind and matter.

Even if God were conceived as the unity of mind and matter (body), there would still be the problem of their relation. In respect to God, mind and body cannot be independent. If they were, then the former would not relate them and be their unity. And this will lead to another mediation and so on. With regard to God then they are unreal appearances. Spinoza's view, made consistent, would approximate to this position.

This unacceptable predicament of declaring the body to be illusory confronts us, it can be averred, because we have abstracted the body from the self and vice versa. It might further be suggested that body and mind are organic to each other: one cannot simply be without the other. If on the previous view (the Cartesian Conception) there is no bond of unity, on the present one there is no ground of distinction. If two things have been always together and will be so too, even the bare distinction of their duality cannot arise. We are not justified in taking them as two. All relation implies a non-implicatory term which is not exhausted in the relation. That must be something in itself, irrespective of the relation. This cannot be the body, for we have no means of coming across the body apart from the self. The self is what is in *itself*.

So we can neither conceive the self and the body as independent of each other nor as mutually dependent. The only alternative that accords with facts is that the body is what it is in relation with the self and nothing apart from it. The body is the unreal appearance of the self, what is mistaken for it. The "rope-snake" is nothing at all without its identification with the rope. It seems to persist and have a ghostly existence or subsistence insofar as it is not totally cancelled. And there is a demand to realise the appearance as mere nothing, *tuccha*.

Alternatively, the self can be viewed as the essence or reality of the body. Initially, they are an indistinguishable whole, a continuum. Later analysis reveals the self as the inner core or the soul and the body as the outer shell. The object itself has, on this conception, to be taken as a degraded or castaway body, i.e., what we were identified with before. If the object were, to start with, an independent entity existing outside the self, the two could never be related. They were in identification with each other initially, as in perception. The self gets dissociated from the continuum only later. This requires elucidation.

III

The thickest and grossest body we have in perception. There we are not conscious of the distinction between subject and object. It may be said that we identify ourselves, for the time being and to a limited extent at least, with the particular object. The particular is an entity whose position is fixed by its relation with all other entities, spatially and temporally, in varying degrees of importance and relevance. It is quite natural for the terrestrial observer to instinctively identify himself with the earth and locate and measure in terms of the earth's position and distance. For him the earth is the body at the time, for though its function is un-noticed, it conditions our sense of the celestial objects. Normally, we are identified with the physical body; and all our sense-experience is conditioned by it. And when we actually perceive, the body temporarily extends, as it were, to the object of perception. The sense-organs are so many tentacles which the physical body shoots forth in grasping the object. But this temporary extension of the body or its identification with the particular is not a conscious process : in perception we are not reflectively aware of the perceiving. And only as we withdraw our identification with the object, do we become reflectively aware of the previous act of perception. It is then that we make the bifurcation of subject and object. The identification with the object well explains the feelingin of being in immediate contact with reality which is the unique characteristic of perception.

This supplies the point of reference or direction to thought. Perception is thus understood on our theory, as an extended body-function.

Owing to the stress of interest there arises, in the presentational field, the distinction between the thing and its quality, the substantive and the adjective. This is the most primary distinction we can think of. It is through the adjective, the universal, that we interpret substance—the "that", which tends to fall outside the "what". Thought emerges with this distinction, as it tries to understand the real through the what. The bifurcation into the subject and the object is also engendered thereby—a distinction absent in the actual state of perception. In perception we identify ourselves with the particular, which for the time being constitutes the extension of our body. In thought we identify ourselves with the concept or the universal, and through that we reach the object mediately, ideally. The communicability of thought is due to the identity and universality of the concept.

Empirical concepts serve to understand particular objects, and they vary in different situations. There may well be forms or Categories of the Understanding and Reason which condition, not this and that but, all objects. The Kantian *a priori*, if they represent the actual state of things, are to be conceived as the almost permanent body of the self. The *a priori*, while they actually function, are not known as such. Nor is it necessary. Their functioning is unconscious. We are so one with them that we are not aware of their presence. Nor do we know *when* we got identified with them. We are as little conscious of their beginning as that of illusion. Nobody can say to himself: "Lo ! let me now fall into illusion"

When they function they are not known as *a priori*; when they are known as *a priori*, they have already ceased to function as such. The consciousness *of* the *a priori* is not consciousness *through* the *a priori*. For, the consciousness *of* the *a priori* cannot itself be conditioned by the *a priori*; if it did, it would invariably lead to a *regressus ad infinitum*. This very knowledge would require the very same or other *a priori*, and these again would be known by others and so on. Rather, we cannot even be aware of the *a priori*. The question may be raised about the kind of knowledge or consciousness that a critique of experience (say that of Kant or Hegel) proposes to give. A critique of knowledge can hardly be knowledge, if by the latter we mean the knowledge of the table, chair etc. The awareness of the implications of judgment is no judgment.

A critique of the *a priori* then means the cessation of the *a priori.* To know the *a priori* as such is at once to be free from it. And this cessation, like the cessation of illusion, is a conscious process. If the *a priori* were the spirit or one with it, there would not be the consciousness of them at any particular time. In that case, we should either be conscious of them always or never at all. But the fact is that the beginning of the *a priori* or their identification with the self is not a conscious process, but their cessation is. The *Critique,* as the analysis of the *a priori,* is their dissociation from the pure self. They are to be understood more as the *Avidyā* of the Vedānta than otherwise. Its beginning and continued identification with the self is a mystery, but its cancellation is reflectively known in spiritual or non-empirical consciousness.

It may be said that a consciousness of *a priori* is purely verbal, purely symbolic without any content. But this would at least show that the word is a more universal and subtle body than even the Categories, and that we become aware of one body through another.

IV

From the above we can surmise that wherever there is reaching, as the awareness of something unknown before, there is body. This is in fact the converse of our definition of body as that through which something is reached. There might as well be a hierarchy or gradation among the several bodies. One body may be gross and particular, another subtler and more universal, another subtler still. They might also be causally linked to one another. The physical body, through which in perception we are identified with the object, may be conceived as the outward expression of the inner tendencies and development of the mind. In fact it is unhesitatingly accepted by the Indian Systems that the physical body with the experiences it enjoys is due entirely to our *karmas,* to our *vāsanās.* These constitute a quasi-permanent body almost indistinguishable from the self. They together make up our personality.

The complex of *karmas* would not itself have come into being had we started our cycle of life with a clean slate. We could not have picked up anything on the way. Wealth might be increased and diversified, not out of nothing, but because of an initial and original outlay, one's own labour or thrift to start with. This initial causal body, by means of which we acquire the complex of karmas and through this the gross physical body, is the body *par excellence*; it is the ultimate and underived means by which we acquire all other things. In religious language, this is called original sin or finitude. The Vedânta would take it as *avidyā* or *kāraṇa-śarira.*

All other bodies are reached through it, and therefore they may be said to have both a beginning and an end. The ultimate body is not acquired; it perishes but is not born; we can put it off but not on. In fact the identification of the self with the original or any other body is a lapse from consciousness. Hence we have called the relation between the body and the self mistaken identity or illusion. As in the case of the illusory appearance, no reason can be given why it should get identified with the spirit, with the real. It is a standing mystery. However, the real problem is not how to relate the body to the self or vice versa, for they are already identified with each other; but the dissociation of the self from the body, the cancellation of this illusion. The endeavour of all spiritual discipline may well be to bring about a sure and lasting freedom from all body, to realise the spirit in its innate purity. And even to have raised the problem of the body is already to be aware, symbolically at least, of the possibility of the freedom of the self from the body.

When we recognise anything *as* body, it is already dissociated from the self and discarded. But this recognition, as it is a new acquisition in experience, is made possible through a subtler and more universal body. Wherever there is reaching there is body. The original body, from the nature of the case, is the last to be discarded. There is some peculiarity about this. This discarding, unlike other discardings, is not of a thinking or discursive kind. For this would, on our conception, lead to a regress of bodies. It might therefore be hazarded that the culmination of spiritual discipline is a non-discursive consciousness beyond understanding and reason. The cessation of the most primordial body is, as accepted by the Vedānta, the Spirit itself.

3.1. REVELATION AND REASON IN VEDĀNTA*

I am deeply grateful to Professor Devasenapathi for inviting me to deliver a course of lectures on Advaita Vedānta in this University. I deem it a great honour. This gives me an opportunity to share my thoughts with you.

The first question that I wish to raise is whether the Vedānta, not necessarily Advaita alone, is a philosophical system based on purely rational considerations or on revelation. Could it be taken as philosophy understood in the light of the Greek tradition as a free, unfettered adventure of human reason in the realms of the supersensuous? Or should it be conceived as a textual interpretation like the medieval Christian scholastic philosophy or even like the Islamic philosophy? The term '*Vedānta*' primarily means the *Upaniṣads* and it is in this sense that Śaṅkara uses this term.[1] He does not use it to designate his philosophy. The Advaita system based on the *Vedānta* has also acquired the name '*Vedānta*'. The secondary signification of the term 'Vedānta' has in a sense suppressed and superseded the primary sense. It should be taken as 'Mīmāṃsā' (*vākyārthavicāra*) or a systematic consideration of all the texts of the *Upaniṣads*. We need not be very squeamish about taking it as 'Mīmāṃsā'. In his second interpretation of the third *sūtra* of the *Brahma-sūtra* (*Śāstrayonitvāt*), Śaṅkara raises the question: What is the source or ground useful in understanding the Real, that which is *pramāṇa* for making the assertions that Brahman is the ultimate cause of the origination, sustenance and cessation of the world.[2] Is the causality of Brahman established by reasoning as is done by the Naiyāyikas? It is not so. It is based on the *Upaniṣads*.

*Reprinted from *Journal of the Madras University*, January 1980.

1. *Brahma-sūtra*, I, i. 1, (introducion): yathā cāyam arthaḥ sarveṣām vedāntānām, tathā vayam, asyām śārīrakamimāṃsāyām pradarśayiṣyāmaḥ. At several places after quoting Upaniṣadic texts, Śaṅkara says, iti vedāntāḥ; iti vedānteṣu etc.

2. *Brahma-sūtra*, I, i. 3. atha vā yathoktam ṛgvedādi śāstram yoniḥ kāraṇam asya brahmaṇo yathāvat svarūpādhigame. śāstrād eva pramāṇājjagato janmādikāraṇam brahmādhigamyate ityabhiprāyaḥ.

The text on which this interpretation of the *Sūtra* is based is found in the *Bṛhadāraṇyaka Upaniṣad.*[1] In the *Bṛhadāraṇyaka*, there takes place a discussion between Yājñavalkya and many others in the court of Janaka. The last one to debate after others have been defeated, is the illfated Śākalya, who persistently questions Yājñavalkya. After answering all these questions, Yājñavalkya gets annoyed and then turns on him and says, "If you do not tell me about the spirit known only through the Upaniṣads, your head will surely fall." Śākalya did not know the answer. He was only a purveyor of secondary knowledge. And therefore his head fell. Śaṅkara says that this narration in the *Upaniṣad* is a myth. It is for the sake of extolling *brahma-vidyā.*[2] The truth that is inculcated is that the ultimate Reality can be known only through the *Upaniṣads.* This knowledge cannot be gained by *tarka* or reasoning.[3] Brahman is known only through scriptural testimony.

In the beginning of the *Bhāṣya* on the *Bhagavad-Gitā*, Śaṅkara speaks of two things which can be known only by revelation. He speaks of *dharma* which is *pravṛtti-mārga* and *Brahman* which is *nivṛtti-mārga.* Why is it that the nature of moral duty or even ritualistic performances of certain sacrifices could not be known by empirical observations and by laws of reasoning ? There is no connection between throwing some oblations into the fire, muttering some recitations of mystic sounds, etc., and getting to heaven. No one can see that connection. And even with regard to moral duty, can one say that honesty, charity, chastity, kindliness, etc., invariably lead to the well-being of the society ? But the causal connection between the means and the end is not empirically observed. Sometimes the so-called moral act does not invariably produce the desired result. One who is upright and virtuous is not necessarily happy. On the contrary, good people are very often seen to suffer. So there seems to be no connection between morality and happiness. Even in the intuitionistic ethics like that of Immanuel Kant, the utmost

1. *Bṛhadāraṇyakopaniṣad* III, ix. 26. tam tvaupaniṣadam puruṣam pṛcchāmi, tam cen me na vivakṣyasi mūrdhā te vipatiṣyatiti.

2. ākhyāyikā brahma-vidyāstutyarthā.

3. *Kaṭhopaniṣad*, I.ii.9. naiṣā tarkeṇa matirāpaneyā proktā'nyenaiva sujñānāya preṣṭha,

that we can expect is to have a kind of formal criterion of duty as the categorical imperative, *i.e.* as that which can be universalised or as that which requires us to treat a human being always as an end and never as a means. These are merely formal criteria. They do not tell us which acts are to be followed and which acts are moral and so on. So there must be some authority, some source, from which we derive the notion of *dharma* as comprising both moral duty and ritualistic or ceremonial acts with which alone, we may say, the Mīmāṃsā is concerned. Therefore in the beginning of the *Mīmāṃsā Sūtra* after stating that *dharma* is something which is to be enjoined, which is of the nature of a command, Jaimini says, "Let us now enquire into the nature of the evidence for these."[1] Then he says that *pratyakṣa* (perception) which is concerned with the contact of sense-organs with the objects, can only reveal to us what is present and cannot tell us something which will happen and which is beyond the purview of the sense-organs. Therefore, Śabara, the commentator, says that only through verbal injunctions can those things be revealed[2] that are past, present, future, something which is hidden, something which is subtle, something which is obstructed. So no sense-organ is competent to tell us of the nature of moral duty. For the same reason, the other means of knowledge like inference are also incapable of revealing to us the nature of moral duty. In the same way Brahman, which is supersensuous reality, cannot be known by perception, because it is not sensuous and has no sensuous qualities. It has no form, no sound, no touch. Hence perception is out of the question in the case of Brahman. Can we know it by inference or by presumption, or by analogical reasoning? No; because Brahman is completely transcendent. There is no connection between Brahman and things which are known through empirical evidences. Paradoxically, Brahman is in a sense the most universally known. It is invariably known as the substantive of every knowledge. But Brahman escapes us by its very univer-

1. *Mīmāṃsā Sūtra* I,i. 2, 3, 4. codanā lakṣaṇo'rtho dharmaḥ; tasya nimitta-pariṣṭiḥ ; satsamprayoge puruṣasyendriyāṇām buddhijanma tat pratyakṣam animittam vidyamāno-palambhanatvāt.

2. *Mīmāṃsā Sūtra* I, i. 2. codanā hi bhūtam bhavantam bhaviṣyantam sūkṣmam vyavahitam viprakṛṣṭam ityevam jātīyakam artham śaknotyavagamayitum. nānyat kiñcanendriyam.

sality, by its very uniformity and by its very all-pervasiveness, by being something which is always present, something which is everything and something which one cannot get rid of. One cannot acquire or abandon it. Suppose we are asked, "What is in this room?" You will certainly count and give an inventory of the persons, chairs, tables, fittings, fans, etc. in the hall; but we will not include the air or light in this room in that list, because they are supplied free and are present everywhere. Brahman which is much more universal, uniform, and unobtrusive than air or light is not known because of its very unobtrusiveness. In a sense we may say that Brahman is known in every knowledge and also we can say that Brahman is not known. Therefore it is taken as that which is something different from the known and different from the unknown.[1] For these considerations, Brahman cannot be the object of perception or any other means of knowledge excepting verbal testimony. Scriptural language is capable of revealing to us what is not present, what is subtle, and so on.

It may be said that we have the power to frame hypotheses even with regard to the things unknown. And also, we can by analogical inference talk about things that cannot be observed directly by the senses. We do not see God with our eyes and yet we can speak of God by inferring His presence by arguments which show that He is the Creator, that He is the First Cause of this world, etc. In the same way it may be analogously said that just as we see everyday an artist creating works of art, even so we can infer the existence of the first cause. We can stretch our imagination and say that the first cause must be immensely great, the greatest in perfection among all creators. The Naiyāyika blindly formulates the inference as follows: This world requires an agent, because it is a product like the pot, table etc. The effect is contingent, that which has a beginning. One can apply this inference to the world. The world as a whole with everything in it can be taken as a contingent effect.

Things are not so very easy as they look, and I should remind you here of what Kant says in his *Transcendental Dialectic* with regard to the ideas of Reason concerning God. He examines every argument, cosmological etc., and says that they cannot

1. *Kenopaniṣad*, I. 3. anyad eva tad viditādatho aviditād adhi.

establish God conclusively. In India the Buddhists, the Jainas, and the Mīmāṃsakas have not accepted the world as an effect. We are begging the question when we say that the world is an effect and that it is contingent. How do we know that it is an effect ? Things in the world might have been produced, might have originated and may cease to exist. Can we ever observe the world originating and ceasing to be ? It means that we must posit ourselves as existing somewhere even before the beginning of this world. Nobody can do that. We may say that Ram, Shyam, Devadatta, are all produced by their parents. But it does not mean that society has a parent. That is a kind of false analogy. On the other hand, what applies to the world as a whole need not be true of the parts of the world. And therefore the theory of creation is not proved. And even if we grant that the world is an effect that needs to be brought into existence by an agent or some material cause other than itself or by something which is both the material and the efficient cause, does it follow that that cause is Brahman or God ? It may be the result of the free play of atoms surcharged with energy, as the Jainas think. The atoms themselves are active. Or it may be the result of the *prakṛti* of the Sāṅkhya, or some other entity. When we leave the sensuous region and go beyond it to account for the origin of the world, we are in the realm of mere conjectures. We have free scope to give our imagination, and no two persons will agree about the actual cause of the world. nd imagination would depend upon man's temperament, his capacity, his prejudice, and so on. This is the negative objection.

There are also positive objections. If there is a God who creates this world, why does He not create all persons happy ?. Is He incompetent to do it ? Or does He not have enough goodness to do this ? We could also have a counter-argument and say, "How can God produce the world unless He is embodied ?" We have not seen any agent who is disembodied. Any agency, and efficient cause, is embodied. On the other hand, natural objects like mountains and rivers are not produced by any agent, by any embodied person; they are already there. They are having their own laws. Nobody bodily takes water from higher places to the lower plains. It flows of its own accord. The trees grow of their own accord. The seasons are changing of their own accord. Nor can we accept the law of parsimony here. We may apply that law to an hypothesis, and say that hypothesis which has the least number of presuppositions is the truer one, is the more acceptable one. But who has invested this law of parsimony with that kind of authority? For aught we know, nature may be lavish. It does not always follow the law of parsimony. And what constitutes *lāghava tarka*, parsimony of concepts, in a particular situation? Who can decide whether a particular hyphothesis has really fewer presuppositions than another? So it is a matter, again, of temperament and taste. All these considerations have been urged by Śaṅkara when he comments on the *sūtra*, *tarkāpratiṣṭhānāt*.[1] Therein he denies the absoluteness of bare, unaided reasoning which is not stable and final. Why? There is no unanimity among those who use bare reasoning as the sole guide. It is not possible to bring together all the logicians, past, present and future, not only in this world, perhaps in other parts of the universe also. How can you bring them together and then make them agree? And even if you bring them together, would they agree? So Śaṅkara asks: who told you that the Sāṅkhya philosopher is the superior person among all the logicians? And there is no finality in it, because what is established by one person is disestablished or overthrown by another person who is more skillful in wielding logic. Again, there is no certainty about reasoning. What worth can we attach to such pretensions or imaginations? So speculative philosophy is based on mere imagination (*utprekṣā*). Further one cannot have any control over reasoning.[2] To guide or regulate it is difficult.

It may be argued that all that Śaṅkara urges about the instability of reasoning, its want of finality, its want of unanimity and certainty is again based on reasoning. He is using reason to discredit reason. To this the answer is: the critique of reason means that reason is both the object of enquiry and the agent conducting the enquiry. This 'of', in the expression *critique of reason* is both accusative and nominative. It means that reason can be reflective and be aware of its own limitation.

1. *Brahma Sūtra* II, i. 11.

2. *Bhāṣya* on *Brahma Sūtra* II, i. 11. yasmān nirāgamāḥ puruṣotprekṣāmātranibandhanās tarkās apratiṣṭhitā bhavanti. utprekṣāyā niraṅkuśatvāt.

Reason can be reflectively aware of its own limitations. Śrī Harṣa and Nāgārjuna used the dialectic to show that any speculative philosophy contradicts itself, that it is not consistent with its own presupposition and that it does not give, any positive insight or intuition into the real (*prajñā*). So reason is not a way of knowing things. But it is a way of arranging, correcting, regulating, systematising thought. It itself cannot generate thought or knowledge. A balance will weigh, but it cannot provide things which are weighed. Measure can measure, but it cannot provide things which it measures. If you are given a heap of fruits, you can arrange them in any way you like. You can make it square, pyramid or any way you like; but the arrangement itself is not the fruit. Similarly, reason is not the faculty of intuition. It does not give new knowledge or insight into the nature of the real. That is the burden of what Śaṅkara says.

We may consider certain objections that may be raised against the position that *śruti* or revelation will give us certain knowledge, infallible insight into the real. It may be argued that *śruti* also cannot fare much better. What is the certainty that we can attach to sentences and verbal knowledge? Does not verbal knowledge require to be corroborated by and conform to other experiences? Suppose a person makes a statement, we ask for the ground for such a statement. We are not satisfied with what one merely says. So also the case must be with *śruti*. To this objection it can be replied that we must admit that any knowledge must be accepted as self-valid. If we accept one knowledge as corroborated by another knowledge and that by another knowledge and so on, then where is the end? If we stop with *some* uncorroborated knowledge, which does not require certification or confirmation by any other knowledge, then we are abandoning the principle with which we started. So in the last analysis we have to accept knowledge as self-valid (*svataḥ-pramāṇa*). We can say that we are not making any special claim in respect of verbal knowledge but it is true of every knowledge. Every knowledge is self-valid unless it is contradicted by other factors. Śaṅkara says: Scripture is self-valid just as the sun is self-manifest with regard to the sensuous objects.[1] It does not

1. Śruteḥ svataḥ prāmāṇyam, raveriva rūpa-viṣaye. cp. *Śloka Vārttika* I, i, 2 (53):
tasmād bodhātmakatvena buddheḥ prāptā pramāṇatā;
arthānyathātvahetūtthadoṣajñānād apodyate.

require any other light. The light of the sun reveals, and that is the end of the matter.

The *Vedānta* or the *Upaniṣad*, being a set of words put in a particular order is composed of sentences which are meaningful and must be the work of some author. Therefore it is subject to all the prejudices and shortcomings of that person. This is one objection. Secondly, as language, it is convention and an arbitrary convention at that . How can you convey anything more than or different from what the convention itself has put into it ? The capacity of language to reveal to us something transcendent, supersensuous, which is beyond convention, as Brahman, is questionable. Language, it is said, is an arbitrary convention established in the past by human beings or as the Nyâya version has it, by divine convention (*Īśvara-saṅketa*). The modern linguistic philosophers say, and the Buddhists also agree, that language is a game with a set of syntactical operative functions and those who belong to that group know how to operate these functions. What is explained here is that we cannot go beyond the limits of language functions in a closed circle. We cannot get beyond into something which is non-linguistic. We can ask for clarification, explanation, simplification; but language itself cannot be taken as revelation of something which is non-linguistic. That is the burden of the whole argument. We cannot jump out of it, as it were, to reality, to God or Brahman.

Let me answer these objections in brief. Language, it is argued, is a convention. It has a certain origin. That is, there was a time when there was no language at all. People must have gathered together in an assembly and in the assembly some smart persons must have said that "crow" stands for crow, that "calf" stands for calf, etc. Now, if this was the origin of language, it can be asked: how did the other persons understand ? To make people understand, you require language. You cannot originate convention without language, and language itself is taken as convention. This is the vicious circle.[1] To escape from

1. *Śabara Bhāṣya on Mīmāṃsā Sūtra*, 1, 1. 5. na hi sambandhavyatiriktaḥ kaścit kālo'sti yasmin na kaścid api śabdaḥ kenacid arthena sambaddha āsīt. katham ? sambandhakriyaiva nopapadyate. avaśyam anena sambandham kurvatā kenacit śabdena kartavyaḥ. yena kriyeta tasya kena kṛtaḥ. athānyena kenacit śabdena

this, one may say that language is not man's convention, but a divine convention. Just as a person gives names to his children or arbitrarily names certain plants and animals which have been discovered by him, so proper names are created by man. But with regard to the common names, man is not the originator and there must be some common agent, who cannot be this man or that man, but God. Let us take it that God has made this convention. How will he make this convention known to human beings? He must reveal these conventions and say: 'let this word stand for this object' and so on. Now how will you make this convention known to others. To understand this convention made by God, people should be already conversant with the use of language.

Here we are back again in the old vicious circle. Hence language cannot be derived from non-linguistic phenomenon. It is a kind of non-derived thing. Modern philosophers have also accepted this. The grammarian philosophers of India hold that nobody has made the word and meaning go together. *Śabda* is *nitya*; *artha* is *nitya*; and *sambandha* is also *nitya*.[1] We do not know when language originated. We live, move and have our being in language. Words must be taken as the *formal* and natural cause of the world. It is said that Prajāpati created the world on the norm of Vedic words. He uttered the word "*bhū*" and the earth was created and so on.[2] This is comparable to the doctrine of Ideas by Plato. *Śabda* forms the eternal formal pattern on which the whole world is created.

Language is also presupposed by the *Upaniṣads* when they say that Brahman is real, that the world is false, and that the jīva is Brahman. The *Upaniṣads* cannot tell us what is false, what is real; they cannot tell us the usage of these words. That is, they cannot perform two functions. They have to convey a message, viz., that Brahman is real and that the world is false; but they have also to give the instrument, the faculty by which

kṛtaḥ; tasya keneti tasya keneti naivāvatiṣṭhate. tasmād avaśyam anena sambandham kurvatā akṛtasambandhāḥ kecana śabdā vṛddhavyavahārasiddhā abhyupagantavyāḥ.

1. siddhe śabdārtha-sambandhe—the very first *Vārtika* commented upon by Patañjali in his *Mahābhāṣya*.

2. *Brahma Sūtra*, I, iii, 28; 29.

we will understand the usage also. So we are asking *śruti* to perform two functions at the same time. They can tell us that Brahman is real and that the world is not real. But the usage of these words 'real', 'false' etc. must have already been known to us. That is what Śaṅkara says. There is no difference between the worldly words and Vedic words. Words and the meaning which we attach to the words are the same as of the Vedic words. This is in full accord with the Mīmāṃsā doctrine[1] on the continuity of the usage of word both in the Vedas and the workaday world.

Now as regards the contention that language is a game, that we cannot go beyond the circle of linguistic conventions, and that we can only ask for clarification and simplification, but that we cannot get any revelation or knowledge into the real, we may ask: do we use words always to clarify? Of course, we ask for clarification sometimes. But primarily language is used to convey something, to convey meaning. It is a wrong philosophy of language to ignore this basic position. The critics cannot claim any peculiar privilege in legislating out of existence the other conceptions of language. What they do is to bring in some other kind of philosophy. The option is not between philosophy and no philosophy (no metaphysics), but between rival metaphysical conceptions. Their standpoint does not appeal to me, and I have shown the way in which primarily language is used to convey meaning, to refer to the objects, not merely to clarify expressions. It means that language is something which can reveal, which can convey, which can stand for things.

Linguistic philosophers also hold that that alone is significant which has an opposite. When we speak of something, we always distinguish, for instance, table from something which is not table. Here we are confronting something which is *all universal* and for which there is no other. Brahman is so universal that there is no other and it has no quality, no attribute. How

1. *Śābarabhāṣya* on *Mīmāṃsāsūtra* I. i. 30. ya eva laukikāḥ śabdāsta eva vaidikās ta evaiṣām arthā iti, kutaḥ? prayogacodanābhāvāt. evam prayogacodanā sambhavati yadi ta eva śabdās ta evārthāḥ. itarathā śabdānyathātve'rtho na pratīyeta tasmād ekaśabdatvam iti. ucyate; prayojanamidam; heturvyapadiśyatām iti. na teṣām eṣām ca vibhāgam upalabhāmahe. ata evaikaśabdatvam, tāñścārthān avagacchema.

can we say that it is this as different from that? It has no connotation, nor does it have any denotation. The very incapacity of Brahman to have connotation and denotation makes all the sources of the knowledge of Brahman insignificant. Even *sat*, *cit* and *ānanda*, are not the qualities of Brahman. Nor are they different Brahmans. Then, how is it to be understood? Only empirical objects could be known, about which statements could be made and distinguished from other objects. It may be argued that "God" is something which is significant. He can be spoken of as a super-person, as a power, as the first cause. But this cannot be applied to Brahman.

To this our reply is Brahman can be spoken of as *what cannot be described*. It is speakable as the unspeakable. We make use of negative language. If, of two things, one has a positive content, quality, etc., and the other does not have them, the thing that does not have them can be distinguished from the thing which has them by the non-possession of these qualities. By not possessing the qualities it is easily distinguishable from things which have them. So *neti neti* is a perfectly valid language. In this process, first of all, we make an ascription, and then we negate it. In the transition from the false ascription to the negation, we become conscious of the ground of which we made a certain false ascription and then negate it. We say that there is something behind, which is a support of this false ascription.[1] So it can be known through negation. Speakability and objectivity are not coincident as the Naiyāyika thinks. The Vedāntist says that the thing need not be an object, but still it can be spoken of. What we speak about need not be known as an object.[2]

Is Brahman completely unknown? It is not completely unknown, because it is known as I. The difficulty here is that we are misapprehending it. But even this misapprehension reveals to us in some form the underlying reality. The illusory is not completely false. There is some ground which is mani-

1. The well known dictum and method of the Advaita Vedānta: adhyāropāpavādābhyām niṣprapañcam brahma pratipadyate.

2. The Advaita distinction between vṛtti-vyāpti and phalavyāpti; that is, a thing may be referred to in thought, but it need not be objectified as *this* or *that*.

fested in this false dascription. If it is completely known, no enquiry is necessary. If it is completely unknown, no enquiry is possible. So the enquiry of Brahman means that we know that we have some apprehension or knowledge of Brahman. Only our knowledge about it is wrong. We are ascribing features to it which it does not have, and by negating these ascriptions we will arrive at the real thing.

Only with regard to the supersensible, scripture is the authority. The sensible objects of the world could be known by perception and other means. Revelation does not mean that we accept all that is stated in the *Veda*. Whatever other religions may say, Hinduism does not hold that all that is stated in scripture is to be accepted as it is. In the *Veda* there may be statements which are repetitive, which are *anuvāda* and statements which are opposed to things that are established otherwise by empirical observations. (*virodhe syād guṇavādaḥ*). We do not accept such statements as valid. There may be statements which are conditionally valid. There may be statements, the principal meaning of which alone is to be taken.[1] Again, there may be statements whose secondary sense alone should be taken. What is the principle for adopting the secondary or the primary sense? And what is the method of ascertaining it? We require consideration by *tarka*, by rules of interpretation (*mīmāṃsā*). Mīmāṃsā is *nyāya*, logic, reasoning. If scriptural utterances contradict our experience and if what is conveyed by them is capable of being observed and known by empirical observation, scripture does not constitute the authority. Scripture is valid only in those spheres which are supersensuous. The acceptance of revelation is subject to our applying thought and logical rules of interpretation to settle the true and final import. When

1. If such statements are taken literally and in their own context, they would be quite insignificant. Therefore, they are related to injunctions and prohibitions (*vidhi, niṣedha*) as either praising or deprecatory statements, respectively. They become significant indirectly either by leading to the performance of injunctions or by restraining persons from doing things prohibited. The doctrine of Arthavāda thus imports a measure of meaning to statements which are praśaṃsā, parakṛtiḥ and purākalpaḥ. According to another classification it is as under: anuvādo'vadhārite;

virodhe guṇavādaḥ syādanuvādo'vadhārite;
hūtārthavādas tadbhānād arthavādas tridhā mataḥ.

food is given, we must chew it and subject it to the process of assimilation by the juices of the stomach. Only then does is become part and parcel of our being. Even so in the case of scripture, the process of assimilation is required. Hence it is said by Śaṅkara that *puruṣa-buddhi-sāhāyyatva* or the aid of the reasoning is necessary for understanding the meaning of scriptural texts. Scripture also declares: "One sees by the sharp intellect." Far from being antagonistic to reason, scripture welcomes it. In fact, without reasoning we cannot understand the true import of scripture. As a matter of fact, I wonder why the Western thinkers have not so far invented the rules of interpretation as far as the Bible is concerned, whereas in India our chief concern has been this. The whole of Mīmāṃsā is a very stupendous creation of rules of interpretation. I am bold to say that there is nothing in the world that can compare with Mīmāṃsā with regard to the systematic way in which texts should be dealt with. For example, issues such as, "What is *vidhi* (injunction)?" "What is *niṣedha* (prohibition)?" "Which is the principal?" "Which is the secondary?" are dealt with in Mīmāṃsā. Leaving alone eschatological considerations like heaven, etc., and taking it merely as exegetical system concerning the rules of interpretation, Mīmāṃsā is a stupendous discipline.

The Vedānta agrees with the Mīmāṃsā. But whereas Mīmāṃsā would reduce everything to injunction relating to ritualistic or ceremonial acts, Vedānta would hold that even those statements in the *Veda* that speak about existent entities are significant. One may say that this acceptance of the rules of interpretation imports a limitation of subjectivity or relativity, because we now open the doors for interpretation; but one cannot help it. We need not feel shy of it. After all, this is a help. The *Veda* is not merely to be repeated by rote but has to be understood; and understanding means taking the help of the rules of interpretation. Philosophical schools differ from one another in respect of the rules of interpretation. Ācāryas also differ. Even among the Ācāryas of Advaita there are differences in interpretations on certain doctrinal matters. In fact the whole of Advaita could not be taken as a single monolithic construction. We find all sorts of views fully expressed, and yet there is a fundamental unity, as Sureśvarācārya says, regarding the basic tenets. Different techniques have been used to bring about the conviction of identity of Brahman with Ātman; and all these techniques are valid.[1] This is reiterated by a late writer, Appayya Dīkṣita.[2] One may also say that after *śravaṇa* there is *manana*. What is the function of *manana* ? *Manana* is *vicāra* (enquiry), and it is a function of the intellect. It has two principal functions: (1) to remove the improbability about the statements and (2) to remove the contradictions.[3] If there is a debate between the Vedāntist and a non-Vedāntist or an atheist or a Christian, it will not do if one argues with one's texts and ask the other disputant to accept them. We have to produce arguments which would be appealing to him, which he should be able to accept on grounds of reason. So on this account also reason is required to meet the objections not necessarily from the Vedāntists but also from atheists and others.

What kind of knowledge does *śravaṇa* give us ? There are two schools here. One says that *śravaṇa* gives us mediate knowledge because it is a species of verbal knowledge. They say that *śravaṇa* is incapable of giving us the immediate intuitive perception of Brahman. This is the view held by Vācaspati Miśra. He says that after *śravaṇa* we have *manana* and *nididhyāsana*. By long practices of contemplation i.e., constant meditation, the mediate knowledge obtained by *śravaṇa* is changed into immediate knowledge. As against this, we have the Vivaraṇa school which says that even *śabda* or verbal testimony can give us immediate knowledge. However, not all verbal knowledge will give us immediate knowledge; but statements about things which are immediate are capable of giving immediate knowledge. We know the story of ten persons who after crossing a river wanted to make sure that all of them had safely crossed the river. Everyone counted others except himself, and they found that the tenth man was missing. A passer-by who came to their rescue said that the tenth man was the person who was counting.

1. *Bṛhadāraṇyakopaniṣad Bhāṣya Vārttika*, I, iv.402.
   yayā yayā bhavet puṃsām vyutpattiḥ pratyagātmani;
   sā saiva prakriyeha syāt sādhvī sā cānavasthitā.
2. prācīnair vyavahārasiddhaviṣayeṣvātmaikyasiddhau param;
   sannahyadbhir anādarāt śaraṇayo nānāvidhā darśitāḥ.
   Siddhāntaleśasaṅgraha, introductory verse.
3. Manana removes asambhāvanā and viparītabhāvanā.

He conveyed that information through words "you are the tenth man" (*śabda*).[1] Hence even words are capable of conveying immediate knowledge.[2]

What is the use, then, of *manana* and *dhyāna*, it may be asked, if *śabda* can generate immediate knowledge? *Manana* and *dhyāna* are *not* required for converting mediate knowledge into immediate knowledge. They help to remove the false ascriptions. We do not find any contradiction between reason and revelation. They are not mutually contradictory; they are, complementary, provided we understand them in a reasonable sense. It is only an exaggerated claim that will put either reason or revelation at the cost of the other, or bring them into conflict with each other. If we take *śravaṇa* as giving us intuitions, giving us knowledge or insight into the supersensuous reality, *dharma* or Brahman, and reason as *vicāra*, as thought that interprets the given, arranges it, corrects it, and regulates it, then there is no difficulty; and we treat them as mutually complementary; one is necessary for the other. Reason lacks substance or content; and *śruti* lacks form. But if we interpret reason as that which gives us not only regulative principles, correct procedures and rules, but also as giving us the stuff or content, as Hegel held, then we cannot reconcile scripture and reason. On the other hand, persons, like the fundamentalists and literalists of the Bible, take every word in the scriptures as certain and true without modification, without distinction between that which is the principal, that which is the secondary, etc., without having a *mimāṃsā* about it. But Vedānta says that the intuitions of the real are given to us by *śruti*, whereas reason will help us to understand *śruti* properly and assimilate what is given to us. Viewed in this way, there is no intrinsic opposition between scripture and reason. Their opposition arises when inordinate claims are made about their respective spheres and modes of knowledge. This stand of the Vedānta is not very different from that of St. Thomas Aquinas and other mediaeval philosophers with regard to the interpretation of the scriptures.

1. daśamastvam asi.

2. The doctrine of *Śabdāparokṣyavāda, Advaita Siddhi* Chap. III, pp. 875-7 (Nirnaya Sagar Press Edn.); *Vedānta Paribhāṣā* I (pp. 53 ff).

3.2. THE TWO DEFINITIONS OF BRAHMAN IN THE ADVAITA*

(*Taṭastha-lakṣaṇa* and *Svarūpa-lakṣaṇa*)

It is a commonplace in the Advaita that there are two definitions (*lakṣaṇas*) of the Absolute Spirit (*Brahman*). These are the Taṭastha (accidental or modal) and the Svarūpa (essential or substantial) definitions. The question is : why the two lakṣaṇas, if one would do ? If the *svarūpa-lakṣaṇa* gives us the essence of Brahman, then why have the Taṭastha at all ? Are they alternatives in the sense that it is a matter of indifference whether we have the one or the other ? Or, if they are complementary to each other, and this may well be the case, which comes first and why ? In the *svarūpa-lakṣaṇa*, it is to be noted, there are at least three co-ordinate definitions: *Sat* (Being), *Cit* (Intelligence), and *Ānanda* (Bliss). Here, too we might ask: Why only three—neither more nor less—, and why these three, and what is the status of each in relation to others ?

These problems are not, to my knowledge, answered or raised in any of the standard expositions of the Advaita. It might therefore be of some interest to attempt an answer to these questions.

I

An example of the *taṭastha-lakṣaṇa* is that *Brahman* is the cause (*kāraṇa*) of the origin, sustenance, and cessation of the world. In the Advaita, cause is interpreted not as the changing stuff but as the unmodified ground (*adhiṣṭhāna*) of the appearance (*vivarta*). The world is not a modification of Brahman but an unreal appearance that is mistaken for it. Of the two definitions, the *taṭastha* must necessarily come first in the order of our discovery of *Brahman*. We know Brahman *only* as we negate the appearance which covers the real from our view. *Brahman* is not one real and the world another beside it. *Brahman* is *the* reality of the world, its very essence. Without negating appea-

*Reprinted from the *Krishna Chandra Bhattacharyya Memorial Volume*, Indian Institute of Philosophy, Amalner, 1958.

rance we cannot know *Brahman*. If we could, there is no point in pronouncing the world false. It may be different from *Brahman*, but on that account it would not be false.

For this reason we find it hard to accept the generally accepted notion that we start with a criterion of reality as non-contradiction, etc., then proceed to sit in judgment over things, and finally to condemn the world as false because it fails to measure up to this criterion of ours. If the criterion is based on first-hand acquaintance with reality, it is not revealed how we have so secretly and securely come to have this experience at the very outset. And having had access to the heart of reality, why have we turned away from it to indulge in a thoroughly gratuitous condemnation of the world ? If, however, the criterion is purely formal, it is inexplicable why we have started with that particular criterion of reality and not with any other, all criterian being equally formal. The entire procedure would then be highly hypothetical: *if* you accept criterion A as the standard, then, c, d, e, are the consequences; and if instead, criterion B were accepted, x, y, z, will be the consequences. In such a case, the starting point cannot be justified; and besides, we shall have nothing whereby to decide between the rival hypotheses. This might be the method of speculative dogmatic metaphysics; it is not the spirit of advaitism.

All this arises because we invert the real order of our discovery. The progression is from the appearance to the real, from the false to the true and not vice versa.[1] There is no passage from the real to the unreal; nor is it needed. Our natural attitude is to take anything that appears as real. For instance, we mistake the body for the self. This is an unconscious process of identification; for none can consciously fall into illusion. Then occurs the shock of disillusionment. Consequent on this, we become reflective. Disillusionment, or the cancelling consciousness, reveals the soul of the appearance by tearing off its superficial vestures as it were. Only this experience provides us with the criterion of the real as *abādhya* (the uncontradicted) and the illusory as *bādhya*; and not any *a priori* formal conception.[2]

1. *Br. Up.*, I. 3. (28). "asato mā sad gamaya, tamaso mā jyotir gamaya, mṛtyor māmṛtam gamaya."

2. Logically, this raises the issue whether we negate because we are already

This explains why Śaṅkara straightaway begins his *bhāṣya* on the *Brahma Sūtra* with the consideration of illusion and ignorance (*adhyāsa* and *avidyā*).[1] Such a procedure must otherwise appear strange, for he is expected first to define Brahman and to treat of it. On our view, however, this is perfectly legitimate. We cannot define Brahman except as the reality of the world, or as what the world is mistaken for. The nature of the mistake and the way to remove it is therefore necessarily a preliminary part of the quest for Brahman.[2] Moreover, knowledge of Brahman is no new information. When it will dawn on us, it would be realised as what was already there—the implicate of all—and as what could have been known before in entirety but for our ignorance. How else shall we term the process except as a species of *discovery* or recovery ? It is literally an uncovering or unmasking process. Self-realisation is a case

aware of the true state of things (x is not y, because it is z) or that the negation itself leads us to the discovery of the truth (x is z, because it is not y). The exponents of the doctrine of significant denial (Bradley and Bosanquet) advocate the former position. Negation, on this view, is reduced to a gratuitous backstroke, as we had already known the true nature of the thing in question *before* we negated. Negation occurs in concrete experience as correction of error or cancellation of a previous misperception. This itself leads us to the correct appraisal of things. It is not always the case that we had been in possession of an affirmative proposition before we made the corresponding negative judgment. When I mistake a distant object for a man, I may come to make the negation, '*this is not a man*', from the continued absence of any movement, etc. Through this negation itself, my curiosity may be stirred, and I may later discover that the mistaken object was but a sign-post, a wayside shrub, or a pile of stones.

1. Later Vedāntins invariably follow this lead. It is Adhyāsa and Avidyā that they begin with, and to these topics they devote greater attention, Cf. the opening chapters of *Vivaraṇa, Saṅkṣepa Śārīraka, Advaita Siddhi*, etc.

2. Padmapāda, of all the commentators, notices the anomaly of beginning with *adhyāsa* (Illusion), while Śaṅkara should have straightaway begun with knowledge of Brahman. He justifies it cogently thus: brahmajñānam hi sūtritam anarthanibarhaṇam, anarthaś ca pramātṛtāpramukham kartṛtvabhoktṛtvarūpam. tad yadi vastukṛtam, na jñānena nibarhaṇiyam, yato jñānam ajñānasyaiva nivarttakam. tad yadi kartṛtvabhoktṛtvam ajñānahetukam syāt, tato brahmajñānam anarthanibarhaṇam ucyamānam upapadyeta. tena sūtrakāreṇaiva brahmajñānam anarthahetunibarhaṇam sūtrayatā, avidyāhetukam kartṛtvabhoktṛtvaṁ pradarśitaṁ bhavati. *Pañcapādikā* on *Brahma Sūtra* I.i.I (Introduction), pp. 10-II. Madras Edition.

of gaining depth without adding to our stock of knowledge (*aheyānupādeya*). Brahma-knowledge is insight, not information.

Our interpretation also explains why Śaṅkara insists, as a pre-requisite for knowing *Brahman* (*brahma-jijñāsā*), that the seeker should have already discriminated between the real and the unreal (*nityānitya-vastuviveka*) and have evinced an attitude of indifference to secular values (*ihāmutrārtha-bhogavirāgaḥ*). On any other interpretation, this should be the *end, not the means*, of knowing Brahman. In the desire to know the Absolute, there is the awareness of having alighted on something unique and valuable. The philosophical consciousness having emerged, it cannot be argued into existence, it is appreciated as a new mode of consciousness different from the secular. As yet, it is vague and undirected. It is the purpose of the two definitions to direct and deepen the spiritual process already incipient in the *brahma-jijñāsā*. They constitute the two stages of the progress. Starting from phenomena, the *taṭastha-lakṣaṇa* leads us to the *existence* of Brahman as their unconditioned ground. The *svarūpa-lakṣaṇa* enables us to penetrate deeper into its *nature*. *The taṭastha-lakṣaṇa* gives us the *that of Brahman*, and the *svarūpa-lakṣaṇa* tells us *what* it is.

II

Spirit is the spirit of things, their inner soul. It is not Spirit and things, i.e. spirit on one side and things on the other. The *Ātman* in the Vedānta is understood as the soul (essence) of all being (*ātmā sarvasya ātmā*). Brahman is the reality of the world; conversely, the world is the appearance of Brahman. This is exactly what the *taṭastha-lakṣaṇa* says. What appears is false, and the false merely appears. It is all surface and no depth. The real never appears; it is all depth, substance and no surface.

There are writers on the Vedānta, some modern exponents especially, who declare the world as appearance, and yet contend that it is somehow real and is an integral part of Brahman. Possibly, they are not quite aware of the implications of the notion of appearance. This implies the distinction between what a thing is *in itself* and what it appears to percipients under certain conditions. If all our perceptions were veridical and absolute, without any subjective (accidental) element in them, or if they were totally subjective, we could not employ the concept of appearance. To call anything an appearance is to be aware of two aspects of a thing, the essential and the accidental. Again, what appears always appears *as* another. It is significant only in the context of mistake. For this reason the Advaita invariably equates the appearance with the false (*dṛśyatvāt mithyā*). We cannot determine what would be the nature and existence of the appearance apart from the conditions under which it appears. Take away the percipient, his ignorance and other auxiliary conditions which engender it, will the appearance still continue to appear? The real, however, will be there without the appearance. Further, to call anything appearance implies evaluation. The appearance, as the false, is what is *rejected* as valueless, and the real is the value. The real and the false are not merely different as red and blue; one is *preferred* to the other.

It does not make much sense then to call the world an appearance and at once to plead that it somehow belongs to Brahman and that it cannot be rejected wholly. Which part of it is rejected and which other part is retained? And of the rejected part too, we cannot plead that it is somehow real, etc. For this would be to reject nothing in the end. And appearance implies, as we have seen, falsity and rejection. It is, however, open to such exponents to question or deny the falsity of the world and thereby not employ the notion of appearance. That is a position opposed to the Vedānta; but it has the merit of not misunderstanding it.

The appearance then is *not* an integral part or aspect of the real. If the "snake" were an aspect of the rope under certain conditions of terrain, light, and perspective, why should it be called false at all? The false is not the transitory (*anitya*). It is not that the rope had put on the snake- modification for a moment, and then had quietly subsided into its old form. It never had that form even when it was thought to have had it; it is not contended that it appears so *now* or that it would do so in the *future*. The appearance is not moored by any fastening to the real; it is just a "floating adjective". The relation between the two is one-sided, not mutual. The appearance implies the real; the real does not imply the appearance. To appear and to appear *in the place of* the real, i.e. be mistaken for it, are one and the same fact. To be real is not necessarily to appear. We can pass from the world to Brahman, but cannot pass back to the world. Formally expressed: the real is the implicate, and not implicatory, of appearance; the appearance is implicatory of the real and not its implicate.

III

It is commonly held that the differentia alone can be the definition (*lakṣaṇa*); and only by *belonging* to the *definiendum* does it serve to distinguish it from the rest. How can the world which is not integral to Brahman, yet define and distinguish it from others? It is not, however, necessary that the definition must be a real property of the *definiendum* to serve as a mark of distinction. Even an assumed mark will do equally well.[1] The bough of the tree may indicate the location of the moon without belonging to it. The crow perching on the house-top does serve as a mark to single out a particular house from among several without forming a permanent fixture therein. Likewise, the world may be *indicative* of Brahman *without being constitutive of it*. There is distinction without differentia. Upalakṣaṇa is lakṣaṇa; even an ascribed or symbolic characteristic may serve as definition (*asad vyāvarttakam upalakṣaṇam*).

We may even assert the converse: all *lakṣaṇa* is *upalakṣaṇa*, all definition is ascription. The reason is that the difference between the mark and the marked will not obtain if the marking characteristic were integral to the latter. The marked (the definiendum) is not just the marking characteristic. It should at least be something more than that ; for there is no point in using a defining mark which merely defines itself. It may, however, be said that the defining mark is *one* part of the thing defined. This would mean that the defined is constituted of two factors—the defining mark and some X. But how can we assert that that is *one* thing which has these two incongruent factors? If the X is taken as another characteristic similar to the defining mark, then what you call a thing is a jumble of two determinate characteristics having no connection with each other.

1. *Brahma Sūtra Bhāṣya*, II. 1. 14 : "tathākārādi-satyākṣara-pratipattir dṛṣṭā rekhānṛtākṣara-pratipatteḥ." Cf. also *Advaita Siddhi*, pp. 440 ff. (asataḥ sādhakatvopapattiḥ.)

If the X is taken as indeterminate it will not be possible to assert any determinate relation between the two factors,—the indeterminate X and the defining mark. It could be identity or difference or both if we choose, and none in particular. And what is the thing which *has* these two factors?

A correct analysis of the relation between the definition and and the definiendum leads us to the conclusion that like the true subject of a proposition which is never a predicate, nor the sum total of all possible predicates, the definition is non-constitutive of the definiendum. *Brahman* is transcendent to thought (*nirdharmaka*), and we can define it only by ascribing features to it. Shorn of technicality, this means that the phenomenalisation of the Absolute is a free act of grace. It is *not compelled* to appear, but *condescends* to appear. The *taṭastha-lakṣaṇa* emphasises the free nature of *Brahman*. Not necessarily connected with the world, *Brahman* is free to appear in other forms, and there is no limit to the forms either. Being the cause of the world etc., is not the only *taṭastha-lakṣaṇa* of *Brahman*. He is the implicate not only of the object but of the knowing subject as well. *Brahman* is like the centre which is reached from the periphery by any of the radii. On the other view of a necessary causal relation between *Brahman* and phenomena, this world would be the only manifestation of *Brahman*. The possible and the actual would be identical as in Spinoza.

A more serious objection to making the relation between the two necessary, or in conceiving the world as an integral part of *Brahman* is that we cannot escape the Kantian antinomies. There cannot be any legitimate passage from the sphere of phenomena to their unconditioned ground. Through the usual modes of relation, cause and effect, part and whole, substance and attributes, etc., there is no solution of the dilemma: either the unconditioned itself will fall within phenomena and thus cease to be the unconditioned, or its existence and nature can only be dogmatically asserted. The dogmatic use of categories beyond their legitimate field of demonstrability invariably gives rise to various and conflicting speculative systems. This conflict engenders distrust in the ability of reason to reach the unconditioned. And yet, the urge to go beyond phenomena is there as ever. This is the consciousness of the transcendental illusion. Advaitism, as it has been pointed out, starts with this in the

Brahma-jijñāsā. Illusion being a fact, all that is necessary for its occurrence must be taken as true. The analysis of any empirical illusion is helpful as providing us a pattern for interpreting the world-illusion. The Vedānta adopts this procedure. (*idam jagat mithyā, dṛśyatvāt; śuktirajatavat.*)

It could not be any possible objection to this procedure that this too involves the illegitimate extension of the categories, &c. For the worst consequence that can be urged against any view is that it is a falsification of the real, that it leads to illusion. The datum for philosophy, according to the Vedānta, is illusion. And illusion itself cannot occur without the ground (*adhiṣṭhāna*) on which false ascriptions are made. The Vedānta thus avoids the antinomies, and yet renders the consciousness of illusion significant by interpreting the ground (the thing-in-itself) not negatively as an unknown X, but axiologically as immanent in experience. It also follows that in the Vedānta, every category, causality, substance etc., gets transformed by the notion of ground and appearance. Historically, too, the Advaita develops its thesis by criticism of other systems; it begins where other systems end.

IV

The key-note of the Vedānta metaphysics is the relation that obtains between the world and *Brahman*, the false and the real. This relation is not only the prius but is the exemplar of all relations. To say that relation is of the nature of the relation between the false and the real is to say that all relation is false. The general formula is : the two terms sustaining a relation are not of the same order, one is *higher*, and the other *lower*; the two terms are neither mutually dependent nor mutually independent ; relation is neither 'internal' nor 'external'. If mutually dependent, we cannot distinguish between the two terms, as they so necessarily imply each other that one cannot exist without the other any time. We cannot even say that there are two terms, as the basis of distinction is lacking. If mutually independent, there is no basis of connection; each term is a self, a self-contained universe as it were. To escape this dilemma, we have to conceive one term as basic and capable of existing apart from its relation to the other and the other incapable of so doing and therefore dependent. One term, the higher, is not exhausted in the relationship; it has a transcendent or non-implicatory existence which is its intrinsic nature. The other term, however, is entirely exhausted within the relation and has no non-relative existence.

To consider in brief the Advaita conception of some relations. *Brahman* as the cause of the world is transcendent; it does not get modified into the effect, though the so-called effect is nothing without it. The effect is thus an appearance (*vivarta*) which is ascribed to an immutable ground (*adhiṣṭhāna*), The Sāṅkhya conception of *pariṇāma* (change) is modified into the *vivarta-vāda*; identity between cause and effect (*sat-kārya-vāda*) gives place to the one-sided non-difference (*ananyatvam vyatirekeṇā-bhāvaḥ*).[1] *Brahman* as substance is a self, the only self that is self-sufficient and self-evident. It does not owe its existence or nature in any measure to other things. Nor is it dependent on being known, for this is the nature of the appearance (*dṛśyatvān mithyātva*). Substance is thus unrelated to particular objects or to the subjective act of knowing. It is not, however, the unknown thing-in-itself; for, though predicates are irrelevant to it, predication itself is not possible without it. It is thus the self-evident (*svayamprakāśa*),—unknown, yet immediate (*avedya* and *aparokṣa*). The universal is the basis of the particulars, and these are false limitations or abstractions. The universal can exist without the particulars, and not vice versa. From the standpoint of the universal, the particulars do not even appear. Only a particular can perceive a particular, for only a limited being identified with a limited object in the totality of things can apprehend the particular. Particulars are necessarily many. But ultimately there is only one Universal Being, *Brahman*. The particulars depend on the Universal without dividing it.

This logic may help us to understand some problems, e.g., the relation between mind and body, or subject and object. We can conceive the self and the body neither as independent of each other nor as mutually dependent. The only alternative

1. *Op. cit.*, II. 1.(14) : "tasmād yathā ghaṭakarakādyākāśānām mahākāśānanyatvam, yathā ca mṛgatṛṣṇikodakādīnām ūṣarādibhyo'nanyatvam dṛṣṭanaṣṭasvarūpatvāt svarūpeṇānupākhyatvāt, evamasya bhogyabhoktrādi-prapañcasya brahma-vyatirekeṇābhāva iti draṣṭavyam."

that accords with facts is that the body is what it is in relation with the self and nothing apart from it. The body is the unreal appearance of the self; the superficial vesture (*kośa*) of the inner core. It is what is mistaken for the self. Alternatively, the self can be viewed as the essence or the reality of the body (*nihitaṁ guhāyām*). Initially, they are an indistinguishable whole. Later analysis reveals the self as the inner core, the soul, and the body as the outer shell. The external object itself has, on this analysis, to be taken as a degraded or castaway body i.e., what we *were* identified with before. The perceiving subject (*aham*; *pramātā*) and the object known (*viṣaya*) presuppose a common, deeper unity that underlies them. Their difference are on the surface, while identity is their real nature. The very possibility of their coming together in the knowledge-context depends on this inherent identity (*abhedābhivyakti*); any particular act of knowing merely removes the obstruction that superficially separates them (*āvaraṇābhibhava*).[1]

V

One is tempted here to digress a little to contrast the Vedānta logic with that of the Sāṅkhya and the Mādhyamika. The Sāṅkhya will no doubt take the relation between cause and effect and other pairs as one of almost reciprocal identity. There is real change : the cause itself becomes the effect (*satkāryavāda*). The substance is determined by the attributes (*dharma*); both the terms sustaining the relation are real. But even in the Sāṅkhya the two terms are not of the same status or order: the substance or the cause is the deeper or more real term.

For the Mādhyamika, both the terms of a relational complex are false; as mutually dependent, they lack an essential nature of their own (*tat tat prāpya yadutpannaṁ notpannam tat svabhāvataḥ*). The relativity of things is their unreality.[2] The cause and the effect are neither identical with nor different from each other, nor both, nor neither.[3] There is no substance without attributes,

1. *Advaita Siddhi*, pp. 453 ff. (dṛgdṛśya-sambandha-bhaṅgaḥ.)
2. *Mādhyamika Kārikā*, XXIV, 18. "yaḥ pratītya samutpādaḥ śūnyatāṁ tāṁ pracakṣmahe; sā prajñaptirupādāya pratipat saiva madhyamā."
3. *Ibid.*, ip. 1. "na svato na parato nobhābhyāṁ nāpyahetutaḥ; utpannā jātu vidyante bhāvā, kvacana" kecana.

nor attributes without substance;[1] the self (*ātman*) is not one with its states; nor is it anything apart from them.[2] Like Bradley, who lays down that qualities are nothing within or without relation and so too relation, the Mādhyamika enunciates his dictum that both those things are unreal which cannot be conceived as either identical with or different from each other.[3]

The Vedāntin will not reject both the terms as relative; he accepts one as the reality or the basis of the other. For the Mādhyamika, the substance and the attributes are equally unreal, as neither of them can be had apart from the other. The Vedantin would say that the attributes are mere ascriptions of substance, the particulars are negations of the universal and are, therefore, unreal by their very nature (*svarūpato mithyā*); but the substance or the universal is inherently real, only its seeming relationship with the attributes or particulars is false (*saṁsargato mithyā*); it has a transcendent nature without the relation.

It is, however, manifestly wrong to hold that the Mādhyamika is a nihilist in the sense of not accepting a real. *Tattva* is accepted by him in unmistakable terms; only it cannot be characterized as *sat* (being) or *asat* (non-being), etc.[4] *Śūnyatā* is the unqualified denial of the predicates of the Absolute. There is no positive identification of it with anything in experience. The Mādhyamika barely asserts the existence of the Absolute as the implicate of all phenomena. He may be said to stop with the *taṭastha-lakṣaṇa*. It is the peculiar merit of the Vedānta that it does not stop with the bare assertion of the reality of the Absolute (Brahman); it also tells us *what* Brahman is.

VI

The *taṭastha-lakṣaṇa* just implies the presence of Brahman as the unconditioned ground of phenomena. It does not give us an insight into the nature of Brahman. This is done by the

1. *Ibid.*, IV. 1. ff.
2. *Ibid.*, XVIII. 1. ff.
3. *Ibid.*, II. 21. "ekibhāvena vā siddhir nānābhāvena vā yayoḥ ; na vidyate tayoḥ siddhiḥ kathaṁ nu khalu vidyate."
4. *Ibid.*, XVIII. 9. "aparapratyayaṁ śāntaṁ prapañcair aprapañcitam; nirvikalpam anānārtham etat tattvasya lakṣaṇam."

svarūpa-lakṣaṇa. In the *taṭastha,* the characteristics of another (the world) are conveniently made to indicate Brahman; it is reaching Brahman from without. The *svarūpa-lakṣaṇa* is a non-relational definition.[1] Here the definiendum and the definition coincide. *Sat* is not a property *of* Brahman; it is not *in* Brahman or *part of it.* Similarly with *Cit* and *Ānanda.* The state of understanding one thing through another has been transcended. The *svarūpa-lakṣaṇa* is thus on a higher level of spiritual consciousness. If the *taṭastha* represents the discursive or the *manana* stage, the *svarūpa* is the intuitive. In intuition, essence and existence coincide. With the lapse of difference on the content-side, the distinction between the content and a subject contemplating it also lapses. It is because of diversity and succession of the presentational field that we are enabled to make the distinction between subject and object; for, if one thing is continuous while the others are varied and interrupted then the former is different from the latter. If, however, the object presented were absolutely unitary and homogeneous and did not show any diversity like substance *and* attribute, etc. the difference between knowledge and the object known lapses. Brahman as *sat* is such a unitary object.[2]

The three terms of the definition, *Sat, Cit* and *Ānanda,* are not synonymous (*aparyāya*).[3] Although they all *denote, not connote,* one and the same entity, Brahman; the difference between them is not verbal; each denotes Brahman differently. The thing excluded, or the mode of approach (the *vyāvartya*), is different in each case; *Sat* excludes *asat* (non-being); *Cit* (will or intelligence) excludes matter (*jaḍa*); *Ānanda* (bliss) excludes *duḥkha* (pain). These terms are not concepts or predicates. It would be less of a mistake to take them denotatively as things or substances. Each is *sui generis,* a Self, Each is identical with *Brahman,* substantially, not conceptually.

1. *Citsukhī,* p. 109. "Saṁsargāsaṅgisamyagdhihetutā yā girām iyam; uktākhaṇḍārthatā yad vā tatprātipadikārthatā.

2. *Bhāmatī,* p. 16. "yeṣu vyāvarttamāneṣu yad anuvarttate tat tebhyo bhinnaṁ yathā kusumebhyaḥ sūtram."

3. *Citsukhī,* p. 111. "aparyāyaśabdānām ekaprātipadikamātraparyavasāyitvam akhaṇḍārthatā. na caivaṁ padāntaravaiyarthyam. vyāvarttyabhedād arthavatvopapatteḥ." Cf. also *Advaita Siddhi,* pp. 675ff.

The logical implications of the *svarūpa-lakṣaṇa* are :

(i) Direct non-relational acquaintance with the thing is the presupposition of knowledge through description, though the order of discovery is just the reverse of the order of implication;

(ii) Second, that the denotation of a term is prior to its connotation or even that the denotation is the true meaning of a term; the connotation is its appearance, a mental replica or symbolic substitute for it. Subject or substance is never a predicate (*dravya* is the *prātipadikārtha*);

(iii) Third, the import of any and every proposition is to assert the existence of the subject, not through predicates or concepts, but without them, in spite of them. "There shines the bright moon"—in this sentence the purpose is not to predicate brightness of the moon, but to single out the moon from its surroundings; brightness, the predicate, merely facilitates this function; it is the thing or substance we are interested in. Not only is existence not a concept, it is even opposed to that. Vedāntism sets its face against all forms of the ontological argument. The Rationalist's device of deriving existence from a specific concept—Perfect Being (Descartes and others), or from a system of concepts—Reason (Hegel). Existence is *not conceivable*; we can only intuit it. If Hegel's is a logic of Ideas or Concepts, the Vedānta's is a logic of existence. Owing to limitations of space, it is not proposed to develop these implications in this paper.

VII

The puzzling question about the *svarūpa-lakṣaṇa* is that there are three *lakṣaṇas* in one: Brahman is triunal. We are expressly warned not to derive one from the other or to sub-ordinate them. The question then is: Why three only, and why these three.

A similar question arises in the Sāṅkhya about the nature of Prakṛti *as sattva, rajas,* and *tamas*: each is Prakṛti and the whole of it too. The philosophers of the Medieval Age in the the West were considerably exercised over the Trinity and also about the so-called attributes of God—Omniscience, Omnipotence, and Goodness. As in God existence and essence are identical, it is truer to say that God *is* Goodness than that God *has* Goodness, &c.

I venture to make the suggestion that *Sat*, *Cit*, and *Ānanda* stand for the three functions of Knowledge, Willing, and Feeling. Spirit is Truth or Knowledge; Spirit is Will; and Spirit is Bliss. Each is *sui generis* and is not to be confounded with the others. Their confusion makes for illusion (*adhyāsa*), and their distinction through reflective analysis (*viveka*) is the spiritual discipline of philosophic insight.

These three spirit-functions may be formulated thus: in knowing the Truth, our attitude is one of discovery or revelation of what is already present; the given is everything. The object of knowledge, as in Truth, is unconstituted by the subjective act of knowing. There may arise a demand to realise the Truth as what is not, and need not be, known. The thing-in-itself, the given, must be known without the mediation of the Categories of thought, without any trace of subjectivity, empirical or transcendental. These usually condition experience; and while from the practical point of view the object known through them may be valid, yet for the lover of truth, Pure Being must be known in its undistorted form. In Willing, the willed content is wholly *through* the willing, not having any being without the latter. This is best exemplified in moral endeavour and in conscious imagination. The demand here will be to realise the *pure act* without any trace of the given (the thing-in-itself) In Feeling, content and consciousness, subject and object, form an indistinguishable whole; the separation of the one from the other would mean abstraction or hollowness and consequennt loss of the feeling tone. As no empirical emotion comes up to this ideal, the demand would be to realise a state of perfect amplitude or fullness (*Paripūrṇatā* = *Ānanda*).

VIII

These functions can be deduced from an analysis of any empirical illusion. Our attitude towards the rope or the ground of the illusion is Knowledge. For, there the rope does exist independent of the knowing act and our subjective ascriptions; it was real even when we were ignorant of it while we were in illusion. The 'snake' on the other hand is as it is in our consciousness (*pratibhāsamātraśarira*); its nature is what appears, nothing hidden or separate from consciousness. According to our scheme, this may be termed feeling; for here consciousness and content form a unity as in any state of pleasure. Considering the history of the emergence of the 'snake', we may say it is a freak. It has no place among empirical objects; it does not belong in any assignable sense to the rope or its surroundings. It seems to have emerged out of nowhere. It may be taken as a creature projected unconsciously by our phantasy. We may say that it has been willed into existence and exists in and through that transcendental act.

We have seen that the *taṭastha-lakṣaṇa*, which is the first stage in the discovery of Brahman, is the consciousness of the world-illusion with Brahman as its implicate. The *svarūpa-lakṣaṇa* represents a further stage in the analysis of illusion, the consciousness of its constitutional structure. We can venture to state that only such an analysis of illusion can give us an *a priori* deduction of the triple nature of Brahman. And it is in accord with the procedure of Advaita as modelling its metaphysical reality on the structure of illusion.

As the Vedāntist analyses illusion from the knowledge-standpoint, he is biassed in favour of the given—the *adhiṣṭhāna* (rope): he makes it the prius of the whole show and calls it real. The other two attitudes involved in illusion, namely the emergence of the 'snake' and its continued appearance in consciousness resulting in the obscuration of the rope from our view, he conveniently puts down as the two functions—*vikṣepa* and *āvaraṇa* of *avidyā*. Illusion or *adhyāsa* is the confusion or the unconscious synthesis of these, the Knowledge and the *avidyā* functions. What is true of the one we take as true of the other and vice versa. In illusion we believe we *know* the 'snake' whereas it is *willed* into existence and is *felt* to be there. The rope is taken to be 'unknown' and non-existent (*nāsti, na prakāśate*), whereas this is true of the 'snake' alone. For, to exist is to be self-existent, independent; and that the 'snake' is not. The Vedāntins do say that in illusion there is the identification of two functions (*vṛttis*)—*pramātṛ-vṛtti* and *avidyāvṛtti* of the *śākṣi*.[1] Cancellation does not bring in any new factor, for that would be a different state having nothing to do with the previous state of illusion. It merely clarifies the datum of illusion by carefully analysing it. What seemed a unitary mass turns out to be a fusion or

1. *Advaita Siddhi*, pp. 652ff.

unconscious synthesis of these functions. Mixed up, they create a mess; separated, each is a self as it were. Illusion will not be possible if there were no confusion of functions or attitudes; nor can there be cancellation, if the datum of illusion were a unitary unanalysable fact.

The world-illusion is thus the confusion of these three functions, each of which has a nature, underived and non-redundant. Though the Vedāntin is biassed in favour of the Knowledge-function and realises Brahman as Truth or Pure Being, it speaks greatly for his analytical skill that he recognises the other spiritual functions and insists on keeping them apart as a self. Being, Act, and Bliss are equally and fully *Brahman*. This does not mean a plurality of Absolutes, as there is no conceptual distinction; all these denote one entity[1], though in diverse ways. *Brahman* is their inexpressible substantial unity.

1. *Ibid.*, p. 676. "yadyapi sarveṣāṁ satyādipadānām *lakṣyam ekam eva* nirviśeṣaṁ brahma, tathāpi nivarttanīyāṁśādhikyena na padāntaravaiyarthyam. Cf. also *Citsukhī*, p. 111.

3.3. THE CONCEPT OF APPEARANCE*

Why should we start with the notion of appearance rather than with the real ? Are we not concerned with the nature of Brahman, which is the real? This is a very pertinent question to ask. One cannot, it should be pointed out, go up to the end and reach the real except as the reality of appearance. Only by cancelling the superficial aspect of that which is sensed can we know anything as real, as its essence. It is not as if the Self is on the one hand and other things on the other. Ātman is *sarvasya ātmā*, the Self of all. *Brahman* or *Ātman* is not one reality among other realities. If it were so, there is no point in calling the world false. Brahman is the reality of the world; and without negating the appearance, we cannot know *Brahman*. Appearance and reality are not two disconnected things. Appearance is the superficial or the surface aspect, and reality is its true essence, its real nature. In the order of discovery, i.e., in the order of our knowing things, appearance comes first, although in the order of existence it is the reverse. For example, when we dig, the more superficial layers that we encounter appear first before we reach the depths, although in the order of physical formation, the deeper layers must have occurred first and the superficial layers later. So the order of discovery is the epistemic order. This explains why Śaṅkara, without any apology, without any explanation, starts straightaway with *adhyāsa*, though he is expected to deal with Brahman. Why should he bother about *adhyāsa*? Padmapāda, the commentator on Śaṅkara's Bhāṣya, has very well explained why Śaṅkara has done this. The knowledge of Brahman will remove ignorance. By this, Śaṅkara implies that there is already *adhyāsa*. *Adhyāsa* and *ajñāna* are to be removed, and only *jñāna* can remove ignorance. Knowledge cannot manufacture things. It is only proper that the *Bhāṣyakāra* should bring out the implication of this position.[1]

*The second of five lectures given at the University of Madras, October, 1976.

1. *Pañcapādikā* on *Brahma Sūtra* I, i, 1 (Introduction) pp. 10-11, Madras Edn. brahmajñānaṁ hi sūtritam anarthahetunibarhṇam, anarthaśca pramātṛtāpramukhaṁ kartṛtvabhoktṛtvaṁ. tad yadi vastukṛtam, na jñānena nibarhaṇiyam.

Advaita is not a theistic philosophy as Śaiva Siddhānta or Viśiṣṭādvaita or any other religious philosophy is. Brahman of Advaita is the ultimately real; it is not God or Person, however exalted He may be, but the absolute Spirit, impersonal Pure Being. So we may say that Advaita Vedānta is the philosophy of Truth or Pure Being. *Mokṣa* is freedom which is not the acquisition of a new dimension, but discarding the false. Freedom is not conferred on us by God. It is our natural and inherent right. It is not through generosity or grace of God that freedom is conferred. For any other system it may be like that. Though other systems call it *mokṣa*, it should be taken as a kind of exalted state rather than *mokṣa*. *Mokṣa* is not an effect or result (*kārya*) at all. Śaṅkara is at pains to make out that all the four kinds of *kārya* are not the ways to *mokṣa*.[1] Freedom could be taken as an attainment only in a figurative sense. It is the destruction of *avidyā* or ignorance; but its accomplishment is only in a negative sense and not in a positive sense. It is a *re*covery or *dis*-covery of our own real Self. It is recovery or realisation of our real nature by casting away our superficial vestures which we have put on unconsciously and beginninglessly. For this recovery, personal God does play a vital role, for it is He who directs our attention to our real nature. In that sense, we would say that God opens our eyes; and it is for us to seek and acquire knowledge. In fact, knowledge is freedom.

There is yet another observation to be made here. If we do not have the experiences of illusion and disillusionment, we cannot start our enquiry into the real. The terms 'real' and 'false appearance' will then have no meaning for us. In a situation in which all our cognitions were completely true without any case of misperception and disillusionment, there could be no enquiry into the nature of Brahman. Possibly, we can have our religious attitudes; we can make complete surrender and submission to God so that we may have some benefits to be conferred on us by God; all that is possible. But the Advaita

yato jñānam ajñānasyaiva nivartakam. tad yadi kartṛtvabhoktṛtvaṁ ajñānahetukaṁ syāt, tataḥ brahmajñānam anarthanibarhaṇam ucyamānam upapadyate. tena sūtrakāreṇaiva brahmajñānam anartha-hetunibarhaṇam sūtrayatā avidyāhetukam kartṛtvabhoktṛtvam pradarśitam bhavati.

1. Śaṅkara's *Bhāṣya* on *Brahma Sūtra*, I, i. 4.

enquiry is not possible without the experience of illusion and the subsequent correction thereof. The dictum, "*jñānānmuktiḥ*" which means release through knowledge applies fully and literally only in the case of Advaita, although the other systems, even the religious systems like Śaiva Siddhānta or Viśiṣṭādvaita, appropriated this concept of *jñānamukti*. I suppose it is not proper, because in those systems the final state is not *mokṣa*, but a kind of exalted state such as *Kailāsa* or *Vaikuṇṭha*. Such a state is not freedom.

Every philosophical system can be derived from one basic principle or standpoint. If we know that principle or basic idea, we may be able to derive all the doctrines as implications of that principle. Let me point out that the Nyāya-Vaiśeṣika, for instance can be derived from one principle, viz., that everything is an object (*viṣaya*). The Śāṅkhya system is derived from the principle that there is change. The Yogācāra system is based on the principle that consciousness (*vijñāna*) alone is real. The basic standpoint of Advaita Vedānta centres round the concept of appearance. The analysis of appearance or illusion tells us about the structure of illusion, about the causes of illusion, what lies behind it and how it can be removed, etc. An analysis of an empirical illusion throws a lot of light upon the concept of appearance.

Advaita Vedānta may be taken as philosophy of truth, i.e., it may be understood in the cognitive attitude. By that it is meant that we should separate it from the attitudes of feeling and willing.[1] The elements of feeling and willing are *avidyā*. But Advaita is concerned with Pure Being. Truth is discovery. We do not add anything to it. We do not distort it by our knowing or not knowing. It is not construction; it is not explanation. It is

1. Knowledge is cognitive experience, and it has to be distinguished from types of non-cognitive experience, such as willing and feeling as exemplified by volitional acts or emotional states of pleasure, pain, anger and lust. What is peculiar about the cognitive attitude is that we want to "see" or "take in" things as they are, as they obtain in reality; we do not want to add or modify or distort the given, and to the extent we do these things, it is not knowledge.

jñānam tu pramāṇajanyam, pramāṇaṁ ca yathābhūtavastuviṣayam, ato jñānaṁ kartum akartum anyathā vā kartum aśakyam.

kevalaṁ vastu-tantram eva tat, na codanātantram, nāpi puruṣatantram. Śaṅkara's *Bhāṣya* on *Brahma Sūtra* I, i. 4.

mere revelation of that which already exists. Knowledge does not add to the things, and true light should not distort the nature of things which reveals to us the pure being. Certainly Truth is not conceived in the Vedānta as the coherence of thoughts. Coherence means consistency in the sense that a statement is backed up or supported by other statements. The whole system is linked together. But what guarantee is there that the initial standpoint or the initial judgement is true? An initial lie supported by another lie, the second lie by the third and the third by the fourth, and so on, do not give us truth. Vedānta will not accept that the nature of truth is coherence of judgements. Nor can it be considered as correspondence. The true judgement, it may be said, is correspondence with the real, with fact. But, then, how are we to ascertain that what obtains in knowledge is the same as what obtains in the real? We will have to say that it is by other experiences, and so on. Hence there will always be a gap between the knowledge and the real. For Vedānta, in the ultimate analysis, knowledge and truth must coincide; that is, we do not know the things by representation, but by *being one with the thing itself.* The *Upaniṣad says*, "One who knows Brahman becomes Brahman" (*brahma veda brahmaiva bhavati*). Rather the converse is true. You know Brahman only when you become or be Brahman. So our subjective act of knowing does not add anything to the object known, nor does it in any way distort it. Knowledge has a revelatory function. It means that the real is hidden; that it already exists, but we do not know it, just as in darkness things exist though we do not know them; and when light is brought in, we recognise that these things had been there already. Brahman exists in its full form, in its infinite form, in its complete form. That is why it is called Pure Being. And knowledge is of Brahman as an existent fact (*bhūtavastu, pariniṣṭhita-vastu*).

From this it follows that there is something hidden, and that there is something which hides. Suppose there is nothing which is hidden. Suppose that there is the cover, but it does not cover anything. The Śūnyavādins, according to Vedānta and other schools, hold that there is only *Śūnya* ultimately. Of course they have rejected the reality of the phenomena and taken them as false. But nothing is real. Vedānta is totally opposed to *Śūnyavāda*. I do think that Śaṅkara and others are correct in characterising Nāgārjuna and others as Śūnyavādins, *from their standpoint.* Vedānta is distinguished from the Mādhyamika school insofar as it takes the ground of appearance to be real. The Advaitins are concerned with knowing the real as non-dual, whereas for the Mādhyamika any ontology is unacceptable.

Vedānta is also opposed to the empirical or humanistic attitude which says that, behind or beyond the empirical things which are seen, there is nothing. All that exists, it is maintained, is what can be observed by sense experience, seen, touched, felt, etc. Vedānta is opposed to this view, because it would mean that there is nothing which is hidden, nothing beyond appearance. If the things were all the time hidden or if the things were all the time open, then we cannot even make the statement that the observed things are all that there are.

I pose the question whether all illusions could be reduced to one type, the rope-snake type or shell-silver type, and whether the analysis of one illusion would suit other types of illusion. Again, even if we accept illusion, what right have we to extend it to the world-illusion ? What right have we to say that the world itself as a whole is an illusion ? Individual things in the world may be illusory, but it does not follow that the world itself is illusory? So Vedānta thinkers should explain this by analogy, by logic, by arguments. Vedānta is committed, as any absolutism is, to a two level theory, i.e., it speaks of the level of the appearance and that of the real. In declaring or judging anything as appearance, we state two things : first that it is not ultimate or the reality which is something behind the appearance, and secondly the appearance is not nothing. This view is opposed to the contention of the realist who takes things at their face value. Things that appear to us are as we cognise them. Realism takes them as we experience them; but according to Vedānta it is appearance of the real. There is a connection, an elastic connection, between the real and the appearance. So Vedānta may be taken as an epistemological dualism. It operates on two levels: the false and the real. This could be said not only for Vedānta, but also for all philosophy. The concept of appearance is basic, because philosophy is *tattva-jñāna*; i.e., we distinguish between what appears and the essence or reality of that appearance. Otherwise, there is no *tattva-jñāna*.

The usage of the terms 'real' and 'false' must have experiential basis. The meaning of these terms must be illustrated and elicited in the context of some concrete experience. We cannot start with a mere formal criterion of the real. What is this real? What is the empirical context which gives that concept of appearance or the real or whatever it is? If we start with a formal criterion, some other person will start with some other criterion, and so on. There is no way of ruling out these criteria. It will then become a matter of taste or temperament. There is no tribunal to which we can appeal to show that a particular criterion is false, or that some other criterion is true. Vedānta does not, therefore, assume the meanings of these key terms, viz., 'real', 'false', but by analysis of the concrete instances of illusion, brings out the meaning of these terms in the context of actual experience.

What is appearance? In the *Advaita-siddhi*, five definitions are given, and they have been accepted as the norm in all Advaita discussion. The order in which they are given is also stated. Now I would raise this question: Are there five definitions? Or could the number be reduced? If we accept several definitions of illusoriness, is there any order in which you could state them? I do not think that this question has been raised in any of the writings of the Vedāntins. However, I am raising this question. To me, there can be only three questions with regard to the false (*mithyātva*) and I shall also state the order in which these questions should be answered. First of all, how and where and when do we know anything as appearance? How do we know that anything is appearance? I suppose, it can happen only in the context of cancellation or negation. When we negate something, the 'snake' for example we come to know the true state of affairs; we see that the 'this' in front is not snake or silver at all. Unless we have the occasion to apply negation, we do not have the concept of *mithyātva*. The concept of illusoriness (*mithyātva*) arises in the first instance only when we annul or negate what has been taken as real. Therefore I would say that "*pratipannopādhau traikālika-niṣedhapratiyogitvam mithyātvam*" should be taken as the first definition of *mithyātva*. The illusory object does not exist even in the place where it appears to exist; it was not, it is not, and it will not be. Even when we perceive the snake in illusion, the snake is not there; or when we discover the rope, it is not there. The illusory snake or the illusory silver was not there at all. This definition of the false is based on the *śruti* text "*neha nānāsti kiñcana*" (There is no plurality whatsoever here). Negative statements like this should be taken as supplying the authority for this concept of illusoriness.

Only when we cancel, we become aware of the 'snake' as illusion. Is this cancellation a kind of destruction or physical disintegration? The answer is: No. Knowledge cancels ignorance. No other thing cancels it. *Jñānanivartyatva* is not physical disintegration or destruction, but annulment of the previous state of illusion by right knowledge. We cannot say that one state of knowledge is removed by another state of knowledge by the mere fact of succession. It is the removal of the previous state through the rise of *knowledge*, not by the efflux of time but by the knowledge of the real state of affairs. Knowledge can arise only by destroying ignorance which was covering the real. The very function of knowledge is revelatory, or discovery, like light. So, knowledge destroys ignorance just as light destroys darkness. It destroys, not piecemeal, but completely. It is not that some residue of ignorance is left over. In fact, our concept of total negation can only happen in the case of knowledge. In the case of physical destruction, we can always say that we convert one state of things into another state. The concept of destruction arises only in the context of illusion which is completely destroyed by knowledge. Only illusion can be completely destroyed, and knowledge alone can do it, neither action nor devotion.

Then the question is posed: What is that which *was* there and which *is not there now*? What is it that has been removed by knowledge? We want to know the ontological status of what appeared. And in answer to that question we have to come to the third definition of illusoriness as *sad-asad-vilakṣaṇatva* (asat once different from the real and different from the unreal). *Anirvacanīyatva* sould not be taken as our incapacity to define it; it is not a subjective incapacity. It only means that the illusory object is not definable either as real or as unreal. The point to be noted here is that we posit a third category, i.e., what is different from the real and the unreal. Real and the unreal are not the only two categories that exhaust the entire universe of discourse.

Objections may be raised against this definition by pointing out that *sat* and *asat* which are contradictories exhaust the whole universe of discourse. If we deny one of them, we ought to accept the other. If we say "This is not *sat*," then we ought to accept that "This is *asat*"; and if we deny *asat*, we have to accept it as *sat*. There is no third alternative at all, whereas the Vedāntin is postulating a third category, which is opposed to logic.

The Advaitin meets these objections by giving his own definitions of *sat* and *asat*. *Sat*, of course, is defined as something that stands unaffected by our knowing or not knowing, that which is not contradicted by our experience. So *sat* is accepted as *abādhyam* or uncontradictable. *Asat* is defined by the Vedāntin as that which never confronts us as *sat*, that which *never appears to us in any experience*, real or illusory. It never poses itself as real. *Sat* is real; and it is not affected by our knowing or not knowing it. *Asat* is something which never even claims to be real. Now we can see that *anirvacanīyatva* e.g., shell-silver, or rope-snake, or a dream object and so on, is different from both *sat* and *asat*. It is different from *sat* because it is sublated; and it is different from *asat* because it is cognized. *Asat* never appears as real, whereas this rope-snake appears to us. It has a history which we cannot deny. Its whole being, however, is exhausted in appearing to us. That is, it is *prātibhāsika* (*pratibhāsamātra-śarīratva*). It does not exist apart from knowing and it is not real at all. The real is something independent of our knowing or not-knowing it, whereas this rope-snake or shell-silver has appearance in our context of illusion. It has no other existence elsewhere. Its span of life is limited to our illusory apprehension. That is why it is called the apparent.

Now let us draw out some of the implications of this concept of appearance. There are two levels. 'Real' and 'false' are not two things; they are stages or aspects, if you like; i.e., deeper and superficial aspects. That is why Śaṅkara calls it *satya-anṛte mithunīkṛtya* (a knot of the true and the false). *Adhyāsa* is the identification of *anṛta* with *satya*. Secondly, there is a loose relationship between these two. The relationship between the superficial aspect and the deeper aspect is something loose. It is not internal or vital. We cannot say that the snake is the real modification of the rope. The rope can exist without the 'snake' that appears; the shell can exist without the 'silver' that appears.

The real does not lose its integrity, even when it is apprehended otherwise. While the false is dispensable, the real is something which is indispensable. The real can exist without the false, but the appearance cannot exist without the real. The relation is one-sided identification. Whereas the false is dependent upon the real, there is no need for the real to depend on anything at all. Without Brahman there is no world. In that sense the world is identical with Brahman, not in any positive sense.[1] It is not the constituting factor of the real. It negates the real. The appearance can indicate the real, but does not constitute it. The relation between the real and false is the exemplar of all relations. It throws light upon understanding all relations like cause and effect, universal and particular, substance and attribute, whole and parts, etc. For the Vedāntin the cause is not integrally connected with the effect. So the cause is unaffected by the effect. It does not become the effect; it is not modified; it is not exhausted; it is not turned as it were into the effect. There is appearance and yet the cause or ground is not in any way touched or affected, much less exhausted by the appearance. Change here is not *pariṇāma*, but *vivarta*, not transformation but transfiguration or emanation. For the Vedāntin the universal is real, the particular is appearance. The universal need not appear as particular, whereas the particular has to depend on the universal. So also the substance can be taken as the ultimate, but it need not have attributes. But attributes have to be based upon substances. So also the whole and parts. The whole need not be determined or limited by parts. But the parts depend upon the whole. Without the whole how can we have parts which are limitations of the whole ? From what we have said above, we generalise that the notion of relation in the Vedānta is that it is not of two the things which are independent or real, as the Nyāya holds. In Nyāya difference is more important. But relation cannot be understood as relation of two things which are independent or which have a nature of their own. Nor can relation be understood as integrally and totally binding the two terms related. Relation is so vital that the terms do not have any existence apart from their relation. In

1. Śaṅkara's *Bhāṣya* on *Brahma Sūtra* II, i. 14. ananyatvaṁ vyatirekeṇābhāvaḥ brahma-vyatirekeṇa jagato'bhāvaḥ.

that sense we have no two different things which are mutually dependent in the Vedāntic concept. If the two things are mutually independent, there is no basis for relation at all; and if they are dependent mutually, there is no distinction or terms as such. So the Vedāntin would say of two terms, one and one term alone is independent and the other term is dependent. The Mādhyamika Buddhists would say that there cannot be shell without silver and *vice versa*; hence both the terms are false, whereas for the Vedāntin one term is false and the other is real. By, 'false' Vedānta means that it is exhausted by being apprehended; and by real it means something which is in existence independent of our knowing.

We shall now consider the evidence for what has been stated above. How do we know that the world is illusory? There are three reasons which are given for the falsity of the world. This world is false, because it is perceived (*dṛśyatvāt mithyā*) just like a picture or the 'rope-snake'. Again, this world is false, because it is inert (*jaḍatvāt*). The third argument is that the world is false because it is limited (*paricchinnatvāt*). The world is limited in space, in time and in respect of things.

Let us have a close look at these arguments. What is *dṛśya*? That which is expressed in any particular mode or manner through concepts or words is *dṛśya*.[1] It is not merely being seen, but something which is expressed in concepts and words as 'this' or "that" or in some other manner. Why should it be false? Why should expression be false? The Vedānta contention is that anything that is concretely expressed through words is false, and conversly the real is something which cannot be expressed. The real is too deep for words and concepts, i.e., we my say that it is all depth and no surface at all, whereas the false is all surface and no depth at all. The real is what is at the back of all these expressions. It is what these expressions are trying to express? Words cannot exhaust the real, much less do they truly represent it. It means that anything that is expressed in language, in culture, in sensation, that anything that is expressed is false to that extent. The way in which the real manifests itself, is a *mode* of expression. The Vedāntin wants to make out

1. *Advaitasiddhi*, pp. 268-9 (Nirnaya Sagar Edn.). śabdajanyavṛttiviṣayatvam eva dṛśyatvam; yadvā saprakārakavṛttiviṣayatvam eva dṛśyatvam.

that this manifestation is not the only expression, but there is something else also. There should be many other things in reality unexpressed. So this world is not the only expression. In that sense, even God, religion and all cultures are but false. The Vedāntin is bold enough to say that even God is false. If you speak of only one religion or one culture or one civilization, it rules out other religions, other cultures, other civilizations whereas this gives you scope for expressing the real. It means that all religions are expressions of the inexpressible Brahman. So civilizations have taken place, they will occur; they are here and many more may come in the world; still Brahman is not affected by them; and yet every civilization, every culture, every religion can be taken as *an expression* of Brahman.

How do we explain that the inert is false? What is *jaḍa* (inert)?[1] It should be taken as *viṣaya*, i.e. object which is different from consciousness or what is *known by* consciousness. It is this which confronts us in experience as *an other*. Why should it be false if it were not self-luminous? Because it depends upon another thing to evidence its own being. It has to depend upon the consciousness for its being. So the implication is that what is self-luminous is real. The real which is self-luminous is not known as object; it need not be known. It is immediately aware of itself. Otherwise, we have to get to some other knowledge to know it. So we may say that there is an ultimate reality which lights up all things, but which is not revealed by anything else. By its light everything is known, but it is not known by anything else. It is therefore said to be *svayamprakāśa* (self-luminous). The object is not self-evident nor independent; it is *jaḍa*; and therefore it is false. Only the self-evident must be taken as the real and the non-self-evident is false.

What is *paricchinnatva* or finitude? It is limitation or restriction. This world is false because it is limited. Limitation is of three kinds. There is first of all spatial limitation. For example, we say, "This is here", "It is there", "It is not here", and so on. Secondly, there is limitation by time. We say: "It is 'now' or 'then' ", "It is not 'all time' or 'always' ." A thing may exist for a longer time or shorter time., but it does not exist always. The world is false because it is limited by time. What

1. ajñānatva; anātmatva; jñānaviṣayatva; asvaprakāśatva is jaḍatva.

is real is the infinite, the eternal, which is not conditioned by time or space or characteristics.

The whole, the *akhaṇḍa*, the unrestricted, the infinite, is the real; whereas the restricted, the limited—in time, space and things is unreal. *Saccidānanda* is the converse of *dṛśyatva, jaḍatva* and *paricchinnatva*. One may ask: "What is the value of these arguments ? Will they bring about conviction ? Will they convince the opponent ? Can we bring home to him this theory that the world is false because it is *dṛśya, jaḍa* and *paricchinna* and so on ?" I would say that these arguments are as good as other philosophical arguments. They are no doubt well formulated, but like all philosophical arguments they do not bring about conviction. Even if we depend on reasoning (*tarka*) based on *śruti*, it does not fare much better, because one can say: "Well, I see the argument; but what makes you think that the world is illusory? In the case of the world we do not see the negation or have the experience of cancellation. So there is a difference between world-illusion and rope-snake illusion." Moreover, one can present a counter-argument. One argument can equally be countered by an equally efficient argument. So what is there to decide between these arguments? Taken by themselves these arguments are not sufficient. They are not sufficient to bring about conviction. But taken along with the intuition given to us by *śruti*, they help us to confirm and to convince by removing the improbability and contradictions; and no opponent can shake you from that position.

Let me summarise what has been stated so far. First of all, with reference to the concept of appearance, there are two levels. The real and the appearance are not two things, but only two stages. They are not to be taken as unconnected or unrelated things; one is deeper, the other is superficial. The real is what is at the back of all things. That which is inexpressible, that which is the pre-supposition, that which is the whole and the infinite is self-luminous. The opposite is false. The relation between the false and the real is elastic. The false indicates the presence of the real. In fact there is nothing which is completely false. False is a part of the real and hence there is a kind of relation between the two. The relation between them is not constitutive but *indicative*. The false indicates the real, and does not constitute an integral part of the real. The relationship between the real and the false exemplifies al relationships.

The manifestations of the real provide the metaphysical basis for toleration of different cultures and religions. It is not as if we tolerate other cultures or religions as part of good manners. It is something deeper than that. We hold that all these cultures and religions are the ways in which the real is expressed. Though no one way can claim to be the only way, all ways are only expressions or versions of the same underlying reality.

3.4. SELF-LUMINOSITY*

The Vedāntic standpoint is based on experience. So it is not open to any kind of doubt or speculation or conjecture. It is not so much concerned with any particular experience, but with that which is foundational to all experience, viz., Brahman, the Ultimate Reality which is the foundational consciousness. The Ultimate Reality is the most intimate Self (Ātman). *Svayaṁprakāśatā* may be briefly defined as "*avedyatve sati aparokṣa-vyavahāra-yogyatvam.*" It means that Brahman-Ātman is not known as an object and yet is immediately aware of itself.

It should be pointed out that this definition of self-luminosity is not a new revelation. It is the most recurrent topic in all the Upaniṣads which speak of the Self as *svaprakāśa, svayaṁjyoti.* In the *Bṛhadāraṇyaka*[1], there is a well-argued discussion between Janaka and Yājñavalkya on this problem. The concept of self-luminosity is based on the *svayaṁjyotirbrāhmaṇa* and Yājñavalkya asks: How can one know the knower? How can one know that by which one knows everything? Where there is duality, there is a possibility of one knowing the other. But when everything is the Self, where does the question arise of one knowing the other? The Upaniṣad says: *na tatra sūryo bhāti na candra-tārakam, nemā vidyuto bhānti kuto'yam agniḥ.* The Self is that where the Sun does not shine, nor the Moon and the stars, nor the flashes of lightening, not to speak of fire. Every other light follows this original light. By that Light everything shines.[2] We have in these texts of the Upaniṣad the whole definition of self-luminosity. The entire *Kenopaniṣad* may be taken as nothing but a thematic discourse on self-luminosity. The question is raised : "*keneṣitaṁ patati preṣitaṁ manaḥ*[3] etc." By whom does the mind function? By whom do the vital airs function? How does speech function? By raising these questions, the *Upaniṣad* conveys the idea that the Self is the eye of the eye, ear of the ear,

*Reprinted from *The Journal of the University of Madras*, Vol. LIII, Nos. 1 & 2 June and July 1981.

1. *Br. Up.* IV, iii. The discussion starts with the question: "kiṁ jyotir ayaṁ puruṣa iti."
2. *Muṇḍaka Up.* II, ii, 9; *Śve. Up.* VI, 14.
3. *Kena Up.* I, 1.

speech of speech, i.e. the Upaniṣad wants to bring out that the Self is something more internal than the outward organs.[1] Again, in the debate between Yājñavalkya and many others in the assembly convened by Janaka, Yājñavalkya is asked: What is that which is unconditionally immediate?[2] Other objects become immediate conditionally. When there is attention and the sense-organ is in contact with them through some external light and when the object is of a particular magnitude, then only these things will be perceived. But the Self is always unconditionally immediate. Janaka asks Yājñavalkya again: "What is the light by which man is guided?" One may answer: By the light of the Sun man is guided. If the Sun is not there, what happens? "The Moon is there", one may reply. Suppose the Moon is not there? "The light of the stars is there", one may answer. If there is no light of the stars, then speech is there to guide a person. We know that by the sound of speech man may be guided in darkness. If there is no speech also, then Yājñavalkya says, the Self which is self-luminous is there.[3] Yājñavalkya then tells Janaka about the three states of experience and the Self which is invariably and uniformly present in all of them.

One who knows the Self gets beyond all fear, because fear is generated by a second; if there is no second, there would be no room for fear at all.

In Śaṅkara and others we find the same doctrine. In a number of places Śaṅkara says that one who denies the Self is the Self.[4] If destruction takes place, it can take place only up to Puruṣa, but Puruṣa cannot be destroyed by any forces of destruction.[5] It is immutable; it is permanent.

I shall base my exposition mostly on Citsukha. He begins with this notion which is the most fundamental one in Advaita by placing it right in the beginning of his treatise. The benedic-

1. *Kena Up.* I, 2. śrotrasya śrotraṁ, manaso mano yadvāco ha vācaṁ sa u prāṇasya prāṇah cakṣuṣaścakṣuḥ.

2. *Br. Up.* III, iv, 1 and *Br. Up.* III, v: yat sākṣād aparokṣād brahma ya ātmā sarvāntaras tam me vyācakṣva iti.

3. *Br. Up.* IV, iii, 6: ātmaivāsya jyotir bhavatītyātmanaiva jyotiṣā iti.

4. ya eva nirākartā tasyaivātmatvāt.

5. sarvaṁ vikārajātaṁ (vastujātam) vinaśyat, puruṣāntaṁ vinaśyati, puruṣastu avikāri, anucchitti-dharmā kūṭastho nityaḥ.

tory verse in the beginning (*mangalācaraṇa*) starts with: "*namaskurmo nṛsiṁhāya svaprakāśa-cid-ātmane*". Then he introduces the discussion on the concept of *svayaṁprakāśatva* It may be stated here that Citsukha shows better appreciation of the importance of this doctrine than any one else. Madhusūdana Sarasvatī closely follows Citsukha, but I do not think that he adds anything very significant to what Citsukha has stated with clarity and depth.

Citsukha's mode of approach is to give, first of all, a preliminary definition and also *prima facie* evidence for it. He gives as many as eleven definitions[1] of *svayaṁprakāśa*, and accepts the eleventh definition. Each definition is framed having in view some opponent or other. During the whole treatment of this topic, Citsukha has in view the Nyāya school as the principal opponent although he does not say it in so many words.

Let me explain first of all what this definition: "*avedyatve sati aparokṣa-vyavahāra-yogyatvaṁ*" means. Though the Self is not an object, yet it has the fitness to be immediately aware of itself. The question arises: what is this fitness? What is this *yogyatā*? Is it a *dharma* (a characteristic or attribute)? First of all, it is absent in the state of *mokṣa* (freedom). In *mokṣa*, the Self cannot be aware of itself as *svayaṁprakāśa*. *Svayaṁprakāśa* is there, but it cannot be aware of itself as there is no other and as there is no challenge or occasion to know itself as such. To meet this objection, it might be stated that fitness (*yogyatā*) belongs to the locus or substrate (*adhikaraṇa*), which does not have the absence of fitness, just as the Naiyāyikas or the Vaiśeṣikas define *dravya* as the substrate of qualities.[2] The Nyāya-Vaiśeṣika holds the view that in the first moment of its existence the substance is *nirguṇa* (*utpannaṁ dravyaṁ ādye kṣaṇe nirguṇaṁ niṣkriyaṁ ca tiṣṭhati*). The cause should precede the

1. atha ko'yaṁ svaprakāśaśabdārthaḥ? kiṁ svaścāsau prakāśaśca svaprakāśaḥ; svasya svayaṁeva prakāśa iti vā; sajātiyaprakāśā-prakāśyatvaṃ vā; svasattāyāṁ prakāśavyatirekavirahitatvaṁ vā; svavyavahārahetuprakā ṣatvaṁ vā; jñānāviṣayatvaṁ vā; jñānāviṣayatve satyaparokṣatvaṁ vā; vyavahāraviṣayatve sati jñānāviṣayatvaṁ vā; svapratibaddhavyavahāre sajātiyaparānapekṣatvaṁ vā; avedyatve satyaparokṣavyavahāraviṣayatvaṁ vā; tadyogyatvaṁ vā.

2. TP p. 9. mokṣadaśāyām ca vivakṣitadharmābhāve' pi kadācit sattvena tadatyantābhāvānadhikaraṇasya, guṇāśrayo dravyam itivat siddheḥ.

effect; at least for one moment the cause must be without the effect. In that moment it will not be called substance because there is no *guṇa.* Though it does not have the *guṇa* at that moment, according to the Nyāya, the absence of *guṇa* is not there. Though the *guṇa* is not actually present, yet it belongs to that locus (*adhikaraṇa*) from which it is not absent.

But, does the Self have any *dharma* at all? Is it not taken as *nirdharmaka* or *nirguṇa* in the Advaita? Can we speak of any kind of *yogyatva* of *dharma*? We can, in empirical usage, suppose or assume such attributes. Citsukha quotes the famous verse of Sureśvarācārya:

"akṣamā bhavataḥ keyaṁ sādhakatva-prakalpane,
kiṁ na paśyasi saṁsāraṁ tatraivājñānakalpitam".

We need not suffer from the incapacity of imagining things. The whole world, Advaita maintains, stands upon *avidyā*. Citsukha also quotes from the *Pañcapādikā*:[1]

"*ānando viṣayānubhavo nityatvaṁ ceti santi dharmāḥ,*
apṛthaktve'pi caitanyāt pṛthagivāvabhāsante".

Ānanda (Bliss), *viṣayānubhava* (experience of objects), and *nityatvam* (eternity) are not separate qualities from the self (*caitanya*), but yet they seem to be separated from the Self and among themselves. So we can also have *yogyatva* like them in the Self.

We have now to explain the nature of consciousness or *anubhūti* which is *svaprakāśa*. What is the *pramaṇa* for this? The evidence for this, as pointed out, is the very essence of experience (*anubhūti*) itself. This point can be conveyed in the form of an argument as follows for the sake of proving it to others: "*anubhūtiḥ svayaṁprakāśā, anubhūtitvāt, yannaivaṁ tannaivaṁ, yathā ghaṭaḥ.*" *Anubhūti* is the *pakṣa*; *svayaṁprakāśa* is the *sādhya*. We cannot give any positive example in support of the argument. This is a *kevala-vyatireki* type of inference as no other entity except the self is self-luminous. If Experience (*anubhūti*) were to be known by another, then it would lose its very nature as *anubhūti*; it will not be considered as *anubhūti* at all. The very nature of *anubhūti* demands that it will not be known by any other, and yet it is *svayaṁprakāśa* (immediately aware of itself).

We may consider some objections raised against this position. First of all there is the objection from the Nyāya point of view.

1. *Pañcapādikā*: Madras edn. p. 23; Calcutta Sanskrit Series edn. p. 67.

For the Nyāya, there is nothing which is not known; even if we say "I do not know this", in a way we know it as we speak about it. A thing which is not an object, which is not known as any object, cannot be found in the universe anywhere. We may state this as a counter-argument. *Anubhūti* is *vedya*, i.e. experience is known, because it is a *vastu* (thing) or padārtha (spoken about). Whatever is a *padārtha* is known, and *anubhūti* is a *padārtha* or *vastu*, therefore it is known. The inference regarding *svayaṁprakāśa* is countered by a different *anumāna* which is the opposite of the first *anumāna*. Experience (*anubhūti*) is known as an object (*vedya*), as it is a thing (*vastu* or speakable), like a pitcher.

The third which is a more formidable objection takes the form : If we are adducing any *pramāṇa* for *svayaṁprakāśatva* of the Self, then it becomes *vedya* If, on the other hand, we maintain that we are not adducing any *pramāṇa*, then there is no proof or evidence for it. It means that the Advaita position falls to the ground by its not being supported by any argument. This is the dilemma which the Advaitin has to face. If we adduce a *pramāṇa*, then *anubhūti* becomes *vedya*; and consequently our definition of *anubhūti* is contradicted. If we do not adduce any *pramāṇa*, then the thesis has no proof and falls to the ground. To take these objections one by one.

Knowability of any object has its opposite, because it is a *dharma*; i.e. whatever we speak about must have its opposite; otherwise we cannot have significant discourse.[1] All significant discourse is possible only when we have things from which we distinguish these. The absence of these things is also possible. We cannot speak of something which is all-pervasive. If there is knowability (*vedya*) only, how will we distinguish *vedya* ? How will *vedya* become significant ? There must be something different, the non-acceptance of which would lead you to undesirable consequences. If we do say that *anubhūti* is *vedya*, then it will lead to certain undesirable consequences. What

1. TP p. 12: vedyatvaṁ kiṁcinniṣṭhātyantābhāvapratiyogi, dharmatvāt, śauklyavad iti sāmānyato dṛṣṭānumānenānirdhārita-dharmi-viśeṣaniṣṭhasyavedyatva-dharmasya prasiddhatvāt. This is in full accord with the contention of the linguistic philosophers that any term in a significant discourse must have its opposite, that from which it is distinguished.

are they? It will lead to the utter unknowability of all things, utter darkness. If *anubhūti* is known by another *anubhūti*, the second by the third and so on, then the whole world will be shrouded in darkness, since the first term is not firmly fixed.[1]

As regards the second objection, i.e., *pratiprayoga* or the counter-argument which shows that *anubhūti* is known as an object, the Vedāntist would say that we must distinguish between *anubhūti* and other things. Let us suppose, for the sake of argument, that *anubhūti* is known. Is it known by another knowledge? First of all, there is a knowledge of a table. Then we have the awareness that there is the knowledge of the table. Then it is also known by a third knowledge. The fourth also will be known by another, and so on. This series of cognitions will chase one another in quick succession, and there will be no end to this series. If knowledge as such is known by another knowledge, evidenced and certified by yet another knowledge, it should go on endlessly. If it is said, as is done by the Nyāya, that we do not pursue the series of knowledge beyond three or four steps (*tri-catur-kakṣā-nādhikā-matiḥ*), then how does that fourth knowledge differ from the first knowledge? If the first and subsequent knowledges remain forever unknown, the whole series will suffer from the same predicament. If the fourth knowledge need not be known, the first knowledge itself need not be known to be aware of itself. So nothing will be known, and hence there will be utter darkness. We may have two or three hypothesis with regard to knowledge. Knowledge or experience is never known or experienced. We do not have any direct knowledge of it like the eye. We see through the eye, but the eye itself we do not see. It is the eye by which we are able to see things, but the eye itself we will not see. Knowledge is that by which we know things but which itself is not known. How then is it known? By familiarity with the object (*prākaṭya* or *jñātatā*). The object has a familiar look. Then, we infer that something has taken place here. We do not have a direct knowledge of that knowledge. This is one position we

1. Either it would lead to a *regressus ad infinitum* (*anavasthā*) or to total darkness (*jagadāndhya-prasaṅgaḥ*), as no member of the knowledge-series is cognised. To escape this predicament, we have to accept that knowledge is self-known. This is the nerve of the argument in accepting the Self-luminosity of knowledge.

can adopt.[1] The second position is that every knowledge has to be known as an object by a separate knowledge, owing to what we may call an introspective act which has for its object the first knowledge. The emphasis is on the knowledge as an object. I have the knowledge of the table. The first knowledge is to be known by a second knowledge in the form: "I know that I know". The second knowledge also would need to be known, by a third knowledge : "I know that I know that I know".[2] But it is a fact that when we know a thing, we do not have any doubt that we know it. When we know anything, we do not doubt that we know it, nor have a contradictory experience to the effect that I do not know it.[3] To know and to be conscious that we are knowing it are one and the same thing. They are simultaneous.

According to Buddhism, the light of knowledge shines when we know the object, and so on. The Buddhists have accepted knowledge as self-luminous (*sva-saṁvedana*). For them, every knowledge is *svayaṁprakāśa*. But there is some difference between the Vedānta conception of *svayaṁprakāśa* and the Buddhist conception of it. The Buddhists take part of the knowledge as subject and part of it as object. Knowledge bifurcates itself into two aspects. But the Vedāntists say that knowledge cannot be bifurcated In fairness to the Buddhists, it should be said that they might have accepted it in the beginning; but later on they also say that the intellect which is the Self does not have parts, but appears *as if* it has the three elements or parts, i.e., the thing grasped, the grasper, and the grasping (knowledge). It means that they too later on came to understand the *svayaṁprakāśa* as what is indistinguishable, as that which does not have any parts.[4]

1. This is the position of the Bhāṭṭa school of Mīmāṁsā.

2. This is the well-known doctrine of anuvyavasāya advocated by the Nyāya.

3. TP p. 16: kiṁ ca, anubhūtir arthaprakāśanasamaye yadi na prakāśeta tathā saty-anantarakṣaṇe jijñāsos tatra sandeho viparyayo vā viparītapramā vodiyāt. na ca kaścid amum adrākṣīnno vā bhavāniti pṛṣṭo'nantarakṣaṇe sandigdhe viparyasyati saṁvidabhāvaṁ vā pramiṇoti, kiṅtu niścinotyeva 'idam aham adrākṣam' iti. tena prakāśamānaivānubhūtir arthair vyavahāraṁ janayatīti yuktam.

4. avibhāgo'pi buddhyātmā viparyāsitadarśanaiḥ, grāhya-grāhaka-saṁvittibhedavān ivopalakṣyate.

We shall now consider the third objection. If we adduce a proof (*pramāṇa*), it is argued, *anubhūti* becomes *vedya* (an object); and if we do not adduce any *pramāṇa*, it means that there is nothing to prove it and therefore the whole thesis falls to the ground. The Vedāntist does not accept the second alternative. He does not say that he does not adduce any *pramāṇa* therefor. He does speak of it, and also he is able to urge certain considerations in support of it; but, it does not mean that on this account it will become an object (*vedya*). We do speak of *svayaṁprakāśa*; we adduce evidence, although it may not amount to any kind of independent proof. It is all the time a rebuttal of the other standpoints or misapprehensions. By removing the misunderstandings, Citsukha is directing our attention to the basic fact of experience and asking us to realize its unique nature, viz., its *svayaṁprakāśatā*. *Anubhūti* is not known as an object and yet it is self-evident. We can speak about something, but it does not become an object. Anything that is spoken about, according to the Nyāya, becomes an object. We speak about a square circle. But does it become an object? We speak about God. Does it become an object? We speak about moral duty. Does it become an object? The Naiyāyika seems to think that any usage of words would mean objectifying the thing. The Vedāntist, however, makes a distinction. He accepts *svayaṁprakāśa* in a symbolic way, but it is not confronted as an object. That which is not known as an object is still something that can be referred to in significant discourse and can be said to be validly known. However, that which is known as "this", as confronting one in a determinate way, becomes *phalavyāpya*. But how do we speak of Brahman? We speak of Brahman as what cannot be spoken of. There is, however, *vṛttivyāpyatva* (knowable through the intellect) even with regard to Brahman, because our ignorance of Brahman can be destroyed *only through the work of a vṛtti*.[1] We cannot say that the very presence of consciousness is inimical to ignorance. If that were the case, the whole world would not have come into existence at all. *Svarūpajñāna* (which

1. Ṭikā, T. P. phalavyāpyatvam eva śāstrakṛdbhir nivāritaṁ, na tu vṛttivyāpyatvam; brahmaṇyajñāna-nāśāya vṛttirapekṣitā.
or. *Pañcadaśī*, VII, 90—phalavyāpyatvam evāsya śāstrakṛdbhir nivāritam VII, 92—brahmaṇyajñāna-nāśāya vṛttivyāptirapekṣitā.

is Brahman) is not inimical or opposed to the presence of *avidyā* and its effects. What is inimical to it is a specific act or mode of knowledge (*vṛttijñāna*). Advaitists give the example of the rays which, when passed through a lens, burn the object; but the rays do not burn by themselves. Consciousness shines everywhere. But it removes ignorance only when it is reflected in the mind or focussed and directed through the intellect (*buddhi*).

There are four grades of speakability. We speak of the concrete objects of the world such as table, chair, tree, mountain, etc. These are objects of commonsense and are literally and directly speakable. The second grade of speakability is with regard to the generalities of the laws, the numbers which govern the operations, the law of gravity, or the laws of thought and so on. No doubt they are speakable, but we cannot point them out as we point out to the chair, table, etc. They are at the back of our discourse and there is no surface for them. Both of these things are literally speakable.[1] When we speak of God or when we come to super-sensuous states like duty, or when we speak of the distinction between falsity and truth—these are symbolic. They are not literally spoken. They are spoken of, but not spoken about. So the distinction between God and creatures or between the false and the true is not scientific or objective. The distinctions between true and false, etc., are not laws, and nothing of the world will be affected if we do not agree to these things. We are stretching the meaning of the words in a metaphorical way when we say that God is the First Cause, is father or mother. Our usage here is metaphorical or symbolic.

Now we come to the fourth grade of speech where an object is spoken as what cannot be spoken. Difference, wherever it may be, presupposes an identity, i.e., difference can only stand on the ground of some identity. But identity itself cannot be spoken of as one of these differences. It can only be referred to as what the differences *are not*. Hence the need for the *neti neti* (not this, not this) method. The demand that Brahman should be taken as *one more thing*, one among the multitude of objects,

1. Only in the first two modes of the speakable can the thing spoken about be in the objective mode, and not in the last two grades of the speakable.

is illegitimate, because we do understand Brahman as the *ground of things*, as the identity underlying all differences. We should not make identity itself one more thing, one among things. If that were the case, we have to ask for another identity. We can drive home the point by giving the example of a platform on which we stand. We cannot ask the platform again to be based on another. If it were so, then, where will that stand? The ground can only be understood as what the things which are supported by it are not. It can only be referred to as what things cannot be, what these things are not. So we require a fourth kind of speech with regard to what is unspeakable; and that is the *neti, neti* speech.

So far we have adduced evidence for *svayaṁprakaśa*. The Ātman is *svayaṁprakāśa*. There is no distinction between the Ātman and *svayaṁprakāśa*. The Ātman should not be conceived as a substance which has the *quality of consciousness* or self-consciousness. The substance-attribute conception is irrelevant or unwarranted here, because consciousness is the nature (*svarūpa*) of the Self. The substance-attribute relation is not acceptable to the Vedāntist. Ātman is not to be viewed as having consciousness, but it *is* consciousness. That is, there is no distinction of substance and attribute in the Ātman. Consciousness is Ātman and Ātman is consciousness. Ātman is *cidrūpa*. It does not know itself as object, yet it is immediately aware of itself always, it is unfailing, uniform awareness itself.[1]

Not only we cannot make the distinction between Ātman and consciousness, but we also cannot make the distinction between one self and another, the third self and the fourth self and so on. So Ātman is not the "I" as opposed to objects and distinct from other "I's". What is *svayaṁprakāśa* is not an object. Its nature is unique. It is always the subject *par excellence*. We cannot ascribe any attribute to it, any feature, any quality, any distinguishing mark.[2] It can be distinguished from other

1. TP p. 21-2: cidrūpatvād akarmatvāt svayaṁjyotiriti śruteḥ; ātmanaḥ svaprakāśatvaṁ ko nivārayituṁ kṣamaḥ.

2. Because Rāmānuja makes a difference between the Self and its knowledge and also identifies the Self with the "I" (*ahamartha*), he is forced to make distinctions and separations between one self and another. For the Advaitist, the "I" is the Ātman (Consciousness) as already delimited and wrongly identified with the inner sense (*antaḥkaraṇa*). The Prābhākara, who accepts

things by the non-possession of these distinguishing marks. Because it has a unique position, it cannot be presented as an object. And so, we cannot distinguish between one self (or consciousness) and another. Ātman is absolute. It follows therefore that the notion of *aham* is due to *adhyāsa*. *Aham* is the first *adhyāsa*.[1] *Adhyāsa* is only a compound, a mis-alliance between this (*idam*) and *not-this* (*anidam*, consciousness), since we are identifying consciousness with *antaḥkaraṇa*; and when the consciousness is thus identified, it becomes an "I", *aham*. If so, we can distinguish many *ahams*. But in itself, consciousness cannot be distinguished from another, because there is no second to it. It is all-pervasive; it is universal, it is unique.[2] It is the Self of all; it is Brahman. Knowing this, one transcends all desire, fear, sorrow, duality, disease, and death. It is the stage of fearlessness, because fear pertains to the realm of the dual. Where is the question of fear when everything is Ātman which is *svayaṁprakāśa*? Attainment of the Self is also the highest human value.

knowledge to be self-luminous, makes a difference between the Self (*ātman*) and consciousness, whereas for the Advaitist they are identical.

1. *Pañcapādikā* : Calcutta Sanskrit Series edn. pp.131-2. : aham iti tāvat prathamo'dhyāsaḥ.

The "I" is not strictly unitary, it is a compound of object (*idam*) and subject (*anidam*). Because, the "I" is distinguished on the one hand from "this" (object) and on the other from one's "I"; there is *compositeness* in its make-up.

2. *Br. Up.* III, v, i. Ānandāśrama Edn. p. 448. atha hainaṁ kaholaḥ kauṣītakeyaḥ papraccha, yājñavalkyeti hovāca yadeva sākṣādaparokṣād brahma ya ātmā sarvāntaras taṁ me vyācakṣvetyeṣa ta ātmā sarvāntaraḥ katamo yājñavalkya sarvāntaro yo'śanāyāpipāse śokaṁ mohaṁ jarāṁ mṛtyum atyeti. etaṁ vai tam ātmānaṁ viditvā brāhmaṇāḥ putraiṣaṇāyāśca vittaiṣaṇāyāśca lokaiṣaṇāyāśca vyutthāya atha bhikṣācaryaṁ caranti.

Also: *Br. Up. IV*, iv,25. dvitīyād vai bhayaṁ bhavati, abhayaṁ vai janaka prāpto'si.

3.5 KNOWLEDGE AND TRUTH*

The framing of the topic poses a preliminary question. It presupposes that we know knowledge or can know it. For how else, it may be asked, can we ascertain whether it is true or not, whether it conforms to its deliverance of the content or otherwise. When and how, if at all, do we become aware of knowledge? We do not admittedly know knowledge either simultaneously, when we perceive an object, or subsequently by a separate act of knowing. We also have no memory of knowledge, not having perceived it in the first instance. When we perceive the table or the tree, it is the table or the tree that we perceive, and not the knowledge and table together or even their distinction. In normal empirical perception, the datum does not appear as distinctly distinguished from the perceiving consciousness, there being no need to separate the two. Nor is it possible to do so. For when I see a patch of colour, I am conscious of the patch of colour only and not at once conscious of my perception of it, or any distinction from it. These two, the colour and my perception of it, cannot obviously be given together. Nor is it true that immediately after the occurrence of a perception, in the second and subsequent moments, there is consciousness of the previous act of perception—the so-called introspection of old time psychology or the *anuvyavasāya* of the *Nyāya*. It is even thought that such introspection intervenes automatically. There is no experiential basis for this introspection. It is not that every act of perception is *ipso facto* followed by a back-stroke of the consciousness of itself. Should not this introspection itself be followed by another which apprehends it as introspection and still by another and so forth indefinitely? There is no evidence of this un-ending series, and a peson's life time will be consumed in one single act of perception.

Moreover, the disembodied act of perceiving, contentless and diaphonous as it is, cannot be an object of thought, for it does not arrest attention, being the act of attention itself. As being

*Reprinted from the Proceedings of the 1975 Indian Philosophical Congress. Delhi: Motilal Banarsidass, 1976.

invariable and uniform, it eludes our grasp. How then do we become *aware of knowledge*, for even to speak of it is, in some measure, to be conscious of it? One way in which we could become conscious of our involvement is the experience of the same objective content in two different ways or stages: first *as believed to be true* and subsequently, *as disbelieved*, or at least as that from which belief has been withdrawn. Without one and the same object appearing in two different stages or modes of apprehension, we may not become aware of our act of attending to it. In the transition of our attitude, as we pass from belief in the reality of the object to disbelief in its reality, we are indirectly aware of our act of attention. If the objective content were to differ in the two stages, or if it were a unitary unanalysable fact, reflection cannot result. Only when what we took to be one thing really turns out to be another on closer inspection, do we scratch our head and become self-conscious. Did I perceive it after all or was I day-dreaming? What was it that I actually perceived? Some such misgivings and searchings of the heart, as it were, describe the attitude of self-reflection. As long as a machine is running smooth and in order, we have no occasion to become inquisitive about its inner structure and functioning. Only as a break happens, we begin to inquire about the economy of each part in the whole and the functioning of the entire mechanism. This is an interesting but somewhat intricate and intriguing topic for investigation. And this is not the place to undertake a fuller analysis of the context of illusion. I may state my conclusion briefly that the consciousness of the false engenders reflection; it makes us turn back upon ourselves.

Knowledge and truth involve each other. We cannot be conscious or be aware of knowledge as such without a previous belief and a subsequent disbelief or at least a re-confirmation of the content. Re-confirmation must be understood as annulment of a previous disbelief. Without the consciousness of the false or at least its suggestion, we cannot affirm anything as true. To speak of the true is to distinguish it from the false. If everything which passes for knowledge were true without exception, or if everything were false without exception, we cannot call any particular knowledge true or false.

II

Knowledge is a cognitive experience, and it has to be distinguished from types of non-cognitive experiences, such as willing and feeling as exemplified by volitional acts or emotional states such as pleasure, anger and lust. What is peculiar about the cognitive attitude is that we want to "see" or "take in" things as they are, as they obtain in reality: we do not want to add or modify or distort the given, and to the extent we do this, it is not knowledge.

The notions of truth and falsity imply that knowledge is a mode of consciousness which is, or should be, determined solely by the object ("*jñānaṁ tu pramāṇa-janyam, pramāṇaṁ ca yathābhūtavastuviṣayam, ato jñānaṁ kartum akartum anyathā vā kartum aśakyam, kevalaṁ vastutantram eva tat, na codanātantraṁ nāpi puruṣatantram*", *Śaṅkara's Bhāṣya on Br. Sūt. I.i.4*; "*na vastu-yāthātmyajñānaṁ puruṣabuddhyapekṣaṃ, kiṁ tarhi, vastutantram eva tat.*" *ibid., I.i.2.*). Consciousness or the subject cognizing must merely reveal or discover the object, neither adding anything to it nor distorting it. To be discovered, the object of knowledge should exist prior to and independent of the knowing; it must be an accomplished fact—a *siddha-vastu*—one that is not brought into being through the knowing itself. If it were simultaneous with knowledge or were created by it, how can any knowledge be true or false? The perception of the "rope-snake" would not be an illusion and would not be recognized as such any time, if the rope (the real) were not taken as existing both *during* and *before* the illusion; it must be something absolutely independent of the knowing of it. The "rope-snake", however, has no existence independent of our knowing, and is totally exhausted in that relationship (*dṛśyatvāt mithyā*). Once this is granted that the object of knowledge should exist prior to it, we cannot also assign any period or limit to its priority. For, to do any such thing, we have to reach a stage when consciousness alone existed and the object was ushered into existence later on, presumably by the former. It is evident that such consciousness is not knowledge; it is willing. However far back we may trace our knowledge, it will always presuppose the object as prior to it. This priority is not primarily temporal, but only signifies the accomplished character of the object.

Similar considerations require that the object of knowledge should not be subject to the accidental conditions of the perceiver. For example, if a certain object were to be known from a certain position at a certain time and by a certain person only, we cannot call that object real, nor that knowledge true. For, we have no means of deciding whether the object is our creation or a joint product of the conditions of the perceiver and those of the object. Thus the object of knowledge cannot be uniquely particular; it must be universal, free from all conditions and accidents. And if this were pushed further, it would mean that strictly speaking, only Pure Being can be said to be the object *par excellence.*

Not only is the object to be independent of our knowing, but we have also to regard the object as not being required to be known by any person or mind. When we know an object we need not at once be conscious of this very knowing. For the object, which alone should determine the nature of consciousness in knowledge, says nothing about its present knownness or its past un-knownness.

The above contentions about the ideal of knowledge run counter to the commonly received principle of idealism that the object is mind-dependent in some way or the other. But all arguments of idealism (e.g. those advanced by Vijñānavāda, Berkeley or Hegel) rely upon feeling and willing and mis-apply them to knowledge. The knowledge absolutist agrees with the realist and with Kant, as against the idealist, that the object of knowledge is or should be independent of the knowing consciousness. There is profound disagreement, however, with realism in another respect. The realist uncritically takes what is ordinarily given as pure knowledge. No actual knowledge in the empirical way is completely free from non-cognitive factors such as imagination, construction, bias and prejudice, etc. Such states appear as knowledge, are taken to be knowledge, but are actually illusion or erroneous perception. It is a necessary demand that we should purify and disassociate knowledge from other factors which are non-cognitive but which masquerade as knowledge. The "rope-snake", for example, is mistaken as knowledge. What we seem to perceive is not given or known; it is a creation or projection of our imagination or fantasy although not apprehended as such in the state of illusion. Thus, knowledge as such is invariably true, and truth is *known* only, not felt or willed. It is only metaphorically that we speak of the truth of a feeling or willing, not literally.

III

It is a very widely held notion that truth can obtain only between propositions, or that it is a function of propositions. For, it may be said in justification of this position, that how else can we ascertain and know anything as true? It is only thought as expressed in language and having a structure (i.e. several elements in a recognisable and ordered configuration) that we can consider and be aware of it as true or truth. As for the question, with what is the proposition to be alligned or compared, two answers might be given: one is that the proposition may be related with other propositions, thus forming a coherent system of propositions; the other alternative is that the proposition may be compared with the object and its correspondence with the latter may be ascertained.

In the first case, what we arrive at is only consistency or logical truth. We only draw implications and more implications and still further implications. There is nothing to justify or validate the original proposition or body of propositions with which we have started. Given these propositions or presuppositions, we can correctly draw the consequences that flow from them. This is eminently the procedure of formal logic. Even a lie may be consistently bolstered up by other lies and these by some others, the whole procedure being sustained by our ingenuity and inventiveness. Such truth is not concerned with conformity of thought with the real, unless we granted the *assumption* that ultimately thought and reality are identical. The real is nothing but systematic or coherent thought. This is what Hegel says. His whole dialectic is a good example of this. The superstructure raised by him should not be taken as in any way validating the assumption, but only as a sustained drawing out of the implications of the assumption. All knowledge is reduced to one mode, that of thought or reason. There is no given or independent fact nor direct, immediate perception. This does offend our sense of truth as discovery of what exists independent of our knowing act.

The other theory is that our knowledge conforms or corresponds, point by point, item by item, to the real given to us in perception or direct acquaintance. Where there is one-one correspondence between the two, there is truth. (*tadvati tat-prakāraka-jñānaṁ pramā*). Some merit in this theory may be accepted; there is recognition of the independence of the real. The difficulty, however, is how can we ascertain that what appears in knowledge is a true transcript of what obtains in reality. We do not, *ex hypothesi*, have the original also before us in knowledge. It may be said primarily that the real is given to us in perception as "this", as the subject of a judgment, and thought only elaborates it (*sarvaṁ jñānaṁ dharmiṇyabhrāntam, prakāre tu saṁśayaḥ*). The persistent question is how we can assert that what appears in knowledge and given expression in language is identical with what we perceived as given reality.

It might well be said that that knowledge which leads to successful activity in our empirical ventures should be taken as valid or true (*saphala-pravṛtti-janakatva*). The criterion of truth is now not correspondence of knowledge and object, but that which leads to successful or uncontradicted activity, i.e. what works in practice. Even a postulate or assumption may work. Here there is no question of absolute truth, but what is useful or leads to desirable results. This may well vary with regard to different spheres of our interest. This is truth according to commonsense and science.

The philosophical question still awaits an answer. It may well be that whatever appears in knowledge as thought-elaboration, and finds expression in linguistic forms, may not be identical with the real. The possibility of discrepancy and deviation is still there. When we look at a building from a distance or from a particular angle, we may get only a perspective. There could be an infinite number of such perspectives, and each one may be useful. No one perspective or a combination of them can claim to be absolutely correct.

The only way to be sure of absolute truth is to get into the skin of the thing, as it were, by becoming identical with it. Here knowledge and its object coincide. This is intuition *par excellence.* There is no possibility of discrepancy or falsity here, because we are not looking at the thing externally, mediately, from a distance or through the mediation of categories, or in a biased or prejudiced way. We know the thing not by representation, but by being it, as it were. Knowledge and the thing known become one. There is, however, a drawback. When we have the intuition we are not at once aware of it *as intuition of the real.* It is indeed a paradox: we have the truth when we are identical with the real, but cannot be reflectively aware that we know the truth. When we are reflectively making the assertion, we are already away from it. Our assertion may be a falsification or a distortion of the real, and is therefore only appearance. To avoid this predicament, the Advaita Vedānta takes recourse to negation. By consciously and systematically negating all thought elaboration and linguistic expression in every form, we arrive at ultimate truth or reality (*adhyāropāpavādābhyāṁ niṣprapañcaṁ brahma prapadyate*). The presupposition behind this is that thought, and this applies to language also, falsifies reality, and by the negation of this falsification or appearance, we alight upon the absolutely real. For a discovery of the real, the appearance is negated. This is possible only if the appearance were in some sense related to the real. All appearance is appearance *of the real* (is indicative, if not constitutive, of the real), and by removal of the appearance we realize the presence of the real as underlying it. A further consequence of this view is that we have recourse to two levels or orders of things; the real and its appearance.

Suppose, for instance, we hold the view that language and thought are closed circles, that they are arbitrary conventions and although we may express one set of terms in other terms, simple or complex, there is nothing behind or beyond these linguistic expressions, like a transcendent reality. Modern linguistic philosophy holds that language is a game or a set of games, and we cannot get out of the linguistic to anything non-linguistic called the real. The quest for absolute truth or the real is meaningless. The world is what it is. The problem of truth or any other philosophical problem is solved by dissolving it, by showing that there is no problem at all. This leads to an unmitigated relativism and indifference towards the great issues of life. Therefore, such a view has to be discarded. The statement that all language is a game is itself not a game, but a veritable statement. There is thus a deep inconsistency in linguistic philosophy.

The stand of the Mādhyamika (*Śūnyavāda*), as understood by

the othodox schools, is not much different. There may be the real, but thought and language are no indication or guide to it. There is falsification, and everything is false, but is it not a falsification *of* the real? Negation of the false does not at once mean the apprehension of the real behind it, as held by the Advaita Vedānta. We can only refute this stand attributed to the Mādhyamika by showing that in all our experience there is no *mere falsity*, which is not at once the falsification *of an underlying ground.* The very impossibility of the false otherwise is the argument.

I have considered in brief some of the principal points of view on Knowledge and Truth. One point clearly emerges out of this. It is not possible to formulate a neutral or universally acceptable position; for any position presupposes or is but an expression of a particular metaphysical stand. This is the nature of all philosophy.

3.6 THE SIX WAYS OF KNOWING

A Review of the Vedānta Theory of Knowledge, by D. M. Datta, George Allen & Unwin Ltd., London, 1932.*

Prof. Datta's book is a pioneer work in some respects; it is not a compendium of all the systems nor is it a general survey of a particular system. For the first time, we are offered a systematic and reasoned exposition of the theory of knowledge in Vedānta. The "*Six Ways*" can adequately be described as a free commentary on the "*Vedānta Paribhāṣā*"; so closely is it followed that the author raises the same objections and gives the same answers as set forth in the *Paribhāṣā*". The six ways or sources of knowledge are Perception, Inference, Comparison, Testimony, Postulation and conscious Non-cognition—to the exposition and critical estimater of each of which one chapter is devoted. The order of the sources adopted by Dr. Datta is slightly different from the usual one, though he does not assign any reason for the deviation except that some sources would appear to have more affinity with some others preceding them in the eyes of western thinkers (p. 15)

Pramāṇavāda, as conceived in the Indian systems, concerns itself primarily with four problems: The number of *pramāṇas*, the specific nature of each, their object and the result that they lead to.[1] There is no unanimity with regard to the conception of *pramāṇa*, though all are agreed that it is a means, a *karaṇa*, which leads to right knowledge. The *karaṇa* can be the sense-organs, as in perception according to the Nyāya; other systems regard that *karaṇa* itself is knowledge, though leading to another. The conception of *pratyakṣa* and other sources, their

*Reprinted from *The Philosophical Quarterly*, January 1933.

1. Cf. *Nyāya-bindu-ṭīkā*-P. 7 (B. Indica). "caturdhā cātra vipratipattiḥ; saṅkhyā-lakṣaṇa-gocara-phala-viṣayā."

Prakaraṇa-pañcikā, P. 38—"svarūpa-saṅkhyārtha-phaleṣu vādibhir yato vivādā bahudhā vitenire; tato vayaṁ tat pratibodhasiddhaye pramāṇa-pārāyaṇam ārabhāmahe."

Parīkṣā-mukha-sūtra-ṭikā I :

"svarūpa-saṅkhyā-viṣaya-phalalakṣaṇāsu catasṛṣu vipratipattiṣu madhye" etc.

number and the object of each are identical in no two systems. The author's procedure is to develop the Vedāntic standpoint on each important topic by a criticism of the views of other systems. The Advaitin, in Mr. Datta's hands, always manages to come out the best, though not in every instance deservedly so. Scant justice is done to the Buddhistic position, and the Jaina is not mentioned at all, inspite of the fact that important and divergent views with regard to the number and nature of *pramāṇa* are held by the latter. The author could have easily availed himself of the excellent special treatises on the subject as the *Pramāṇa-naya-tattvālokālaṅkāra*, *Prameya-kamala-mārtaṇḍa*, *Sammati-tarka*, etc. This however should not seriously affect the merit of the work as a whole; it is but secondarily a comparative study.

Parallels to logical and epistemological doctrines in the west are always drawn, and many of them are suggestive. It may be said that the work is addressed particularly to a reader of western philosophy, and the author's aim is to make the Vedānta position plausible and acceptable even to adverse critics like the realists. For instance, the peculiar contention of Vedānta that the *antaḥkaraṇa* is matter and that it assumes the form of the objects is plausibly compared with the Gestalt theory of the mind, without at the same time ignoring the differences. In the given account of the *pramāṇas*, the reader is not likely to miss anything of importance; he can safely trust himself to the guidance of Dr. Datta.

In his account of *pratyakṣa*, which is deservedly treated at some length, Prof. Datta brings out clearly the special features of the Vedānta conception. The immediacy of Knowledge does not depend upon its being engendered by the senses as it is generally held, but on the nature of the presented object. So the seemingly verbal knowledges "You are the tenth" and "that thou art" etc. are consistently upheld to be immediate and perceptual. The governing condition of knowledge being perceptual is the immediacy of the object to the apprehending consciousness engendered either by the manifestation of the identity or by the rending of the intervening veil between the object and the *pramātṛ* brought about by the *vṛtti*. Here the author very profitably discusses the several alternative theories regarding the precise function of the *vṛtti*; these alternative conceptions are consequent on different conceptions of the Ego, *Jiva*. A fuller and reasoned account of them is to be found in the *Advaita Siddhi* (chapter on *prati-karma-vyavasthā*) and *Siddhāntaleśa* (Part I, pp. 146 ff. Chow. Edn.) to both of which the author makes references. The perception of the *sākṣi* differs from that of the *Pramātṛ* in the sense that the former does not require any other *vṛtti* to engender the contact between him and the objects. The objective condition of anything being immediate (*viṣayagata-pratyakṣatva*) is that the existence of the object should be identical (not-different) from that of the apprehending consciousness; this is the main plank of all idealism. This condition is always present with regard to the illusory object, but is brought about at a certain finite time and to a certain extent with regard to the empirical objects by a suitable *vṛtti*. Some minor tenets, that the *antaḥkaraṇa* is not an *indriya* or that it is not partless, the non-acceptance of the universal and the *alaukika sannikarṣa* etc., are all very well expounded.

One great defect in the work has however to be noted. The peculiar standpoint of the Vedānta that these modes of knowledge are merely empirical and cannot be ultimate has nowhere been clearly emphasised and reasoned out. The question is about the falsity of *pramātṛtva* —signifying thereby the several empirical cognitions. Allied with this is the relation of the *pramātṛ* to the *sākṣi*; why is the former said to be *adhyasta* or superimposed on the latter ?

To elucidate the criticism. The conception of *pramātṛtva* implies two things: that something is, and can be, known; and also that a preference is exercised even among the known. Knowing is a simpler relation than knowing as true or false. Logically, before a choice can be exercised both the alternatives are to be known. Such a simple cognitive relation alone is involved when we know pleasure and pain or introspect into our states. Another explicit instance is the apprehension of the illusory object. In all these, the object apprehended is immediate and completely possessed by consciousness; there is nothing transcendent, and no process is involved in knowing. The existence and the knowledge of feeling are coincident. The apprehension of the *sākṣi* is therefore primordial, direct and intuitional. It involves no relations. In contrast, all the functions of the *pramātṛ* are relational; even perception is relational; it is a judgment that is based upon the intuition of the *sākṣi*. The latter's knowledge is neither false nor true (*sākṣi-jñānasya satyāsatyāviṣayatayā*), while that of the *pramātṛ* implies the application of a standard. And the standard is set up by the relationship of the *antaḥkaraṇa* and the body to the objects. Those that satisfy the requirements of the body and can be reacted by it are called real; the nacre-silver, though directly given, is unreal because it does not satisfy such a requirement. From the side of the spirit or pure consciousness, the exaltation of this accidental standpoint of the *antaḥkaraṇa* to the status of the true and the real should seem irrational and unjustifiable in the extreme. The highest truth is not *a* standpoint; there to know is to *be* that. In the *pramātṛtva*, however, not only the distinction between subject and object but also distinctions in the objective itself are involved. Though unjustifiable from the point of spirit, its identification with the *antaḥkaraṇa* is the essential condition of there being empirical or relational modes of knowledge. Only a limited and specific entity can enter into relations with other entities equally limited, and vary those relations. On the hypothesis of this identification with the *antaḥkaraṇa* can the existence of various *pramāṇas* be explained. What is in immediate contact with my body and senses is perceptual to me at this time; what is reached through a process is mediate. In empirical perception, the resultant knowledge is a judgment, and the *karaṇa* is the intuition of the *sākṣi* which possesses the object immediately and directly. In inference, a judgment itself is the symbol or the starting point; a known relation between two entities is the *karaṇa*. In testimony, the known relation between words and their meanings is the symbol; in comparison, the knowledge of similarity is the *karaṇa*. In *arthāpatti*, a negative relation is made the symbol, while in *anupalabdhi* the conscious non-perception of anything is the symbol. Dr. Datta himself could have arrived at all this had he not arbitrarily confined his task to *pramā* only. For, it is no exaggeration to say that the Vedāntic theory of knowledge is based entirely on an analysis of illusion and similar states.

Coming to inference, the features that distinguish the Vedānta from the Nyāya conception are mainly three : the non-acceptance of *parāmarśa* as a *vyāpāra*, the contention that the *kevalavyatireki* type of *anumāna* is a separate *pramāṇa*—*arthāpatti* and the total disallowance of the *kevalānvayi*. The first two are not peculiar to Vedānta alone. The last contention deserves more attention than is paid to it. Why cannot we have any inference which would be true of the entire universe of things? Nyāya thinks it is possible, because all are objects of thought (*prameya*), knowable. Vedānta denies this, as there is one thing at least which is not knowable—knowledge. Of this, all characters can be denied without contradiction; for the characters are knowable, while knowledge is not, and hence the relation between the two is unprovable. The Nyāya acceptance of the *kevalānvayi* is based on the assumption common to all realism that knowledge of an object is but another object.

The author's suggestion that *upamāna* is a kind of immediate inference—conversion—is striking. But he does not take a firm stand, being easily scared away by the prejudice against immediate inferences in the west. The question of the proper terminology apart, the vital point is: in passing from 'A is like B' or 'A is equal to B' to 'B is like A' or 'B is equal to A' what is the process involved, and what guarantees its validity? Is the principle reducible to any other source? We are not concerned here with a few stray cases as the examples '*go*' and '*gavaya*' would lead us to believe, but with such axioms as "things equal to each other are themselves equal" etc. Such a knowledge is of course valid, at least as valid as the sources of knowledge. Inference cannot lead us to the converse of any proposition; for the major premise required for any inference would itself beg the question, as has been very well pointed out in the *śikhāmaṇi* which deserves to be quoted here.[1]

Comparison represents a stage prior to inference, enabling as it does to formulate general connections. Dr. Datta's confining *upamāna* to 'A is like B' when the likeness is percieved and not to others has little textual or other support. For, the *karaṇa* is simply the knowledge of A's (Gavaya's) similarity to B (Cow) and not the perceptual knowledge of similarity.[2] The similarity

1. *Śikhāmaṇi* p. 203. idamatrākūtam. kimatra sāmānyavyāptir mūlam, viśeṣavyāptirvā. nādyā, yattadbhyāṁ ananugatatvena sāmānyavyāpter anumānānaṅgatvāt. na dvitīyā, yo gavaya-niṣṭha-sādṛśyapratiyogī sa gavaya-sadṛśa iti viśeṣavyāpteḥ prāgajñānāt. kiṁ ca nānumānāt tatsambhavaḥ gavaya nirūpitagosādṛśyarūpa-sādhyāprasiddheḥ etc. etc."

2. Ved. Pari. p. 201. "Tatrānvayavyatirekābhyāṁ gavayaniṣṭhago-sādṛśya-jñānaṁ karaṇam, goniṣṭha-gavaya-sādṛśya-jñānaṁ phalam"

may itself have been inferred or given by testimony; but given the knowledge 'A is like B' by *upamāna* alone do we arrive at the resultant knowledge 'B is like A' etc. And just as a perceived similarity does not necessitate the engendered knowledge being considered perceptual, the verbal similarity too need not lead to a verbal knowledge.

With regard to *anupalabdhi*—better expressible as conscious non-cognition, Prof. Datta supports the narrow view of the *Paribhāṣā* that it is confined to cases of perceptual non-existence only. What guarantees, it may be asked, the exhaustiveness of alternativeness under any head? What source of evidence assures us that these are the only *pramāṇas* and there is no seventh. Our test is not a mere appeal to perception but to all others. They fail to acquaint us with any other and the absence of all the five sources consiciously felt is itself a guarantee that nothing exists. The view of the older Vedāntins agrees with that of the Bhaṭṭa as expressed in the famous couplet :

pramāṇapañcakaṁ yatra vasturūpe na jāyate.
vastusattāvabodhārthaṁ tatrābhāvapramāṇatā.

To think that non-existence can be given by other sources as well is to deprive *anupalabdhi* of all status. Each *pramāṇa* must lead to some knowledge not derivable from other sources; only then, can each *pramāṇa* keep its exclusive character.

The last book is devoted to verbal knowledge. Among many other topics it discusses the meaning of words (*śakti*, *lakṣaṇā* and *vyañjanā*), the origin of symbolic function, the nature of sentence (*vākya*) and the factors that engender a complete coherent meaning. The highly technical doctrines—*anvitābhidhānavāda* and *abhihitānvayavāda*—are lucidly set forth. In this chapter, there is only one thing to which I should take exception. I have always considered it a gross mistake on the part of the Advaitins not to have recognised the true significance of the Sphoṭa theory. Instead of acclaiming the grammarian as a kindred spirit that has reached the Absolute through the word-essence, the Vedāntin has chosen to ally himself with the Mīmāṁsaka in condemning the *sphoṭa* theory. Its significance has not been properly understood. Words and sentences are thought to be constituted of discrete parts—the syllables and words etc. But that we are at all able to construct relative wholes out of discrete entities presupposes an a priori knowledge of the whole;

for it is that alone which guides the grouping of only certain elements (lacking unity in themselves) in a certain order only. To contend that this presupposed whole itself is an entity created out of parts is to fail curiously in critical thinking. Dr. Datta has only too readily allowed himself to be led away by the weight of authority—one other instance of his engineering a position for the Vedāntin at all costs.

On the whole "*The Six ways of Knowing*" is well done. Dr. Datta has handled the materials with skill and moderation. His work should prove of much value to the expert and the general reader alike in understanding the Vedānta theory in a comparative way. The language of the book is clear and simple; though it could have easily been more compact and terse without at once sacrificing clarity. Dr. Datta has however thought it better to err on the right side. The work is well documented. "*sākṣi-bhāṣyaṁ*" is obviously a misprint for sākṣi-bhāsyam,' though the mistake is repeated four times (on pages 58, 77n. 129 and 179.)

4. TYPES OF INDIAN REALISM*

A. General Considerations

I

Realism is a characteristic philosophical stand-point. It is neither science nor even specially favourable to, or supported by, science. As philosophy, it is a theory of the totality of things and seeks the ground, not of this or that but, of all phenomena in something that is transcendent. As such, the propositions of realism are, by their very nature, unverifiable. And any proposition that is unverifiable in principle is not science, e.g., the proposition that the object is but an idea or that it is constituted of atoms or that it is an evolute of primordial matter (*prakṛti*) etc. It is evident that science can find no use in its procedure for these and similar concepts, as the concepts of the object, subject, relation etc. To say "this is an object" is not to convey any information which can be made use of either in science or in practical life. It is impossible to say anything about the *world as a whole* which would not be an unverifiable theory. Bereft of any scientific value, realism, and for the matter of fact all philosophy, can have but a spiritual value. And by this standard alone can the claim of any philosophy be adjudged. To adduce that scientific investigations support realistic views would be, on our view, not to know what is philosophy about.

Our enquiry is mainly epistemological. We are interested in the logical development of each system, in the way by which they arrive at their conclusions. Our task would be to grasp the principles and the main concepts that are basic to each system and to show how other tenets have consistently developed out of them. Such a study will have value in showing up the distinctive feature of each philosophical attitude; it will also be possible then to fix the relative position of each in a scheme.

The types of realism considered here are mainly four : the Nyāya (including the Vaiśeṣika), the Mīmāṁsā Schools, Buddhistic realism (as exemplified in the Vaibhāṣika and Sautrān-

*Reprinted from *The Philosophical Quarterly*, October 1935, July 1936.

tika schools) and the Jaina theory of *anekāntavāda*. Each of these has distinctive features of its own, and it is even interesting to see how opposed they could be in their fundamental notions. These realisms are schools of thought rather than speculations of individuals. Each system has been cultivated for centuries, and some of them are still in vogue. It is difficult to point out to individuals as the originators of particular doctrines in every case, though certain differences in tenets have continued to exist within each system itself. We are not interested at present in any historical development of each system, nor even in its detailed structure. Again, though it should be easy to adduce textual support for statements made here, documentation is avoided; it might hinder our seeing the general standpoint and its implications.

Though realistic, the Sāṅkhya is left out of consideration. It is not quite a type of realism, for it takes phenomena as in some way due to the entanglement of the subject (*puruṣa*) with the object (*prakṛti*), though the latter is free in a material sense. This can hardly be subscribed to by any realism. It is nevertheless true that the Sāṅkhya is neither consistent nor even thorough in carrying out this doctrine, and the absolutism of the Vedānta arises as a direct criticism of the insecure Sāṅkhya position.

A word has also to be said about the non-inclusion of many of the non-Advaitic schools of Vedānta. Most of them are synthetic systems on a religious basis, and some, e.g. the Mādhva System, are frankly realistic and are but variations of the Nyāya. They do not exhibit differences of type, and so are left out of account here.

II

All realistic systems exhibit certain common characteristics which cannot fail to strike us. They are, one and all, pluralistic; and this is so not by any accident. It is not meant that they are necessarily dualistic, as they have to make a distinction between thought and reality, but that even their objective ultimates are plural, many. This pluralistic tendency is nowhere more thorough-going or consistent than in the *anekāntavāda* of the Jainas—a radical and alternate type of realism. How precisely this pluralism follows in each system from its ultimate position and its implications will be elucidated later.

The second common feature of these systems is that they are dogmatic. It is not that they use no arguments or adduce no proofs for their contentions, but only that they are not critical, not self-conscious enough. They do not necessitate the rising to a level of consciousness higher than that of common-sense or discursive thinking. This they fail to attain because they are not sufficiently free from some fundamental presuppositions under which each of them suffers. They cannot simply look upon the world, for a moment even, as false, as suspect at least; and criticism is impossible without this suspension of belief. All this is in contrast to the idealistic schools which are critical and absolutist and necessitate the rising to a higher level of self-consciousness. It follows from the non-requirement of a higher consciousness that the ordinary sources of knowledge, perception and inference, are all that are needed to reach their ultimate conclusions in the realistic systems. The Vaiśeṣikas and the Bauddhas do not admit any other. It is true that the Nyāya speaks of four kinds of *pramāṇa*, but that is more by way of enumerating the sources of knowledge commonly used than as an actual use of these sources in arriving at its tenets. No tenet of the Nyāya is reached by testimony, *śruti*. The realistic schools of Mīmāṁsā do require, for many of their doctrines, testimony and actually propound the theory that testimony gives us knowledge not attainable by the other sources. But this too, as we will show, does not necessitate the rising to a higher level of consciousness. The Vedānta may be said to interpret phenomena in the light of *śruti*, while the Mīmāṁsā interprets *śruti* in terms of phenomena; for all its canons of interpretation are mostly derived from common-sense and logic. It does not necessitate any recourse to a non-empirical consciousness as in the Vedānta. Realism does not make any distinction between phenomena and noumena—*vyavahāra* and *paramārtha*; it is not compelled by its logic to do so. Realism is necessarily empirical.

The third general observation that can be made is that the ethical doctrine of salvation—Mukti—sits loose in the realistic systems. If the world of phenomena which is coincident with misery[1] were due to some complication of the subject with the

1. It is well-known that the Buddhists take everything to be essentially pain—sarvaṁ duḥkham. It is interesting to see Udyotakara, from the side

object, i.e. due to illusion, we can understand logically its cessation. But the entire endeavour of the realistic systems is directed in proving that the self has no hand in the phenomenal game. We might very well know the self as we know any other object, but it will not help to free the self. It is not involved at all in phenomena and does not constitute them. It is free and isolated as any object is from other objects. And this very knowledge that the self is not involved or does not constitute phenomena is itself bereft of any spiritual value; a scientific one it could not have at all. It fails in the very purpose of philosophy. The salvation-doctrine is put in merely to be in consonance with the general outlook of the Indian mind; the logic of the systems does not lead to it. All this comes to mean that realism does not conceive the self as spirit, as a function forming matter, but as a species of matter or object. In the last resort, it is even sought to be denied as in Buddhism. The implication of this position is that we can deal with the object as a whole without at once explicitly relating it to any privileged entity as the subject—the main plank of all realism.

III

It may be interesting to consider each system as conceiving reality on the pattern of a particular type of judgment. A certain amount of artificiality is inseparable from any architectonic scheme, but it might be found helpful notwithstanding.

The Nyāya conceives reality as a perceptual judgment of the affirmative type. The perceptual judgment has a distinct accomplished aspect about it lacking in other judgments, which involve a process or movement. In the percept there is nothing in the making; everything is presented as already spread out to be seen at a glance, as it were. With the Nyāya, terms no less than relations are objects presented; the self and its functions, knowledge etc., are equally objects, presentable in a literal sense. Negation, with the Nyāya is not the consciousness of a no-fact, but the perception of a negative fact, non-existence being conceived as quite perceptual on a par with existence. Even parti-

of Nyāya, giving expression to the same idea : "ekaviṁśati-prabheda-bhinnaṁ punar duḥkhaṁ, śarīraṁ, ṣaḍindriyāṇi, ṣaḍviṣayāḥ, ṣaḍbuddhayaḥ, sukhaṁ, duḥkhaṁ ceti" (N. S. I.i.1.)—practically the entire phenomena.

cularity, which we should take as traceable, in the last resort, to the relationship of the percept with the ego, the percipient, is conceived here as a unique character ever present with the object (*viśeṣa*). Subjective functions are petrified into objective entities, for that is a sure way to ensure the independence of objectivity.

Underlying all this is the supposition that everything that is speakable is knowable, objectively real and independent; these three, *abhidheya*, *jñeya* and *prameya*, are all-embracive and coincident—Kevalānvayi. Can we not, however, speak of something which we may not be said to know, the self for instance or even the square-circle? But it is taken for granted that because we speak of the no-fact, e.g. the 'rope-snake,' in the same way as we speak of the fact, both are objects and that in the same way. What is assumed unconsciously but nevertheless invariably is that there is a perfect parallelism between thought and language, psychic state and its verbal expression, and that for every verbal expression there is an actual thought corresponding to it. It is not realised that there can be verbal expression for which there is, or can be, no thought, e.g. the square-circle. Again, similarity of expression is no evidence of the similarity of the mode of apprehension. We speak no doubt of the absence of a thing and about knowledge itself, but the apprehension in these cases is different from perceiving the table. It will be found that the Nyāya crystallises language into tenets and very often the appeal is to the particular mode of speech, as in the case of *samavāya* ("*iha-pratyaya-hetuḥ*"), the universal and for the distinction of substance and quality. Empirically minded, there is no attempt in the Nyāya to critically appreciate the relationship between thought and its verbal expression. A detailed exposition of this position shall be taken up later in dealing with each system.

To the Mīmāṁsā, only the imperative (*vidhi*, *codanā*) is significant. A statement of the mere existence of fact is valueless; we cannot proceed with it. Fact acquires significance only as it lends itself to be utilised in the carrying out of an injunction (*bhūtaṁ bhāvyāya upadiśyate*). Injunction (the imperative) is the verbal activity which induces the practical activity of another towards an objective and is of the general form—"Do this to attain that." The activity of the imperative is verbal; it is a peculiar power of the word. Its objective is the activity of the person commanded, and the means by which it evokes a response in the injuncted is the knowledge of the imperative on the part of the commanded. The activity of the commanded has three aspects: it is directed towards the attainment of an end—*svarga* etc.; the means are the performance of certain specifically enjoined acts, sacrifice etc.; and as the performance is a process, it would naturally demand a manner of bringing it about in a particular sequence (*iti-kartavyatā*). Such is the nature of the imperative—*bhāvanā*, and all phenomena are significant as they play their respective roles in this scheme of activity, in the performance of *dharma*.

Mīmāṁsā has its rise in religious consciousness and is a realism rooted in religion—*dharma*. Religious consciousness is distinguished from other purposive endeavours inasmuch as its end is not perceptible, it is unseen—*adṛṣṭa*. The observance of the rules of hygiene or of the laws of state are purposive no doubt but their results are directly perceptible, and the relation between the act and the result can be easily demonstrated. Bathing in the Ganges may be good for health; but one may not be actuated by this motive; one may consider the bath as holy, as having some peculiar and unassignable significance. In this case, the result and the connection between the result and the act are undemonstrable and unseen. The act here is symbolic of the end. A symbolic act is very properly termed rite or ceremony. Take away the symbolic or ceremonial character of religion, we would have efficiently eliminated religion.

Now what is the source of this religious consciousness ? By this we ask for the evidence which tells us that certain symbolic acts performed in a certain way lead to results not perceptible. We can easily see that perception and inference cannot yield such knowledge as they are tied to the percept. Only revealed testimony can give us the imperative which alone, as we have seen, is significant. By its own logic Mīmāṁsā is led on, as will be shown later, to the self-validity of all knowledge, the eternity and impersonality of verbal symbolism, the eternity of sound and meaning and the peculiar conception of creation etc.

The Buddhist of the realistic school conceives reality on the pattern of the hypothetical judgment, sequentially. The import of this is the denial of the existence of any unconditioned static being. This is precisely the main tenet of Buddhism, embodied in the formula: "If this, then this" (*asmin sati idaṁ bhavati*), and its application to all phenomena in the doctrine of dependent origination—*pratītya-samutpāda*. This predilection for the hypothetical, for considering things sequentially, is due to the Buddhists' approaching metaphysics from the standpoint of moral consciousness. Moral consciousness is the consciousness actuated by ends; it is the consciousness of a rational sequence between the act and the end. It militatesa gainst two things: an act not issuing in a sequence but just being a static inefficient being and an end emergent at random without any antecedent; the first would mean the uselessness of any act, and the second is the very negation of any moral endeavour. These two antitheses of moral consciousness are a free rendering of what the Buddha characterised as eternalism and nihilism—*śāśvatavāda* and *ucchedavāda*.

The justification of the Buddhistic realism is the fact of causation. Being—an immutable self-identical entity—cannot figure as the antecedent or the consequent in the hypothetical judgment; it is outside the causal circle, and so not real. Only the impermanent (kṣaṇika), the unique (*svalakṣaṇa*) is the cause. It will be seen that these characteristic Buddhistic doctrines lead on to others—to the denial of substance, self, and the substitution of it by a group or series of groups (*skandhas*), the rejection of the universal except as a mere idea (*kalpanā*) and the acceptance of only two sources of knowledge, one for the unique and the other for the series—*santāna*. Phenomenal world is the flow of the diverse elements (the Dharmas) in an impure sequence (*sāsrava*) and *nirvāṇa* is the cessation of their sequence, the isolation of the *dharmas*.

The denial of substance, the ego, and the doctrine of universal momentariness etc. have been very severely criticised by the orthodox schools. But one finds that the criticism is from an altogether different point of view, and so does not go to the root of the matter—the fact of causation itself. The internal criticism is from the absolutist schools of Buddhism, especially from the Mādhyamika. In the very first chapter of the *Mādhyamika Kārikā*, the realist notion of causation is refuted. The cause cannot be either being or non-being or even a combination or negation of both; it is the purely indeterminate-*śūnya*.

The Jaina conceives reality on the model of the disjunctive judgment. To him other systems appear one-sided, blind to other aspects, and this exclusiveness is what is sought to be avoided by the *anekāntavāda*—the alternate pluralism of a unique sort. The disjuncts or alternatives are anekānta : they are indifferently exclusive and not exclusive; they do not preclude their combining to form a new alternative, which does not, however, supersede them but is merely another alternative. For instance, reality is either sat or asat or both either alternatively or at once; the last alternative admits of being conceived with the three previous ones, making thereby a sevenfold disjunction. The Jaina type of realism may be considered as the radical and most consistent carrying out of the realistic thesis and constitutes perhaps its *reductio ad absurdum* as well.

IV

In contrast to these types of realism, the absolutist systems—Vedānta, Mādhyamika and Vijñānavāda—conceive reality as approached only through negation or the cancellation of the world-illusion. The negative judgment is, strictly speaking, not *a* judgment at all but the *negation* of judgment. Like cancellation, negation is a criticism of our unconscious and unreflective position, and thus stands on a higher level of reflective consciousness. The several absolutisms are so many different interpretations and formulations of negation.

The Vedānta, committed as it is to the supremacy and absolutism of Being, interprets illusion as the transference of the being of one to another, to non-being, and cancellation as the annulment of this false relation of non-being to being. We become aware of the true nature of being as we cancel the illusion. The Mādhyamika takes illusion as the emergence of the unreal and its appearance at once as the real, the real in his system being the indeterminate—*śūnya*. The 'rope-snake' is by its very nature unreal and not so because something else is real; it is entirely unrelated to the real. With the Vijñānavādin, negation applies only to the "this" aspect or externality of the appearance; its essential unity and identity with consciousness is reinstated through cancellation.

It might be seen that these are three alternative modes of interpreting negation; and each is incommensurable with the others. One thing they all have in common: they deny multiplicity; phenomena are illusion, and reality is apprehended through negation, cancellation.[1]

B. Nyāya-Vaiśeṣika

The Nyāya-Vaiśeṣika is easily the most intelligible of all the types of Indian Realism. It is nearer to common-sense than any other system. There is a surprising comprehensiveness and neatness about its tenets without loss of rigour. This is due in great measure to the close modelling of the categories on every-day speech. Nyāya crystallises linguistic forms into doctrines. Hence its great hold upon our empirical mind. We are all Naiyāyikas first and continue to be so unless by a special effort we free ourselves from the empirical habits of our mind.

I

Idealism may be said to idealise or subjectify the object. In absolutism the object is annulled and reduced to the spirit. Realism directly traverses this position by objectifying the subject. This may take either of these two forms : consciousness of an object is but a particular cross-section or selection of the objective field or that it is another object. The former view is that of Holt and other thorough-going realists. The latter is that of the Nyāya. We may become aware of the knowledge of an object by the same or by a different mode of knowing, e.g. the inner sense. In both the cases, knowledge is an object—*viṣaya*—*par excellence*. And this because we speak of the subject as we speak of the object. It is not, however, realised that speech symbolises the object and the subject in quite different ways. The one is a symbol for a presented content, and the other is a symbol for what is not and cannot be so presented. The subject or spirit is symbolised as what cannot be symbolised.

1. For instance, the negative judgment, "This is not silver," is differently interpreted, owing to emphasis on one aspect or the other. On the Vedāntic view, the this (rope) is not *silver*; its supposed silver character is negated. The Vijñānavādin negates the "thisness" alone of the silver; *this* is not silver; its essential unity and identity with consciousness is made evident thereby. To the Mādhyamika both the "this" and the "silver" are equally false, for the one appeared inseparable from the other, and negation applies equally to both : *this* is not *silver*.

The advantage of reducing the subject or knowledge to a species of the object is obvious. The independence of the object is secured. One object is not just another object; each has an individuality of its own. The flower-vase may be on the table; but it is existentially different from and independent of the table and *vice versa*. As objects, they are equals and enter into relationship on a reciprocal basis. Each has a specific and inalienable nature of its own. It is not, as with idealism, that the nature of an entity is what it is in virtue of its relation to consciousness or coherence with other entities. This conception of each object as what is distinct and independent of other objects is necessary, if the object is to be independent of the mind. Otherwise, the very purpose of conceiving mind as an object would be valueless. For as mind is an object, any other object, it might be urged, is what it is in relation to this object—the mind. The independence of the object of all subjective influence logically implies the individuality and distinctness of each object. Realism in fact invests every object with a self-hood; each object is significant by itself. This is in contrast to the idealistic tendency to subjectify the object and therefore necessarily to conceive significance as one with coherence or relatedness with other contents.

The implications of the realistic view are interesting.

(1) All relation, including the knowledge-relation, is externally, accidentally, related to the terms. It does not make or unmake the terms. Nor, conversely, do the terms make the relation.

(2) Relation is a relation of distincts. Distinction is the ground of their relation, not their unity. Terms must be something in themselves, definite and distinct from all others, before they could enter into relation. Their nature is complete without the relation, which therefore can only be an accident to them.

(3) This leads to atomism on the one hand; for the entities are discrete, and the whole which they form can only be a mechanistic juxtaposition of parts lacking the characteristics of a genuine whole. On the other, it necessitates an infinite regress, as the relation is virtually a *tertium quid*, itself requiring to be related to its terms and so on. In principle there can be no distinction between term and relation on the realistic thesis. They do not perform different functions; both are presented as static and already spread out.

(4) On any realistic view—and all realism knows only one category, the object—it is difficult to give any meaning to the negated fact, the illusory. There are several attempts on the part of realism to explain illusion in purely objective terms. But we cannot explain illusion without bringing in belief and subjectivity. Any formulation of this would mean a criticism of realism itself. This would be taken up after an exposition of all the types of realism.

II

The fundamental presupposition of the Nyāya-Vaiśeṣika is that all is definable, knowable as object. This underlies the conception of *padārtha*, literally meaning of words. Both the Nyāya and the Vaiśeṣika Sūtras begin with a complete enumeration of the classes of the speakable; ostensibly nothing is left over. But there is little attempt to justify such a formulation. Fact-hood and speakability coincide in these systems. This is by no means a passing doctrine. For many of its chief tenets, e.g. *sāmānya*, *samavāya*, and the difference between substance and its attributes, Nyāya and Vaiśeṣika adduce as proof only modes of speech. In the later phase of the Nyāya, this doctrine of the coincidence of fact and speech assumes the form of a valid type of inference—the *kevalānvayi*. All is knowable, because speakable Several definitions of *vyāpti*, as in the *Tattvacintāmaṇi*, are sacrificed, because they do not cover the *kevalānvayi*, the all-embracive inference.

Is an all-embracive universal inference possible? It is conventionally stated that we infer knowability from speakability, and *vice versa*. The nature of this so-called inference is gravely open to doubt. In inference there is a passage from one premise to another; at least a distinction is involved between the ground and the consequence, the *hetu* and the *sādhya*. No distinction is conceivable if both these are coincident as the speakable and the knowable. There is no relation and certainly no process. Relation is not possible without distinction, and distinction implies the existence of a non-implicatory term, one that has an existence outside the relation. There is no ground of distinction between two terms which are invariably and necessarily co-existent mutually; the absence of neither can be conceived. We cannot even speak of them as two. All distinction is to be conceived primarily as the difference between being and non-being. Relation is denied here as there can be no conceivable distinction between the speakable and the knowable. There is not a speakable which is not a knowable or *vice versa*. But it may be said in objection against the above view that difference may be a positive relation between two positive terms, as the difference between the blue and the red. Difference, relation, on this view then is *not conceived* or felt but *perceived* as presented along with the things. The differents and their difference are literally perceived. It is a matter for empirical observation and formulation to take note and specify the differences. This view also implies that no thought-function is needed to make the distinctions. They are already there embedded in the things. The object stands self-analysed to the last distinction as it were. We are merely to take note of it passively.

Even granting all this, the universality of the inference can still be questioned. How do we perceive the universal relation (the coincidence) of the speakable and the knowable? There is no one perception which can possibly embrace all speakable and knowable; nor even can an ensemble of particular perceptions perform the miracle. *Sāmānyalakṣaṇa* perception also can be of no appreciable avail here. One might even concede that the speakability and knowability of all objects can thus be perceived as related.[1] What of the speaking and knowing self? In any act of perception, the percipient cannot himself be cognised. Nyāya would have too easy an answer. The percipient (the knower) can subsequently be cognised and thus known, as in introspection (*anuvyavasāya*). But such a step assumes the identity of the knower and the known—an identity which, from the nature of the case, cannot be proved. What is knowledge in the first stage comes to be known as an object in the later stage. All this comes to mean that Nyāya reduces the subject to the object, and without such a tacit assumption its position cannot be substantiated. The *kevalānvayi* inference is thus, on analysis,

1. This itself is a very big concession. For there is no generic character present in all objects by which anything can be known as object. Only when we contrast the object or distinguish it from something that is not object (i.e. the subject), do we at all get the notion of the object in general. A purely objective attitude can give us no concept of objectivity.

shown to be identical with the convenient but untenable reduction of the subject to the object, though ostensibly it is put forward as proving it.[1]

III

It is interesting to trace the far-reaching implications of the conception that all is knowable as object. All the chief tenets of the Nyāya seem to follow from this.

1. Knowledge and the self are knowable like other objects; the knowledge of an object is but another object. Though existentially knowledge and its object are two different entities, they do not differ in kind. The knowability of knowledge is reflected in the doctrine of introspection—anuvyavasāya. Each knowledge is cognised by a subsequent knowledge. There is no self-conscious and self-valid cognition—*parataḥ prakāśa* and *parataḥ prāmāṇya.*

This view leads to certain insuperable difficulties. If the cognition of an object were another fact and is thus required to be evidenced by a subsequent cognition, why should not the latter be again cognised and so on *ad infinitum.* And there can be no last member to the series, except arbitrarily. For *ex hypothesi*, a new fact (object) is precipitated at each stage, and all the necessary and sufficient conditions for introspection are present at each successive stage.

That such a series of cognitions, one chasing the other in quick succession, lacks experiential basis must lead us to reject the conception of the knowability of knowledge. On the Nyāya view, the occurrence of knowledge is not at once its evidence; it is conceived as evidenced, as any other object is, by a subsequent cognition. Knowledge too then is as unconscious and dead as any object. The doctrine of *parataḥ prāmāṇya* easily follows from this. Actually, however, there is no conscious gap between the occurrence of knowledge and its apprehension as such. To have knowledge is at once to know it as knowledge. Knowledge is not known by a separate act of cognition.

1. Vedānta which denies knowledge (Brahman) to be knowable is led logically to reject the *kevalānvayi* as a valid type of inference. Cf. *Vedānta Paribhāṣā*, p. 177 :

"tacca anumānam anvayirūpam eva, na tu kevalānvayi. sarvasyāpi dharmasyāsmanmate brahma-niṣṭhātyantābhāva-pratiyogitvena, atyantābhāvāpratiyogisādhyakatvarūpa-kevalānvayitvasyāsiddheḥ."

2. The same confusion is exhibited with regard to the other self-functions, e.g. desire, feeling and will. They are taken to be known as objects of the inner sense, *mānasa-pratyakṣa*. But to will, to feel or to desire is at once to be conscious of the willing, feeling and desiring. It is not that an appreciable time lapses between the occurrence of these phenomena and our awareness of them. They do not begin by existing unknown and come to be known subsequently. In that case the knowledge of the interval would itself be inexplicable, as one of the termini would always be unknown. An object may, for aught, exist unknown, i.e. independent of our consciousness and later be known. The knowing does not make the object. The existence or occurrence of the object is not its being known. Such a distinction is available in the case of the object, as existence and knowledge are not simultaneous. Again, the truth-claim of an object implies its independence of the subjective act of knowing. The severance of existence and awareness is not conceivable in the case of willing, feeling and knowing itself. To have a feeling is at once to be aware of it as feeling; it has no existence apart from its awareness. It is self-evident. And thus there is no question of its being made aware of by a separate act of cognition.[1] There is no possibility of any regress either. The difficulties on the Nyāya view arise because the subjective is not recognised as different from objectivity or fact-hood, because the subjective is dogmatically assumed as a species of the objective.

3. The knowability of knowledge leads to another curious result. In the first stage when we know an external object, knowledge is obviously conceived as a relation, as connecting the self with the object. Knowledge functions as a relation between the subject and the object. Subsequently, in *anuvyavasāya* knowledge is known as object. This is tantamount to holding that relation is known precisely in the same manner as the terms it relates. In fact, Nyāya is not conscious of any problem in the apprehension of relation. It is readily taken as

1. Cf. The doctrine of sākṣi-bhāsya. The several functions of the mind (*vṛttis*) are immediately apprehended by the pure subject (*sākṣī*) without the intervention of any other *vṛtti*. In all such cases, consciousness and exsitence coincide i.e. there is no *ajñāta-sattā* (unknown existence). See *Vedānta Paribhāṣā* pp. 69ff.

known, as presentable together with the terms it relates. Relation is not conceived as a function, as an activity or category which implies and in some measure conditions the terms. It is something static and inert; itself another content beside the two contents, it is a veritable *tertium quid.*[1]

4. As relation is presented as an object on a par with the terms, it does not constitute the terms nor is constituted by them. Two objects which are simultaneously together cannot constitute each other; neither involves the other, though they happen to be together. *Samavāya* or inherence has to be understood as a mechanical and external combination of determinate and discrete entities.

It would be wrong to conceive, as it is done by some, *samavāya* as internal relation. A relation is internal when it satisfies these two conditions: (1) The terms comprising the relation are what they are within the relation; they are non-significant except as so related; (ii) and the relation itself cannot subsist between any other terms. On the Nyāya theory however the nature of the terms is not affected by the relation; they preserve their identity and significance within and without the relation and *vice versa.* Relation is a combination of two entities which already have a distinct nature of their own.

In other systems, viz. the Sāṅkhya and the Vedānta, the relation between substance and its quality is viewed as one of identity,[2] for the quality is but the determination of the indeterminate substance. It is the indeterminate substantive that presents itself as the determinate adjective. There is real conditioning or categorisation here. Such however is not possible on the Nyāya theory. Substance (*dravya*) and quality (*guṇa*), in Nyāya, are distinct and discrete entities, they belong to distinct classes and are not necessarily understood through each other. The quality is *in* (not of) the substance, the *in* being a permanent

1. The usual criticism (urged by Śaṅkara and others, Br. Sūtr. II. ii.13) that *samavāya* would require another relation to relate it to the terms and so on *ad infinitum* is quite in point. For relation, in Nyāya, is conceived not as *relating*, but as a third fact inserted in between the two terms. A purely objective view of relation cannot but lead to such anomalies.

2. In the Sāṅkhya the identity is real, while in the Vedānta it is illusory.

fixture or glue between the two. It is true that the quality is conceived as produced in the substance. But the relation of cause and effect is also of the same nature, external. It is a relation of two distincts juxtaposed.

5. The effect is emergent *in* the cause (*yasmin samavetaṁ kāryam utpadyate*); it is an other to it. There is no genuine creation : the cause does *not* produce the effect. The material cause, in Nyāya, is not therefore self-creative as in the Vedānta and Sāṅkhya[1]; it does not put itself forth as the effect. The emergence of the effect is not due to any self-activity of the material cause. The efficient cause, the motive force is necessarily an external agent. Logically therefore the agent (the *nimitta kāraṇa*) must fall outside the material cause; one thing cannot be both at once. Again, the material cause is not only inactive but cannot be a single unitary entity. If that were so, why should it not be self-creative; for would it not then be self-sufficient, containing all the necessary ground of the effect within itself? It is not self-active, creative, just because by itself it does not constitute the sufficient and all-inclusive condition of the effect. For, *all the necessary ground* (*sāmagri*) being together, if the effect did not emerge, it will never emerge. Paucity of material is the lack of self-sufficiency. Efficient activity (*nimitta*) merely collects together or brings into operation the *several* material factors. Thus the material out of which anything is produced cannot be one single entity, but always a plurality. Causation is the putting together (*asamavāyi kāraṇa*) of bits of matter (*samavāyi kāraṇa*) by a transeunt agency (*nimitta*) which cannot but be external to the materials. Nothing is a self-sufficient cause; the material units of any effect are also plural. Causation is thus the mechanical combination of discrete bits of matter: it is *ārambha*, not *pariṇāma*.[2]

1. The effect is thus the self-manifestation (*abhivyakti*) of the causes, and the relation between the two is one of identity (*satkārya-vāda*). In Vedānta, this identity is illusory, and this is the difference from the Sāṅkhya theory.

2. The argument in this section may be thus summarised. Relation in Nyāya is the relation of two distincts which are different from each other. The effect is a new entity that emerges *in* the cause. The latter does not create or transform itself into the effect. The efficient or active cause must thus lie outside the material cause and *vice versa* (the *samavāyi kāraṇa* cannot at once be the nimitta too and *vice versa*). This exclusion of the *samavāyi* and *nimitta*

For the Buddhist change is the emergence of the unique. Change is without any residue, total. Nothing is permanent or immutable. The relation between the cause and the effect is pure difference without any ground of unity or identity. The Sāṅkhya believes in real becoming, in one thing actually transforming itself into another. Cause and effect are identical and it is even urged that the effect is nothing new; it is already contained in the cause. In the Vedānta there is no real becoming, but only a semblance, an illusion, of it. The Naiyāyika keeps very close to common-sense. He accepts change, the coming into being of some non-being (the whole or the effect), but he also accepts the immutability of being (the ultimate parts or atoms). The combinations are impermanent, but not their ultimate constituents. The atoms are self-existent and immutable entities, veritable selfs as it were. They carry the burden of the Universe in the Nyāya system.

The atomic theory has come for a thorough criticism at the hands of other systems, especially the Vedānta (Br. Sūt. II. ii, 11-17). Most of the arguments are too well-known to need elaboration, e.g., the impossibility of the contact of indivisible (partless) atoms, their imperviousness to any external influence etc. We are, however, interested in showing that the adduced proof for the atom is a *petitio principii*. The atom cannot even be inferred legitimately.

As all phenomena are necessarily to be derived by the putting together of bits of matter, we are forced to seek the ultimate elements out of which things are combined. Shall we stop with the *tryaṇuka*—the body of the least perceptible size? Prudence would suggest this course. But there is a very compelling reason why we cannot stop with the tryaṇuka. For then the perceptible size would be unconditioned—underived and ultimate. And if one perceptible size be considered ultimate, why not others too? This would mean an end to all explanation, to *ārambhavāda* itself. We are thus necessitated by the demand to explain, by reason itself, to seek the ground of the perceptible in something that is non-perceptible, in the transcendent. Nyāya extends the

would further imply that the self-sufficient cannot be the cause, for why should it then look to the nimitta, containing all within itself? Because the material and efficient causes are separate, the cause is neither self-creative nor unitary.

familiar argument that an object of any perceptible magnitude is composed of parts. The least perceptible size is also composed of parts, which are medium-sized (*madhyama parimāṇa*). And the latter are constituted of parts which are not further divisible nor perceivable; for otherwise there would be a *regressus ad infinitum.*

Is the argument, the inference from the perceptible to the non-perceptible, valid? At first sight it appears to be a legitimate extension of the argument from the causal relation of two objects of perceptible size. But really it is not sound. For why should not the argument be extended *ad infinitum*, without our alighting upon the atoms? How will you apply the clincher at some stage and say, we stop here, as the parts of this whole are further not divisible? It is urged that otherwise the biggest thing and the smallest scruple will be of the same size (*meru-sarṣapayoḥ sāmyaprasaṅgaḥ*); difference in magnitude will be obliterated; for everything, the greatest and the least thing included, will have an infinite number of parts. But this objection would appeal to one who has already accepted that things of perceptible size are made up of smaller parts put together. But this is the very thesis—*ārambhavāda*—at issue, and hence cannot be availed of in the very progression of its proof. "Again there is a breach of the law of continuity in assuming infinite hardness and absolute indivisibility to emerge suddenly when a certain stage is reached in division."

If the atom-hypothesis were the only way of explaining phenomena, the argument might be valid. This is far from being so. From the nature of the case however there can be several other alternatives claiming at least equal validity. Instead of supposing bodies (wholes) as generated out of discrete parts we may conceive them as limitations of one primordial and ubiquitous matter (*prakṛti*), or even as false superimpositions upon universal being. These are genuine alternatives with greater plausibility. It may well be that it is our initial prepossession that inclines us to favour one theory as against others. Still, the Naiyāyika has no right to put his argument in so assertoric a form. It should read thus : *If* it were accepted that wholes are conditioned by discrete parts, then it is a fact that atoms constitute the ultimate parts. Even then, there are genuine difficulties about their combination and interaction etc. The atom cannot strictly be said proved, known by either perception or inference or even by testimony. In fact, for the Nyāya-Vaiśeṣika, the atom is unproved, but thought to be self-evident.

It was stated that Nyāya invests the object with self-hood, egoity. Nothing shows this up more clearly than the queer doctrine of unique particularity—*viśeṣa.* The problem of particularity is forced upon us in this way. The objects of experience are not mere universals or even their particular combinations, as these would still be universal. In that case we could never perceive, or remember any object as *this* or *that.* The *this* and *that* are incommunicable and unique characteristics that endow the objects of experience with individuality and fact-hood. In a sense, the problem of all philosophy may be said to be the showing how universals get concretised, become particular and acquire a local habitation. The Kantian functions may be understood as representing the several stages of "concrescence" through the categories of the understanding and sensibility.

Nyāya tries to solve the problem of the particular by positing the category of *viśeṣa.* The argument is somewhat thus. The particularity of phenomenal objects, e.g., two tables which are bound to be products, is due to the particular and individual nature of their constituent parts. *This* table is different from *that* one, because the parts that go to make the one are different from those of the other. And this can be applied to the parts and the parts of those parts and so on *ad infinitum,* till the atom. What can distinguish one atom from another atom of the same class? Not the possession of certain characters, qualities etc., for these would belong equally to all the atoms of one class. What is the ground of distinction between one liberated soul and another, between all eternal substances in general? Nyāya finds the ground of particularity in a simple eternal character, *viśeṣa,* residing in the atom and other eternal substances. But how is one particularity—*viśeṣa*—differentiated from other particularities? Nyāya boldly declares that each particularity is unique and self-distinguished (*svato vyāvṛttaḥ*). There are as many, qualitatively and numerically different, *viśeṣas* as there are eternal substances. The boldness and enormity of this conception is astounding. Is not this tantamount to saying that each atom has a self-identical and self-distinguishing egoity of its own, by virtue of which it keeps its individuality, identity and uniqueness amidst others ? Only, the egoity is *objective* and lacks experiential basis.

Particularity cannot be conceived as a character or quality which always belongs to an object in itself, even when it is out of all relation with other entities. A particular is invariably one amidst a multiplicity. The *this* or *that* is what is picked up and distinguished from among its fellows. Only in a complex situation can a particular be encountered. As a matter of fact the entire range of entities appear as its adjectives; the *this* is related to all entities, of course in varying degrees of relevance and importance. A particular can be defined as that in whose composition all other entities enter with varying degrees of relationship and significance. Taken by itself, no entity is particular. In Whitehead's words, there is the "ingress" of all entities in the constitution of the *this*.

Particularity has thus to be conceived as a sort of relational property which an object acquires when in relation with other objects. It will also be readily seen that this aspect of it does not belong to it by nature, i.e., its relationship with other objects is not fixed forever. For, now one object is particular, now another. What is *this* now and that *to me*, may not be so at other times and to others. In the objective sphere itself, there is no principle of preference or choice why a certain object is made the substantive, the principal and the rest its adjective or background. The choice of a certain object from among others is due to the selective attention of the percipient. Anything that is in immediate contact with the embodied percipient is *this* and *now* to him. And due to the freedom of the percipient, now one object, now another, is *this* or *that.* Nothing is *this* or *that* forever and out of all relation to the percipient and to other objects in the presented field. It follows from the above that the particular cannot be independent of experience. A universal can be so, for it is the essence of the Universal, as an intelligible character, to be free; it does not depend upon its being known by me or anybody. The highest universal is entirely free of all experiencing; it need not be presented at all. Conversely, the ultimate particular is dependent entirely on being experienced, on the perception of the embodied self. If we had no bodies and if there were no space-time functions, i.e., the world of other coordinate entities, no entity would be particular.

It is seen that particularity has to be traced in the last resort to the percipient who is but the embodied ego. Each ego is different, because each is a personality, free and self-active in some measure. No two egos would react to the same situation identically; and it may even be maintained that they do not perceive any situation alike. Particularity is not sought to be explained in the sense of being derived from that which is not already so. It is only traced to its ultimate and legitimate source, the ego. In taking the ego or the personified self as the principle of particularity, we bring it within the reach of immediate experience. No ego is derived from any other ego; each is unique, and this uniqueness is not a matter of postulation but actually felt and lived. Nyāya relegates this self-function to the *viśeṣa*, thus betraying its inveterate tendency to objectify and deaden spirit-functions.

It was pointed out in the introduction that Nyāya conceives reality on the pattern of a perceptual judgment. The foregoing would have shown how, for Nyāya, all things are presented as accomplished, readymade and static. The self and all thought-functions are objectified, materialised.

(APPENDIX)

[A brief outline of the theory of judgment in Nyāya may be indicated here. All the Nyāya categories can be shown to be implied in the structure of knowledge as conceived by this system. (Such an attempt has already been made elsewhere, vide "The theory of Judgment in the Indian Systems" (1), *Phil. Quarterly*, Jan. 1933).]

According to Nyāya a judgment, e.g., "The table is brown" is not expressible with less than three factors, which are different from one another; and they are the subject (the substance), the predicate (the qualities) and the relation of inherence between the two by which the predicate is relevant to the subject. Most of our waking experience can, with little difficulty, be cast into this form. In the example chosen, even if we stop with 'the table' we are still left with a judgment. We are determining the object before us as falling within the class of objects called 'tables.' In the scholastic language of the Nyāya, we have here the particular 'table', sustaining the relation of inherence to the universal 'tablehood' present in it. All the categories of Nyāya-Vaiśeṣika have to be derived from one of these three. There are things in which others inhere, those that are so dependent and the fact of inherence itself. Hence objectivity—the knowable—must be docketed in one or the other of these three pigeon-holes.[1] Knowledge and *Ātman* are also objects. It is quite in keeping with this conception that everything is knowable that the *kevalānvayi* type of inference is accepted in Nyāya. Vedānta which denies knowledge to be knowable is led logically to reject the *kevalānvayi* as a valid type of inference.

Now as Nyāya holds that all judgments are constituted of these three factors, it has to show that they are not only distinct and different from each other but are also 'given' separately in some cognition. Else, the assertion would be a false abstraction lacking experiential basis. Nyāya, therefore, accepts the *nirvikalpa* form of knowledge—a state previous to all judgmental or relational mode in which the two terms are apprehended in isolation. The argument adduced is very simple. A knowledge of a whole constituted by parts i.e., any relational mode, presupposes a knowledge of the component parts. This very knowledge cannot in turn be relational, as this would lead to an infinite regress. The close similarity of this with the argument adduced for the existence of the atom is too patent to be missed. We can also mention another objective counterpart of *nirvikalpa* knowledge. It is the fact that in the first moment after its production each substance is quality-less in isolation. The *Ātman* in the emancipated state is also of this type. If 'A r B' were the symbol of a relational mode, A and B standing for the terms and 'r' for the relation, in the *nirvikalpaka*, which necessarily precedes all knowledge, A and B are apprehended separately. It must be borne in mind that Nyāya does not consider these differents and their relation as false abstractions. The relational mode can itself become the object of another and later knowledge, and so on. We not only know that the table is brown but also know that we know it to be so. For the rise of this introspective knowledge—*anuvyavasāya* or later determinate knowledge—it is evident that the first determinate or relational

1. *viṣayatā* is threefold : it is either *viśeṣyākhyā*, or *viśeṣaṇatākhyā* or *saṁsargākhyā*

mode of knowledge must have already taken place; for in the second stage it is made the object. It is theoretically possible to continue this objectification of knowledge to any extent, but after the introspective mode—*anuvyavasāya*—there shall be nothing new. All our purposes are served with the three stages only, namely the *nirvikalpa*, the *savikalpa* or *vyavasāya* and the *anuvyavasāya*.

Some very patent implications of such a theory of judgment can be drawn, and these are important for our purpose.

i. The Nyāya countenances the doctrine of external relations. That the same elements, terms, can occur in different combinations without thereby losing their identity or undergoing any change is the essence of the doctrine of external relations. As such, it is opposed to the doctrine of internal relations which contends that the terms comprising a relation are so organically united that they are what they are within this very relation and cannot be had in their identical nature outside this relation. The terms, no less than the relation, cannot be repeated elsewhere. But for Nyāya both the terms as well as the relation can be repeated in different combinations without loss of identity. In the *nirvikalpa* which, as we have seen, precedes all judgment, the two terms constituting the judgment are present in isolation; yet they do not lose their nature. The judgment (*vyavasāya*) itself appears as a constituent in the introspective mode (*anuvyavasāya*). At each stage the combination is different, yet the constituents are the same. As this is true of knowledge—one object, it is true of all other objects. Nyāya, therefore, believes in the existence of wholes constituted by parts, which enjoy an identical existence before and after the combinations. They can also occur and recur in some other combination. The parts and the whole are both real in an unmitigated sense, and they are different. We thus see Nyāya deriving everything from atoms; the whole world is a combination of the ultimate parts. Nyāya advocates what is called technically *ārambhavāda*. The cosmological principle with Nyāya is not evolution, but collocation.

ii. Let us consider the relation of the two terms in the judgment. The subject and the predicate are different. Were they identical, they should be interchangeable, i.e., propositions true of the one must also be true of the other, and propositions not true of the one must also be not true of the other and *vice versa*.

The relation between the terms is not a mere name for the two things; for, as we saw, in the *nirvikalpa* stage the two appear in their isolation, and yet there is no judgment. It is thus a third something, which being there the predicate becomes relevant to the subject. A positive definition of it cannot be given. Relation is an object of thought which never becomes the subject or the predicate of any proposition.

The function of relation is as much to separate as to connect; it is a third something which comes between the relata. If relation were no entity or were reducible to either of the terms, there shall be no judgment, no characterisation of the substantive by the qualities. In that case, the character will not be relevant to the characterised; they will be two independent entities having nothing to do with each other. Relation is also not a fixable content; it is what Johnson very aptly calls the 'characterising tie.' It follows that no difference can be made in it; we cannot have many characterising ties. If in each judgment the relation too were *ipso facto* different, the subject would be distinguished not only by the predicate—the qualities but also by the relation; this is to say that the relation would itself become a quality, and unless some other relation were posited, this quality itself would be irrelevant to the subject. The characterising tie being thus a contentless and independent entity, it is not only one but underivable and eternal. It is present wherever the two—substantive and adjective—are present. This is why *samavāya* is considered one and eternal; it is not waiting to be ushered into existence with the terms, but is uniformly present; it only gets related to particular sets of terms when they come into being. This doctrine of *samavāya* brings out more clearly than any other that the Nyāya ontology is merely the characteristics of the judgment given a metaphysical status.

iii. It was mentioned that no judgment in Nyāya is complete without at least three stages—the *nirvikalpa*, *savikalpa* and *anuvyavasāya* which can be symbolised as 'A, B', 'A r B', and '(A r B)' respectively. It can be seen very readily that the identity of the terms A and B occurring in these situations should be guaranteed if all the three were to refer to the *same* situation. Consistently therefore, Nyāya would have universals not only for the substantive (*dravya*) but for the adjectives (qualities and action) as well. *Both* the terms in the judgment, as they are repeated, shall have to be recognised as the same, and this is impossible without an identical and unchanging entity enduring unaltered inspite of the different collocations. The universal is not needed with regard to the relation—*samavāya*, which, as seen, is one and unaltered. It—the universal—is also not necessary with regard to itself. It is also clear that the connection of the universal (*jāti*) with each of the terms A or B, is more vital and immediate than their relation to each other in a judgment; for it is the presence of the universal which makes them what they are, A or B. And unless they were distinct and recognisable in themselves, they could not enter as elements in a judgment. Though Nyāya takes this relation of the terms in a judgment too as *samavāya*, the difference is brought out when it is realised that the universal is eternal and ever-present and awaits but the emergence of the particular to get connected with it. The adjective—quality or action—however, gets related to the substance only after the second moment of the latter's existence. Moreover, the substance under certain situations, e.g. the *Ātman* in a state of release, can exist without the qualities, while it can never be bereft of the universal.

iv. The terms in a judgment are not mere universals brought together. If so, the repetitions of the terms in the three stages mentioned are not possible. How is the first occurrence of A distinguished from its second one ? Not through the universal, for that would go to prove their identity, and not their difference. Nor even through the possession of characters, for though this might be possible after a judgment has been formulated, after a subject has been characterised, it is unavailing when it is being characterised. This is to say, this help is not available to us in the *nirvikalpa* and *savikalpa* stages of the judgment. Nyāya, therefore, seeks to account for the ultimate particularity of the substantive (*dravya*) by the bold assumption of a category called particularity (*viśeṣa*) which is numerically and inherently different in each ultimate particular substance—*antya-nitya-dravya-vṛttayo viśeṣā anantā eva*; *te ca svato vyāvṛttāḥ*. Particularity cannot be a class-concept; for then it would defeat the very purpose for which it is intended. We may therefore state that the subject of any judgment which is not itself an implicit judgment or a complex is to be distinguished by the possession of a unique *viśeṣa*—particularity. With regard to the predicates (qualities etc.), this difficulty does not arise; for they can be distinguished through their relation with the substantive—*dravya*; only the latter is required to be presented first. The primacy of *dravya* in the system is thus accounted for.

To sum up : Our analysis of the Nyāya theory of judgment has shown that the judgment consists of three irreducible and distinct factors—the substantive, the adjective and the relation; the relation between the terms can be said to be external in the sense that the terms can figure in other situations without thereby losing their identity. This raised a further question : how is the identity of the terms in the various stages known and tenable ? Nyāya accounts for it by the assertion of universals not only for the substance but for the qualities as well. No term, however, is a mere universal; the several repetitions of each in the different stages of a judgment will in that case be indistinguishable. So, a category of particularity to distinguish the ultimate subject is posited by Nyāya in the *viśeṣa*. Each term in a judgment is thus complex : there is the universal inhering in a particular. This relational mode is more primary and vital than the relation of the terms themselves in a judgment. We have, in the course of the analysis elucidated the doctrines of *samavāya*, *sāmānya* and *viśeṣa*, showing how they are based upon the theory of judgment.

v. As a consequence of the assumption that knowledge is knowable, i.e. as object, it follows that the content of knowledge is comparable with its object, like any two other objects. Nyāya, therefore countenances only the Correspondence Theory of Truth, and is committed to the doctrine that no knowledge is self-evident and self-valid. The validity of each judgment depends on its correspondence with the object. But every form of correspondence is faced with a dilemma. If truth were a certain one-one relation between a knowledge-content and the objects, we have two closed, though parallel, spheres which have nothing to do with each other, and we have no means of even asserting that the one corresponds with the other. If the two were identical, the question of relevance of knowledge should not arise. Nyāya finds a nexus in the 'subject' or the *dharmi* which is 'given' once for all. It cannot be doubted or mistaken (*sarvaṁ jñānaṁ dharmiṇyabhrāntaṁ, prakāre tu saṁśayaḥ*); doubt or mistake pertains only to the proper characterising of the subject. This is to say that not all thought is false but only some later elaborations.

At each stage, the Nyāya theory of judgment is faced with a *regressus ad infinitum* that is fatal to the establishment of difference between the character and the characterised and also to the assertion that knowledge itself is an object—the two basic assumptions of Nyāya. It seems to get over the difficulty only by the further assumptions of *sāmānya* and *viśeṣa*. Subject to these limitations the theory is workable and represents perhaps a fairly coherent form of realism.

5.1 NĀGĀRJUNA'S REFUTATION OF MOTION AND REST*

Nāgārjuna's refutation of motion and rest presents several interesting features and raises some big issues. Zeno denied motion; he did not disturb rest. Nāgārjuna performs the seemingly impossible task of denying both at once. Zeno's argument, repeated in all the famous examples, rests on the infinite divisibility of space without taking into consideration a similar circumstance with regard to time. His arguments do not bring out any epistemological or metaphysical standpoint; Nāgārjuna's do. An attempt will be made to elucidate his general standpoint, after a presentation of his dialectic against motion and rest.[1]

1. Motion is denied by showing the untenability of the factors indispensable for its generation—viz. the space traversed, the mover and the commencement of motion. To take each in turn :

What is traversed ? Not that which has been already traversed; nor even that to be done so; there is no third division of space as 'the being traversed'. When a footstep is put forward, it divides the space exactly into two—the one already traversed and the other yet to be done so. It will be pointed out that there is some such space that *is being* traversed; for that is the place where activity is present; and this activity does not pertain to the traversed or that portion yet to come. But as the activity belongs to the moving body and not to the space, this too will not help us to distinguish that space, unless we accepted motion in both—two motions in the space covered and in the moving body. If there were only one motion—namely, that of the moving body—how can the space, though unrelated to motion, be still said to be 'being traversed' ? There is nothing to differentiate it from other spaces. With two motions, two

*Reprinted from *The Philosophical Quarterly*, October, 1933.

1. Section I of this paper is an analysis of Chapters II & VIII of *Mādhyamika Kārikā*, while the other sections are based on the general standpoint exhibited in the whole book, esp. in Chap. I.

moving bodies shall have also to be accepted, unless we hold that motion can exist disembodied, apart from the moving body. We here come to an impasse. There is no space which is being traversed. The divisions in space are relative and unreal; from the standpoint of knowledge no such distinctions are tenable.

Motion is possible, because there is the mover in which it inheres. We must make the distinction between the two. But is the mover intelligible with or without the motion ? Can we say that the mover moves ? He is either motionless in himself apart from the motion, or has a motion other than the motion which inheres in him. In the first case, we have the contradiction of a mover without motion; in the second, there are two motions, for it is a *mover* that *moves,* not a non-mover as in the first case. But this too is unpalatable; disembodied motion cannot be contemplated.

It may be thought that these difficulties are really about the locus of motion, whether it resides in a body which is itself bereft of motion or not, and have nothing to do with motion at all. When and where does motion begin ? Not at the place already traversed, nor even in the space yet to come; and we have seen that there is no such space like 'the being traversed', for this would involve two motions and two bodies. When does motion begin ? Not when a body is at rest; for at that time, before the commencement of the activity, there is no space that is being traversed or that traversed etc. Can there be motion in the space not yet traversed ? This is a veritable contradiction; motion is to commence where it does not exist. Without motion, the divisions of space into the 'traversed' etc., are untenable. It would be seen that on the basis of these distinctions can motion be conceived to arise, and only with its commencement are such distinctions tenable, involving thereby a vicious circle.

2. Motion does exist, it might be asserted, for, its opposite—rest—does do so; that exists whose opposite exists, as darkness and light, or as this side and the other side. Logically, therefore, a denial of motion involves that of rest as well. It is here precisely that Nāgārjuna proves himself a truer dialectician than Zeno.

Here too, as in the case of motion, the indispensable factors are denied. Who rests ? Not the mover, nor the static—the non-mover; and there is no third who can rest. The static does not rest, for it is already stationary; there are no two rests, as these would involve two stationary bodies. It is a flat contradiction to say that the mover rests, when a mover is impossible without motion; when any body rests, it is, *ipso facto*, not a mover. It will be said that rest is possible, as cessation from motion is possible. The mover can stop; stopping is an opposite activity. Not so; for, whence will he stop ? Will it be from the space already traversed, yet to be traversed, or that which is being traversed ? Now this activity brought in to ensure rest is on a par with motion, and will be assailable on that score. There is no motion in all these three spaces for the said reasons; and hence there can be no cessation of it.

Rest is possible, for it can be begun, it might be said. But is it begun when someone is at rest, or not at rest, or when about to rest ?—precisely the very alternatives considered in connection with the commencement of motion.

A general difficulty about motion is that it can be conceived neither as identical with the mover nor different from him—the difficulty of all predication. If identical, the subject and his activity cannot be distinguished; but to assert this identity a distinction is necessary. If activity be different from the subject, the latter can exist without activity and *vice versa*; motion should be possible without the moving body. Nāgārjuna comes to the conclusion that both those things do not exist which can be conceived neither as identical with nor as different from each other. ("*ekībhāvena vā siddhir nānā-bhāvena vā yayoḥ; na vidyate tayoḥ siddhiḥ kathaṁ nu khalu vidyate*", *Mādhyamika Kārikā*, Ch. II, 21.)

3. What is the general principle involved in this dialectic against motion and rest ? It is undertaken from the standpoint of pure immediacy of experience, and is a consistent solipsism of the 'present moment'. Santayana has very admirably developed this method in his *Scepticism and Animal Faith*. Far from being self-contradictory, solipsism of the present moment is the only attitude that demands radical evidence—experience—for any assertion; it is not to be frightened into acquiescence of universally believed notions. Confine yourself at any time rigorously to the immediately given; the distinctions of space into the traversed, yet to be traversed, etc., and of motion as originating, progressing and ceasing cannot arise; for these

issue out of relating, out of positing characters that transcend the immediately given. All such relating and positing involve a vicious circle. Distinctions in space are possible on the commencement of motion, which itself cannot be understood without these very distinctions it engenders. The Mādhyamika Dialectic is a call to purify the given object of thought of all beliefs in the transcendent, of dogmas. It finds that when such a purification is effected, no assertion—affirmation or negation—is possible. Everything is *śūnya*. The Mādhyamika cannot have any thesis of his own—positive or negative.

4. This raises two fundamental issues : Is Criticism of any thesis possible without any counter-thesis; and can all the alternatives under any head be rejected, without thereby violating the Excluded Middle ?

It is commonly held that to criticise a theory, we should have a rival theory or standpoint of our own, or that some tenets should be held in common by the disputants. But the acceptance of a common tenet, a common platform cannot serve to favour any of the rival hypotheses; nor does a special tenet or thesis particular to each party fare any better; for to claim peculiar strength on the basis of a special tenet will cut both ways. How then is any hypothesis to be demolished at all ? It is by pointing out that all the consequences of the hypothesis contradict either the hypothesis, or are mutually contradictory. The holding of a rival hypothesis is not only unnecessary but is clearly irrelevant. Nor is it necessary that the consequences of a hypothesis should be believed in by the party which urges the objections, but merely that the consequences should be shown to be implied in the hypothesis to the satisfaction of the party concerned. This is the only way by which we can confute an opponent. The absurdity of his position must be brought home to him. The Mādhyamika claims to do nothing else. He is a *Prāsaṅgika*—having no tenet of his own and not caring to frame a syllogism of his own. "An opponent in putting forward a thesis is expected, as he is a believer in pramāṇas, to validate it; he must prove to his opponent the validity of that very argument by which he himself has arrived at the right conclusions. . .But the case of the Mādhyamika is different; he does not vindicate any assertion in order to convince his opponent. He has no reasons and examples which he believes to be true."[1] Every endeavour of the Mādhyamika is, therefore, exhausted in reducing the opponent's position to absurdity on principles and consequences which the opponent himself would accept. So we may answer the first question by forcibly asserting that to criticise a position it is not only unnecessary but irrelevant to advance another position.

It might be urged that criticism is the applicat on of certain logical canons—the valid sources of knowledge etc. These at least shall have to be accepted even by the Mādhyamika. But for a critic of knowledge, for a Transcendentalist, there are no first principles, no inviolate axioms which he should respect, or at which he should arrive at the end of his enquiry. If the first principles and the valid sources of knowledge are themselves under discussion, will it do to start by unquestionably accepting them? Just as this enquiry can proceed without being saddled with the acceptance of any dogma, other enquiries can fare equally well. Formal Logic may proceed on certain assumptions, but a self-conscious dialectic cannot, without being false to its position, accept them.

5. Another line of objection may be adopted to confute the Mādhyamika. When one alternative is rejected or accepted the other is, *eo ipso* accepted or rejected, else the Excluded Middle is violated. The Mādhyamika flagrantly violates the rule; we find him cutting down all alternatives that are exclusive and exhaustive. For instance, four alternatives are framed by him with regard to causation, but none is accepted :

"Neither out of themselves (*svataḥ*), nor out of others (*parataḥ*) nor from both (*ubhayataḥ*), nor at random (*ahetutaḥ*) have entities sprung into being" (Mādh. Kār. 1. 1.) Here too both motion and rest have been denied. The Mādhyamika alone is not the sinner in rejecting the Excluded Middle. Kant does not accept this when he formulates his antinomies and rejects them both, e.g. "the world has a beginning in space and time" and that "the world has no such beginning" etc. Hegel himself does not recognise it; had he done so, he should have chosen either Being or Non-Being instead of seeking a third.

i. No logical flaw is involved in not observing the Excluded Middle. If any one wants to vindicate this law, he must not

1. *Mādh. Kārikā*, Ch. 1, I. pp. 16ff. (B. B. Edn).

only resolve the antinomies which any dialectic presents, but show that in rejecting one alternative we do so by covertly accepting its contradictory or *vice versa.*

ii. The law of Excluded Middle assumes a sort of omniscience and makes capital out of our ignorance. That any two alternatives together exhaust the realm of discourse and that no third is possible cannot be known from the alternatives themselves. Such is not the case with the law of Contradiction; it derives all its force from the material in hand, what is actually presented to us. We can, even on the strength of immediate experience, say that both the contradictories cannot be true. Excluded Middle too, it will be urged, does not presume anything more than the particular kind of disjunctives called the Contradictories—as Being and Non-Being, Affirmation and Negation. Such contradictory alternatives can easily be recognised by any one. To this our reply is that the doctrine of Contradictories conceived by Formal Logic is defective; for, it is always possible to suggest one other alternative in all cases; besides being and non-being, we can admit the Indefinite; affirmation and negation do not exhaust all attitudes towards an assertum; we may not assert anything at all, but simply entertain a datum without these two modes. The contention is not merely academical. Consider for instance the two propositions—"An integer between 3 and 4 is prime"; "An integer between 3 and 4 is composite, not prime." Neither of these propositions is true, though they are contradictories in the formal sense. Can the Excluded Middle help us here ? For, this is a case where *no* adjective, no alternative can be predicated without absurdity. The illusory snake is another example; it cannot accept the predicates Sat or Asat, for it is not an existent.

If we want to formulate the contradictory of any proposition 'S is P', it is not merely 'S is not-P' but also 'S is not'—i.e. the proposition is contradicted if the subject does not exist. It is clear that because there are two contradictories to any position we can never pass from the denial of the position to any one of the contradictories or *vice versa.* This is tantamount to giving up the Excluded Middle.

A formal objection, pointed out by Johnson, can also be raised against the law. If it were true, the existential import of a proposition and that of its obverse must be neither less nor more.

'S is not P' says nothing about the existence of S or of P; the proposition will be valid even if they had never existed. What is required is that the combination SP should not be found, and this is available with or without the existence of these terms. Now following formal logic, we shall be told that 'S is not P' can be positively rendered into 'S is non-P'. But this is more than a mere verbal change. The new proposition affirms a negative predicate of a subject S. If S were not an existent the proposition would be meaningless, as it would be even if there were no P and non-P. But as we have seen, the original proposition gives no guarantee of the existence of S or P. The obverse imports, tacitly under cover of an indubitable law, existential matter not to be found in the original proposition. The obverse will be valid, only if one implied premise 'S is' is supplied. Therefore it is clear that the principle on which obversion is based, namely the Excluded Middle, is not valid. 'S is not P' does not commit us to any position, while 'S is non-P' commits us to the existence of S and possibly of P and non-P. It is apparent that Excluded Middle is not a purely formal principle, but a device to serve a metaphysical doctrine, in which to negate a judgment is taken as affirming a negative pedicate. It seems to be a very cheap device for asserting the existence of any subject. As a matter of fact it does not question the existence of the subject; its only trouble seems to be confined to the assignment of a positive or negative predicate; the fundamental question of the existence of the subject of a judgment is left to take care of itself.

The Mādhyamika, on the other hand, questions the very existence of the subject of which there may be any dispute about the proper predicate. And as the subject cannot be discussed or known apart from the predicates, he formulates a general rule—that a subject, an entity of which all assignable positions, predicates, either taken singly or collectively, are inadmissible, does not exist. If the existence of the subject is not assumed at the outset, non-existence is also not presumed, but everything is decided on its own merits. The Mādhyamika finds that he can formulate at least four theses or alternatives in any case. One can assert existence of a subject, or deny it, or assert both existence and non-existence, or assert neither existence nor non-existence. It will be seen that the first is the Realist thesis; the second is purely negative, the third is a synthetic position, say that of Hegel or of the Jaina, the fourth is the purely agnostic thesis. All these, singly and collectively, are wrong and Tattva is that which escapes all these predicates.

"*na san nāsan na sadasan na cāpyanubhayātmakam;*
catuṣkoṭi-vinirmuktaṁ tattvaṁ mādhyamikā viduḥ"

5.2. BUDDHISM AND CONTEMPORARY INDIAN THOUGHT*[1]

Quite a considerable part of contemporary Indian thought is concerned with Buddhism either in the form of expositions and specialist studies or as inspired by it. The revival of interest in Buddhism is understandable.[2] It has profoundly influenced the philosophy and religion of India down the ages. The interest in Buddhism is not merely historical, a matter of curiosity and national pride. Thinkers find in Buddhism plentiful suggestions for solving the social and religious problems that afflict us today. The 2500th Anniversary of the Lord Buddha's Parinirvāṇa (Great Decease) has served as an additional stimulus to this interest.

The abiding value of Buddhism lies, I think, in its typifying certain distinct norms of thought. These norms are not outmoded; no religious or philosophical norm is. They may not exactly be in fashion now. But fashions, like the seasons and the weather, change quickly, and the so-called outmoded forms have a curious and persistent way of coming back. The philosopher should not succumb to changing fashions, but has to fix his attention on the abiding norms. There are elements in Buddhism which are capable of being disengaged from their purely historical and accidental environment and applied to the present-day conditions.

The purely moral and humanistic attitude of Buddhism strongly appeals to the modern man. In Buddhism we have a religion without God, without any extraneous appeal to revelation and dogma. It takes its stand on the Law (*Dharma*)

*Reprinted from Revue Internationale de Philosophie, no. 37. 1956.

1. I am deeply grateful to the Editor, Professor J. Lameere, for asking me to contribute a paper to the Special Issue of the *Revue Internationale de Philosophie*. He was also good enough to suggest that I might write on the ContemporaryInterpretation of Buddhism.

2. The present writer has dealt with the Revival of Buddhistic Studies in a Report submitted to the Unesco last year. Some material from that Report (unpublished) appears in this article.

as an intrinsic and universal Norm of all existence. The enthusiastic welcome that it received in the 19th century and is still continuing to receive is in a great measure due to this moral standpoint. The egalitarian stand taken by Buddhism, as contrasted with the hierarchical pattern of Brāhmanism, in regard to the cultivation of Spiritual life is in closer conformity with the ideals of today. Mahāyāna Buddhism is justly celebrated for the ideal of the Bodhisattva. And this is an answer to the oft-repeated but untrue accusation that Hindu religions are more intent on private salvation and do not concern themselves with the good of fellow-beings. If anything, the spiritual ideal is more universal and non-sectarian.

I

The Problem of Interpretation

A number of leading contemporary Indian thinkers and scholars have attempted to interpret Buddhism, its religion and philosophy. They have also tried to assess the nature and extent of the influence exerted by and on Buddhism by other modes of Indian thought. These questions are considered here in brief. Does all Indian philosophy stem from one original source—the Upaniṣads? And are all Indian religions variations of the Vedic? Following the lead of Professor Radhakrishnan, the foremost Indian thinker of today, there is a large and impressive body of opinion favouring the unilinear tradition and development of Indian thought.[1] In the estimation of the Buddhist and non-Buddhist (Jaina and Brāhmanical) orthodox tradition, the differences between the two are radical. To my mind both these estimates seem to suffer from the fallacy of over-simplification. Probably, the truth lies some-where in the middle. A careful analysis would reveal that Hinduism (Brāhmanism) and Buddhism belong to the same genus; they

1. Professor Radhakrishnan has stated and re-stated this interpretation in several of his works: *Indian Philosophy*, Vol. I, pp. 360ff., *Gautama the Buddha* and more recently in the *Philosophy of Sarvepalli Radhakrishnan*, Reply to Critics, pp. 837 ff. In a recent collective work brought out by the Govt. of India, 2500 *Years of Buddhism* many writers follow this view. In the Radio Broadcast Talks from New Delhi by several leaders in connection with the Buddha Jayanti Celebrations, this view has been reiterated.

differ as species. In a sense, they are complementary to each other; one emphasises what the other lacks or slurs over. Without basic affinity they would have been completely sundered from each other; without differences they could not have vitalised and enriched each other. In view of the difference in their basic standpoints and the mode of their historical development, we should be alive to their differences as much as we affirm their affinities.

Both Brāhmanism and Buddhism are types of spiritual religion. They try to realise a state of utter negation of the ego, the abolition of selfishness. Positively, it is the attainment of the universal where all differences and conflicts cease and where there is concord and harmony. Again in both, the highest state is attained by a non-discursive intellectual intuition, a kind of mystic absorption. A strenuous spiritual discipline is enjoined as the indispensable means to attain it. The highest state of realisation called by various names (*brahman*, *nirvāṇa*, *śūnyatā*, *tathatā* etc.) is really the ineffable absolute which is transcendent to thought, but which is thoroughly immanent in all beings. Both religions have always believed in the Law of Karma as the Law of the Universe and as the arbiter of human destiny.

To consider the differences in philosophy. All systems of Hindu thought subscribe to the *ātma-vāda*—the conception of reality as Being, substance and permanent. In its most radical form, as in the Vedānta of Śāṅkara, it denied the reality of change, and characterised it as appearance. The Buddhist schools rejected the reality of the soul or substance (*anātmavāda*) and conceived the real as Becoming. The real for them is sequential, momentary, incessantly perishing and emerging. There is no inner and immutable core in things; everything is in flux. For the Buddhists, the notions of soul, substance, universal and identity are thought-constructions, subjective. This constructive activity of thought, however, is transcendental in character, not empirical. Belief in the soul or the substance (*ātman*) is a basic wrong notion (Avidyā, ignorance) which is at the root of all suffering. Salvation would result if the belief in *ātman* is abandoned. For, only as we take anything as abiding and identical do we become attached to it, cling to it; we are also averse to things that are opposed to it. The result is tension and conflict. For the Vedānta, which may be considered as the most consistent form of Brāhmaṇical thought, ignorance is just the reverse; it is the conceiving of the real as changeful, different and particular. And when we realise the real as truly universal and identical (differenceless), as *ātman*, do we get freed of limitations and reach Brahmahood.[1]

The religious differences are no less basic and striking. The source of religious inspiration in Brāhmanism is the revelation as given to us in the Vedas; in Buddhism it is reason. Not that Brāhmanism is antagonistic to reason or is unmindful of its value; but it is only revelation which can give us intuitions of the transcendent. The function of reason is to analyse and to clarify and, if necessary, to defend and to remove apparent contradictions. The role of reason is somewhat negative, like the hedge that protects the growing field of corn from depredation by stray cattle. Innovations are only interpretations of the given truth, and originality is not so much the discovery of new truths as of meanings and emphases. The entire mode of devlopment in Hinduism is authoritarian and traditional. We could even take it as theological in character. The core or the initial knowledge is of divine inspiration; but it does not remain an imposed belief, but one which is to be realised in one's intimate experience (*anubhavāvasānatvād brahmavijñānasya*).

In contrast to this, Buddha asks us not to receive anything on trust or to accept any authority, but to test it by reason and experience. He himself did not owe allegiance to any authority, Vedic or non-Vedic.

The reason for the difference in the two inspirations takes us to the heart of each religion. Buddhism, earlier Buddhism at least, believes in self-effort. Its spiritual discipline has little or no place for seeking outside help or divine guidance. Salvation is strictly a sustained and heroic act on the part of man himself. It is not an act of God or a cooperation between man and God. We have here a religion without God, a perfection of self-discipline and self-analysis. The fundament is the Autonomy of the Moral Law (*Karma*). Buddha was thus led to deny two opposed standpoints: Naturalism or Nihilism

1. I have dealt with the differences of the two traditions in my book, *The Central Philosophy of Buddhism* (Allen and Unwin, London), especially in Chapters I and III.

(*ucchedavāda*) which totally denied the Moral Law (free act and its result), reducing man to a fortuitous conglomeration of natural forces; and Eternalism (*śāśvatavāda*), the Transcendent Freedom of God (and even of an unchanging Soul, Ātman) who is above the Moral Law (*Karma*). Acceptance of Naturalism would have meant the denial of the freedom of will even in the phenomenal sphere and the acceptance of the chance-origin of the universe. Suffering then cannot be accounted for, and will prove incapable of removal. Acceptance of Eternalism (really the Super-Naturalism of God) is the acceptance of a Non-phenomenal Transcendent Freedom to start with; it would have meant the acceptance of some entity exempt from and impervious to the Moral Law, one which cannot be related to the Moral as its cause or effect. The Moral Consciousness itself does not evidence it as in any way essential to it. Buddha took his stand, like Kant, on the Moral Act, the immanent freedom that is felt by man in his endeavours to better his condition. Even man's suffering is evidence of his inherent freedom; a stone-pillar does not suffer. This felt immanent freedom can be made absolute by right effort, conduct as well as by insight into the Moral Law. It is Buddha's genius that perceived the Inexorability and Universality of the Norm (*pratītya-samutpāda*). And the perception of the Norm itself has a reformative and regenerative effect on Man. The Moral is here raised to the status of the Spiritual: immanent freedom as felt and exercised in human involvement is perfected into the transcendent freedom beyond the phenomenal, into *nirvāṇa*. The immanent leads, through its inner dynamism, to the Transcendent Freedom of *nirvāṇa*.

For Buddhism the fundament is the moral consciousness and the spiritual urge is for purifying the mind of its passions (*viśuddhi-mārga*). The fundament of Brāhmanism is God-consciousness; and the goal is exaltation or deification. The Vedas, which are the fountain-source of all forms of Hinduism, are literally intoxicated with the Idea of God, of a Transcendent Being ever Free and ever the Lord, supernatural and superhuman. The Vedic seers had an unusually quick, and open sensitiveness to the transcendent being. They try to grasp Him now as Agni, now as Indra, now as Varuṇa, Viṣṇu or Rudra and in hundred other ways. These are predicates or characteristics of Godhead rather than substantive entities in their own right. The Vedic seers are conscious all the time that the super-abundance of the Deity cannot strictly be bound. Aditi is the unbound; and all Gods as Ādityas partake of the Limitless. Each deity is the upholder of the cosmic order (*ṛta*). The Vedic seers had an almost overwhelming sense of the Infinite impinging on us. Religion was for them not the laboured suppression of passions, of control and regimen as in Buddhism, but the relationship with the transcendent through prayer and devotion. This *en rapport* relationship with God is what distinguishes Hinduism from Buddhism. And this consciousness has never left it at any stage of its long history. Newer deities emerge; rather, the older ones are given new names and are worshipped in newer forms; but the same pattern remains. This may be theism, but it is not a theism of the semitic type. It is rather pantheism; the difference between God and Man (creatures) is not absolute.

The Deity is not discovered by man by a self-effort; it is the Deity that freely chooses to reveal itself. Man just receives and realises it. He is saved by this relationship, his sense of kinship and identity with the Transcendent Spirit, Freedom. Practice of moral virtues and concentration of mind have value as enabling one to perceive this inherent identity, just as a clean mirror is able to entertain the image without distortion. The purity of the mirror is not however the source of the image, and is merely ancillary to the reflection. As realising the accomplished fact, Spiritual achievement for Brāhmanism is symbolic, not laboured and literal as in Buddhism.

The differing interpretations of Buddhism imply difference in the conception of philosophy. Is philosophy the ability and insight to perceive the identity and unity of things, even to the extent of ignoring difference ? Or, is it the discovery of distinctions that things as well as systems of philosophy exhibit. The Vedānta attitude (Professor Radhakrishnan is a good example of this) is one of non-distinction; it is the seeing of unity everywhere. A third view is the dialectical attitude which does not take sides, which does not speculate and press for this or that conception, but merely stands aside and is self-consciously aware of the dialectical play of reason. This may be considered as moving on a higher plane, as a philosophy of philosophies

II

Relation of Buddhism and Vedānta

There has been considerable research on the influence of Buddhism on the Brāhmaṇical systems of thought and *vice versa.* The contending views on this question either seek to deny influence altogether or assert it to the extent of bodily incorporating tenets. Here too a balanced view may be considered as possibly nearer the case.

As Buddhism and Brāhmanism were not moving in closed compartments and as there is ample evidence of lively interchanges between them, mutual influence may legitimately be surmised. The precise nature of it, however, has to be determined. Influence, it must be clearly understood, is not necessarily borrowing or acceptance of doctrines from others. That too is influence which stimulates the systems to modify, revise or even to re-affirm their doctrines. Influence may be expressed as much through opposition as by acceptance. In this sense alone have the Brāhmaṇical systems, Vedānta and Nyāya, been influenced by Buddhism and *vice versa.*

Again, great religions do not bodily borrow from others. They gradually, and in their own way, assimilate from other modes of thought elements that can be organically woven into their own fabric of thought. They keep true to their basic principles, and any modifications introduced have to be in conformity with them. They cannot simply jump off the rails as it were.

Attention should also be paid to the inherent dynamism present in each system of thought which impels it to develop along certain lines irrespective of outside influence. Inadequate appreciation of this factor explains, to a considerable extent, the unjust accusation that the development of Mahāyāna is foreign to Buddha's thought or that Śaṅkara's non-dualism, his *māyāvāda*, is not the genuine teaching of the *Upaniṣads.*

There is no doubt that almost a revolution occurred in the Upaniṣadic tradition (*ātmavāda*) as well as in the Buddhistic (*anātmavāda*) in the course of their long development. Buddhism which, in its earlier phase, was a radical pluralism became in the Mahāyāna a radical absolutism with different conception of Buddha and the Bodhisattva ideal. How could this occur ?

Two answers are possible: one that of borrowing from or being influenced by the Upaniṣadic thought where absolutism and theism are such dominant features; the other hypothesis would deny external influence and seek to account for the revolution as the result of an inner dynamism in Buddhist thought itself. These two views are not exclusive, and perhaps the truth lies somewhere between the two.

It is possible, nay probable, that Buddhist thinkers came gradually to realise that behind the phenomenal play of the many and varied forces, there was a subjacent ground that is transcendent to thought. *Nirvāṇa* which was conceived as almost annihilation—the stoppage of all life-forces—receives new meaning as the Unceasing, Unacquired Foundational Reality; the world is its free appearance. That it cannot be described or understood in terms of the empirical far from making it unreal makes it out as the only reality. It is indispensable and is the goal of all endeavour. The Upaniṣadic Brahman is obviously the model from which the *Tathatā* or *Śūnyatā* has been drawn. Competent scholars, like Kern, Keith, Stcherbatsky and Radhakrishnan among others, have drawn pointed attention to the probable influence of the Upaniṣadic thought on the emergence of the Mahāyāna.

I attach somewhat greater importance to the dynamism inherent in Buddhism itself which engendered the revolutionary change. It was stated that earlier Buddhism believed solely in self-effort and was actuated by the moral consciousness. In this sense, Gautama the Buddha was, paradoxically enough, the first and last Buddhist; he alone conceivably could free himself without external aid or guidance. With regard to others, his followers, his own advent exercised a profound influence; they had both his precept and example before them. The personality of Buddha introduces into Buddhism an active religious element of great importance. Completely free after his Enlightenment, Buddha still continues to be a Person. His life and acts are solely for the sake of others (*parārtha-sampadaḥ Tathāgatāḥ*). His activity however does not bind him; he is completely free and egoless. Buddha is the embodiment of Freedom and Grace. Buddha functions very much like Īśvara in this regard in Buddhism. Theism enters Buddhism implicitly, through the personality of Buddha. We know from the history of Buddhism that the fundamental difference between the Sthaviravāda (representing the Hīnayāna phase of Buddhism) and the Mahāyāna centered round the Supermundane Personality of Buddha (*lokottaravāda*).

The subject of the relationship between Brāhmaṇical and Buddhist systems in itself is a vast and interesting field of study. Material of importance is to be found scattered in the polemic śāstra-literature of the different systems. Regarding the relation of the Vedānta to the Mahāyāna some definitive work has been done recently.[1] Although the hypothesis of the evolution of Vedântic absolutism by a criticism of he Sāṅkhya dualism and the earlier Vedānta of the pre-Śaṅkara commentators cannot be ruled out, it happens that the Mādhyamika and Yogācāra absolutisms had already been evolved in Buddhism. We have undeniable evidence of the Mādhyamika and Yogācāra influence in the *Māṇḍūkya Kārikā*. The whole problem has been ably and thoroughly treated by Professor Bhattacharya in his *Āgama Śāstra of Gauḍapāda*. (Calcutta, 1943).

It is, however, difficult to conceive how the philosophers belonging to the ātma-tradition could borrow doctrines from those of the opposed anātma-tradition. The Vedāntists stake everything on the reality of the ātman and accept the authority of the Upaniṣads; the Buddhists denied the reality of the ātman (soul, substance, the permanent, the universal) in any form. The barrier was always there. Besides, it is readily assumed that there is no difference between the absolutisms of Nāgārjuna, Śaṅkara and the Yogācāra. A closer analysis should bring out their differences as much as their generic affinity. Consistently with the above contention, we could only expect the Vedāntin to have profited by the technique or method of the Mādhyamika. He had before him the Mādhyamika distinction of *paramārtha* and *saṁvṛti*, the Noumenon and Phenomena, and of the Mādhyamika method of reaching the real by negation of the unreal. The Mādhyamika and Yogācāra also had a theory of illusion to account for the emergence of appearance. Knowledge of this turn in Buddhism must have sent the Vedāntin

1. Reference may be made to Dr. Mahadevan's treatment of the subject in his: *Gauḍapāda, A Study of Early Vedānta* (Madras, 1951) and Dr. Murti's *The Central Philosophy of Buddhism*, Chapter IV.

back to his own texts and enabled him to perceive the truer meaning of the Upaniṣads in Advaitism. There has been borrowing of technique and not of tenets.

III

The Problem of the Absolutes

Consideration of the relation of the Vedānta to the Mādhyamika and the Yogācāra idealism leads us to the question of the correct appraisal of these absolutisms. Are these identical in essence and differ only in name?[1] Or, do these absolutisms stand for ultimate incommensurable types? The problem is of great philosophical value, as it brings to the surface basic differences in the conception of philosophy. Its importance is not confined to the context of Indian Philosophy.

As absolutisms, the Mādhyamika, Vijñānavāda and Vedānta exhibit some common features as to their *form*; they differ in the mode of their approach, and possibly with regard to that entity with which they identify the absolute. In the actual state of the Absolute, they may be identical; at least we have no means of asserting their difference; silence is their most proper language. The centre of the circle may be reached from the periphery by any of the possible radii; short of reaching the very centre, persons adopting different radii may genuinely feel that they are on the right path to the centre and that the others are not. For, each votary may see the centre looming ahead of him; but he cannot, from the nature of his predicament, see that others also may be reaching the centre through their particular modes of approach.

In all these systems, the absolute is transcendent to thought, totally devoid of empirical determinations (*nirdharmaka, śūnya*). The Absolute is immanent too, being the reality of appearance. The Absolute is but the phenomena in their essential form. It follows that the absolute is realised only in a non-empirical

1. See Radhakrishnan, *Indian Philosophy,* Vol. I, pp. 662 ff. For a different view see Das Gupta, *Indian Idealism,* p. 79. See also Murti, *The Central Philosophy of Buddhism,* Chap. XIII (pp. 311-28.), Dr. A. K. Chatterjee, *The Yogācāra Idealism,* Chap. X, pp. 235 ff., Dr. P. T. Raju, *Idealistic Thought of India,* pp. 251 ff.

intuition called variously, *prajñāpāramitā*, *lokottarajñāna*, and *aparokṣānubhūti*. The nature of this experience is that it is a non-discursive, immediate and unitary cognition; here essence and existence coincide. They further agree with regard to the nature and status of phenomena which are appearance. Engendered by a beginningless non-empirical ignorance (*avidyā*), the appearance can be completely negated by the true knowledge of the absolute. The nature of *avidyā* and its orientation to the absolute differ in each system. Every absolutism is really an *advaita* or *advayavāda*, non-dualism; they do not establish the absolute, but just reject duality as illusion. And the rejection is dialectically made and not on the basis of positive arguments. Otherwise, *that* on the strength of which the absolute is established will stand out as another reality. What is rejected as illusory differs in these systems: the Mādhyamika negates the conceptualist tendency; for, this is what falsifies reality which is Intuition (*prajñā*); the Vijñānavāda negates objectivity; for this makes *vijñāna* appear infected with the duality of subject and object; the Vedānta negates difference; the real is Universal and Identical.

By implication every absolutism has to formulate the distinction of Reality and Appearance and the two truths (*paramārtha* and *vyavahāra*). All three agree in their ideal of spiritual discipline. It is knowledge (*prajñā*, *brahmajñāna*) that frees us; other factors are auxiliary to this. The state of *mukti* (*nirvāṇa*) is a complete identity with the Absolute.

The differences of the absolute, at least in the manner of their approach, should not be overlooked. Absolutism, all philosophy, starts with the reflective consciousness, and reflection is engendered by the consciousness of falsity or illusion. We become self-conscious of our activity only when the thing attended to turns out to be other than what it appeared at first sight. Every absolutism may therefore be understood as a mode of the negative judgment, as negation of illusion. There is difference with regard to the illusion with which they start, and the standpoint from which they negate the illusory. By implication, this entails a difference in the way that the relation between the real and the appearance is conceived in each system.

"The Vedānta and Vijñānavāda start with an *empirical illusion*, the 'rope-snake' or the dream-object and extend this analysis analogically to the world-illusion which is super-imposed on the real. The Vedānta analyses illusion from the knowledge-standpoint; the illusion consists in wrong characterisation, in mistaking the given as something else; the 'this' which is given is misperceived as the 'snake'. Even for being mistaken, the 'this' must be there as the substrate, independent of our knowing. The 'snake' is however exhausted in the knowledge-relation itself, and it is therefore an appearance.

The Vijñānavāda analyses illusion from an opposite angle; for it, the 'given' is appearance, and the ideating consciousness alone is real. The appearance of something, the 'this', independent of the act of cognition, is negated; and the true nature of the appearance as identical with the projecting consciousness is reinstated.

In both the Vedānta and the Vijñānavāda, the analysis of empirical illusion is extended analogically to the world. But what will tell us that the phenomenal world itself is illusory, for here obviously we have no experience of an actual cancellation to justify this, as we had in the example of an empirical illusion ? An empirical illusion (of the form 'this is snake') does not of itself necessitate being universalised of all phenomena. The problem must present itself in all its universality. Both Vedānta and Vijñānavāda have therefore to take the cue from some extra-logical mode of cognition: the Vedānta gets it from revelation (śruti) which declares that the *ātman* (*Brahman*) alone is real; the Yogācāra depends on the deliverance of the trance-states where the object drops out leaving consciousness as the sole reality. This is made the norm for judging phenomena.

The Mādhyamika starts, not with an empirical illusion, but with the Transcendental illusion, as exhibited in the inevitable conflict of opposed standpoints and philosophies. He addresses himself primarily to the *views* about the real; only indirectly, he is concerned with the things or reality; for the views criticised are views of the real. The Mādhyamika approach is solely that of a critic of experience. Dialectic or criticism itself is philosophy; while for the Vedānta and Vijñānavāda dialectic is enlisted in the service of philosophy.

What is negated ? If the form of illusion is set down as : 'This is snake', the negating or cancelling consciousness is of the form : 'This is not snake'. For the Vedānta, the *not* applies to the 'snake'. This is *not snake*, i.e. *This* is real, but its ascribed snake-character is false. For the Vijñānavāda, the 'not' applies to the *this*, 'The snake is *not this*', i.e. the 'snake' is *not* out there as *this*, as an object independent of the projecting Ideation of consciousness, but is identical with that latter. The 'this' (given thing, Being) is real for the Vedānta, and the 'snake' as a creature of projective imagination is appearance. For the Vijñānavāda, it is just the reverse: the 'this' as an other, independent of consciousness, is appearance; and the 'snake' is real, being the mode of constructive Ideation. Both have this common feature however. From the context of illusion they reject one aspect—the appearance—(the 'snake' by the Vedāntin and the 'this' by the Vijñānavādin); it is totally false, unreal (*svarūpato mithyā*, *parikalpita*). They however retrieve and salvage the other part, the real or the prius of illusion (the 'this' by the Vedāntin and the 'snake' by the Vijñānavādin); only its relationship with the appearance is false (*saṁsargato mithyā*); the *paratantra* (the stream of consciousness) is false to the extent of the imputation of the object (*parikalpita*); but in itself it is identical with the Absolute (*parinispanna*).

Logically, the above analysis means that although the relation may be false, both the terms are not false, but only one; there is an absolute or non-relative term. The general formula is: the two terms sustaining a relation are not of the same order, one is *higher* and the other *lower*: the two terms are neither mutually dependent nor mutually independent; relation is neither 'internal' nor 'external'. If mutually dependent, we cannot distinguish between the two terms; as they so necessarily imply each other that one cannot exist without the other any time. We cannot even say that there are two terms, as the basis of distinction is lacking. If mutually independent, there is no basis of connection; each term is a self, a self-contained universe as it were. To escape this dilemma we have to conceive one term as basic, and thus capable of existing apart from its relation to the other; while the other is incapable of so doing and therefore dependent. One term, the higher, is not exhausted in the relationship; it has a transcendent or non-implicatory existence which is its intrinsic nature; the other term however is entirely exhausted within the relation, and it has no non-relative existence.

For the Mādhyamika negation applies to both the 'this' and the 'snake': *this* is not *snake.* The 'this' cannot be had apart from the 'snake', for we know the 'this' only as identified with the 'snake' (predicate) and not in isolation; the 'snake' too can be had only as identified with the 'this' (substrate, subject) They are relative to each other, and this constitutes their falsity. Neither the constructive Ideation of the Vijñānavāda, nor the Pure Being (of the Vedānta) which allows, as the Passive ground, for the superimposition to occur, is real for the Mādhyamika.[1]

The Mādhyamika Absolute (*Śūnyatā*) has to be understood as the Reflective Awareness of the dialectical play of reason, of the 'is' and 'not-is'; it is none other than this critical consciousness. To deny this is to deny critical reflection. That would be to hold that we can *do* a thing, but *cannot know that we do it* : *we do it*: that we can theorise and speculate, but *cannot know that we theorise or speculate.* This amounts to a contradiction, for the denial itself betrays *knowledge* of the theory.

Brahman is the Absolute or Pure Being; and the method of approach is from the standpoint of knowledge. *Vijñaptimātratā* is Pure Act (Transcendental Ideation) and the approach is from the standpoint of the Will Consciousness. *Śūnyatā* is *Prajñā*, non-dual Intuition, and the approach is from the standpoint of philosophical reflection or criticism. It is that contentless and positionless awareness itself. Brahman and Vijñaptimātratā too are contentless; for in Pure Being there is no *other* from which it could be distinguished and related. Nothing can be predicated of it, and one cannot even speak of it literally. Can we still continue to call it Being, *vijñāna*, or by any other term? In the end every consistent absolutist is reduced to the Mādhyamika position of 'No-position'. The differences pertain to the mode of approach, to the standpoint from which these systems reach the Absolute, like the centre of a circle which is reached from the periphery by different radii.

It is evident that there are differences in the approach to the absolute in the Vedānta, Vijñānavāda and the Mādhyamika. Whether these absolutes are really incommensurable even in the ultimate state is more than what we can aver. If we cannot assert their differences, we are equally precluded from asserting their identity.

1. *The Central Philosophy of Buddhism*, pp. 322-24.

It remains a significant fact that in both the traditions (Buddhistic and Brāhmanical), the absolute is reached in diverse ways. Why this passion for the Absolute, when admittedly it does nothing on the empirical level. The mosaic pattern of Indian culture provides the answer. It is perhaps the only way to reconcile varieties of religious and philosophical types without sacrificing the underlying unity. And this may not be without value in the present-day world. India is a world in miniature, and the Indian experiment deserves to be tried on a larger scale.

Unification of the multifarious and even conflicting cultural patterns by reducing them to a single uniform type may not easily be possible. And even if possible, it is not desirable; the world will lose its vitality and richness. The very process of unification is bound to leave permanent trails of bitterness and discord. On the other hand, individualism cannot be pushed on to the extent of each individual constituting a self-contained universe, a law unto himself. Human civilization has already given the answer. It has taken the form of cultural groups or communities. Within each community, however, there is the incessant tension between the claim of the individual and the well-being of the whole, as there is among the different communities at large. Spirituality in the last analysis would lie in the conformity (or complete identity) of the good of the ego with the good of the Whole (God or Godhead). This unconditional humility or self-surrender is an unmistakable implication of all Indian absolutism. It carries with it the capaçity and the open-mindedness to appraise and appreciate other paths and points of view.

5.3 SAṀVṚTI AND PARAMĀRTHA IN MĀDHYAMIKA AND ADVAITA VEDĀNTA*

It has been the fashion to consider that the differences between the Mādhyamika *śūnyatā* and *Brahman* are rather superficial and even verbal, and that the two systems of philosophy are almost identical. At least Professor Radhakrishnan thinks so, and Stcherbatsky's and Dasgupta's views are not very different. I hold a contrary view altogether: that inspite of superficial similarities in form and terminology, the differences between them are deep and pervasive. Both Mādhyamika and Advaita agree that the absolute is transcendent to thought, totally devoid of empirical determinations (*nirdharmaka, śūnya*). "The Absolute is immanent too, being the reality of appearance. The Absolute is but the phenomena in their essential form. It follows that the absolute is realised only in a non-empirical intuition called variously, *prajñāpāramitā*, *lokottarajñāna*, and *aparokṣānubhūti*. The nature of this experience is that it is non-discursive, immediate and unitary cognition; here essence and existence coincide. They further agree with regard to the nature and status of phenomena which are appearance. Engendered by a beginningless non-empirical *avidyā*, the appearance can be negated completely by the true knowledge of the absolute. The nature of *avidyā* and its orientation to the absolute differ in each system. Every absolutism is really an *advaita* or *advayavāda*, non-dualism; they do not establish the absolute, but just reject duality as illusion. And the rejection is dialectically made and not on the basis of positive arguments. Otherwise, *that* on the strength of which the absolute is established will stand out as another reality. What is rejected as illusory differs in these systems: the Mādhyamika negates the conceptualist tendency (*vikalpa* or *dṛṣṭi*); for this is what falsifies reality which is Intuition (*prajñā*); the Vijñānavāda negates objectivity; for this makes *vijñāna* appear infected with the duality of subject and object; the Vedānta negates difference (*bheda*); the real is universal and identical .

*Reprinted from M. Sprung (ed.), *Two Truths in Buddhism and Vedānta*. 9-26. (c) D. Reidel Publishing Company, Dordrecht-Holland, 1973.

By implication every absolutism has to formulate the distinction of Reality and Appearance and the two truths (*paramārtha* and *vyavahāra*). Scriptures too are interpreted on this basis—*nitārtha* (*para*) and *neyārtha* (*apara*). The Vedāntic doctrine of three 'truths' and the admission of the *prātibhāsika* is necessitated by the fact that it first analyses an empirical illusion (an illusion which is cancelled in our ordinary experience even) and applies this analysis analogically to the world-illusion. The position of Vijñānavāda is similar. The Mādhyamika, however, addresses himself directly to the world-illusion as presented in the conflicting philosophies and points of view. He is concerned with what has been called by Kant the Transcendental Illusion.

All three agree in their ideal of spiritual discipline. It is knowledge (*prajñā, brahmajñāna*) that frees us; other factors are auxiliary to this. The state of *mukti* (*nirvāṇa*) is a complete identity with the Absolute.[1]

1. The Differences Between Mādhyamika and Vedānta

(1) It must not be forgotten that the Vedānta and the Mādhyamika belong to two different traditions—the *ātman* tradition of the Upaniṣads and the *anātman* tradition of the Buddhists. The Vedānta is a complete and consistent formulation of the *ātman* doctrine of the Upaniṣads which conceive reality as pure being, as not subject to change and as one identical universal being. *Brahman* is the soul or spirit of things, their essence or reality. Change and particularity are taken as appearance of the underlying *ātman* or *Brahman.* This I have called the substance view of reality.

As opposed to this, Buddhism began with the rejection of the soul or substance and conceives the real, as becoming, as a continuum of momentary entities. The Vibhajyavāda of Buddhism is the critical analysis of concepts and linguistic usage. It rejected and relegated soul, substance, the universal and the whole as mere words without any backing in fact. The Mādhyamika philosophy is the complete and consistent formulation of the sceptical attitude that was born with Buddhism. Not only is the soul or substance unreal (*pudgalanairātmya*) but the so-

1. *The Central Philosophy of Buddhism,* George Allen and Unwin, 1955, pp. 321-2.

called 'elements', accepted by the earlier Ābhidharmika Buddhism is equally false (*dharmanairātmya*). Denial or rejection must be complete; everything is *śūnya*, void or devoid of any intrinsic nature of its own (*niḥsvabhāva*). The Mādhyamika dialectic is the most consistent and complete formulation of the critical analysis which began with Buddhism.

Although there have been lively skirmishes between the two traditions, there has been no comingling or compromise of positions on either side to any appreciable extent. It is my contention that there could not be acceptance of any doctrinal content by either side from the other as each had a totally different background of traditions and conception of reality. The Vedāntists stake everything on the *ātman* (*Brahman*) and accept the authority of the Upaniṣads. We have pointed out the *nairātmya* standpoint of Buddhism and its total opposition to the *ātman*, the permanent and universal, in any form. The barrier was always there. In the circumstances, we can at best say that presumably there has been borrowing of technique and not of tenets.

(2) For the Mādhyamika the dialectic itself is all philosophy. After the refutation of all views or standpoints through *reductio ad absurdum* arguments (*prasaṅgāpādanam*) there is nothing else to know. There is no knowledge of anything as the underlying reality. *prajñā* is the negation of all views (*śūnyatā* of all *dṛṣṭis*) and *prajñā* is the critical awareness itself without any object or content known.

In the Vedānta the dialectic is in the service of philosophical knowledge. The dialectic is used to refute difference or duality (*bheda, bhedabuddhi*) which hides the real and is *avidyā* (ignorance) *par excellence*. In this the Advaita follows the Upaniṣads in decrying difference. When difference is removed, the underlying reality of *Brahman* shines out. Although *Brahman* is not an object of knowledge, there is some sense in speaking of *knowing Brahman*. It is not knowledge through representation or discursive thought, but knowledge by *being* the thing known (*brahma veda brahmaiva bhavati*). When the superficial differences are rejected, what remains is the identical, universal Pure Being. We realize the absolute *Brahman* in negating the false ascriptions of it.

(3) Dialectic in the Vedānta starts with the analysis of an empirical illusion (for example the rope-snake), and this analysis

is extended analogically to the world illusion. The Vedānta undertakes a very careful and elaborate analysis of empirical illusions and even criticizes the theories of illusions, with the purpose of elucidating the notions of Real, (*sat, satyam*) and the False (*mithyā, anṛta*) and to bring out the relationship between the two. It takes the Real as the unsublated (*abādhya*) as what maintains its nature unchanged throughout its entire existence. The False (appearance) on the other hand is what is sublated as it is subject to the negation of the former, that is "it was not, is not, and would not be". It is negated or removed, not by physical factors but by right knowledge, (*jñānanivartyatvaṁ vā mithyātvam*). Its status is that it is neither Real nor utterly unreal (*sadasadvilakṣaṇatvam*). The utterly unreal (*asat, tuccha*) is defined as what never appeared as real anywhere. Thus the Real and the False are not contradictories, they are contraries. The False is at once different from the Real insofar as it is sublated in experience, and different from the utterly unreal (like the sky-lotus, hare's horn, son of a barren woman, etc.) as it did not not appear as real, but did appear and was mistaken for the real. It is technically called *anirvacaniya.* The Vedānta further holds that whereas the False presupposes the Real as it is mistaken for it and without the ground or substrate there could not be appearances, the Real does not need to appear and can be without the appearance. The relation between the two is one-sided. This question will be considered later on. It is the contention of Vedānta that there can be no illusion without a real basis or substratum (*sadadhiṣṭhāna*).

What compels us to extend the logic of an empirical illusion to the world? Even granting the occurrences of empirical illusions and accepting the Vedānta analysis of such illusions, why should the world be taken as illusory? The Vedānta adduces some arguments why the world could be taken as illusory. The world is false because it has a determinate character or form, like the 'shell-silver'. A determinate character is an elaboration or thought-interpretation of what is directly or intuitively known and therefore is dependent on the latter. The thought elaboration may deviate from the intuitively given. A second argument is that the world is false because it is not self-evident (*jaḍa*); only the self-evident (*svayamprakāśa*) is real. The self-evident is what is not object and yet immediately and unconditionally aware of itself. A third argument is that the world is false, because it is limited (*paricchinna*) in space, in time and in regard to its nature. Only the infinite is real (*ananta, ānanda*). All worldly objects arise as limitations of the Infinite Being (*Brahman*). The Real is therefore defined as *sat* (being), *cit* (consciousness), and *ānanda* (bliss), understood negatively of course as what is different from non-being, from the unconscious and from the painful.

Although the Vedānta gives arguments for the falsity of the world, its conviction is based, initially at least, on the scriptural texts and later on confirmed by reasoned thought and by direct experience.

As distinguished from the Vedānta position, the Mādhyamika does not start with the analysis of an empirical illusion and then extend it analogically to the world illusion. Although the Mādhyamika characterizes things as illusory and gives examples, as castles in the air (*gandharvanagara*), mirage (*marumarici*), the stem of a banana tree, ball of foam (*phenapiṇḍa*), hair-ringlets in space (*keśoṇḍuka*), and of course the son of a barren woman, etc., he nowhere, to my knowledge, gives an analysis of any empirical illusion to point out what constitutes their illusoriness, as Vedānta does. Nor does he criticize other theories of illusion. He also does not draw any distinction between the false (illusory) and the utterly unreal (*asat*) such as hare's horn or the son of a barren woman. The Vedānta does make out a clear and convincing case of distinction between the *mithyā* (false) and the *asat* (unreal).

The Mādhyamika starts with the world-illusion itself in all its directness and universality. The world-illusion is presented to the Mādhyamika as the total and persistent conflict of Reason—the interminable opposition of philosophical viewpoints as actually propounded by speculative philosophies. He is concerned with the Transcendental Illusion. Their antinomical conflict on every issue of importance is an eye-opener. Criticism or *prajñā* emerges. The primordial opposition or contrast in the Mādhyamika is between *dṛṣṭi* and *prajñā*, between dogmatic or speculative philosophy and criticism, which self-consciously refuses to take positions. Nowhere does the Mādhyamika concern itself directly with issues like god, soul, matter, creation, etc., but only indirectly in his criticism of the philosophical views about these. For instance, in rejecting the different theories of causation the Mādhyamika has rejected causation as a constitutive feature of the real.

It must, however, be said that the Mādhyamika dialectic, being a criticism of philosophical standpoints, can get under way only when the different systems have already been formulated. It cannot be an original system. This may make the Mādhyamika philosophy appear adventitious, as it has to depend on the chance-emergence of different systems and their opposition. It has, however, been shown thatt he conflict is necessary and implicit in Reason itself. The Mādhyamika system may be later in time, but its emergence is logically necessary; the inner dynamism of philosophical consciousness leads to th transcendentalism of the Mādhyamika. Philosophical knowledge for him is not a body of doctrines, but their criticism and rejection.

II. Advaya and Advaita

The Mādhyamika absolutism is an *advayavāda*. *Advaya* is knowledge free from the duality of the extremes (*antas* or *dṛṣṭis*), of 'is' and 'is-not', being, becoming, etc. It is knowledge freed of conceptual distinctions. *Advaita* is knowledge of a differenceless entity—*Brahman* (Pure Being). *Advaya* is purely an *epistemological* approach; the *advaita* is *ontological*. The sole concern of the Mādhyamika *advayavāda* is the purification of the faculty of knowing. The primordial error consists in the intellect being infected by the inveterate tendency to view Reality as identity or difference, permanent or momentary, one or many, etc. These views 'cover' or 'obscure' reality and the dialectic administers a cathartic corrective. With the purification of the intellect by *śūnyatā*, intuition (*prajñā*) emerges. The Real is known as it is, as *tathatā* or *bhūtakoṭi*. The emphasis is on the correct attitude of our knowing and not on the known.

From the ontological standpoint of the Advaita Vedānta, the emphasis is on the thing known. When that is universal and devoid of difference (duality) the knowing faculty too gets concentrated and lost in it (*brahma veda brahmaiva bhavati*); *Brahman* experience is non-dual. The primary aim of the Vedānta and the Vijñānavāda is to seek the truly real and suffuse the mind exclusively with it to the extent that the mind becomes one with the real. Dialectic is employed to demolish difference (*bheda*), plurality (*dvaita*) and particularity (*pariccheda*), thereby indirectly establishing the reality of Pure Being as changeless, universal and self-evident. The Vijñānavāda uses dialectic to disprove the reality of the object and plurality; it thereby indirectly establishes the sole reality of consciousness (*vijñāna*).

The Vedānta not only has an ontology but it also has a full-fledged theory of *avidyā* or *māyā* and gives an explanation of the world of *jīvas* (individuals) and matter. It has a cosmology, although this has an epistemic status only.

For the Mādhyamika the ontologization of categories of thought is the very worst sin one could commit; it is *dṛṣṭi* which it is the function of *śūnyatā* to remove. It is not therefore surprising that he has no doctrines about god, man, matter, creation, etc. Also he does not speculate about the nature of *avidyā*, to whom does it belong and what is its object, etc. The Advaita Vedānta schools, however, have interesting theories about these points. The Mādhyamika has a few things to say about *viparyāsa* (wrong belief or superimposition) and this will be considered later.

We may ask the question : Why is it that the Mādhyamika rejects every alternative standpoint and why does the Vedānta consider the world false (an appearance)?

The Mādhyamika has to make his rejection of views universal; he cannot refute some views, but has to include all philosophies actual (already formulated) and possible (anticipate future philosophies in a general way). He has thus to schematize and bring all philosophical views into his net of the four-cornered conspectus of negation (*catuṣkoṭi*). Universality and completeness is claimed for this much in the strain of Kant's critique or Hegel's dialectic. The question is not of the topical soundness of the schematism, but of the quality and daring, almost of the pretentious nature of the claim made by the Mādhyamika. Without this claim for universality, the Mādhyamika criticism would not be a *dialectic of all philosophy*. Why are all views rejected ? What is the principle on which it is done ? Any fact of experience, when analysed, reveals the inner rift present in its constitution. It is not a thing in itself; it is what it is in relation to other entities, and these in turn depend on others. This process thus proceeds indefinitely and leads to a regress. Practically minded commonsense does not care to go deep. Philosophical systems, in their anxiety to uphold their own views, slur and gloss over the inherent flaw and instability of their contentions. For instance, in causation we must differentiate between the cause and the effect and at the same time identify them. The relation between the two cannot be conceived as identity, difference or both; nor can we give it up. Nāgārjuna says: "Neither of those things is established (as real) which cannot be conceived either as identical or different from each other."[1]

The principle is enunciated in almost every chapter of the Madhyamaka Kārikā. The substance-view thinks that it could have substance without attributes or modes; the modal view believes that it can dispense with substance altogether. There is, however, no attribute without substance nor is substance without attribute. They are not intelligible even together; for how can we then distinguish them? Nāgārjuna, in discussing the relation between a person and his emotions (*rāga* and *rakta*), says that they are not anything either together or separately; likewise, no entity is proved (to exist) as together or separately.[2] There is no self apart from the states (*upādāna*), nor are the latter without the self that gives unity to them; nor are they anything together.[3] The relation between fire and fuel (*agnīndhana*) is examined at length by Nāgārjuna to illustrate this predicament. Fire is not fuel, lest the consumer (agent or *kartā*) and the consumed (object-*karma*) should be identical ; nor is fire different from fuel, for it cannot be had without the latter.[4] All entities, like the Self and its modes (*ātmopādā-*

1. MK. II, 21.
ekībhāvena vā siddhir nānābhāvena vā yayoḥ;
na vidyate tayoḥ siddhiḥ kathaṁ nu khalu vidyate.
MK. XXI, 6.
sahānyonyena vā siddhir vinānyonyena vā yayoḥ;
na vidyate tayoḥ siddhiḥ kathaṁ nu khalu vidyate.
2. MK. VI, 10.
evaṁ raktena rāgasya siddhir na saha nāsaha;
rāgavat sarvadharmāṇāṁ siddhir na saha nāsaha.
3. MK. X, 16.
ātmanaś ca satattvaṁ ye bhāvānāṁ ca pṛthak pṛthak;
nirdiśanti na tān manye śāsanasyārthakovidān.
4. MK. X, 1.
yad indhanaṁ sa ced agnir ekatvaṁ kartṛkarmaṇoḥ;
anyaś ced indhanād agnir indhanād apy ṛte bhavet.

nayoḥ kramaḥ) as well as particular empirical things such as table and chair, are completely covered by this analysis.[1]

Again, it is pointed out that the agent is dependent on the act; and this in turn depends on the agent. All things are to be understood as on a par with the agent and the act.[2] If the definition (*lakṣaṇa*) were different from the definiendum (*lakṣya*), the latter would be bereft of any distinguishing mark; and if both were identical, then there would be the absence of both as such.[3] There is no whole apart from the parts and *vice versa*.[4] Things that derive their being and nature by mutual dependence are nothing in themselves: they are not real.[5]

Relation has to perform two mutually opposed functions; as connecting the two terms, in making them relevant to each other, it has to identify them; but as connecting the two, it has to differentiate them. Otherwise expressed, relation cannot obtain between entities that are identical with or different from each other.[6]

These insuperable difficulties impel us to the conclusion that cause and effect, substance and attribute, whole and parts, subject and object, etc. are mutually dependent, relative; hence they are not things-in-themselves.[7]

1. MK. X, 15.
   agnīndhanābhyāṁ vyākhyāta ātmopādānayoḥ kramaḥ;
   sarvo niravaśeṣeṇa sārdhaṁ ghaṭapaṭādibhiḥ.
2. MK. VIII, 12, 13.
3. Prasannapadā 64.5, 6.
   lakṣyāl lakṣaṇam anyac cet syāt tad lakṣyam alakṣaṇaṁ;
   tayor abhāvo 'nanyatve vispaṣṭaṁ kathitaṁ tvayā.
4. MK. IV, 1.
   rūpakāraṇanirmuktaṁ na rūpam upalabhyate;
   rūpeṇāpi na nirmuktaṁ dṛśyate rūpakāraṇaṁ.
5. *Prasannapadā*, p. 200.
   parasparāpekṣā siddhir na svābhāvikīti
6. MK. XIV, 8.
   na tena tasya saṁsargo, nānyenānyasya yujyate

   Cf. Bradley: "Relation presupposes quality, and quality relation. Each can be something neither together with, nor apart from, the other; and the vicious circle in which they turn is not the truth about Reality." *Appearance and Reality*, p. 21.
7. MK. XVIII, 10.
   pratītya yad yad bhavati na hi tāvat tad eva tat

What is relative is subjective, unreal. The categories are so many conceptual devices (*vikalpa, prapañca*) by which Reason tries to apprehend the Real that cannot be categorised and made relative (*buddher agocaras tattvam*). Reason (*buddhi*) is therefore condemned as falsifying the real (*saṁvṛti*). No phenomenon, no object of knowledge (*bhāva* or *abhāva*) escapes this universal relativity.[1]

Relativity or mutual dependence is a mark of the unreal. A Hegel would have welcomed this inherent dependence of things as the dialectical necessity of Reason working through the opposites, differentiating and at once unifying them. For him that is the mark of the Real. And this, because he does not go beyond Reason; in fact, for Hegel, Reason and Real are identical. For the Mādhyamika, reciprocity, dependence, is the lack of inner essence. *Tattva*, or the Real, is something in itself, self-evident and self-existent.[2] Reason, which understands things through distinction and relation is a principle of falsity, as it distorts and thereby hides the Real.[3] Only the Absolute as the unconditioned is real, and for that very reason it cannot be conceived as existence (*bhāva*) or non-existence (*abhāva*) or both or neither together.

For the Mādhyamika everything is self-inconsistent and nothing can be salvaged out of it. For the Vedānta falsity is a mistake (imposition of one thing on another), and there could not be any mistake without a core of truth or reality. The rope is mistaken for a 'snake'; *Brahman* is mistaken for the world.

MK. VII, 16.

pratītya yad yad bhavati tat tac chāntaṁ svabhāvataḥ.

Bodhicaryāvatārapañjikā (BCAP) p. 352, pratītyasamutpannaṁ vasturūpaṁ saṁvṛtir ucyate.

Thus, pratītyasamutpāda is equated with śūnyatā. See MK. XXIV, 18.

1. MK. XXIV, 19.
apratītya samutpanno dharmaḥ kaścin na vidyate;
yasmāt tasmād aśūnyo hi dharmaḥ kaścin na vidyate.

2. MK. XVIII, 9.
aparapratyayaṁ śāntaṁ prapañcair aprapañcitam;
nirvikalpam anānārtham etat tattvasya lakṣaṇam.

3. Bradley comes to the same conclusion: "The conclusion to which I am brought is that a relational way of thought—any one that moves by the machinery of terms and relations—must give appearance, and not truth." *Appearance and Reality*, p. 28.

The 'snake' is false because the rope alone is real. There cannot be a mere mistake; it is always grounded on something real.

Ultimately, the entire world of appearance rests on the ground of *Brahman.* There is thus no context of illusion which cannot yield reality as its substratum. We have only to remove the cover of appearance to find behind it the real.

III. The two Truths : Saṁvṛti and Paramārtha

All Mādhyamika treatises[1] take the two truths—*paramārtha-satya* and *saṁvṛtisatya*—as vital to the system; some even begin their philosophical disquisitions with the distinction. According to Nāgārjuna, "Those that are unaware of the distinction between these two truths are incapable of grasping the deep significance of the teaching of Buddha."[2] The doctrine is already well-developed in the *Aṣṭasāhasrikā* and other Prajñāpāramitā texts besides *Saddharma Puṇḍarika, Samādhirāja* and similar Mahāyāna Sūtras.

Paramārthasatya, or Absolute Truth, is the knowledge of the real as it is without any distortion (*akṛtrimaṁ vasturūpam*).[3] Categories of thought and points of view distort the real. They unconsciously coerce the mind to view things in a cramped, biassed way, and are thus inherently incapable of giving us the Truth. The *paramārtha* is the utter absence of the function of Reason (*buddhi*) which is therefore equated with *saṁvṛti.* The Absolute truth is beyond the scope of discursive thought, language and empirical activity; and conversely, the object of these is *saṁvṛtisatya.*[4] It is said: "The *paramārtha* is in fact

1. Some chief references where this doctrine is discussed: MK. XXIV; *Madhyamakāvatāra* by Candrakīrti (MA) VI, 23 ff; *Bodhicaryāvatāra* by Śāntideva, IX, i ff; BCAP pp. 352 ff.

2. MK. XXIV, 9.

ye' nayor na vijānanti vibhāgaṁ satyayor dvayoḥ;
te tattvaṁ na vijānanti gambhīraṁ buddhaśāsane.

3. BCAP. p. 354.

paramaḥ uttamo 'rthaḥ, paramārthaḥ akṛtrimaṁ vasturūpaṁ,sarvadharmāṇāṁ niḥsvabhāvatā.

4. From *Satyadvayāvatāra* as quoted in BCAP p. 366; see also *Prasannapadā,* pp. 374-5.

yadi hi paramārthataḥ paramārthasatyaṁ kāyavāṅmanasāṁ viṣayatām upagacchet, na tat paramārthasatyam iti saṅkhyāṁ gacchet. saṁvṛtisatyam the unutterable (*anabhilāpya*), the unthinkable, unteachable etc."[1]

Devoid of empirical determinations, it is the object of the innermost experience of the wise.[2] It is so intimate and integral that we cannot be self-conscious of it.

Saṁvṛtisatya is Truth so-called; truth as conventionally believed in common parlance. Candrakīrti gives three definitions of *saṁvṛti*. As the etymology shows, *saṁvṛti* is that which covers up entirely the real nature of things and makes them appear otherwise. In this sense it is identical with *avidyā*—the categorising function of the mind—Reason. *Tattva* is the unconditioned (*nirvikalpa* and *niṣprapañca*). It may also mean the mutual dependence of things—their relativity. In this sense it is equated with phenomena, and is in direct contrast with the absolute which is by itself unrelated. The third definition of *saṁvṛti* is that which is of conventional nature (*saṅketa*), depending as it does on what is usually accepted by the common folk (*lokavyavahāra*).[3] It is the truth that does not do any violence to what obtains in our everyday world, being in close conformity with

eva tad bhavet, api tu, devaputra, paramārthasatyaṁ sarvavyavahārasamatikrāntaṁ nirviśeṣam asamutpannam aniruddham, abhidheyābhidhānajñeyajñānavigatam, etc.

1. From *Pitāputra Samāgama* as quoted in *Śikṣāsamuccaya* by Śāntideva (ed. by Bendell) (Bib. Buddhica I), p. 256; BCAP. p. 367.

yaḥ punaḥ paramārthah so 'nabhilāpyaḥ, anājñeyaḥ, aparijñeyaḥ, avijñeyaḥ, adeśitaḥ, aprakāśitaḥ etc.

2. BCAP, p. 367.

tad etad āryāṇām eva svasaṁviditasvabhāvatayā pratyātmavedyam, atas tad evātra pramāṇam

kutas tatra paramārthe vācāṁ pravṛttiḥ kuto vā jñānasya. sa hi paramārtho parapratyayaḥ śāntaḥ pratyātmavedya āryāṇāṁ sarvaprapañcātītaḥ.

3. *Prasannapadā* p. 492. 10-12.

samantād varaṇaṁ saṁvṛtiḥ, ajñānaṁ hi samantāt sarvapadārthatattvāvacchādanāt saṁvṛtir ity ucyate; parasparasaṁbhavanaṁ vā saṁvṛtir anyonyasamāśrayeṇety arthaḥ; atha vā saṁvṛtih saṅketo lokavyavahāra ity arthaḥ, sa cābhidhānābhidheyajñānajñey ādilakṣaṇaḥ.

It is in the first sense of *saṁvṛti* as *avidyā* that Śāntideva identifies *saṁvṛti* with *buddhi*. BCA. IX, 2; this is the same as *dṛṣṭi*. See also MA VII. 28. mohaḥ svabhāvāvaraṇād dhi saṁvṛtiḥ, satyam tayā khyāti yad eva kṛtrimam, avidyā hi padārthasatsvarūpāropikā svabhāvadarśanāvaraṇātmikā saṁvṛtiḥ. MA. p. 23.

linguistic conventions and ideas. It is the object of the ignorant and the immature. *Paramārthasatya* is unsignified by language and belongs to the realm of the unutterable, and is experienced by the wise in a very intimate way.[1]

In calling it '*lokasaṁvṛti*', it is implied that there is some appearance which is '*aloka*'—non-empirical, i.e. false for the empirical consciousness even. Cases of optical and other illusions, distorted perceptions caused by diseased and defective sense-organs, experiences in abnormal states of the mind and dream-objects are examples of the '*aloka*' or *mithyā saṁvṛti*.[2] This corresponds to the *prātibhāsika* of the Vedānta.

IV. Avidyā

The first definition of *saṁvṛti* is that it covers entirely the Real and in this sense it is *avidyā* or *viparyāsa*. For the Mādhyamika not only difference but identity too is *avidyā*; the real is neither one nor many, neither permanent nor momentary; neither subject (*vijñāna*) nor object. These are relative to each other and are equally unreal. The Real is purely indeterminate, and all attempts to identify it with Being, Becoming, Consciousness, etc. are *vikalpa*, subjective devices. Nāgārjuna says: "If the apprehension of the impermanent as permanent is illusion, why is the apprehension of the indeterminate as impermanent not illusion as well."[3]

In the Abhidharma, Vedānta and Vijñānavāda systems particular concepts or ways of viewing the real are *avidyā*. For the Mādhyamika, *avidyā* is much wider and more general in scope; conceptualization as such (not merely particular concepts), any view without exception, is *avidyā*. Reason or intellect (*buddhi*) as the faculty of conceptual construction is *avidyā* (*buddhiḥ saṁvṛtir ity ucyate*).

1. BCAP, p. 360.
abhūtārthadarśināṁ pṛthagjanānāṁ mṛṣādarśanaviṣayatayā samādarśitātmasattākam.
MA. VI, 23.
samyagdṛśāṁ yo viṣayaḥ sa tattvaṁ; mṛṣādṛśaṁ saṁvṛtisatyam uktam.
2. MA. VI, 24, 25, 26.
vinopaghātena yad indriyāṇāṁṣ aṇṇām api grāhyam avaiti lokaḥ; satyaṁ tal lokata eva śeṣaṁ vikalpitaṁ lokata eva mithyā.
3. MK. XII, 14.

Avidyā for the Mādhyamika is itself unreal, it is *māyā*. If it were real, its products too would be real and there could be no question of negating, or even changing the world process. Nāgārjuna puts the matter dialectically thus: "If the passions belonged to one as an integrally real part of one's nature, how could they be abandoned; the real cannot be rejected by anyone. If the passions did not belong to anyone, how could they be abandoned; for, who could abandon the unreal, the non-existent? It is concluded that *kleśas*, *karmas* and their results are of the stuff of fairy castles, mirages and dreams."[1]

The Vedānta offers full explanation of *avidyā*, evidence for its presence and the way it functions. *Avidyā* is the principle of creativity (the *śakti* of *Brahman*) by which the non-dual eternal Being, becomes, 'appears' as many and is differentiated. It is a beginningless quasi-positive entity, though not eternal, and is of the nature of Name and Form (*avyaktanāmarūpa*). It functions in an *a priori* way. The empirical world is a joint product of *Brahman* and *avidyā*. It belongs to *Brahman*, as only a conscious being capable of knowledge can be ignorant. And that can be only undifferentiated universal Pure Being (*nirvibhāga citi*); for particular beings (*jīvas*) presuppose difference which is the function of *avidyā*.

In the last analysis, *avidyā* or *māyā* represents the freedom of *Brahman*, to appear as the world or not to appear, or to appear in any other form. It is the principle by which the Transcendence of *Brahman* is safeguarded and yet there is the world appearance as from *Brahman*. *Māyā* has an epistemic status only. The relation between *Brahman* and *māyā* is one-sided identity: *māyā* depends on *Brahman*, but *Brahman* can be free of *māyā*.

As in the case of the Absolute, the doctrine of two truths also is liable to misinterpretation. There are not two different spheres or sets of objects to which these apply. There would then be no point in calling one *saṁvṛti* and the other *paramārtha*; the two might be different, but one would not be less real than the other. The difference is in our manner of looking at things. All things put on two forms owing to the manner of our apprehension: one is the *tattva* which is the object of right knowledge and

1. MK. XXIII, 24, 25.

the other is the object of false knowledge. In fact, there is only one Truth—the *paramārthasatya,* as there is only one real—the Absolute. The other —*saṁvṛtisatya,* is truth so-called in common parlance; it is totally false from the absolute standpoint.

It might be asked, if *saṁvṛti* is ultimately to be rejected and not retained in the *paramārtha,* why consider it at all? We should concern ourselves with the *paramārtha* alone. But can we do so without taking the help of the *saṁvṛti* (*vyāvahārika*) ? If we had been already rooted in the Absolute (*paramārtha*), there should not be any occasion or use for *saṁvṛti.* The *paramārtha,* however, can be understood and realized only negatively, *only as we remove the saṁvṛti,* the forms which thought has already, unconsciously and beginninglessly, ascribed to the real. The Real is to be *un*covered, *dis*covered and realized as the reality of appearances (*dharmāṇāṁ dharmatā*). In the order of our discovery, the removal of *saṁvṛti* must precede our knowledge of the *paramārtha.* The *paramārtha* is the end or goal that we seek to attain, and *saṁvṛti* is the means; it is the ladder or the jumping board which enables us to reach that objective. It is therefore stated that *saṁvṛti* is the means (*upāyabhūta*) and *paramārtha* is the end (*upeyabhūta*). Basing ourselves on *vyavahāra* do we advance to the *paramārtha.*

The Four Holy Truths have to be understood as included in these two: *nirodhasatya* as *nirvāṇa* is *paramārtha* and the other three including the *mārga,* are within *saṁvṛti.* Even the spiritual discipline (*mārga*) undertaken for attaining *nirvāṇa,* exalted and purifying as it is, is within *saṁvṛti.* So too, the four fruits of the discipline are within *saṁvṛti.* The Prajñāpāramitā goes so far as to say that even Buddhahood is illusory like a dream or *māyā*; if there were anything higher than that even, it has to be pronounced to be within *saṁvṛti.* The reason is that the scope of *saṁvṛti* is co-terminus with the range of concepts and words, with any kind of distinction and duality.

V. Conception of Relation in the Mādhyamika and Vedānta

For the Mādhyamika, both the terms of a relational complex are false; as mutually dependent, they lack an essential nature of their own. The relativity of things is their unreality. The cause and the effect are neither identical with nor different from each other, nor both, nor neither. There is no substance without attributes, nor attributes without substance; the self (*ātman*) is not one with its states; nor is it anything apart from them. Like Bradley, who lays down that qualities are nothing within or without relation and so too relation, the Mādhyamika enunciates his dictum that both those things are unreal which cannot be conceived as either identical with or different from each other.

The Vedāntist will not reject both the terms as relative; he accepts one as the reality or the basis of the other. For the Mādhyamika, the substance and the attributes are equally unreal, as neither of them can be had apart from the other. The Vedāntist would say that the attributes are mere ascriptions of substance, the particulars are negations of the universal and are, therefore, unreal by their very nature (*svarūpato mithyā*); but the substance or the universal is inherently real; only its seeming relationship with the attributes or particulars is false (*saṁsargato mithyā*); it has a transcendent nature without the relation.

The general formula applicable to the Vedānta is: the terms sustaining a relation are not of the same order, one is *higher*, and the other *lower*; the two terms are neither mutually dependent nor mutually independent; relation is neither 'internal' nor 'external'. If mutually dependent, we cannot distinguish between the two terms, as they so necessarily imply each other that one cannot exist without the other any time. We cannot even say that there are two terms,as the basis of distinction is lacking. If mutually independent, there is no basis of connection; each term is a self, a self-contained universe as it were. To escape this dilemma, we have to conceive one term as basic and capable of existing apart from its relation to the other and the other incapable of so doing and therefore dependent. One term, the higher, is not exhausted in the relationship; it has a transcendent or non-implicatory existence which is its intrinsic nature. The other term, however, is entirely exhausted within the relation and has no non-relative existence (*prātibhāsika, pratibhāsa-mātraśārīratvam*).

VI. Views on Language

I may very briefly indicate the function of language in the two systems. For the Mādhyamika language is a conventional set of symbols which has no reference outside this convention to any referent, to fact or reality. The meaning of a term or concept is another term or concept. That is, we never get out of the convention. This is *saṁvṛti* as *lokavyavahāra*, as conformity with linguistic conventions and ideas. Speech has no revelatory function.

The Vedānta on the other hand holds that though *literally* we cannot speak of *Brahman* as meant by the word, it can still *indicate* the presence of *Brahman* in a metaphorical or symbolical way (*lakṣyārtha*). In fact, it is through the Scriptural Word (*vāk*), that we initially derive our knowledge of *Brahman*. *Brahman* is known only through the Upaniṣads.[1] In the last analysis, *vāk* (speech) and *Brahman* may even be identical.

VII. Śūnyatā as Freedom

It is the contention of the Mādhyamika that the final release is possible only through *śūnyatā*—by the giving up of all views, standpoints and predicaments. The root cause of *duḥkha* in this system, is the indulging in views (*dṛṣṭis*) or imagination (*kalpanā*, *vikalpa*). *Kalpanā* is *avidyā par excellence*. The real is the indeterminate (*śūnya*); investing it with a character, determining it as 'this' or 'not this' is to make the Real one-sided, partial and unreal.

Nāgārjuna analyses the nature of bondage and freedom thus : "Of constructive imagination are born attachment, aversion and infatuation, depending (respectively) on our good, evil and stupid attitudes. Entities which depend on these are not anything by themselves. The *kleśas* are unreal."[2] "Freedom (*mokṣa*) is the cessation of *karma* and *kleśa* (acts and passions); these arise from *vikalpa* (imaginative construction); this ceases with the knowledge of their falsity (*śūnyatā*)."[3] *Śūnyatā* is the antidote for all *kleśas*. When the real is not misapprehended as an *ens* or as a non-*ens* there is cessation of *kalpanā* and the cessation of *kalpanā* is *nirvāṇa*. Thus the abandonment of all views and standpoints is the means to freedom; it is a disburdenment and a

1. Śaṅkara's *Bhāṣya* on *Brahma Sūtra* I, i, 3.
tam tu aupaniṣadaṁ puruṣaṁ pṛcchāmi
2. MK. XXII. 1, 2.
3. MK. XVIII, 5.

great relief. It is Freedom itself. It is for this soteriological purpose that *śūnyatā* is taught and practised. It is a species of spiritual regeneration. But we should not take the cure of the disease as one more reality. Both the disease (*saṁsāra*) and its cure (*śūnyatā*) are equally within phenomena. We are therefore warned not to consider *śūnyatā* to be another *dṛṣṭi*.

For the Vedānta, '*Tat tvam asi*' (That thou art), '*aham Brahma asmi*' (I am Brahman), is the saving knowledge which engenders freedom through knowledge of identity between the Self (*ātman*) and *Brahman* (Universal Being). But this saving knowledge is itself phenomenal.

In both the Mādhyamika and the Vedānta freedom is the abandoning of the egoistic standpoint and attainment of the universal. The attainment is conceived somewhat more positively as Brahmahood, while the Mādhyamika will not allow us to characterize it in any manner in keeping with his *śūnyatā*.

VIII. Conclusion

I have interpreted *śūnyatā* and the doctrine of Two Truths as a kind of Absolutism, not Nihilism. Nāgārjuna's 'no views about reality' should not be taken as advocating 'a no-reality view'. I find myself, therefore, unable to accept Dr. Streng's interpretation that Nāgārjuna does not accept, even by implication, any ultimate Reality and that there is no Absolute in his system. All absolutism need not be of the Vedāntic type, and I have drawn, in the course of this paper, the difference between the Vedānta and the Mādhyamika philosophies. I have pointed out that the Mādhyamika is epistemological in his procedure while the Vedānta is ontological. The former is an *advayavāda* (no two views), while the latter is an *advaita* (no two things). The Mādhyamika does not allow us to characterize and clothe the real in empirical terms and concepts (*prapañca, vikalpa*); even *nirvāṇa* or the *tathāgata* should not be theorized about. In the final resort *śūnyatā* by which all things are pronounced unreal, is itself not an end, an entity, but only a means, a remedy to cure a malady. All this is acceptable. But does this 'no view about reality' amount to a 'no-reality view'? That would be a species of nihilism. Both Nāgārjuna and Candrakīrti very vigorously protest against construing *śūnyatā* as "*abhāvārtha*"[1]

1. MK. XXIV.

(nihilism). *Tattva* (The Real) is accepted and is even defined "as transcendent to thought", as non-relative, non-determinate, quiescent, non-discursive, non-dual.[1] True, the Absolute does not possess any attribute of its own, but its presence can be indicated even by an ascribed mark (*samāropāt*). It is asked: "How can the *anakṣara* (the Inexpressible) be understood and taught (declared)?" The Absolute is known as the reality of the appearances, what they falsely stand for.[2]

What happens to the distinction between the Two Truths, the *paramārtha* and *saṁvṛti*? In Dr. Streng's view the *paramārtha* would itself be a species of the conventional and having done its business of rejecting the conventional truths it will itself collapse into nothing. For him, the distinction between the two is only provisional and tactical. There cannot be anything outside the conventional. In reality there is no distinction, and this basic contention of the Mādhyamika has to be given up. In pronouncing everything as *śūnya* does not Nāgārjuna rely on an absolute criterion of the Real as *aparapratyaya* (non-dependent) and *prapañcopaśamam* and *śivam* (free from speech elaboration and benign)? "All things are relative" (*pratītyasamutpannam*). Is this a statement which is itself relative or is it a perception of Truth (*prajñā*)? If the former, its relativity cannot rest on itself nor on the things of which it is a statement. If it were to rest on some other higher statement, this will only lead to a *regressus ad infinitum*. To avoid all this, it is more consistent to take it as a *perception*, (not a logical statement) of truth.

Dr. Streng accepts that *śūnyatā* serves a soteriological purpose and is religiously motivated. In that sense it differs from modern positivism or linguistic philosophy. But how can this purpose be secured if nothing is left over as Real, after the rejection of all things as relative? It is as if a man suffering from headache were told to cut off his head. Of course, he vould be 'cured', for he will have nothing to complain about. In our view, both the headache and its cure and the antidote will be of the same phenomenal order; but the head would remain.

1. MK. XVIII, 9.
2. *Prasannapadā* p. 264, 6, 7 and BCAP, p. 365.
   anakṣarasya dharmasya śrutiḥ kā deśanā ca kā
   śrūyate deśyate cāpi samāropād anakṣaraḥ.

The solution offered by Nāgārjuna to the problem of suffering is really to say that there is no problem, or the problem is of our own making. Even this has to be realized through a spiritual discipline culminating in this conviction. The Vedānta also says the same thing. We are all *Brahman*, only we do not know that we are so. "The individual illusorily thinks he is not free and wants to be free. To his consciousness, accordingly, there is the necessity of a *sādhanā* or discipline to attain freedom. This discipline must be such as will lead him to realize that his bondage is an illusion and that he is eternally free."[1]

1. K. C. Bhattacharyya, *Studies in Philosophy*, Vol. I, p. 118, Progressive Publishers, Calcutta.

5.4 VEDĀNTA AND BUDDHISM*

The title of the Seminar, "Vedānta and Buddhism" is posed as a kind of comparative or related study of these two basic philosophies. It would not do to consider either of them in isolation. The related study could possibly be historical, a chronological and sequential tracing of each (Vedānta and Buddhism) as they influenced each other's development. Such a study would really form part of cultural history and should be based on literary documents and historical evidence. It would also be largely conjectural and somewhat speculative. I surmise some participants would be concentrating on this aspect of the problem. They might be able to throw light on several points in this question : (1) Whether, and to what extent early Buddhism was independent of Upaniṣadic thought; (2) how a philosophy and religion which was radically pluralistic and atheistic (rather antitheistic) could become as absolutistic and even theistic as in the Mahāyāna; (3) whether this was purely the development of an inner dynamism or was prompted, partly at least, by external influences and (4) lastly whether and in what measure the characteristic development of the classical Vedānta of Gauḍapāda and Śaṅkara was not itself influenced by the Mahāyāna philosophy (Mādhyamika and Yogācāra-Vijñānavāda). Extreme loyalists, on either side, are prone to deny or belittle any such mutual influence. It may, however, be surmised that as Buddhism and Vedānta were not moving in closed compartments and as there is ample evidence of lively interchanges between them, mutual influence may legitimately be surmised. The precise nature of it, however, has to be determined. Influence is not necessarily borrowing or acceptance of doctrines from others. That too is influence which stimulates the systems to modify, revise or even to reaffirm their doctrines. Influence may be expressed as much through opposition as by acceptance. In this sense alone have the Brāhmaṇical systems, Vedānta and Nyāya, been influenced by Buddhism and vice versa.

*Reprinted from *Seminar Papers*, The Centre of Advanced Study in Philosophy, Banaras Hindu University, 1968.

Attention should also be paid to the inherent dynamism present in each system of thought which impels it to develop along certain lines irrespective of outside influence. Inadequate appreciation of this factor explains, to a considerable extent, the unjust accusation that the development of Mahāyāna is foreign to Buddha's thought or Śaṅkara's non-dualism, his Māyāvāda, is not the genuine teaching of the Upaniṣads.

There is no doubt that almost a revolution occurred in the Upaniṣadic tradition (*ātmavāda*) as well as in the Buddhistic (*anātmavāda*) in the course of their long development. Buddhism which, in its earlier phase, was a radical pluralism became in the Mahāyāna an as radical absolutism with a different conception of the Buddha and the Bodhisattva ideal. How could this occur ?

Two answers are possible, one that of borrowing from or being influenced by the Upaniṣadic thought where absolutism and theism are such dominant features; the other hypothesis would deny external influence and seek to account for the revolution as the result of an inner dynamism in Buddhist thought itself. These two views are not exclusive, and perhaps the truth lies somewhere between the two.

Owing to my own inadequate equipment in this regard, rather than to the unimportance of the subject, I shall deal with this only marginally, if at all. My interest lies in an analytic study of these two systems or two traditions as examples of the basic radical types of philosophy.

Does all Indian philosophy stem from one original source—the Upaniṣads ? And are all Indian religions variations of the Vedic ? Following the lead of Professor Radhakrishnan, the foremost Indian thinker of today, there is a large and impressive body of opinion favouring the unilinear tradition and development of Indian thought. In the estimation of the Buddhist and non-Buddhist (Jaina and Brāhmaṇical) orthodox tradition, the differences between the two are radical. To my mind both these estimates seem to suffer from the fallacy of over-simplification. Probably, the truth lies somewhere in the middle. A careful analysis would reveal that Hinduism (Brāhmaṇism) and Buddhism belong to the same genus; they differ as species. In a sense, they are complementary to each other; one emphasises what the other lacks or slurs over. Without affinity they would have been completely sundered from each other; without differences they could not have vitalised and enriched each other. In view of the difference in their basic standpoints and the mode of their historical development, we should be alive to their differences as much as we affirm their affinities. My main purpose in this paper is to throw into relief the basic differences between Buddhism and Advaita Vedānta.

As philosophers we should try to understand and appreciate each standpoint intrinsically from within; no attempt should be made to reduce or assimilate other systems of thought to the one familiar to ns. The world would be poorer if we reduce all differences to a dull uniformity. It would be difficult to find two philosophies so different as Vedānta and Buddhism. Buddhism has special claim to our attention as a very sustained philosophy of Becoming, of taking reality sequentially as a process. It took Time seriously and was not afraid of facing the consequences.

All systems of Hindu thought subscribe to the *ātmavāda*—the conception of reality as Being, substance and permanent. In its most radical form, as in the Vedānta of Śaṅkara, it denied the reality of change, and characterised it as appearance. The Buddhist schools rejected the reality of the soul or substance (*anātmavāda*) and conceived the real as Becoming. The real for them is sequential, momentary, incessantly perishing and emerging. There is no inner and immutable core in things; everything is in flux. For the Buddhists, the notions of soul, substance, universal and identity are thought-constructions, subjective. This constructive activity of thought, however, is transcendental in character, not empirical. Belief in the soul or the substance (*ātman*) is a basic wrong notion (*avidyā*, ignorance) which is at the root of all suffering. Salvation would result if the belief in *ātman* is abandoned. For, only as we take anything as abiding and identical do we become attached to it, cling to it; we are also averse to things that are opposed to it. The result is tension and conflict. For the Vedānta, which may be considered as the most consistent form of Brāhmaṇical thought, ignorance is just the reverse; it is the conceiving of the real as changeful, different and particular. And when we realise the real as truly universal and identical (differenceless), as *ātman*, do we get freed of limitations and reach Brahmanhood. In both the Ego is transcended : in Buddhism this is done by denying it altogether; in the *advaita* by universalising and identifying it with God or Brahman.

Religious or practical differences determine the nature of philosophical differences.

II

The Two Patterns of Indian Religious Thought

A great philosopher of the West—Kant—speaks of the two appalling infinites—"the starry Heavens above and the Moral Law within man." The 'starry heavens' is not to be understood as the mere immensity of physical Nature, but the *mysterium tremendum* of the Author of the Universe. The two infinities symbolise the two basic patterns of religious consciousness—one being God-centered and the other man-centered. In a sense, Hinduism (Brāhmaṇism) and Buddhism may be taken as illustrative of these two basic patterns.

The source of religious inspiration in Brāhmaṇism is the revelation as given to us in the Vedas; in Buddhism it is reason. Not that Brāhmaṇism is antagonistic to reason or is unmindful of its value; but it is only revelation which can give us intuitions of the transcendent. The function of reason is to analyse and to clarify and, if necessary, to defend and to remove apparent contradictions. The role of reason is somewhat negative, like the hedge that protects the growing field of corn from depredation by stray cattle. Innovations are only interpretations of the given truth, and originality is not so much the discovery of new truths as of meanings and emphases. The entire mode of development in Hinduism is authoritarian and traditional. We could even take it as theological in character. The core or the initial knowledge is of divine inspiration; but it does not remain an imposed belief, but one which is to be realised in one's intimate experience (*anubhavāvasānatvād brahmavijñānasya*).

In contrast to this, Buddha asks us not to receive anything on trust or to accept any authority, but to test it by reason and experience. He himself did not owe allegiance to any authority, Vedic or non-Vedic. This initial doctrine was modified later, and Buddhists themselves acquired a considerable body of scriptures in the teaching of Buddha, and philosophical disputes were quite often settled by exegetical considerations.

The reason for the difference in the two inspirations takes us to the heart of each religion.

The fundamental principle in Buddhism is the autonomy of of Moral Law (*Karma*)—the freedom that we feel and exercise in our actions and which determines what we are and what we would be. The Law is moral, i.e., it is not a natural or mechanistic operation of brute necessity. Nor is it the dictate of an inscrutable and capricious Person—God. The moral Law is impersonal; it has absolute authority, no matter whether it is fulfilled frequently or seldom or not at all, its authority is innate and underived. The moral Law is perfectly autonomous.

This was not an altogether new idea discovered by Buddha or Mahāvīra. The Ṛg Vedic hymns speak of the Ṛta and Satya, the Order and Truth of the universe; the Deities Indra, Agni and Varuṇa are invariably spoken of as Dhṛtavrata (upholders of the moral order), as *satya dharma*, as *dharmasya goptā*. It is not, as in the Semitic religions, God's fiat that makes anything moral or good. There is an innate propriety in things, their *dharma* or nature. The Deities only reveal and uphold this order; they do not create the order. The impersonality of the Law of Karma was also first developed as a cosmic principle by the Mīmāṁsakas who were the first to deny a personal god. Unfortunately, the *Karma* or *Dharma* they understood and were interested in was ritualistic or ceremonial acts. It was *Karma* (performance of what the Gītā terms *dravya yajña*) and not duty or moral *karma*. And it was with the latter that the Buddha and Mahāvīra were concerned.

Taking his stand on the autonomy of the Moral Law, the Buddha was led to deny two opposed standpoints : one Naturalism (*svabhāvavāda* or *ucchedavāda*) which totally denied, as is done by the Cārvāka or the Ājīvika, the moral Law (free act and its result, *Karma* and *Karmaphala*), and reduced man to a fortuitous conglomeration of natural forces. The other oppo ed standpoint is that of Eternalism (*śāśvatavāda*) which stood for the Transcendent Freedom of God (and even of an unchanging Soul or *ātman*) who is above the moral Law (karma). The Buddha characterises both *ucchedavāda* and *śāśvatavāda* as species of Inactivism.

Salvation or rather Freedom is freedom from moral evil, from passions and their defilement (*saṁskāra*); spiritual discipline is the path of purification (*viśuddhimārga*) and this is achieved through self-effort and self-regeneration. There is no place for outside help or divine guidance. Salvation is strictly a sustained and heroic act on the part of man himself. It is not an act of God or a cooperation between man and God. We have in Buddhism, at least in early Buddhism, a moral religion, a universal religion without God, a perfection of self-discipline and self-analysis. As the spiritual discipline is a catharsis or eradication of passions, the goal is described negatively as Nirvāṇa.

The position of earlier Buddhism was considerably modified in the Mahāyāna. Buddha becomes to all intents and purposes a Divine Person—the free phenomenalisation of the impersonal Absolute or *Dharmakāya*. This revolution enters Buddhism through the unique position of the Buddha and his personality.

III

Philosophy of Becoming (Universal Flux) and the Conception of Dharma (Entity)

Buddhism is a very consistent and rigorous form of the philosophy of Becoming. It takes the Real as Becoming, as dynamic and is opposed to the conception of the Real as Being or Substance. In the beginning this was stated as a principle of observation, especially in the context of moral consciousness. Existence is declared *anicca*, *anatta* and *dukkha* in the Pali Canons. "All things are composite and the composite is transitory and painful." Later on this was formulated in rigorous logical form and deduced from Universal Causation.

The Real is the efficient (*arthakriyākāri*). The permanent as the non-efficient is unreal. Efficiency can be either simultaneous or successive. If simultaneous, all the effects being completed at once, it may be asked whether the permanent exists after the first moment or not. If it does, it should produce the same effects in the second and succeeding moments, thus giving rise to an interminable series of the same effect from one cause. This is an absurdity. If it does not produce this series, though continuing to exist in the succeeding moments, then it is evident that there is a manifest difference in its nature between the first and other moments; for, in the first moment it is efficient (samartha), while in other moments it is not so (*asamartha*) with regard to the same effect. *That cannot be one of which two or more opposed characteristics are predicated.* Nor is the permanent efficient successively, e. g. A first produces X, then Y, then Z. It should be asked whether A is capable of producing Y when it is producing X. If it could do so, A would precipitate all the effects at once, and the second alternative will have been reduced to the first one of simultaneous production. If it is not capable, it will never produce the effect, as a piece of stone cannot produce the sprout, given any length of time. If we still think that A is one and the same entity in two or more moments, then it is both efficient and inefficient at once with regard to the same effect.

It may be objected that a cause (e.g. the seed) is the same; only, the efficiency is owing to the presence or absence of auxiliaries. But do the auxiliaries (*sahakāri*) mean anything to the permanent ? The mere inoperative presence of them will not bring about any result. They must therefore first *modify* the seed before it can sprout; it is the seed as *changed* that produces the effect. If the modification were an integral part of the seed, it should have that always. If it were not, then the seed would have two natures—one, what it is in itself and the other, what it becomes in response to its auxiliaries. But accepting two natures of a thing is really to accept two things, according to the Buddhist dictum. Thus things are different every moment; difference of time is difference of things; at no two moments is a thing identical. Existence is momentary (*kṣaṇika*).

The same conclusion can be enforced by the consideration of decay and destruction. The vulgar notion is that a thing will continue to exist unless it is destroyed by opposite forces. But if a thing is not capable of destruction by itself, no amount of external influence can affect it, much less reduce it to nothing. The blow from a stick destroys the pitcher, it may be said. But if destruction were not inherent in the pitcher, the blow should mean nothing to it; it should continue to exist untouched as before, like empty space. If the destruction were inherent to the pitcher, the blow of the stick is merely an occasion for its cessation, it does not bring it about. Consider for a moment what is meant by the ageing or decaying of a thing. It is not the case that a thing continues to exist unaffected for any stretch of time and then suddenly begins to change. It changes every moment, uniformly, unperceivedly, relentlessly. Change or even birth is death every moment; the thing must become different at every moment of its existence. *Permanence of a thing is an illusion*, like the oneness of the flame or of the stream. Existence is flux. A thing is a point-instant, having neither a 'before' nor an 'after'; it has no span temporally; there is no duration. Cessation is inherent in things and is entire (*ahaituko niranvayo vināśaḥ*).

Precisely the same logic is applied to refute the reality of the whole (*avayavi*). What constitutes one thing? We might hold with common sense that the table is one entity, the tree is one, though they may consist of parts. But the table is partly seen and partly not, as it is impossible to see all the parts at once. Parts of the tree move and some other parts do not; a part of it is in shade and a part of it is sunlit. How can that be one entity to which two or more opposed characteristics (e.g. seen and unseen, moving and unmoving, dark and sunlit) are ascribed? It is not possible to escape this logic by stating that what is moving is one part and what is not moving is different from it. For, both the parts belong to the *same* thing; the characteristics of the parts belong to the thing—the whole—of which they are parts. Therefore there are as many things as there are distinguishable parts or aspects. An entity has no extensity or complexity of content. The oneness of many things (parts and aspects) is illusory as the oneness of a heap of corn. Horizontally, spatially, a thing has no expanse. It is not only an instant (*kṣaṇika*) lacking duration, but a spatial point lacking all magnitude and diversity as well.

By the same logic we are led to the denial of the universal (*sāmānya*) or identical aspect of things. Each entity is discrete and unique (*svalakṣaṇa*). The existence of the universal, uniform and identical, in all the particulars is beset with insuperable difficulties. How can one entity exist in a number of particulars separated by distance of space and time, in entirety, untouched by what happens to the particulars? Moreover, in cognising a thing, we do not certainly cognise it (the particular) and its duplicate (the universal). Wherefrom does a universal, say cowhood, enter into a new-born cow? Where does it go when the cow dies? All existence, for the Buddhist, is particular; the universal is a thought-construct, a vikalpa. The philosophy of Becoming leads to Nominalism (*apohavāda*).

The real is momentary; it is simple, unitary; it is particular, unique. This view militates against the conception of the real as permanent, as substance, as universal and identical. All things, physical and spiritual, exhibit this pattern; there is no exception. It is not, as in the Sāṅkhya, that while the object changes, the self does not change. Nor is change considered as the change of a permanent underlying substance that is continuous in the effect. Change is the *replacement* of one entity by another; it is the cessation of one and the emergence of another. Existence is the momentary flash into being and subsidence into non-being of material and mental states—feelings, perception, volition etc. No doubt the states can be grouped under various combinations into skandha, dhātu and āyatana etc., but the combination is not real over and above the constituents. The components are real (*vastusat*); the combination is appearance (*prajñaptisat*). What we usually take as the self or the soul (ātman) can be analysed, without residue, into the several mental states, citta and caitta. There is no abiding and continuous self over-lapping these states and in which they inhere. The *pudgala* or the individual is an appearance; it constitutes the primary ignorance (*avidyā*; *satkāya-dṛṣṭi*).

There is not, in the whole range of philosophical literature, a more rigorous and complete formulation of the philosophy of Becoming. Heracleitus just propounds the basic principles. Hume gives an account of the self which is largely Buddhistic, but he fails to give an adequate explanation of mental life in terms of this philosophy and is even afraid of the consequences of his position. William James, Bergson, Whitehead and Charles Hatshorne and some of the vogues of Existentialism explain some aspect or other of Becoming, but nowhere do we have a full and consistent account as in Buddhism.

The arguments used by the Buddhists are apagogic in character; they do not directly prove their position; but indirectly do so by disproving the opposite theory. To be cogent, it must be shown that there are only two alternatives in any situation; rejection of one would mean the recovery or acceptance of the other. Apart from this, I do not think that the Buddhist arguments are less cogent and convincing than that of any other philosophy. The Sāṅkhya, for instance, adduces only apagogic proof for its satkārya theory. The metaphysics of Universal

Flux entails a radical theory of knowledge and logic. It is committed to a thorough-going nominalism and the doctrine of two exclusive modes of knowledge. The latter is deduced from the two orders of reality (*mānadvaividhyam meyadvaividhyāt*)—the unique particular (*svalakṣaṇa*) which alone is ultimately real and the other the phenomenal entity which is the object of empirical reference and communication (*sāmānyalakṣaṇa*).

Both the philosophy of non-dual Being and Universal Becoming depart to a great extent from commonsense notions. They had to formulate two orders of existence and to work out a consistent two-level theory. What is real for one is appearance for the other and vice versa. For the Advaita the real is the nitya (eternal, permanent) and the changeful is appearance. For the Buddhist, it is just the reverse.

IV

The Advaita and the Mādhyamika Absolutism

Scholars of Mahāyāna Buddhism and the Advaita Vedānta have not failed to notice some resemblances between them. In fact, many of them were so impressed by this that they have taken the Advaita Vedānta to be little different from the Mādhyamika or the Vijñānavāda. It is true that these systems are absolutisms and that they reach absolutism through dialectic and negation; that they have to formulate a doctrine of two truths and that they have a consequential and complementary spiritual discipline leading to *nirvāṇa* or *mokṣa.* It is, however, necessary to take a closer look to find out whether the categories they employ really mean the same thing. I shall confine my observations to the Mādhyamika and the Advaita Vedānta.

1. The Advaita is a philosophy of Being; it is a sustained investigation having Brahman (God) as the subject of its enquiry. Philosophy is therefore *brahma-jijñāsā* or *brahma-vidyā.* It has no other content or concern. Brahman is Universal Being; and as foundational and undeniable, in any context whatever, it is necessary Being. We cannot acquire or appropriate it, for we are never outside it. Knowing Brahman or Being is unlike knowing any empirical object, e.g., chair, table, for these could well be absent or appear in a changed form. Again, in knowing empirical objects, we invariably apply a universal or an essence

through which they are made intelligible. In a sense they are instances of the essence or the universal. Sometimes, they are contrasted with their opposites or contraries. There are no instances, exemplifications of Universal Being; for, from the nature of the case, there could not be two or more such beings. Brahman is unique and by itself (*ekam eva advitiyam*), a Real Individual. It also follows that it is not known through any essence or representation, there being no need for it in this case. It is known in itself, self-evident, as being intelligible without mediation (*svayamprakāśa*). So if we know being anywhere any time we know it in itself entirely and directly (*sakṛd vibhātam*). It might, however, be sought to be held that this is still hypothetical. Do we know being at all or know it only sometimes? We cannot help knowing Being and we know it invariably. At least in one case, with regard to the 'I' (Self) we know it undeniably, for denial itself is affirmation in this context. It can also be stated that in knowing any object (chair, table, etc.) I am aware of Being. The Vedānta therefore holds that Being or Brahman is the *object of every cognition*, any experience whatever (*sarvapratyayavedya*).

It is also held at the same time that Brahman is not known or that it is transcendent. This is true in a different way. If we are asked to enumerate or describe the things in this room, we would count the chairs, tables, the men and women, the ceiling fans, etc. But we would invariably fail to take note of the air, the light or the space itself. These things escape our notice by their sheer unobtrusiveness, invariability and pervasiveness. By their non-concreteness and invariability, they fail to arrest our attention. In fact, the obtrusive objects occupy our attention instead. To perceive the pervasiveness and underlying features, we have to abstract or withdraw from the surface things. To be aware of Being, as Being, universal and invariable, we have to *see through* or put away the surface things or think them away. Dialectic or negation is employed to remove the undergrowth and thus to uncover the ground of Being. Negation is p ocedural and not an end in itself. The primary distinction for the Advaita is that of Appearance and Reality. They are not to be taken as two separate things, but as non-different. The Advaita Vedānta is a two-level philosophy.

It may appear that I am formulating a species of the

ontological argument in my account of Being (*Brahman*). This is true in a way. But here the accent is not on any *concept* or idea of Being, but the actual, intimate and direct acquaintance with Being itself or in the objective attitude.

Though not literally true, it is still not unmeaningful in the Vedānta to speak of knowledge *of Brahman.* The 'of' is an accusative genitive (*brahmaṇa iti karmaṇi ṣaṣṭhi*). The attitude is basically objective and ontological. Brahman is the object of philosophy and the only object of philosophy. Although it is free from empiricality, or contingent features, Brahman is not itself *śūnya* (Void or Nothing). We may become explicitly aware of *Brahman* (Being) through negating what it is not (*neti neti, adhyāropāpavāda*); but in itself it is not Negation or non-Being, although men of weak perception may misconstrue it so (*digdeśa-guṇa-gati-phala-bhedaśūnyaṁ hi paramārthasad advayaṁ brahma manda-buddhīnām asad iva pratibhāti*).

In the Mādhyamika, there is nothing to know. Philosophy is not the knowledge of any entity, Being or Becoming (Process), universal or particular, etc. Philosophy is the consciousness of its own activity or function; philosophical consciousness comes of age as it were. This is achieved by the refutation of views (*dṛṣṭis*), not of some views regarding things (even God or Tathāgata included), but by a thoroughgoing negative dialectic. The Mādhyamika has to make his rejection of views universal, i.e., not merely refute some views, but all philosophies actual (already formulated) and possible (anticipate future philosophies in a general way). He has thus to schematise and bring all philosophical views into his net of the Four-cornered conspectus or Negation. Universality and completeness is claimed for this much in the strain of Kant's critique or Hegel's dialectic. The question is not of the logical soundness of the schematism, but of the quality and daring, almost pretentious nature of the claim made by the Mādhyamika. Without this claim for universality, the Mādhyamika criticism would not be a *dialectic of all philosophy.*

The dialectic is here not a means which leads to a knowledge of any entity (Brahman or God), but is an end. Dialectic itself is philosophy. The starting point of the Mādhyamika is not an existential situation; it emerges with the philosophical views or formulations as actually propounded by speculative philosophies. Their antinomical conflict on every issue of importance is an eye-opener; criticism or *prajñā* emerges. The primordial opposition or contrast in the Mādhyamika is between *dṛṣṭi* and *prajñā* (dogmatic or speculative philosophy and criticism which self-consciously refuses to take positions). Nowhere does the Mādhyamika concern himself directly with issues like God, Soul, matter, creation, etc. but only indirectly in his criticism of the philosophical views about these.

I am not here concerned with examining the particular arguments adduced by Nāgārjuna or any other Mādhyamika in each case, nor even with the soundness of the *reductio ad absurdum* method in general. I should, however, like to demonstrate the possibility, nay even the necessity, of the distinction between *dṛṣṭi* and *prajñā*. There have always been philosophies, conflicting philosophies, and philosophers have also disputed about their philosophies. Philosophical disputes not only mean differences, perhaps incommensurable differences, but also imply an impartial tribunal to which the disputants appeal. This need not be a third party external to the disputants but a higher light of reason or *prajñā* in each of the disputants (the distinction between Phillip drunk and Phillip sober). In fact, *dṛṣṭi* and *prajñā*, like the Vedāntic Reality and Appearance, are not to be understood as two separate things, but two stages or levels of the same entity; the difference is in the higher degree of analytic clarification and self-consciousness (*prajñā*).

The Mādhyamika Absolutism is an *advaya-vāda* and the Vedānta is an *advaita-vāda*. *Advaya* is knowledge free from duality of the extremes (*antas* or *dṛṣṭis*) of 'is', 'not is', being and becoming and their derivatives. The duality here includes more alternatives also. It is knowledge freed of conceptual distinctions. '*Advaita*' is knowledge of a differenceless entity—Pure Being, Brahman. *Advaya-vāda* is solely a dialectical approach; the *advaita-vāda* is ontological. The sole concern of the Mādhyamika is the purification of the intellect of its inveterate tendency to *view* or conceptualise things.

The two Absolutisms differ in the use of negative dialectic. In the Vedānta it is used to disclose the underlying Being by uncovering the superficial vestures or forms in which it is clothed. This means that no situation, even the worst context of error and illusion, can be totally false. There is a core of reality within and this is a residuum which no negation can corrode. For the

Mādhyamika, however, nothing can be retrieved or salvaged from any error-situation. Both the alternatives, all alternatives, are equally and totally false. What is left over is the negating consciousness that is aware of the dialectical play.

2. For the Mādhyamika, both the terms of a relational complex are false; as mutually dependent, they lack an essential nature of their own (tat tat prāpya yadutpannam *notpannam tat svabhāvataḥ*). The relativity of things is their unreality. The cause and the effect are neither identical with nor different from each other, nor both, nor neither There is no substance without attributes, nor attributes without substance; the self (*ātman*) is not one with its states; nor is it anything apart from them. Like Bradley, who lays down that qualities are nothing within or without relation and so too relation, the Mādhyamika enunciates his dictum that both those things are unreal which cannot be conceived as either identical with or different from each other.

The Vedāntin will not reject both the terms as relative; he accepts one as the reality or the basis of the other. For the Mādhyamika, the substance and the attributes are equally unreal, as neither of them can be had apart from the other. The Vedāntin would say that the attributes are mere ascriptions of substance, the particulars are negations of the universal and are, therefore, unreal by their very nature (*svarūpato mithyā*); but the substance or the universal is inherently real, only its seeming relationship with the attributes or particulars is false (*saṁsargato mithyā*); it has a transcendent nature without the relation.

The general formula applicable to the Vedānta is : the terms sustaining a relation are not of the same order; one is *higher*, and the other *lower*; the two terms are neither mutually dependent nor mutually independent; relation is neither 'internal' nor 'external.' If mutually dependent, we cannot distinguish between the two terms, as they so necessarily imply each other that one cannot exist without the other any time. We cannot even say that there are two terms, as the basis of distinction is lacking. If mutually independent, there is no basis of connection; each term is a self—a self-contained universe as it were. To escape this dilemma, we have to conceive one term as basic and capable of existing apart from its relation to the other, and the other incapable of so doing and therefore dependent. One term, the higher, is not exhausted in the relationship; it has a transcendent or non-implicatory existence which is its intrinsic nature. The other term, however, is entirely exhausted within the relation and has no non-relative existence.

3. Any absolutism such as the Advaita Vedānta and Mādhyamika is a two-level theory. Some relationship has to be posited between the two levels or orders; for otherwise, they would fall asunder and each would be an absolute, an unrelated world by itself. In the Vedānta we have the basic duality of Appearance and Reality; in the Mādhyamika of *dṛṣṭi* and *prajñā*. In the order of disclosure or discovery. we proceed from appearance to the real and from *dṛṣṭi* to *prajñā* which is their *śūnyatā*. The order of original formation, however, is the reverse of this. The transition from appearance to the real (Being) or from *dṛṣṭi* to *prajñā* is a conscious and sustained negation (neti neti and *śūnyatā* of *dṛṣṭi*). The transition from the real to appearance or from *prajñā* to *dṛṣṭi*, however, could only be posited or presumed as what must have transpired prior to any empirical experience. Both the Vedānta and the Mādhyamika would call this transition (from the Real to Appearance or from *prajñā* (*śūnyatā*) as *Avidyā* or *māyā*.

The functioning of *avidyā* can only be presumed as it is not overt and empirical. Much like the 'Unconscious' of Freud or the 'original sin' of Christian theology it is not known at the time of its formation, but is revealed at the time of its unearthing or dissipation. We may even compare it with the *a priori* synthesis of Kant.

The Mādhyamika very briefly defines *avidyā* as what hides the real from us and projects the unreal thing in its place (*abhūtaṁ khyāpayaty arthaṁ bhūtam āvṛtya varttate*; *avidyā jāyamāneva kāmalatāṅkavṛttivat*, BCAP, p. 352). He does not elaborate it and does not offer any satisfactory explanation. This may be in keeping with his manifest disinclination to propound any constructive theory.

The Vedānta offers full explanation of *avidyā*—evidence for its presence and the way it functions. *Avidyā* is the principle of creativity (the *śakti* of *Brahman*; *vikṣepa śakti*) by which the non-dual eternal Being becomes, 'appears', many and differentiated It is beginningless though not eternal, and it functions in an *a priori* way. Roughly stated, the empirical world is a joint product of *Brahman* and *avidyā*.

This principle of contingency and creativity, which with Being, engenders the existence of various objects of the temporal world, is indeed a necessary condition of phenomena; but it is contingent in Being; it is in Being but not of it.

Otherwise, if *Māyā* or the principle of Contingency, were an integral part of *Brahman* (Being) i.e.if Brahman is necessitated to become many, everything (even the most trivial occurrence in the world) would be determined and necessary. This would be Spinozism or Hegelianism. The distinction between the necessary or eternal Being on the one hand and the contingent constituents of the world on the other is obliterated. There would not be any temporal process or creation, but only a logical sequence or equation. Any species of integralism is subject to this predicament. Nor can we deny or fail to concede the existence of the eternal, necessary Being. For this is undeniable and self-evident. We cannot abolish the two levels and reduce them to one alone. Nor can we integrate them by any logic. The relation between the necessary and the contingent is itself contingent, not necessary. The relation between *Brahman* and *Māyā*, between eternal Being and its diversification, is a *synthesis in depth* and not in a horizontal or unilinear comprehension.

Discussion on Prof. T. R. V. Murti's Paper

Thakur Jaidev Singh : To resolve the difficulty with regard to Śūnya, we have to ask as to how the term came into vogue. '*Śūnya*', from the root '*śvi*' means "to swell". Similarly, '*Brahman*' means "to grow big", "to swell". Great mathematicians were using '*śūnya*' and '*ananta*' in their mathematics. '*Śūnya*' is the matrix of all numbers. Varāhamihira says that what makes all numbers swell is '*śūnya*'. Just as there is no alteration in the infinite Immovable, even so there is no change in *śūnya* either by addition or substraction. It is rather curious that this term "*śūnya*" should have been seized upon by Mādhyamika. Likewise in the Upaniṣads, the height of thought culminates in '*neti, neti*'. Brahman is co-terminous with Śūnyatama. Both Vedānta and Buddhism were influenced by these two trends of thought present in Upaniṣads. The Vedānta emphasized the *via positiva*, i.e. Brahman. But Nāgārjuna has nothing to say regarding his own position. When we want to make any assertion about reality, we find ourselves landed in self-contradiction. Mādhyamika does not use the term '*śūnya*' in the sense of mere sophistry or nothing. If you want to know the truth, you have to transcend *vikalpas*. *Nirvikalpa* can be known only by *prajñā*, rather than through the discursive intellect.

Prof. Mahadevan in his reply had observed that Śaṅkara could not be unaware of Nāgārjuna and Mādhyamika, but if you turn to *Vedānta Sūtra*, *śūnya* is dismissed in 3 or 4 sentences. Probably the texts of *śūnyavāda* were not accessible to him. Śaṅkara did not assess the opinion of the opponent. It was on the concepts of *ātman* and *śūnya*, that the battle-royal was waged. However, it is when they approach the analyses of *ātman* that these extremes meet. In Buddhism itself Reality is called *viśuddha*. Buddha was conscious of some *Atta* which was different from the *Atta* used in common parlance.

Prof. R. Ramanujachari : According to Prof. Chubb Mādhyamika had some commitment. According to Prof. Hartshorne their four-fold scheme is not complete. The steps that Nāgārjuna taught are bound to fail, for he too had his own philosophical position. In Prof. Murti's paper, however, there is a fair measure of agreement between Vedānta and Buddhism.

Dr. R. Panikkar : How does the Mādhyamika know that beyond the four possibilities there is no other possibility, if the law of excluded middle does not hold ? Let me offer the concepts of two philosophers, concepts which are not affected by the dialectical method. (1) A principal Aristotlean concept, viz. that there is dynamic Being, which is partly moving and partly at rest. Between Being and not-Being there is this dynamic Being. (2) Heidegger, talking about Identity and Difference, seeks to show that no thinking of identity is possible without difference, and *vice versa* : both are correlative. My conclusion is that those two tides of Indian philosophy are not like two opposite streams, so that one could belong either to one side or to the other side. Identity and difference are correlative.

Prof. Robinson : I would like to ask whether or not sustaining a theory of error is possible in Mādhyamika ? Do not some *dṛṣṭis* need to be restated by the Mādhyamika ? Does Prof. Murti really believe that Mādhyamika transcriptions of historical views are justified or valid ? I would further like to be enlightened as to how does Prof. Murti explain the differences between

Vedānta and Buddhism? Is it possible that the differences are only apparent? Differences may stand out from different axiomatics or necessary pre-suppositions. To what extent does Prof. Murti consider the differences to be axiomatic?

Prof. Hartshorne : If Buddhism is a philosophy of Becoming, then that Becoming is most truncated and one-sided.

Dr. Brahma Swarup Agarwal : I would like to seek a clarification. On the one side there is a philosophy of Being, on the other side there is a philosophy of Becoming. I would like Prof. Murti to clarify how does he effect a compromise.

Dr. R. S. Misra : Buddhism is Nirvāṇa-oriented. In my view, '*Pratityasamutpāda*' can be studied as an ontological law. In earlier Buddhism we find *pudgala nairātmya* which has no basis in our moral consciousness but in ontological consciousness. I suspect there is some influence of Kant's Categorical Imperative in this Buddhist version. I find that Prof. Murti identifies Dialectic with philosophy and philosophy with *prajñā*, and these three are taken as synonymous. But I don't think that dialectic can be taken as an end in itself. Dialectic is penultimate knowledge. I agree with Prof. Murti that dialectic means rejection of all *dṛṣṭis*. Philosophy is reason, but reason is buddhi, and there is something beyond buddhi. Prof. Murti identifies dialectic with reason. Reason becomes so self-conscious that it negates *dṛṣṭis*, but reason is conscious of the duality between *dṛṣṭis* and their self-awareness. Moreover, reason belongs to the epistemological level, whereas *prajñā* pertains to the ontological level. How is the transition made from the epistemological to to the ontological?

Dr. (Miss) Karuna Bhattacharya : I would like to ask whether negative consciousness is the tattva accepted by Mādhyamika? Then again, how can negating consciousness be non-dual? Further, if the world is left untouched by Mādhyamika, in that case is it a philosophy without metaphysics?

Prof. T. R. V. Murti : I am grateful to Prof. Jaidev Singh for his observations. If, *Brahman* and *śūnya* mean the same thing, then Vedānta and Buddhism might be coming nearer, but in philosophy we have to make a distinction between the Mādhyamika approach and the Vedānta approach : between Śūnya and Brahman.

Prof. Ramanujachari is displeased with the Mādhyamika

for attacking all. Well, if things depended on our liking or disliking, it would all be easy. But if there is reason, there is an appeal to that; it is not a matter of mere whim.

Prof. Chubb has given a fine demonstration of what Mādhyamika does. What is philosophy? According to Prof. Chubb philosophy starts with a certain commitment, it elaborates certain commitments: in saying this, has he not exemplified Mādhyamika position? There is no philosophical commitment here but awareness of commitments, of what philosophers are doing. But there must be some name to this kind of activity. Whenever there is another view set against yours, you can't decide, and there is doubt regarding both the views. Dispute cannot be decided by taking sides or by throwing weight on any one side. This dispute leads to suspension of judgement. All the pronouncements are coloured by certain fundamental commitments. Each one has his abhiniveśa. Commitment is never made in a conscious manner. We don't start as neutral, but we can become aware of our commitment. This *awareness* of commitment is *prajāñ*; what is denied are the *dṛṣṭis*. Mādhyamika cannot be taken as one more position, otherwise it will itself be a competitor in the field. *prajñā* itself is not one more *dṛṣṭi*.

Dr. N. K. Devaraja : What is the Mādhyamika equivalent of reason?

Prof. Murti : reason with small 'r' is *buddhi*, Reason with capital 'R' is '*prajñā*'. I don't take these two—*dṛṣṭi* and *prajñā* as two entities but as two modes of the same consciousness. *Prajñā* is *śūnyatā*. If you take it as a *dṛṣṭi*, it is the worst kind of *dṛṣṭi* you could think of. So, *śūnyatā* should not be considered as a *dṛṣṭi*, but as awareness of all *dṛṣṭis*. So *śūnyatā* is the Absolute.

Prof. Chubb: I would like to ask whether pre-suppositionless awareness can remain presuppositionless if it goes further and refutes other views?

Prof. Murti : This presuppositionless awareness is the result of all these refutations. According to Vedānta you cannot be self-conscious unless there is some obstruction in your position. Dialectic is another name for refutation. There is dialectic when you are being aware of the fundamental presuppositions of others, and so it is universal. Unless the refutation is universal, it cannot be dialectic. Dialectic is a position conscious of its own presuppositions.

As for Prof. Hartshorne's query, the answer is that Mādhyamika *catuṣkoṭi* is adequate for all positions. As Hegel takes the fundamental positions and puts them on his dialectical map, so also in Mādhyamika all philosophy—past, present and future—are taken into account.

Coming to Dr. Panikkar's remarks, in case his thesis is : "if you reject this, then you accept the other", then I reject this thesis.

Regarding Prof. Robinson's questions, what Mādhyamika says relating to avidyā is not very illuminating. When dialectic has finished its function, there is still the phenomenological problem of how a dṛṣṭi is made possible. How does *prajñā* become a *dṛṣṭi*? Vedānta answers this question by explaining how avidyā works.

In Buddhism the interest is primarily epistemological, whereas the whole interest in Vedānta is ontological.

Dr. R. S. Misra : *Prajñā* is *nirvāṇa*, but it is not self-conscious reason.

Prof. Murti : Where Mādhyamika ends, Vedānta begins. As for Dr. Misra's observations on Moral Law and Buddhism, *Pratītya samutpāda* is a formal statement of the law of Karma. Buddha all the time laid emphasis on self-effort : there is no room for grace in Buddhism; there is only the working of the Law. The law of Karma accounts for all diversities in the world. *Prajñā* and Reason are one and the same, but at different levels of self-consciousness.

As for Dr. (Miss) Karuna Bhattacharya's question, my answer is that philosophy is not Silence. If there is a philosophy of Silence, it is still talk about Silence.

5.5 RADHAKRISHNAN AND BUDDHISM*

I. Radhakrishnan's Approach to Buddhism

Of All the significant services rendered by Radhakrishnan to our understanding of Indian philosophy his interpretation of Buddhist thought is by no means the least. His appreciation of the importance of the subject is evinced by his devoting approximately half of the first volume of his *Indian Philosophy* to Buddhism. First published in 1923 and revised subsequently in 1929, this is Radhakrishnan's basic work on the subject. He returns to the topic whenever he has an opportunity to do so.[1] When invited to deliver the British Academy Lecture, under the Henriette Hertz Trust, on a Master Mind, he chose—not Śaṁkara or Rāmānuja, but Gautama the Buddha. For,

"In Gautama the Buddha we have a master mind from the East second to none so far as the influence on the thought and life of the human race is concerned, and sacred to all as the founder of a religious tradition whose hold is hardly less wide and deep than any other.[2]"

He approaches the subject in the best traditions of Hinduism :

"Though a Hindu by religion, I have the highest respect for the great Gautama and the attractiveness of his message. This attitude of reverence for the majesty and winsomeness of Buddha's personality is the normal one for the intellectuals of India....His influence on India's thought and religion has been profound and latterly very much on the increase.[3]"

Buddhist studies are still far from complete or adequate. The fact that no large additions or drastic modifications are

*Reprinted from *The Philosophy of Sarvepalli Radhakrishnan*, edited by P. A. Schilpp, New York : Northwestern University, Tudor Pub., 1952.

1. In 1933 Radhakrishnan inaugurated the Don Alphina Ratnayaka Trust Lectureship, in Colombo, Ceylon, with his discourse on "The Teaching of Buddha". (Reference to this work will hereafter be abbreviated: TB.) And, on the invitation of the Chinese Government in 1944, Radhakrishnan delivered a series of lectures on Buddhism and Hinduism in various university centres in China.

2. GB, 1.

3. TB, 2.

called for in Radhakrishnan's exposition and appraisal of Buddhism is sufficient proof of the abiding value of his work in this field. He has created, in Indian universities, a lively interest in Buddhist studies and has guided research work on comparative and critical studies of Buddhist systems. The writer of this essay owes a great debt to Professor Radhakrishnan for his inestimable help and advice in his study of the Mādhyamika philosophy.[1]

There are admitted difficulties in Buddhistic studies. For one thing, their vastness is frightening. An extensive literature, canonical, exegetical, and systematic, covering a period of more than fifteen centuries, is scattered in a score of languages, Pali, Sanskrit, Chinese, Tibetan, and several Mongolian languages. Its complexity is equally formidable; the schools and sub-schools are bewildering in their number and in the twists and turns of their thought. The greatest difficulty, however, is caused by the absence of a continued tradition which might set aright many an incorrect interpretation. For a considerable time to come, therefore, our knowledge of Buddhism is bound to be tentative and patchy. In spite of these discouraging factors, it is the duty of the historian of philosophy to reconstruct and relive the past. Radhakrishnan's basic approach to Buddhism, as to any other philosophy, is that of a constructive philosopher. He enunciates this in his *Indian Philosophy* : "The historian of philosophy must approach his task, not as a mere philologist or even as a scholar, but as a philosopher who uses his scholarship as an instrument to wrest from words the thoughts that underlie them."[2] I find myself in complete agreement with this mode of approach.

It is not possible, nor even desirable, to go over the ground covered by Radhakrishnan in such masterly fashion. I propose confining myself to indicating Radhakrishnan's standpoint on some important problems connected with Buddhism and to showing how far one might accept his lead.

The first question to claim our attention is the relation (not merely historical) of orthodox Hindu (Brāhmanical) thought to Buddha and Buddhism. Secondly, we may consider the

1. This will shortly be published under the title, *The Central Philosophy of Buddhism,* by George Allen & Unwin, London.

2. Ind. P. I, 671.

development of the several Schools belonging to Hīnayāna and Mahāyāna Buddhism. An allied question is their relation and logical affinity to the corresponding Brāhmanical systems. The peculiar feature of Buddhism as a religion requires consideration in order to bring out its distinction from Brāhmanism. Lastly, the spread and disappearance of Buddhism from the land of its birth is to be accounted for. In the absence of an adequate explanation this might remain a puzzling phenomenon.

These problems do not exhaust the questions which call for interpretation or information. Purely literary and linguistic questions have, of course, no place here. It would also be fascinating to trace the spread of Buddhism outside India, in Ceylon, Burma, China, Tibet, etc. But this topic properly belongs to the history of religions. Biographical and chronological details are not considered here. Our knowledge in these matters is still largely conjectural, and for a philosophical understanding of Buddhism they are not essential.

The main feature of Radhakrishnan's treatment lies in the fact that he fully demonstrates the unity and affinity of Buddhism with Brāhmanism. This is indeed the case; for, Buddhism has to be understood as a growth or modification of Hinduism. Both belong to the same genus. It is also, however, necessary to establish their specific differences. Radhakrishnan does not, it appears to me, sufficiently emphasize their differences; in fact, he even tends to minimise them. This is evident especially in his treatment of the relation between the *Upaniṣads* and Buddha and to a certain extent also between the absolutisms of Mādhyamika, Yogācāra, and Advaita Vedānta. The view suggested here is that, although their generic identity is undeniable, the specific differences are equally undeniable. This seem to me essential for a balanced appraisal of Indian philosophical systems.

II. Buddha and Upaniṣads

What is the distinctive nature of Buddha's teaching? Is it the same as that of the *Upaniṣads*?[1]

1. Radhakrishnan deals with this topic in his Ind. P, I, 360ff, 676ff; GB, 28ff; and TB.

All our accounts agree that Buddha taught the Four Holy Truths: the Truth of suffering, its Cause, its Cessation, and the Path leading to its Cessation. For him all empirical existence is pain, and no being is exempt from the Law of Karma. "Birth is sorrow. Decay is sorrow. Sickness is sorrow. Death is sorrow....To be conjoined to things which we dislike, to be separated from things which we like—that also is sorrow."[1] Sorrow is not uncaused or self-caused; fori n either case it could not be removed. Buddha rejected all philosophies that were inconsistent with the possibility of Freedom from Suffering and with the endeavour towards such freedom. He was therefore not only opposed to materialism or nihilism, which advocated the fortuitous origin of things and denied the existence of the Soul apart from the body, but also to those conceptions which took the Soul as a permanent substantial existence impervious to change. Discarding these as the two principal extreme and false views, Buddha taught the Dharma (Law) from the—so-called—Middle position (*majjhena dhammam deseti*). An unchanging eternal soul is a stumbling block to our spiritual life; in that case we would be neither the worse nor the better for our efforts. This would lead to inaction and stagnation. Nay more; the ātman is the root-cause, of all attachment, desire, aversion, and pain. When we take anything as a self, as a substantial and permanent entity, we become attached to it and dislike other things which are opposed to it. Substance-view is ignorance *par excellence*, and from it proceed all passions. (*satkāyadṛṣṭi-prabhavāḥ sarve kleśāḥ*). Denial of ātman or Substance is the very pivot of Buddhist metaphysics, as it is of its doctrine of salvation. The oft-recurring strain in the Pali Canons is that things are transitory: "How transient are all component things; growth is their nature and decay. They are produced; they are dissolved again; to bring them all into subjection that is bliss."[2]

Buddha formulated the Holy Eightfold Path for purifying the mind of passions, anger, lust, craving, and aversion, and to enable it to perceive the Truth. Buddhist spiritual discipline has always been of the three-tier type—Virtues, Concentration

1. GB, 16.
2. *Mahāparinibbāna Sutta*, vi, 10.

of Mind, and wisdom (*śīla, samādhi and prajñā*). It repudiated the mechnical performance of ritual and sacrifice as meaningless. There is no appeal to extraneous inducements, rewards or punishment; there is no invocation to God. The entire dicipline is a severe form of self-culture, directed towards the elimination of all craving, of all clinging to the 'I' and the 'Mine'. Insight into the nature of the Real as *anātman* (substanceless) is the final stage of the path of purity. On the attainment of this enlightenment (*bodhi*) one becomes an *Arhat* ('Saint); this itself is *Nirvāṇa*. Final Release (*Parinirvāṇa*) follows on the cessation of the aggregates of mind and body-functions which constitute the stream of individual life.

Though real, the state of *Nirvāṇa* is inexpressible. "There is the not-born, the not-become, the not-created, the not-compounded....If there were not this not-born,......there could be no escape from this world of compounded things."[1] It is even spoken of in more positive terms as "a reality beyond all suffering and change, as unfading, still, undecaying, taintless, as peace and blissful. It is an island, the shelter, refuge and the goal."[2] We are expressly forbidden to consider *Nirvāṇa*—the state of the *Tathāgata* (The Perfect One) after death—as annihilation. It is one of the four sets of questions declared inexpressible by the Lord. The earlier schools, however, tended to conceive *Nirvāṇa* negatively as a state of extinction comparable to the blowing out of a lamp. In the Mahāyāna Schools (Mādhyamika and Yogācāra) it was taken as the underlying ground identical with the phenomenal world in essence. This latter conception is probably in greater accord with Buddha's real teaching.

It is also on record that Buddha affected silence when questions of a metaphysical nature were asked; he declared them inexpressible. They are invariably enumerated as fourteen and always practically in the same order. Actually, there are four sets of questions, three of which have four alternatives each, whereas the last one concerning the soul has only two. The questions are: whether the world is eternal, or not, or both, or neither; whether the world is finite (in space), or not, or both or neither; whether the Tathāgata exists after death, or does not,

1. *Udāna*, viii, 3.
2. *Saṁyutta Nikāya*, IV, 368ff.

or both, or neither; whether the soul is identical with the body, or different from it. For a correct understanding of Buddha and Buddhism it is essential to have a proper appraisal of this 'silence.'

Such in brief outline is the teaching of Buddha as it can be gathered from the earliest works, the Pali and Sanskrit Canons. It is difficult to decide how much of it could be attributed to Buddha himself and how much to later accretion. This topic has proved a fruitful field for scholars on which to exercise their ingenuity. Did Buddha accept the *Upaniṣadic* (*ātma*) tradition? and, if so, to what extent?

Some Orientalists, like Mrs. Rhys Davids, try to discover a simple 'soul-affirming' primitive teaching of the Master as distinguished from the 'soul-denying' later scholasticism and monkish elaboration. Others, like Poussin, Beck, etc. aver that Yoga and practice of virtue, without any metaphysic, formed the original teaching of Buddha. Many consider him even as an agnostic and take the 'silence' as decisive in this regard.

It is no doubt true that Buddha and Buddhist schools paid great attention to the practice of virtue and concentration of mind. They brought to light deeper and subtler distinctions, and gave us a minute map of the entire terrain of our inner life. However, there is nothing peculiarly Buddhistic about this. We have all the ingredients, if not the detailed prescriptions as well, of a moral code in the Śikṣāvallī of the *Taittiriya Upaniṣad* and similar texts. Yoga-practice was much older than Buddhism. Buddha himself was taught Yoga, all our accounts agree, by two Sāṁkhya teachers, Ālāra Kālāma and Uddaka Rāmaputta. It is an accepted tenet of Indian Philosophical systems that an impure and distracted mind is incapable of perceiving the truth. To reduce Buddhism to a technique of mind-concentration or a code of morals amounts to a failure to appreciate the individuality of Buddha's genius and his metaphysical insight. It is the failure to discern that even a way of life implies a view of reality.

Radhakrishnan interprets Buddha as accepting the *Upaniṣadic* tradition. He bases this interpretation on the following grounds. Buddha cannot be understood except in the historical setting of his age. "Great men are as much the creatures as the creators of their era."[1]

1. TB, 4.

"Those who tell us that for the Buddha there is religious experience but there is no religious object are violating the texts and needlessly convicting him of self-contradiction. He implies the reality of what the *Upaniṣads* call Brahman, though he takes the liberty of giving it another name, *dharma*, to indicate its essentially ethical value for us on the empirical plane. The way of the Dharma is the way of the Brahman.[1]"

"And when the Buddha asks whether anything which is changeable and perishable can be called the self he implies that there is somewhere such a self. . . When the Buddha asks us to have the self as our light (attadīpa), the self as our refuge (attasaraṇa), surely he is referring not to the transitory constituents but the universal spirit in us.[2]"

"As a matter of fact, nowhere did Buddha repudiate the *Upaniṣad* conception of Brahman, the absolute. In the *Kathāvatthu*, where different controversial points are discussed, there is no reference to the question of the reality of an immutable being. All this indicates, if anything, Buddha's acceptance of the *Upaniṣad* position.[3]"

The 'silence' of Buddha unmistakably implies a Transcendent Reality as the foundation of all phenomena. Radhakrishnan rightly rejects the agnostic and the nihilistic interpretations of the silence. Moreover, it is not true that Buddha's attitude was merely suspension of judgment and that he was awaiting a more favourable opportunity to publish the truth. He tells us expressly that he has taught the truth without reservation and without any distinction of the exoteric and the esoteric; unlike a tight-fisted teacher, he had kept back nothing. Nor is Buddha's silence ignorance of metaphysics. He was not only conversant with the philosophical speculations of the time, but was himself a metaphysician of no mean order. By his penetrative analysis he had reached a position which transcended and annulled the dogmatic procedure of Reason. His rejection of speculative metaphysics was deliberate and sustained. Criticism itself is philosophy for him. Radhakrishnan unerringly indicates the nature of Buddha's silence: "If the Buddha declined to define

1. *Saṁyutta Nikāya*, i, 141; GB, 49.
2. *Ibid.*, 51.
3. Ind P, I, 682.

the nature of the Absolute or if he contented himself with negative definitions, it is only to indicate that absolute being is above all determination."[1]

"Why, then, did Buddha not admit in express terms the reality of the absolute? Buddha refused to describe the absolute, for that would be to take a step out of the world of relativity, the legitimacy of which he was the first to question in others. The absolute is not a matter of empirical observation. The world of experience does not reveal the absolute anywhere within its limits.[2]"

This correctly represents the Mādhyamika standpoint, which is the real heart of Buddhism. All that I would like to add to this analysis is that Buddha's implicit acceptance of a Transcendent Reality does not mean that he accepted the *Upaniṣadic* tradition, for nowhere does he identify it with the ātman. For, ātman must mean a permanent substance.

On the other hand, we have to state that Buddha and Buddhism can be understood only as a revolt not merely against the cant and hollowness of ritualism—the *Upaniṣads* themselves voice this unmistakably—but against the ātman-ideology, the metaphysics of the Substance-view. Buddha nowhere acknowledges his indebtedness to the *Upaniṣads* or to any other teacher for his characteristic philosophical standpoint. Though reference is made several times to Brahmā, the deity, Brahman is never referred to. On the contrary, Buddha always speaks as one initiating a new tradition, as opening up a path never trod before. In the *Brahmajāla*, the *Sāmaññaphala Suttas* and elsewhere, current philosophical speculations are reviewed, and all of them are rejected as dogmatic and as inconsistent with the spiritual life. This is not the way of one who continues an older tradition. If the ātman had been a cardinal doctrine with Buddhism, why was it hidden under a bushel so that even the immediate followers of the Master had no inkling of it? The *Upaniṣads*, on the other hand, blazen forth the reality of the ātman in almost every line.

1. GB, 59.
2. Ind. P, I, 682f.

Passages must not be counted, but weighed.[1] We must consider the entire body of texts together and evolve a synthesis, weighing all considerations. We require a synoptic interpretation of the Buddhist scriptures. It is necessary to make a doctrinal analysis of the contents and to assess their value philosophically.

Nothing is gained by the theory of a soul-affirming primitive Buddhism followed by a soul-denying scholastic Buddhism. Even if,—what is impossible—it could be proved that the historical person—Gautama the Buddha—did teach a soul doctrine, fundamentally at variance with the doctrines we associate with classical Buddhism, we should still have to explain Buddhism and to relate it to the *Upaniṣadic* tradition. Excluding Buddha from the charge of preaching the denial of the ātman might save *him* from any 'guilt.' But the question is not a personal one. We should merely have added one more problem: in the act of

1. Radhakrishnan quotes the *Mahāparinibbāna* passage "*attadīpa attasaraṇa*" and translates it: "Be ye as those who have the self as their light. Be ye as those who have the self as their refuge. Betake yourselves to no external refuge. Hold fast to the truth as to a refuge." (GB, 11). This interpretation is not borne out by the context. There was no doctrinal discussion of the soul or the self. Buddha was telling Ānanda that he had become old, eighty years of age, and that he had taught all that he knew without reservation and that he did not hold anything up his sleeve like a "tight-fisted teacher." Therefore, the Order should do well without him. "Ānanda, be a lamp unto yourself, be a refuge unto yourself; seek not any outside help (*anaññā-saraṇa*) in this matter." To treat this passage as inculcating a metaphysical tenet about the self is not warranted by the context. Radhakrishnan himself translates it elsewhere (Ind. P, I, 428) in the usual way as: "Be ye lamps unto yourselves; be ye a refuge to yourselves." The *Dhammapada* text: "attāhi attano nāthā" and similar ones admit of the interpretation that the empirical reality of the self as a doer and enjoyer of the consequences is accepted. The Mādhyamika teachers have made commendable efforts to reconcile these texts. According to Nāgārjuna, Buddha has affirmed the existence of the ātman against the materialist; for there is the continuity of Karma and its result, act and its responsibility; he has denied it as against the eternalist who takes it as an immutable identical essence; he has also said, from the ultimate (*paramārtha*) standpoint, that there is neither the self nor the not-self. Buddha, like a skilful physician, always graduated his teaching according to the need and the capacity of the taught. Radhakrishnan himself makes pointed reference to this interpretation in his Ind. P, I, 389. Much cannot be built on the use of such terms as '*brahmacariya*', '*brahmapada*' and '*brahmavihāra*,' for they connote purity, blessed state and serenity; they have lost all implications of a *Brahman* (*ātman*) metaphysics.

bridging the difference between the *Upaniṣads* and Buddha, we would have increased the distance between Buddha and Buddhism immeasurably. We cannot find any sufficient or compelling motives for the alleged distortion of the original teaching. Either the monks were too stupid to grasp the master's basic teaching, or they were too clever and fabricated and foisted on him an opposite doctrine. Neither of these alternatives can seriously be entertained. Why and when precisely the falsification is supposed to have occurred is not specified. *Prima facie*, those systems and schools of thought which owe allegiance to the founder of this religion have a prior and greater claim to represent and understand Buddhism than the moderns who are removed from him by centuries of time as well as by distance of culture and outlook.

The entire development of Buddhist philosophy and religion is proof of the correctness of the *anātman*-interpretation of Buddhism. There is no Buddhist school of thought that did not deny the ātman; and it is equally true that there is no Brāhmanical or Jaina system which did not accept the ātman in some form or other. It may be objected that the ātman which the Buddhists deny is the material self identified with the body or with the particular mental states, and that such denial does not touch the position of the Vedānta or the Sāṅkhya. But Buddhism never did accept the reality of the ātman, of a permanent substantial entity impervious to change. The Real for Buddhism is Becoming. And any species of the ātman-view must take it as a changeless identical substance. The Buddhist schools differed among themselves to a great degree; but at least one thing they have in common—the denial of any permanent substance (*ātman*). It is a mistake to think that the Mahāyāna schools reversed the denial of the ātman and re-affirmed its reality. If anything, they are more thorough in carrying out the anātman-doctrine. They deny not only substance (pudgalanairātmya), but extend the denial to the Elements too (dharmanairātmya), which the Hīnayāna schools had uncritically accepted as real.

The Buddhists are not the only ones to take their philosophy as a 'no-soul doctrine.' Jaina and Brāhmanical systems too invariably characterise Buddhism as denying the ātman (substance or soul). The modern exponent may not feel committed to the estimate of Buddhism by Buddhists and others. But he is required to pause and explain the unanimity with which Buddhism has been taken as a 'no-soul doctrine.' He is also required to consider the teachings of Buddha in relation to Buddhist schools of thought, which *prima facie* have the right to be considered as embodying the founder's tenets. This problem is at least as important as relating Buddha to the *Upaniṣads*.

A possible objection to the view that Buddha denied the soul might be that it may seem contradictory to his other doctrines accepted as basic, such as the efficacy of Karma, of the adoption of spiritual life and the attainment of *Nirvāṇa*, and of the doctrine of rebirth. Karma without a permanent agent who wills and reaps the fruit of his action seems inconceivable. And, what is the value of spiritual life if there is none at the end of it? Buddha's doctrine would be the acceptance of pain without *any one who* feels it, a spiritual discipline without any person who undertakes it, and a final release (*nirvāṇa*) without any being to enjoy it. Such an absurdity, it might be said, could not have been seriously meant by Buddha.

But, Buddha himself was fully aware of these alleged absurdities. He *replaced* the soul by the theory of a mind-continuum, with the psychical states rigorously conditioned as to their nature by the causal law governing them. According to him this alone provides for progress (change, efficacy) and continuity (responsibility), inasmuch as each succeeding state (good or bad) is the result of the previous state. Thus it avoids, on the one hand, the futility of Karma, which is an inescapable predicament of the acceptance of a permanent soul, and nihilism which follows from the non-acceptance of continuity, on the other. Rebirth does not mean the bodily transportation of an individual essence from one place to another. It only means that a new series of states arises, conditioned by the previous states. Memory and recognition are also similarly explained. If there are difficulties on the Buddhist hypothesis, the difficulties on the other hypotheses are equally formidable.

In every aspect of things we find two opposing standpoints. In causation, we may emphasise the emergence of the effect as something new and different, or we may emphasise its necessary connection and continuity with the cause. In any presented object, we may attend to the particular and the changing, or to the universal and the abiding feature. The latter may be termed the static or space-view of things and the former the dynamic or the time-pattern. On the first view, change and difference may be taken as appearance; on the second, the permanent and the universal will be appearance. One emphasises unity, the other difference. What is real for one is appearance for the other and *vice versa*. The Buddhist and the Brâhmanical schools each evolved a coherent metaphysic and epistemology in consonance with their respective standpoints. It is not contended that Buddha himself formulated the anātman-doctrine in systematic form, with all its implications fully worked out. It is, however, suggested that he gave the inspiration and the impetus to the *anātman*-view, which came to be formulated in such sharp contrast to the ātman-view. That there are insuperable difficulties on either conception of the real, on any conceptual pattern, no one realised perhaps more strongly than did Buddha. He was thus led to discredit all attempts at *conceiving* reality, and in consequence to reject all speculative metaphysics. This is the real meaning of his 'silence.' To this conclusion he would have been led because two or more opposed points of view were tried and found unsatisfactory. If the ātman-tradition alone had held the field, Buddha could not have arrived at his characteristic 'no-metaphysics' position. The systematic form of this 'silence' is the Mādhyamika system. This system could arise only after the two traditions had developed sufficiently to make it possible for the conflict between them to be appreciated in all its intensity and universality. That alone could engender the dialectical consciousness.

Indian philosophy must be interpreted as the flow of these two vital streams of thought—one having its source in the ātman-doctrine of the *Upaniṣads* and the other in the anātman-doctrine of Buddha. Each branched off into several sub-streams with a right and a left wing and several intermediary positions. There were lively sallies and skirmishes between them, but no commingling or synthesis of the two traditions. One took Being as real, the other Becoming; for the former substance typified the real, for the latter the modes. In their extreme form, the former denied the reality of Becoming, the latter that of Being.

The relation of Buddha to the *Upaniṣads* may be stated thus. For both, phenomenal existence is imperfection and pain; they are also one in placing before us the ideal of state which is beyond the possibility of pain and bondage. The *Upaniṣads* speak of it more positively as a state of consciousness and bliss; Buddha emphasises the negative aspect of it: nirvāṇa is the annihilation of sorrow. Both have to speak of the ultimate as devoid of empirical determinations, as incomparable to anything we know: silence is their most proper language. They also agree that no empirical means,—organisational device, sacrifice or penance,—can be of any avail: Only insight into the nature of the real can take us to the goal. For the *Upaniṣads*, the ātman is real; its identification with the body, with the mental states, or with any other empirical object is accidental. Only by negating the wrong identification, its unreal limitations, can we know its real nature; ātman is brahman; it is all that is. No fear, aversion, or attachment could afflict it. Buddha reaches this very goal of desirelessness, not by the universalisation of the 'I' (*ātman*), but by denying it altogether. For, only as we consider anything as permanent and pleasant, i.e., take it as a self, do we get attached to it and are averse to things that are opposed to it. The *ātman* is the root-cause of all passions; and this notion has to be rooted out completely to attain *Nirvāṇa*. For Buddha, then, the self is a primary wrong notion. Buddha does not speak of the knowledge of any specific entity as the saving knowledge. For him the awareness of the nature of pain and its cause is itself the knowledge which sets man free. Times without number we are told that the Tathāgata knows what is pain, how it arises and how it ceases. This can mean that for him the saving knowledge is the self-conscious awareness of the world-process; to realise the inexorability of the Causal Law is to stand aside from it. "Freedom is the knowledge of Necessity." Again, the *Upaniṣads* appear to start with an intuitive or extra-philosophical knowledge of Brahman and then lead the disciple to that knowledge by arguments and analogies. They are not aware, except in a vague form, of the conflict in Reason; theirs is not a dialectical approach. Buddha, on the other hand, is more rational in his procedure. Buddha ascends from the Conflict of Reason to the inexpressibility of the absolute. Both reach the same goal of final release, but by different means. The spiritual genius of Buddha carved out a new path, the negative path.

I am happy to find that there are observations in Radhakrishnan's writings which indicate the difference between Buddha and the *Upaniṣads*: "If there is a difference between the teaching of the *Upaniṣads* and the Buddha, it is not in their views of the world of experience (saṁsāra) but in regard to their conception of reality (nirvāṇa) "[1]

"The fundamental difference between Buddhism and the *Upaniṣads* seems to be about the metaphysical reality of an immutable substance, which is the true self of man as well..... It is true that Buddha finds no centre of reality or principle of permanence in the flux of life and the whirl of the world, but it does not follow that there is nothing real in the world at all except the agitation of forces."[2]

Is not a *fundamental metaphysical difference* the source of all other differences? If Buddhism is "only a restatement of the thought of the *Upaniṣads* with a new emphasis,"[3] it is desirable to emphasise this 'emphasis,' especially because it is of a fundamentally metaphysical nature. The *Upaniṣads* and Buddhism belong to the same spiritual genus; they differ as species; and the differentia are the acceptance or rejection of the ātman (permanent substance).

III. Development of the Schools

Nowhere is our knowledge of Buddhism more deficient than in the emergence and growth of the schools. Of most of the early ones we know next to nothing, and the little that we know is not very intelligible. Early Buddhist historians like Vasumitra, Vinītadeva and Bhavya speak of 18 different Schools, all rightly claiming to embody the true teaching of the Master. Of these, only four main schools deserve consideration: Sthaviravāda (Theravāda), Sarvāstivāda, Mahāsaṅghika, and Sāmmitīya; others are off-shoots of these. The differences began to manifest themselves soon after the death of Buddha, and the first recorded division of the Buddhist Order occurred at the Council of Vaiśāli. The rise of the schools is proof that the teaching of Buddha was sufficiently rich and pregnant with metaphysical

1. GB, 33.
2. Ind. P, I, 375.
3. *Ibid.*, 676.

possibilities, but was not sufficiently definite. The basic teaching, its anātmavāda (denial of substance), is differently interpreted by the different schools. As Radhakrishnan says :

"Philosophy is a natural necessity of the human mind and even the Buddha did not succeed in compelling his hearers to adopt an attitude of suspended judgment on the ultimate questions. In the absence of definite guidance from the teacher, different metaphysical systems were fastened on him early in the career of Buddhism."[1]

I venture to think that the correct approach is to consider Buddhism as a *matrix of systems*, rather than as one unitary system. It does not exclude legitimate different formulations. The attempt to treat Buddhism as one unitary system is a species of over-simplification and engenders a partisan spirit in writers; they begin taking sides with one or the other school of Hīnayāna and Mahāyāna, and consider *that* as *the* teaching of the Buddha. Such procedure prevents a correct understanding of the development of Buddhist philosophy. It would be less fallacious to consider Buddhism as a critical tendency or direction rather than as a finished system.

Each of the systems of Hindu thought (Sāṅkhya, Yoga, Nyāya, Vaiśeṣika, Vedānta and Mīmāṁsā) is treated by Radhakrishnan with sufficient thoroughness and definiteness in separate chapters of his *Indian Philosophy*. We should naturally expect the same thoroughness with regard to at least the four classical schools of Buddhism: Vaibhāṣika (Sarvāstivāda), Sautrāntika, Mādhyamika and Yogācāra (Vijñānavāda). This is, however, not the case. The reason for this is two-fold. Paucity of material is still a great handicap: many of the basic works of some of the systems are not available either in the original language or in translation, although important works are being published from time to time. It would, therefore, be necessary to revise one's exposition and evaluation of the systems with the constantly increasing addition to our knowledge.[2] It is also incumbent

1. GB, 64.

2. Since the publication of *Indian Philosophy* (vol. i) in 1923 and its revision in 1929 the following are some of the important original works that have been made available: *Tattva-Saṅgraha*, (2 vols.), *Abhidharmakośavyākhyā* of Yaśomitra (complete Tokyo Edn.), *Catuḥśataka* of Āryadeva, *Madhyamakāvatāra* of Candrakīrti (in part), *Abhisamayālaṅkārāloka* of Haribhadra, *Madhyānta-*

upon one to make a determined and consistent effort to understand the Buddhist systems from their own inherent and internal standpoint, instead of looking at them through the eyes of the Nyāya-Vaiśeṣika or the Vedānta. They should not be considered as halting approximations to the Advaita Vedānta. I may, possibly, be wrong, but one gets the impression that Radhakrishnan evaluates every system of philosophy, including schools of Buddhism, in terms of the Advaita Vedānta of Śaṅkara. This is understandable since the Advaitism of Śaṅkara represents a very consistent and complete form of Absolutism; and absolutism, some (among them Radhakrishnan) would maintain, is the end of all philosophy. I should like to state that the Mādhyamika, and the Vijñānavāda too, are equally commendable attempts, though from a different approach. A necessary implication of this is that philosophical differences are ultimate and are, therefore, perhaps incommensurable. Refutation and criticism, indulged in by systems of philosophy, ostensibly in order to annul differences and to unify the systems, only serve to distinguish and differentiate them.

There wer e three principal turning-points in the history of Buddhism. The earlier realistic and pluralistic phase, comprising the Hīnayāna Schools: Theravāda and the Vaibhāṣika (Sarvāstivāda). This can be called the Ābhidharmika Philosophy. The Sautrāntika, as a critical realism, is a partial modification of this earlier dogmatic realism. The middle phase is the dialectical absolutism of the Mādhyamika system founded by Nāgārjuna and Ārya Deva (2nd cent. A.D.). The third is the idealism of the Yogācāra, systematised by Asaṅga and Vasubandhu (4th cent. A.D.) and continued by Dignāga and Dharmakīrti.

The *Śālistamba Sūtra* says : "Whosoever sees the *Pratītyasamutpāda* (Law of Dependent Origination) sees the Buddha and whosoever sees the Buddha sees the *Dharma* (Truth or Reality)."[1] Nāgārjuna expresses himself similarly: "One who perceives truly the Pratītysamutpāda realises the Four Sacred Truths, Pain, its

vibhāgaṭīkā of Sthiramati (Nagoya Edn.) *Pramāṇa Vārttika, Hetubinduṭīkā* and *Vādanyāya* of Dharmakīrti. Some other works like Nāgārjuna's *Mahāprajñāpāramitā Śāstra* and Asaṅga's *Mahāyānasaṅgraha* etc., are available in French translation.

1. *Śālistamba Sūtra*, opening passage.

Cause, Cessation and the Path."[1] Buddhism has always been a *Dharma*-theory based on the *Pratītyasamutpāda*, and every Buddhist system has claimed to be the Middle Path. *Pratītya-samutpāda* has, however, received different interpretations at different times. The earlier Buddhism of the Ābhidharmika systems took it as denying the permanent ātman and at once establishing the reality of the separate elements. *Pratītya-samutpāda* is the causal law regulating the rise and subsidence of the several elements. The Middle Path is the steering clear of both, Eternalism (substance or soul) and Nihilism (denial of continuity). The Mādhyamika contends that this is not the correct interpretation of the doctrine. *Pratītyasamut-pāda* is not the principle of temporal sequence, but of the essential dependence of things on each other, i.e., the unreality of separate elements. The entire Mādhyamika system is a re-interpretation of *Pratītyasamutpāda*. This is now equated with *śūnyatā*—the empirical validity of entities and their ultimate unreality.[2] The Middle Path is the non-acceptance of the two extremes—the affirmative and the negative views—of all views. In the Vijñānavāda, Śūnyatā is accepted, but with a modification. The formula now is : That which appears (the substratum, i.e., consciousness) is real; the form of its appearance (the duality of subject and object) is unreal. The Middle Path is the avoidance of both, the dogmatism of Realism (acceptance of the reality of objects) and the Scepticism of Nihilism (the rejection of object and consciousness both as unreal).

The Sarvāstivāda is a radical pluralism erected on the denial of substance and the acceptance of discrete momentary *dharmas*. '*Dharma*' is the ultimate factor or element of existence—a sense which the term has only in Buddhism. *Dharmas* are ultimate, as they are simple and not compounded of simpler entities. A thing (e.g., chair, tree, man) is an aggregate of these elements; the aggregate or the whole is not a reality, one more reality as in the Vaiśeṣika. The elements are impermanent: they are momentary and durationless. There is no inherence of one element in another, hence no substance apart from qualities; no matter beyond the separate sense-data, and no soul beyond the separate

1. *Mādhyamika Kārikā*, XXIV, 40.
2. *Mādhyamika Kārikā*, XXIV, 18.

mental data (*dharma* = *anātman*)....The *dharmas* are classified and defined in the Abhidharma treatises, notably in the *Abhidharmakośa* of Vasubandhu. The Sarvāstivāda lists 75 *dharmas* in all, 72 conditioned phenomena and unconditioned noumena.

According to the Abhidharma conception there is a real transformation of the unconditioned into the unconditioned noumenal state through the force of insight. Nirvāṇa is conceived almost as a state of negation or extinction of the phenomenal forces. This implies that *Nirvāṇa* and phenomena (*saṁsāra*) are totally different. The Mādhyamika controverts these points.

The dogmatism of the Ābhidharmika, its tendency to hypostatise subjective notions and words into objective realities and especially its doctrine of the existence of the elements at all times, evoked criticism from other schools. The Sautrāntika, which discards the Ābhidharma works and bases itself on the direct discourses (*sūtras*) of Buddha, represents the systematic form of this criticism.

The Sautrāntikas cut down the inflated list of dharmas drawn by the Vaibhāṣika. Not only did they reject the past and the future phases, but also Space, *Nirvāṇa*, and the non-mental forces. In the final analysis, a list of 43 elements was drawn up.

The real contribution of the Sautrāntika to the development of Indian thought is the discovery of the subjective—the transcendental function of the mind in constructing the empirical world. Dignāga (5th cent.) and Dharmakīrti (7th cent.) have formulated a rigorous and revolutionary logic and epistemology along Kantian lines. There are two modes of knowledge, immediate and mediate; they are mutually exclusive and exhaustive taken together. The function of the one is to *receive* or acquaint us with the given, and that of the other is to *think* it through concepts. Their respective objects are the particular and the universal; the particular alone is real; the universal is a thought-construction having merely conventional reality. Experience is the synthesis or identification of these two heterogeneous factors. Hindu writers invariably characterise the Sautrāntika as advocating that the external object is inferred, not directly perceived. This is not exactly correct. The essence of representationism is that we do not directly perceive objects, but are aware of our ideas only (the copies of things). The Sautrāntika emphatically asserts, however, that we are in direct contact with the real in perception. His doctrine only means that the subjective factor in knowledge is mistaken for the objective, the thing-in-itself. This mistake is not, however, empirical in origin. The Hindu misconception might have arisen from the fact that the Sautrāntika considers determinate perception (*savikalpa-pratyakṣa*) as mental construction.

One would like a fuller treatment of the Sautrāntika logic and epistemology in a work of the dimensions of Radhakrishnan's *Indian Philosophy*. This is all the more desirable because the corresponding Nyāya epistemology has been treated with such thoroughness and because the Sautrāntika logic has played such a great part in deepening Indian Philosophy. Fortunately, Dharmakīrti's basic treatise, *Pramāṇavārttika*,—long thought lost in the original—has lately been discovered and published; we also have his shorter *Nyāyabindu* and *Hetubindu*; Stcherbatsky has made a notable contribution to the subject by his *Buddhist Logic*.

In the second phase of development there was a revolutionary change in Buddhism: from the earlier radical pluralism it became as radical as absolutism. The part played by some of the philosophical schools, notably the Sāmmitīyas and the Sautrāntikas, which proved to be a sort of transitional link, must be mentioned. Universally condemned as heretical by all other Buddhist schools, the Sāmmitīyas held tenaciously to their doctrine of the Individual (*pudgalātman*) as a quasi-permanent entity, neither completely identical with the mental states nor different from them. However halting this conception may have been, it is evidence of the inadequacy of a stream of elements to account for the basic facts of experience—memory, moral responsibility, spiritual life, etc. The theory of elements is discredited: the mental states cannot completely substitute the *ātman*: a permanent synthetic unity must be accepted. Of course, the Sāmmitīyas could not attain to the fully critical position of the Mādhyamikas, viz., that there are no states without the self, nor is there a self without states, and therefore both are unreal since they are relative. The Sautrāntika by his insistence on the creative work of thought directly led to the dialectic of the Mādhyamika and to the idealism of the Yogācāra. To the former it became clear that the subjective was much deeper and wider in scope. Not merely the categories of substance, but causality, change, being and non-being were equally subjective. The Yogācāra takes the constructivity of thought to prove that the object itself is a construction of thought. We have the Western parallel of the Fichtean and Hegelian idealistic criticism of the Kantian dualism of the thing-in-itself and the categories of thought. The other in thought (object) is itself a creation of consciousness; the dualism of subject and object presupposes a non-dual consciousness which alone is ultimately real.

Radhakrishnan gives a full and very sympathetic account of the Mādhyamika and Yogācāra absolutisms, especially of the former. His interpretation and evaluation of these two great systems shows his unerring understanding and insight. I shall undertake to point out some differences between these systems and the Advaita Vedānta.

The absolutism of the Mādhyamika is established by the dialectic. Dialectic is the consciousness of the interminable and total (antinomical) conflict in reason and resolution of the conflict by rising to a higher level of consciousness. In Hegel, the conflict is resolved by synthesising the opposites in a higher, more comprehensive, unity which is their identity. The Mādhyamika dialectic tries to remove the conflict by rejecting both the opposites, whether taken singly or in combination. The Mādhyamika is convinced that a conjunctive or a disjunctive synthesis of views (as in the Jaina theory of the *anekānta*) is merely another view; it labours, therefore, under the same difficulties. Rejection of all views is the rejection of the competence of reason to comprehend reality. The Real is transcendent to thought. Views are not rejected on any positive grounds nor because another view is accepted. The rejection is based solely on the inner contradiction implicit in each view. Four alternatives are possible on any subject. The basic alternatives are two: Being and Non-Being, Affirmation and Negation. From these, two others are derived by affirming or denying both at once. It may be thought that while avoiding the two extremes, the Mādhyamika accepts a middle position between the two. No; he does not hold any third position; the middle position is really no position, since it is beyond concept or language. How does the Mādhyamika reject any and all views? He uses only one weapon. By drawing out the implications of any view he shows its inherent self-contradictory character. The dialectic is a series of *reductio ad absurdum* arguments. Every thesis is thus turned against itself; it is self-convicted, not counter-balanced. The Mādhyamika disproves the opponent's thesis, but he does not prove any *thesis* of his own The principle of the dialectic is that the relative is unreal; mutual dependence is a mark of the unreal. Reason which understands things by way of distinction and relation is a principle of falsity, for it distorts and thereby hides the real. In causation, for instance, we must differentiate between the cause and the effect and at once identify them; the relation between them cannot be conceived as either identity or difference or both, nor can we give it up. Nāgārjuna says : "Neither of those things is established (as real) which cannot be conceived as either identical with or different from each other."[1] The substance-view believes that it could have substance without attributes or modes (as in the Advaita Vedānta;) the modal or anātman-view entertains the opposite belief that it could dispense with substance altogether (as in the Ābhidharmika and Sautrāntika systems). There is, however, no attribute without substance nor any substance without attributes. They are not intelligible even together; for, we could not then distinguish them. There is no whole apart from the parts and *vice versa.* Things that derive their nature and being by mutual dependence are nothing in themselves, they are not real.

Philosophical consciousness attains its fruition through the working of its inner dynamism, through the three moments of the dialectic: dogmatism, criticism, and intuition. In its natural speculative employment, philosophy is dogmatic; this finds expression in the various systems of thought. As this invariably leads to conflict, philosophy becomes critical, self-consciously aware of the assumptions and inadequacies of reason. This is the consciousness of the relativity of phenomena, their unreality. Phenomena are Śūnya, because they are dependent and are thus devoid of the essence of reality. The completion of criticism effectively does away with the speculative or conceptual function of reason. Philosophy then culminates in intellectual intuition. Here knowledge (reason) and its object (the real) coincide; there is non-duality. This too is *śūnyatā,* since *prajñā* or the Absolute is devoid of duality (free from 'is' and 'is not')

The great contribution Radhakrishnan has made to our

1. *Mādhyamika Kārikā,* II, 21; XIX, 6.

understanding of Buddhism is his unequivocal interpretation of *śūnyatā*. This is the fundamental concept of Buddhism. The whole of Buddhist Philosophy turned on this concept. The earlier realistic phase of Buddhism, with its rejection of substance and uncritical erection of a theory of elements, was clearly a preparation for the fully critical and self-conscious dialectic of Nāgārjuna. Not only is the Yogācāra Idealism based on the explicit acceptance of Śūnyatā, but the critical and advaitic trend in the ātman-tradition is also traceable to this. Thanks to Radhakrishnan's lead, the nihilistic interpretation of *śūnyatā* has come to be rightly discredited. It is now generally accepted that *śūnyatā* stands for the Transcendent Ground inexpressible by thought-categories. It is thus devoid of empiricality, not void or nothing. As Radhakrishnan says :

"About the ultimate reality we cannot say anything. To attain truth we must cast aside the conditions which are incompatible with truth. The absolute is neither existent nor non-existent, nor both existent and non-existent, nor different from both non-existence and existence. To the Mādhyamikas reason and language apply only to the finite world. To transfer the finite categories to the infinite would be like attempting to measure the heat of the sun by the ordinary thermometer. From our point of view the absolute is nothing. We call it śūnyam, since no category used in relation to the conditions of the world is adequate to it. To call it being is wrong, because only concrete things are. To call it non-being is equally wrong. It is best to avoid all descriptions of it Thought is dualistic in its functions, and what is, is non-dual or advaita."[1]

The Absolute is not one reality set against another, such as the empirical. The Absolute looked at through thought-forms is phenomenon. The latter, freed of the superimposed thought-forms, is the Absolute. The difference is epistemic (subjective), not ontological. Nāgārjuna declares, therefore, that there is not the least difference between the absolute and the world. Transcendent to thought, the absolute is, however, thoroughly immanent in experience. A distinction has to be made between what is by itself and what appears to the finite intellect. Nāgārjuna declares that those, who do not distinguish between the uncondi-

1. Ind. P, I, 663f.

tioned truth and the conventional, do not understand the heart of Buddha's teaching.

The Māḍhyamika dialectic, which culminates in intuition, is, however, the fruition not only of the theoretic consciousness, but it is the fruition of the practical and the religious consciousness as well. The dialectic as non-conceptual knowledge takes us beyond the possibility of phenomenal existence; it is freedom itself; (Nirvāṇa). The dialectic as *Prajñāpāramitā* is identified with the *Tathāgata*, the *Ens perfectissimum*, which all beings are in essence and which they attain by spiritual discipline. Religion is the mystic pull of the Transcendent (the Ideal) on the actual. The dialectic consummates the union of all beings with the Perfect Being.

In Vijñānavāda, *Śūnyatā* is accepted, but with a significant modification; it rejected as unreal the duality of subject and object with which consciousness is apparently infected. For the Mādhyamika, phenomena are unreal because they are mutually dependent; he considers the *logical* constitution of a thing and finds it lacking in essence. The Vijñānavādin views it *psychologically*: the object cannot stand by itself; it is nothing without the consciousness on which it is superimposed; but consciousness can exist without the object. It is *vijñāna* that can undergo modifications, and it can purify itself by getting rid of the superimposed duality. With his bias in favour of *vijñāna* as the sole reality, the Yogācāra criticises the Mādhyamika for denying the reality of *vijñāna*. His most effective argument against the Mādhyamika is that everything may be dialectically analysed away as illusory; but the illusion would imply the ground on which the illusory construction itself would have to take place. Accepting the Śūnyatā of the *Prajñāpāramitās* and even protesting that they interpret it more correctly, they give substance to the Śūnya by identifying it with Pure Consciousness that is devoid of duality. They consider themselves the true Mādhyamika—adopting the middle course between the extremes of Nihilism and Realism. The Yogācāra school is the third and last comprehensive synthesis of Buddhist doctrines. It could certainly incorporate the Vaibhāṣika 'dharmas,' taking them as mind and mental states; the Yogācāra even increased the number of '*dharmas*' to a hundred.

Vijñāna then, is *real*, not apparent; but *vijñāna alone* is real, not the object. It is however infected, without beginning, by the primordial ignorance of duality (the subject-object relation). Owing to this ignorance, which is aided by subsidiary passions, *vijñāna* is defiled and undergoes modifications. The modifications are three-fold: *ālaya*, *manovijñāna* and *viṣayavijñāna*. They are the different stratifications of consciousness. Ālaya can be compared, as Radhakrishnan so happily does, to the Unconscious, deep and potential. The *manovijñāna* is the transcendental process of intellection or categorisation, the activity of the mind, by which the potential is actualised, and experience is synthesised. The third mode of consciousness comprises the six kinds of sensa, including introspection. The external object is a projection of consciousness; there arise from it the apprehension of such things as houses, trees, mountains, etc., as existing independent of consciousness; but they do not so exist. Dream-objects are concrete examples of this false projectivity. The object is unreal by its very nature. Although the tree may have no external existence, it might at least be thought that the "tree-idea" exists as a subjective fact. Unlike Berkeley and other subjective Idealists, however, the Vijñānavādin rightly holds that, with the unreality of the object, the idea too loses its distinctive character as this or that idea. The modifications of consciousness, including the *ālaya*, are called *paratantra*, the Dependent. They are unreal in so far as they depend on the object for their determinate character. They are, however, not unreal in themselves. For, they are unreal only in the form in which they appear to us, being infected, as they are, with a false duality. Shorn of this duality, by the force of insight and intuition, they are the Ultimate. Hence the subjective world of ideas is said to be neither identical with nor different from the Absolute; not identical, because it is infected with the duality of subject and object; and not different because the Absolute is none other than this, being free from the false duality. The *Pariniṣpanna* (Absolute) is also called *dharmatā* or *tathatā*, the *Thatness* of things. It is of one undifferentiated nature like space and is identical with the essence of things, the *dharmakāya* of the Buddha.

IV. Influence of Buddhist Philosophy

Influence does not necessarily mean acceptance or borrowing of doctrines. That too is influence which stimulates the systems of thought to modify, revise, or even re-affirm their original stand-point. Influence may be expressed as much by opposition as by acceptance. In this sense alone the Vedānta, the Nyāya, and other systems of the Brāhmanical tradition have been influenced by Buddhism, and *vice versa.*

The subject of the relationship between Brāhmanical and Buddhist systems in itself is a vast and interesting field of study. Material of importance is to be found in the polemic scattered in the Śāstra literature of the systems. Encouraging work has been and is being done to trace the influence of the Sautrāntika on the Nyāya-Vaiśeṣika and of the Mādhyamika and the Yogācāra on the Advaita Vedānta.[1]

It is generally admitted that the Sāṅkhya was the first system of philosophy to arise in India; and in its earliest formulations this is pre-Buddhistic. The Sāṅkhya grew as the first synthesis, on a rationalistic basis, of the chief tenets of the Upaniṣads. The Sāṅkhya shows no Buddhistic influence. On the other hand, the Sāṅkhya itself exerted considerable influence on Buddhism. The teacher of Buddha, Āḷāra Kālāma and Uddaka Rāmaputta, were Sāṁkhya philosophers. Change or becoming is the central problem in Buddhism, as in the Sāṅkhya; but with this difference: in Buddhism this and every other problem was approached from the predominantly ethical point of view. There is no doubt that the Ābhidharmikas had before them the developed Sāṅkhya and that they moulded their own system closely on the Sāṅkhya model. "Viewed as a step in the evolution of Indian philosophical thought," says Stcherbatsky.

"Buddhism was probably preceded by a fully developed form of the Sāṅkhya system in the elaborate thoroughly consistent shape of an Indian science. Both doctrines are sometimes called radical systems, because the one adheres to the doctrine of eternal existence only, while the other maintains universal impermanence. It is out of place here to go into a more detailed comparison of both systems. Their close affinity has not escaped the attention of scholars. What I should like to insist upon is the fact that a close connection may be expressed not only by

1. Reference may be made to Stcherbatsky's *Buddhist Logic* (2 vols.), and to Professor Vidhushekhara Bhattacharya's *Āgama Śāstra* of Gauḍapāda as cases in point.

points of similarity, but also by opposition, nay by protest.[1]"

We may consider the Ābhidharmika conception of '*dharma*' as the Buddhist version of the Sāṅkhya conception of *prakṛti*. The *dharma*, like *prakṛti*, is a space-time entity, though, unlike *prakṛti*, it is a momentary durationless point-instant. The Sarvāstivāda explanation of the mode of existence of an entity in all the three times (past, present and the future) is inspired by the Sāṅkhya.

The great contribution Buddhist thought made to Indian philosophy was the discovery of the subjective, the theory of mental construction and appearance. Whereas the Sāṅkhya took only the relation between *puruṣa* (spirit) and *prakṛti* (matter) as appearance, the Buddhists with their anātman-bias relegated substance, the permanent, the whole, and the universal to the realm of the subjective. They maintained that these were merely thought-constructions lacking reality. Not empirical in origin, these are *a priori* forms which the uncritical mind superimposes on what really are momentary particular elements of existence. Thus is created the illusion of the soul, the permanent, the whole, and the universal. The Sautrāntika elaborated a very consistent and rigorous epistemology on these lines. The Mādhyamika, as we have seen, extended and deepened the emphasis on the subjective.

This revolution in Buddhist thought exerted a decisive influence on subsequent philosophy. Each system began remodelling, reforming and re-adjusting its tenets in the light of this disturbing and devastating discovery of the subjective. Systems with a monistic bias, such as the Vedānta and the Vijñānavāda, accepted the subjective, the *a priori* function of thought, and profited by the result. But they restricted the subjective to certain limits. They seem, therefore, to condemn the extremism of the Mādhyamika—his so-called nihilism. The Advaita Vedānta with its insistence upon the reality of Pure Being, its identity and universality, defined *avidyā* as that which makes Being appear as Becoming, the Universal as particulars, the identical as different. For the Vijñānavāda, *āvidyā* consists in the transcendental activity of the mind whereby the non-dual consciousness projects a false duality of subject and object.

1. Stcherbatsky, *Soul Theory of the Buddhists*, 824.

Both absolutisms employ dialectic to safeguard their absolutism, though not for establishing it in the first instance. Their absolutes partake of the form of the Mādhyamika *Śūnyatā* in being transcendent to thought and being accessible only to non-empirical intuition. They also have recourse to the device of two kinds of truth and two texts by which to explain apparent inconsistencies in experience and in the scriptures.

The reaction of the realistic and pluralistic systems was to reject the subjective and to re-affirm their realism all the more vehemently. The Nyāya and the Mīmāṁsā on the one hand and Jainism on the other take thought-forms as forms of the objectively real also. Thought, for them, *discovers* or *represents* things in a different medium; it does not distort or construct. For the absolutist systems, thought distorts reality and makes it appear as something other than what it really is. They had thus to make the distinction between what is *in itself* and what merely *appears*; they had thus to accept the notion of two types of truth and the distinction between phenomena and noumena. The realist systems required no such distinction; their reals are merely systematised or crystallised forms of empirical thought; they are very close to empirical moulds of experience.

The initial phase of the Nyāya-Vaiśeṣika shows no Buddhist influence. From its inception it has been a realistic pluralism, advocating atomism and the mechanical combination and separation of things. The influence of Buddhism made it still more realistic; it tended to make the Nyāya-Vaiśeṣika a very consistent and self-conscious realism. The Nyāya-Vaiśeṣika, which emerged at the end of its centuries-long duel with Buddhist systems, rigorously establishes the objectivity of relations, of the whole, of the universal, and even of negation. It minimised and even denied the work of thought. It objectified and externalised all thought-forms and put them up as categories of the object. One has to look into the polemic found in the works of Vātsyāyana, Udyotakara, Vācaspatimiśra, Jayanta, Udayana, Śrīdhara and a host of others in order to realise the truth of this remark. The Nyāya thus brought its ontology and epistemology into full accord with its basic principle. The Nyāya resisted the critical and subjectivistic attitude of Buddhistic schools all along the line

In the rise of the Mahāyāna, with a religion and a philosophy radically different from the Hīnayāna and even opposed to it, the influence of the Upaniṣadic tradition has been surmised, and with some justification. Kern sees distinct parallels between the *Bhagavadgītā* and the *Saddharma-Puṇḍarika.* Stcherbatsky says: "That the Mahāyāna is indebted to some *Aupaniṣada* influence is probable."[1] Radhakrishnan suggests this at several places: "*Bhūtatathatā* is the absolute which persist throughout all space and time as the basis of all. This universal eternal substratum answers to the Brahman of the Upaniṣads."[2]

The Dharmakāya answers to the impresonal absolute, the Brahman of the Upaniṣads. It is not so much the body of the law as the fathomless being or the norm of all existence. When the absolute principle assumes name and form we have the transformation of the Dharmakāya into the Sambhogakāya. The substance which persists becomes the subject which enjoys. The Brahman is now the Iśvara. He is the God in heaven, determined by the name and form, omniscient, omnipresent, omnipotent, the Ādi Buddha, supreme over all the Buddhas. When we pass to the Nirmāṇakāya, we get the several manifestations of this one activity into avatārs, or incarnations.....So far as the Mahāyāna is concerned, there is practically nothing to distinguish it from the religion of the *Bhagavadgītā.* The metaphysical conception of Dharmakāya, the or ultimate foundation of existence, corresponds to the Brahman of the Gītā. As Kṛṣṇa calls himself the Supreme One, even so Buddha is made into a Supreme God.[3]

This defines the nature of the possible influence. The earlier atheistic and positivistic phase of Buddhism is transformed into a pantheism with a host of deities; a radical pluralism becomes an absolutism. The influence might have been with regard to the absolute as the transcendent ground of phenomena, an idea which is well-defined in the Upaniṣadic conception of Brahman; the conception of Godhead and the doctrine of *bhakti* (personal devotion) may be traceable to the theism of the *Bhagavadgītā.* If there was borrowing, it was, in any case, only indirect and circumstantial. It is more probable that Buddhism, impelled

1. Stcherbatsky, *The Buddhist Conception of Nirvāṇa*, 51.
2. Ind. P. I, 593f.
3. Ind. P. I, 599.

by its own inner dynamism, was heading towards absolutism in metaphysics and pantheism in religion.

To appreciate the possible influence of the Mādhyamika and the Yogācāra on the Advaita Vedānta, we have to understand the nature of the revolution in Upaniṣad thought ushered in by Gauḍapāda and Śaṅkara. Pre-Śaṅkara Vedānta is best described as a monism; it is not an absolutism or non-dualism. For, it did not find any incompatibility in ascribing a real modification of Brahman to the world of phenomena; Brahman has real parts or aspects and possesses attributes; he has both form and no-form. Mokṣa (Freedom) is not through knowledge alone; karma (performance of enjoined duties) is a co-ordinate means. In Gauḍapāda and Śaṅkara, all this is repudiated. Brahman does not change; there is only an appearance of that. Brahman is transcendent to thought and no predicates can apply to it; there can be no real parts or aspects of Brahman, for it is an Infinite Whole and not made up of parts. The cause of bondage is our wrong identification with the body or mental states, owing to which there arises the false distinction of 'I' and 'Thou.' This wrong notion of difference is to be annulled and this can be attained only by enlightenment or knowledge. The advaitism of Śaṅkara is a conscious and sustained rejection of duality and difference. Brahman is established not positively, but by the denial of duality. In essence all these ideas are present in Gauḍapāda's *Māṇḍūkya Kārikā*. In the first three chapters of the book, he shows, by appeal to texts and arguments, that non-duality (advaita) is the real import of the *Upaniṣads* and that duality is an appearance, etc. The question is: If pre-Gauḍapāda Vedānta is monistic, not advaitic, then how could it suddenly take an absolutist turn ? Two hypotheses are possible: one that of borrowing, or at least copying, from the absolutism and dialectic already well-established in the Mādhyamika and the Vijñānavāda; and second, that, owing to its inherent dynamism, the Upaniṣadic tradition also was heading towards absolutism. There is nothing incongruent about either hypothesis, nor are they mutually exclusive.

Radhakrishnan clearly defines the nature and extent of the influence:

We need not say that the Advaita Vedānta philosophy has been very much influenced by the Mādhyamika doctrine. The *Alātaśānti* of Gauḍapāda's Kārikā is full of Mādhyamika tenets. The Advaitic distinction of vyavahāra, or experience, and paramārtha, or reality, correspond to the saṁvṛti and paramārtha of the Mādhyamikas. The Nirguṇa Brahman of Śaṅkara and Nāgārjuna's śūnya have much in common. The force of avidyā introducing the phenomenal universe is admitted by both. The keen logic which breaks up the world into a play of abstractions, categories and relations appears in both. If we take an Advaita Vedāntin like Śrīharṣa, we find that he does little more than develop the Mādhyamika theory, expose the self-contradictions of the categories we work with, such as cause and effect, substance and attribute, and deny the reality of things on account of the impossibility of explaining them.[1]

One cannot fail to be struck by points of close similarity between the *Kārikā*, especially the IV Chapter of it and Mahāyāna works. These fall under three heads: use of technical terms which have significant meaning only in Buddhist philosophical literature; verses which are almost verbatim quotations or adaptations from well-known Mādhyamika and Yogācāra works; and third, such doctrines as non-origination, the non-predicability of the four kinds of alternatives of the real, the object as the creation of the mind, etc. The conclusion is irresistible that in the *Māṇḍūkya Kārikā*, Gauḍapāda, a Vedānta philosopher, is attempting an advaitic interpretation of Vedānta in the light of Mādhyamika and Yogācāra doctrines. He even freely quotes from and appeals to them. This conclusion is, however, subject to two important reservations, one textual and the other doctrinal. To take the first. We have proceeded on the assumption that all the four chapters of the *Māṇḍūkya Kārikā* are by a single author. The different parts of it, however, are loosely connected; they may have been the work of different authors. Moreover, only the IVth Chapter shows indisputable Buddhist influence. This might well have been the work of a Buddhist, since it begins with a salutation to Buddha and ends with another; there is no reference to the ātman or the Upaniṣadic texts here, such as we have in the previous chapters.

It is also difficult to conceive how philosophers belonging to the ātman-tradition could borrow doctrines from those of the oppo-

1. Ind. P. I, 668.

sed anātman-tradition. The Vedāntins stake everything on the reality of the ātman and accept the authority of the Upaniṣads; the Buddhists denied the reality of the ātman (soul, substance, the permanent, the universal) in any form. The barrier, therefore, was always there. Besides, it is readily assumed that there is no difference between the absolutisms of Nāgārjuna, Śaṅkara and the Yogācāra. A closer analysis should bring out their differences as much as their generic affinity. Consistent with the above contention, we could only expect the Vedāntin to have profited by the technique or method of the Mādhyamika. He had before him the Mādhyamika distinction of *paramārtha* and *saṁvṛti*, of texts into *nītāratha* (primary) and *neyārtha* (secondary) and of the Mādhyamika method of reaching the real by negating the unreal. The Mādhyamika and Yogācāra also had a theory of illusion to account for the emergence of appearance. Knowledge of this turn in Buddhism must have sent the Vedāntin back to his own texts and enabled him to perceive the truer meaning of the Upaniṣads in Advaitism. The upshot of all this, therefore, would seem to be that there has been borrowing of technique rather than of tenets.

This leads us to the intrinsic problem about the correct interpretation of the three absolutisms, the *Śūnyatā* of Nāgārjuna, the Vijñaptimātratā of the Yogācāra, and the Nirguṇa Brahman of Śaṅkara. Do they differ merely in name ? I should like to suggest that, although agreeing with regard to the *form* of the absolute, these absolutisms differ considerably in the mode of their approach and in the nature of the entity with which they identify the absolute. This may also explain why these systems criticise each other and distinguish their respective positions so sharply. In all these systems, the absolute is transcendent, i.e., totally devoid of empirical determinations. The absolute is immanent too, because, it is the reality of appearance; the absolute is but the phenomena in their essential form. They all speak of the absolute as realisable in a non-empirical mode of intuition called variously, Prajñāpāramitā, lokottarajñāna and aparokṣānubhūti. They further agree with regard to the nature and status of phenomena as appearance. Every absolutism is really an advaita or advayavāda, i.e., non-dualism; they do not establish the absolute; they merely reject duality as being illusion.

The differences among the absolutisms, at least in the manner of their approach, should, however, not be overlooked. The Vedânta starts with an extra-logical or theological revelation of the Vedânta texts (Upaniṣads) about the sole reality of the âtman; and this is attempted to be realised by means of rational thought and contemplation. The Mâdhyamika takes hold of the dialectical consciousness which emerges logically in the conflict of viewpoints. The Yogâcâra is convinced of the sole reality of consciousness on the basis of the experience of trance-states, where consciousness continues to exist even though the object may be absent. The Vedânta and the Vijñânavâda begin with an analysis of an empirical illusion,—such as misperceiving a piece of shell for silver,—and then apply that analysis to phenomena as a whole. For the Vedânta, the real is the given, answering to the 'this' in the illusion-context: 'This is silver.' The 'silver,' as subsisting within consciousness only, is appearance. The Vedânta analyses illusion from the standpoint of knowledge wherein the object is or should be independent of the knowing act; knowledge merely discovers or reveals the given being and does not create it. The Vijñânavâdin approaches this problem from an opposite angle; the given ('this') is an unreal or free projection of consciousness, which latter alone is real. *Vijñāna* (consciousness) is understood not as Pure Being (static), but as creating and constructing the object out of itself by a free act. *Vijñāna* can be construed as Cosmic Will, much like the Absolute Ego of Fichte. Differing from both the Vedânta and Vijñânavâda, the Mâdhyamika addresses itself directly to the transcendental illusion created by the opposition of standpoints; it reaches the absolute through this dialectical consciousness. If *Brahman* is Pure Being (static and permanent), *vijñāna* is Creative Force or Will. *Śūnyatā* of the Mâdhyamika is identified with nothing that we empirically experience; it is the Critical or Reflective Awareness itself.

V. Buddhism as a Religion

Many might be tempted to consider Buddhism, at least its Hīnayâna phase, as a positivism in religion. It denied revelation, did not accept God, and, repudiating grace and personal devotion, relied entirely on knowledge and works. If religion means the consciousness of a Supreme Personal Reality and our intimate relation to that Reality, then Hīnayāna is not a religion. This position is radically modified in the Mahāyāna, which accepted the divinity of Buddha. Even Hīnayāna can be considered as a religion in so far as it canalises every aspect of man into the non-worldly ideal of salvation (*nirvāṇa*). As Radhakrishnan puts it :

"The essential quality of religion is to deal with the invisible environment of absolute worth. If this unseen environment or absolute reality does not exist, religion has no basis and no meaning. This reality is for the Upanisads absolute wisdom, and for Buddha it is the moral order. Whether we call it the order of truth or the order of righteousness, it is absolute in its claim. Religion is nothing more than the recognition of this claim. . . . Schleiermacher says: The only way for a truly individual religion to arise is to select some one of the great relations of mankind in the world to the Highest Being and then, in a definite way, make it the centre and refer to it all the others. The absolute can be apprehended by man in numberless ways. Each religion emphasises a special way and is in a sense a special intuition of the infinite, though the whole is always present in each. The Buddha emphasised the ethical aspect of the infinite and the ethical striving of man. Round these are organised the metaphysical and mystical truths of Buddhism.[1]"

Both Brāhmanism and Buddhism are types of Spiritual Religion. They try to realise a state of utter negation of the ego, the abolition of selfishness. Positively, it is the attainment of the Universal where all differences and conflicts cease and where there is perfect concord and harmony. Again in both, the highest state is attained by mystic intuition, a kind of non-discursive intellectual absorption. A strenuous spiritual discipline is enjoined as the indispensable means to it. All this is brought out with fullness and clarity in Radhakrishnan's account of Buddhism as a religion. I should now like to define the differences between Brāhmanism and Buddhism as religions.

The source of religious inspiration in Brāhmanism is revelation as given to us in the Vedas; in Buddhism it is reason. Not that Brāhmanism is antagonistic to reason or is unmindful of the value of reason; but it is only revelation which can give us intuitions of

1. TB, 22f.

the transcendent; the function of reason is to analyse and clarify the revealed truth. Innovations are only interpretations of the given truth, and the entire mode of development is authoritarian and traditional. Buddha asks us not to receive anything on trust nor to accept any authority, but to test it by reason and experience. He himself did not owe allegiance to any authority, Vedic or non-Vedic.[1]

A curious paradox arose soon after Buddha's death. His discourses, edited, codified and preserved, attained the sanctity of Canons or Scriptures like the Vedas. Buddhists began to be as much exercised over exegetical considerations as were their Brāhmanical compatriots. Owing to the diversity of languages in which the Discourses of Buddha were preserved and the want of an accurate system of oral transmission, their dictional purity, obviously, could not attain the standard of the Vedas. This was remedied in the course of time; and disputes came to be settled, in the orthodox Hindu fashion, by appeal to texts. The *Kathāvatthu* (3rd cent. B.C.) adopts this method in deciding issues. The situation continued to be fluid for a long time, however. New canons of the Mahāyāna began to make their appearance not very long after the death of Buddha, and soon their number became a veritable flood. Both Hīnayānists and Mahāyānists appealed to the Word of Buddha; the former were literalists and conservative, the latter were liberal and progressive. Even the Word of Buddha is defined by the Mahāyāna as what is not incompatible with the Norm and whatever is well-said.

Orthodox Hinduism does not rest on any historical fact nor on the advent of any person; its incarnations are mythological and legendary, and the non-appearance of any or all of them would not affect it. It is not an historical religion. Buddhism, on the other hand, is an historical religion. The advent of the human Buddha (Gautama) is vital to it. Buddha is but an exalted human teacher. The advantage of having a human teacher as the founder of a religion is obvious; it makes for concrete and intimate personal relationship. There are, on the other hand, also distinct disadvantages: with the lapse of time the personal intimacy ceases to be felt, and doubt arises about the founder's historicity; legends and exaggerations complete the process.

1. *Majj. Nik. Sutta* 26; *Saṁyutta Nik.*, II, 105.

By dynamic necessity, therefore, Buddha came, in the course of time, to be deified like any other founder of a new religion. The divinity of Buddha came to be the chief ground of difference between the Mahāsaṅghikas and the Sthaviravādins.

If we look at the *Nikāyabheda-Dharma-Mati Cakara Śāstra* of Vasumitra, we come across the following passages. The fundamental and common doctrines of the Mahāsaṅghikas, the Ekavyavahārika, the Lokottaravāda and the Kaukkuṭika schools are:—The four schools unanimously maintained that the Blessed Buddhas are all supermundane, the Tathāgatas have no worldly attributes, the words of the Tathāgatas are all about the Turning of the Wheel of Law, Buddha preaches all doctrines with one utterance, in the teaching of the Bhagavān (Buddha) there is nothing that is not in accordance with the Truth, the physical body of Tathāgata is limitless, the majestic powers of Tathāgata also are limitless, lives of Buddhas are limitless and Buddha is never tired of enlightening living beings and awakening pure faith in them, etc.[1] We can see in these rather undeveloped notions the incipient stages of the Mahāyāna Buddhology, Śūnyatā and the Bodhisattva ideal which came to be developed with such thoroughness in the *Prajñāpāramitā*, *Saddharmapuṇḍarīka*, and other treatises.

The conception of Buddha as God is as foundational in religion as is that of Śūnyatā in metaphysics. It represents the dehistorization of Buddha; Mahāyāna just escapes being an historical religion. In one sense Buddha loses some of his concrete personal character inasmuch as he is now identified with the *dharmakāya* (the Absolute) or *śunyatā*; he is one of the numerous free phenomenalisations of the Absolute. In another sense, Buddha becomes more human: he is the inner essence of all beings and Buddhahood is latent in all; every being is a *bodhisattva* destined, in the fullness of time and effort, to attain complete Buddhahood. By a logical necessity, therefore, "the Buddhas were subjected to a six-fold process of evolution: they were multiplied, immortalised, deified, spiritualised, universalised, and unified."[2]

The dual nature of Buddha as one with the Absolute (*śūnya*)

1. Kimura, *Hīnayāna and Mahāyāna*, 86f.
2. Har Dayal, *The Bodhisattva Doctrine*, 28.

and at the same time actively pursuing the welfare of beings supplies the philosophical basis for the theological conception of the *trikāya* of Buddha. The three bodies or aspects of Buddha are: the *dharma-kāya* or Cosmical body, which is his essential nature as one with the Absolute; the *sambhogakāya* is the body of Bliss, by which he contemplates and enjoyes himself as a Divine, Glorious Person; and the *nirmāṇa-kāya* is the body which he assumes as an act of grace in order to teach the Law and save beings. Gautama the Śākyamuni is merely one of the countless manifestations of the Buddha.

The need for a mediator is felt in all absolutism; Vedānta has recourse to *Īśvara*, distinct from *Brahman*, to account for the revelation of truth; in the Mādhyamika and Yogācāra that function is performed by the *Tathāgata*. It is not a necessary part of Truth that it should be known and declared as truth: it is not constituted by our knowing or not knowing it. The Absolute (Brahman or śūnya) does not reveal itself, being the Truth itself; and finite beings confined to the phenomenal sphere do not know the truth. Only a being who enjoys a sort of amphibious existence, having one foot in phenomena and the other in the Absolute, can possibly know the Absolute and reveal it to others. But *Īśvara* or the *Tathāgata* is a lower principle than the Absolute, which is the impersonal reality of all beings. Though this position is common to both the Vedānta and the Mahāyāna, there are, however, some differences. To *Īśvara* is assigned not merely the function of revealing the Truth; creation, sustenance, destruction, and other cosmic functions are also performed by him. In Buddhism, the Law of Karma takes the place of *Iśvara* in this regard. *Iśvara* reveals the Truth to phenomenal beings through some extra-ordinary mechanism of communication, probably in the beginning of creation; he does not incarnate himself as man for this purpose. The Tathāgata, on the other hand, descends from his divine plane and takes birth among men, conforms to their modes of life, gains their sympathy, and reveals the truth through ordinary modes of communication. The Tathāgata is, to all intents, Man perfected by the destruction of ignorance and passions. The most characteristic feature of God in Mahāyāna Buddhism is the *mahākaruṇā*; Great (Compassion) that is prepared for any sacrifice for any being and for all time. This active and unceasing effort for the welfare and final release of all beings makes the *Tathāgata* a very loving and lovable God. It is easily one of the purest and most exalted conceptions of Godhead. Not that *Īśvara* is not conceived as benign and loving, but that the ideal of *Mahākarunā* and *sarvamukti* (Salvation for all) is not so intimately and intensely expressed there as in Buddhism.

It is not to be supposed that Buddhology was a complete innovation of the Mahāyānists. It is present in implicit form in the Pali Canons too. In the *Mahāpadāna* and the *Mahāparinibbāna Suttas*, we have an account of the spiritual lineage of the Buddhas. The Mahāyāna is the unequivocal expression of these anticipations. In its philosophy, Mahāyāna is an absolutism; in religion it is a Pantheism, a diversity of divine beings with a background of Unity of Godhead. There is greater affinity between Mahāyāna and Brāhmanism than between the former and Hīnayāna.

Though Hīnayāna cannot, on philosophical grounds, find any place for God, Buddha serves the same purpose which God performs in other religions. There are temples, in all the Southern countries professing Hīnayāna, where the image of Buddha is worshipped more or less in the Hindu fashion. Every form of ritual and worship in the Brāhmanical religion is symbolic and mystical; they stand for the transcendent. In Hīnayāna it is mostly relicworship, the veneration of the physical remains of the historical Gautama or his Saints; Stūpas have been erected on these relics (teeth or bones). The need felt by the common man for a personal god was too strong to be resisted. However, scholars and monks in these countries would still in theory profess atheism, strict governance of the law, etc., although in practice it is otherwise.

Buddhism is a religion of the elect, despite the fact that it was thrown open to all without distinction of caste or status. It is expressly meant for the few who choose the life of the monk and conform to the rules of the Order. The layman was not expressly provided for in this scheme. His function seems to have been to provide food and raiment to the Order and to listen to the discourses of the monks. The benefit of Buddhism to the layman is, therefore, indirect and circumstantial. The content of the Buddhist religion is principally, if not wholly, spiritual. There was no ceremonial, social or juridical side to it. In other religions, ceremonies are enjoined on the birth of a child, at the time of marriage, funeral, etc. The *Gṛhya Sūtras* of Brāhmanism are devoted to this aspect of life. Festivals and services also form an integral part of other religions. The religious society is also usually governed by a code of law, governing inheritance, adoption, etc.; the *Dharma Śāstras* perform this juridical function in Hindu society. It is not owing to an oversight or to disinclination that such rules were not framed for the lay society in Buddhism. Buddha himself formulated minute rules regulating every aspect of the life of the monks comprising the Order. The *Vinaya Piṭaka* is a massive code which even to-day regulates the life of Buddhist monks. The conclusion is forced on us, therefore, that the content of Buddhism is chiefly spiritual. It was not committed to any specific social or racial milieu, as is the case in Brāhmanism.

This freedom from the social setting enjoyed by Buddhism is at once an asset and a drawback. It could address itself exclusively to a compact and well-disciplined order. It could also be easily transported to other environmental conditions, since it was not tied to any rigid social cast like orthodox Hinduism. Buddhism is Hinduism meant for export. Only the spiritual message needed to be propagated in other countries. Buddhism could thus take on the colour and hue of the societies and racial groups to which it spread. This accounts for the wide diversity of its forms. It could synthesise and fuse with varied racial and social structures, as in China with Confucianism and Taoism, in Japan with Shintoism, in Tibet with Lamaism, not to speak of its divergent forms in the Southern countries of Asia. In this sense, Buddhism is more universal in its appeal than orthodox Hinduism. But this should not blind us to the fact that it was an exclusive religion. It did not accept alternative paths or modify its teachings according to tastes and temperaments. The Councils and Synods held from time to time were meant to define the Orthodox Norm and persecute heresy by the application of sanctions.

The Mahāyāna differed greatly from Hīnayāna in this regard. It was not only more liberal and prolific, but it also could genuinely provide for different approaches. As the Ultimate is Śūnya, devoid of empirical determinations, it could be reached by not merely one official path but by several. The gradation of teaching according to the spiritual bias and capacity of the individual is a great tenet of Mahāyāna. This is the celebrated doctrine of Buddha's "excellence in the choice of means (*Upāya-Kauśalya*). Buddha does not blindly, mechanically, prescribe one remedy to all and sundry; he varies and graduates it according to the need and the occasion. The indeterminacy of the absolute allows freedom of approach.

VI. The Spread and Disappearance of Buddhism

Orthodox Hinduism was content to leave the propagation of religion to unofficial agencies. In consequence, all its institutions were decentralised. But Buddhism, from its very inception, believed in organised and directed effort. Buddha founded the First Church in history. It is not that the order of monks was his innovation. There were literally countless groups of recluses and homeless wanderers in India before and during the time of Buddha. Moreover, many of the rules adopted by Buddha for his Order were admittedly borrowed from current practice, e.g., the institution of observing the Fortnightly Convention. But such a great and closely knit organisation, actuated by a single purpose, shows Buddha as a unique organiser and administrator. The *Vinaya Piṭaka* may well be compared to the *Laws* of Plato, although Buddha is concerned here to lay down detailed rules not for any imaginary city-state on earth but for the monks bent on achieving freedom from earthly existence.

The speed with which the message of Buddha spread and the succession of high-souled men of incessant energy whom the Order could attract to its ranks are attributable to the unique personality of Buddha, to his universal spiritual message, and to the efficiency of the Order. "The causes of the success of Buddhism as a religion are the three jewels or *triratna*, of (1) Buddha; (2) the dharma or the Law; and (3) the saṅgha, or the brotherhood." :[1] The *saṅgha*, as a devoted body of selfless men drawn from all ranks, especially from the highest classes, not only carried the message far and wide in India, but spread it in distant countries. They were the first missionaries in history.

1. Ind P. I, 473.

The missionary spirit contributed considerably to the spread of the gospel. Buddha bade his disciples: "Go into all lands and preach this gospel." Tell them that the poor and the lowly, the rich and the high, are all one, and all castes unite in this religion as do the rivers in the sea.[1]

Buddhism had a universal appeal; it did not require, as was pointed out above, any specific social or caste background. And there was the Order charged with the task of spreading and preserving the teaching of the Master. But the factors which made for its rapid spread were themselves also the cause of its decline in and disappearance from India.

We must discount all accounts of persecution of Buddhism by orthodox Hinduism. As Radhakrishnan says: "Buddhism died a natural death in India. It is an invention of the interested to say that fanatic priests fought Buddhism out of existence. . . . The violent extermination of Buddhism in India is legendary."[2] Persecution of different religious groups and sects is totally contrary to the Indian spirit. Buddha preached for over forty years after his enlightenment; and, during all that time, he freely moved about the country. We do not hear of any molestation or persecution. He was received everywhere with reverence and honour, even by those who disagreed with him. In fact, he received injury from a faction in his own Order instigated by his cousin Devadatta. The Jaina Order too offered him some opposition. But no mention is made of any civic or other disability imposed on the Saṅgha at any time during its existence. Stray cases of persecution on either side cannot be ruled out; but it is more likely that the Buddhist Order was militant and intolerant. Any organised and deliberate persecution does not appear to have occurred.

Moreover, external persecution has never resulted in extinction. A religion with such vitality and dynamism could not be stamped out by unfavourable circumstances; for, it could not only rise above the circumstances, but also could effectively mould conditions to its own norm. The causes for the disappearance of Buddhism must, therefore, be inherent and internal. Two principal causes might have contributed to the decline and dis-

1. Ind P. I, 475.
2. Ind P, I, 607f.

appearance of Buddhism from India; one, the secularity of the Order, and the other that Buddhism was never rooted in the soil, since it had only a spiritual content. When this spiritual content became indistinguishable from a resurgent Hinduism, there was no *raison d'être* for Buddhism's separate continuance.

The Monastic Order was certainly a potent source of strength. But it was inherently secular, unspiritual; all organisation is so of necessity. Individual monks could not have belongings or own houses; but the Order could and had to acquire property. So long as the monks were few, they could subsist on alms by begging from house to house. But to feed by means of alms several hundred monks gathered in some of the Vihāras was a difficult problem. They had also to set up establishments near flourishing towns and cities instead of residing in solitary places, as the first monks had done. The Order also needed quite a number of men to perform necessary secular duties in order to maintain a few monks who could then attend to their spiritual affairs. It is recorded that Buddha had to make the following appointments: "I sanction a Bhikkhu endowed with five qualities....as Food-controller....I sanction a Superior of Lodgings who will know what is assigned and what is not assigned.... I sanction a storehouse keeper and a receiver of robes."[1] As some of the Vihāras were fair-sized towns, they must have presented problems in sanitation, transport, and other civic amenities. Thus the world, which the monks had ostensibly renounced, comes in through the back door.

Moreover, a different psychology motivates the Order. What one would not do for his individual gain, one would do in the interests of the Order. He would be importunate and callous when it concerned the Order. The impersonality of the Order could, therefore, easily deaden the monks' moral susceptibilities. The interests of the Order would also preclude exposing the failings of its members. Thus the Order becomes a vested interest. Rivalry and competition for position are inseparable from an Order. It becomes a power, and "power corrupts." We also know from history that many of the Heads of the Vihāras wielded considerable power and interfered in the politics of the states; and, in view of their international affiliations, they even conspired at times with foreign invaders.

1. *Cullavagga,* VI, xxi.

An Order is secular and unspiritual by its constitution. A spiritual Order is a standing contradiction. It could exist only by an unceasing compromise between two opposing forces, selfishness and altruism. As long as there was a preponderance of the unselfish element in the Order, it could forge ahead as a real spiritual force. But when the rot set in, as the egoistic trends soon asserted themselves, the Order became a potent source of evil. The Lord (Buddha) must have perceived the inevitable decay of the Order, when he is reported to have said, on the occasion of the admission of women to the Order, that his *dharma* would have lasted a thousand years, but now its life would be shortened to five hundred, because of the admission of women. Actually, Buddhism has lasted much longer than the predicted period. But there was a limit to its usefulness determined solely by its own inherent reasons.

The other reason for the disappearance of Buddhism from India is to be found in its special form. We should not forget that Buddhism was never a rival religion competing with or contending against Hinduism, as Islam and Christianity are and have been doing. Its difference from Brāhmanism was solely on the spiritual plane. It had no rival social and legal institutions. It is wrong to think that Buddha or Buddhism was opposed to caste as a *social* institution. It is true that in the Order of Monks there was no distinction of caste, and caste-values had no meaning. But this does not mean that Buddha ever preached a crusade against caste. According to the Canons, Buddhas could be born in the Brāhmaṇa or Kṣatriya caste, and not in any other. The popular notion that there was a period called Buddhist India, when the majority of people were converted to Buddhism and that on the revival of Hinduism they were reconverted to Hinduism has no basis in fact. As has been pointed out already, Buddhism had a spiritual side only and the layman was never converted to Buddhism, as one can speak of conversion to Christianity or Mohammedanism. Indeed the *upāsaka* expressed his spiritual or moral sympathy; but he was never required to renounce in theory or practice the religion he had been following; there is no mention of any formula or ritual of conversion, and there was nothing to distinguish him from his Hindu brethren. Initiation into the Order of Buddhist Monks is a different matter altogether; there were elaborate ceremonies for that. Only the Monastic Orders could be called specifically Buddhist at any time, and they must have formed a microscopic community. The moral and spiritual influence of the Order on the layman was, however, enormous and continuous.

Since Buddhism confined itself to the spiritual side, it had no separate roots in the general society. With the emergence and spread of the Mahāyāna philosophy and religion and the resurgence of the Vedānta religion and the Advaita philosophy, the difference between them must have become almost indistinguishable. "Buddhism and Brāhmanism approached each other so much that for a time they were confused and ultimately became one. Slow absorption and silent indifference, and not priestly fanaticism and methodical destruction, are the causes of the fall of Buddhism."[1] This analysis of Radhakrishnan is eminently reasonable and true.

The disappearance of Buddhism, as a separate entity, from India is no measure of the disappearance of its influence, however. It has profoundly influenced the philosophy and religion of India. It has deepened our spiritual life and has given us a purer ethics. The absolutist and critical trend in Indian philosophy is largely owing to Buddhism. The Dialectic as a weapon of refutation and as a spiritual mode of approaching the Absolute is distinctly a contribution of the Mādhyamika. In the field of epistemology, the debt that the Nyāya, the Vedānta and the other systems of thought owe to the Sautrāntika is immense. To crown all, we have with us the ideal of the *Bodhisattva*, unceasingly active in the well-being of all creatures, high and low; he is a shining example of egoless personality.

Professor Radhakrishnan's own philosophy stems as much from the absolutism of Śaṅkara as from that of Nāgārjuna. His ethical ideal of the philosopher realising his unity with all beings, not in retirement from the world into a private enjoyment of his own freedom, but in bringing spiritual freedom to others, is as much the ideal of Sarvamukti of the Advaita Vedānta as it is of the Mahāyāna.

1. Ind. Phil. I, 608.

5.6 THE METAPHYSICAL SCHOOLS OF BUDDHISM*

I. The Rise of the Schools

The tendency to split and diversify itself into Schools and sub-Schools appeared very early in the history of Buddhism. The *Kathā-vatthu* (c. 246 B.C.) discusses the doctrinal differences of the Schools, which must have been quite well-established by then. The first recorded division of the Buddhist congregation occurred about a hundred years after the Buddha's *nirvāṇa* at the Council of Vesāli. There the *elders* (*sthaviras*) ex-communicated the 10,000 Vajjian monks, ostensibly on the interpretations of the ten minor[1] rules of discipline; the real grounds were doctrinal. The Vajjian monks formed themselves into the great *order* (*Mahāsaṅghika*)[2] The beginnings of the Mahāyāna can be discerned in this schism. From the *elders*, the Sarvāsti-vādins and the Sāmmitīyas separated themselves in course of time. Each of these comprised within it several sub-Schools.

Early Buddhist historians like Vasumitra, Vinītadeva and Bhavya speak of the eighteen different Schools,[3] all rightly

*Reprinted from *History of Philosophy Eastern and Western*, edited by S. Radhakrishnan, London: George Allen & Unwin, 1952.

1. See *Dīpa-vaṁśa*, p. 35; Buston's *History of Buddhism*, Vol. II, pp. 91 ff.

2. *Dīpa-vaṁśa*, p. 36. In the Northern accounts the origin of the Mahāsaṅghika is given differently.

3. Though all authorities are agreed about the number 18, there is discrepancy with regard to the individual names and the classification. Buston (*History of Buddhism*, Vol. II, pp. 97 ff.), relying on *Bhikṣu-varṣāgra-pṛcchā* and Vinītadeva, enumerates thus: The Pūrvaśaila, Aparaśaila, Haimavata, Lokottara-vādins and Prajñapti-vādins belong to the Mahāsaṅghika School; the Mūla-sarvāstivādins, Kāśyapīya, Mahīśasaka, Dharmagupta, Bāhuśrutīya, Tāmracaitīya and Vibhajya-vāda belong to the *Sarvāsti-vāda*; Jetavanīya, Abhayagiri-vāsins, and Mahāsthaviras form the School of Sthaviras; the Kurukullakas, Avantaka and Vātsīputrīya belong to the Sāmmitīya sect. Reference may also be made to Vasumitra's *Nikāyālambana Śāstra* (Nanjio nos. 1284-6), translated into English by Masuda (*Asia Major*, Vol. II, 1925); Max Walleser's *Die Sektem des alten Buddhismus* gives Vasumitra's (pp. 24 ff.) and Bhavya's (pp. 77 ff.) account of the Schools; Rockhill's *Life of the Buddha*, pp. 181 ff., gives translations from Tibetan sources. The *Kathā-vatthu*, its commentary and the *Dīpa-vaṁśa* (pp. 37-8) give the Pāli or Southern version.

claiming to embody the true teaching of the *master*. Of these only four main Schools deserve consideration: *Sthavira-vāda, Sarvāsti-vāda, Mahāsaṅghika* and *Sāmmitīya*; others are off-shoots of these.

The *Sthavira-vāda*, predominant at first, gradually declined in importance and influence from the time of the 3rd *Council* (Aśoka's reign) till it disappeared altogether from the mainland of India; it, however, continues to thrive in Ceylon, Burma, Thailand. The *Sarvāsti-vāda* was the most dominant and influential School; it had its ramifications all over the country, including Kāśmīra and Gāndhāra. The Sāmmitīyas (Vātsīputrīyas) must have been a prosperous sect with a considerable following. No original works of this sect have been preserved, and there is the disadvantage of having to derive our all too meagre knowledge of this School from its opponents. Universally condemned by the other Schools as heretical, they held tenaciously to the doctrine of the Individual (*Pudgala-ātman*), a quasi-permanent entity, neither completely identical with nor different from the mental states.[1] The importance of this School is as a transitional stage between the one-sided modal standpoint of the other Schools and the no-position of the Mādhyamika. It is, however, the Mahāsaṅghikas who can be definitely termed the precursors of the Mahāyāna religion and philosophy.[2] The implicit differences of the Schools regarding the conception of the *real* (*dharmas*), *nirvāṇa*, the *buddha-kāya* and *individual* or *universal* salvation (*Bodhisattva ideal*) became accentuated and clearer. In their age-long disputation and the clash of ideas, the classical Buddhist systems grew to maturity.

Buddhism is not one unitary system but a matrix of systems. Their internal differences notwithstanding, no School of Buddhism conceived the real as *substance* (*ātman*), permanent, identical and universal. Conversely, all non-Buddhist systems, including the Jaina, accepted the reality of the *ātman* in some form or the other. *Nairātmya* (substancelessness) is the generic idea of Buddhism that is sought to be understood and interpreted by the several Schools, which thus constitute its species.

1. *Abhidharma-kośa* (Appendix), *Pudgala-viniścaya* (Trans. by Stcherbatsky —*Soul Theory*), *Kathā-vatthu* first section; *Madhyamaka-kārikā* IX and X.

2. See Kimura, *Hīnayāna and Mahāyāna*, pp. 12, 15, 67, 115 ff. N. Dutta, *Three Principal Schools of Buddhism*, p. 3 f.

In the earliest *realistic* phase, the rejection of *substance* (*pudgala-nairātmya*) was interpreted to mean the reality of the separate elements (*dharmas*). *Thera-vāda* and *Sarvāsti-vāda* (Vaibhāṣika) are the chief exponents of this dogmatic pluralistic phase. The classical Sautrāntika is a critical edition of this realism. It evolved a rigorous epistemology on Kantian lines. By its critical and subjective trends, the Sautrāntika paved the way for the Mādhyamika and the Yogācāra systems.

The Mādhyamika philosophy, systematized by Nāgārjuna (*c.* second century A.D.), represents the second and central phase of Buddhist thought. It denied the separate reality of the elements also (*dharma-nairātmya*); if the substance is a thought-construct (unreal) the modes and attributes are equally so. If the real cannot be conceived as the permanent, the attributes are equally so. If the real cannot be conceived as the permanent and universal, as the Sāṅkhya and the Vedānta do, it cannot be conceived as momentary particulars either, as the earlier Buddhism does. The Buddha has taught the doctrine of momentariness only as a stepping-stone[1] to the final teaching of the relativity of things (*śūnyatā*).

Like Śaṅkara's Advaitism on the *brāmaṇical* side, the Mādhyamika revolutionized Buddhism. It is a sustained attempt to synthesize the teachings of the Buddhist Scriptures by the adoption of the transcendental (*paramārtha*) and the phenomenal (*saṁvṛti*) standpoints. The Mādhyamika dialectic was born of the criticism of the two radical viewpoints—the substance-view of the *brāhmaṇical* systems and the modal view of earlier Buddhism. And like the Kantian dialectic, the Mādhyamika is a critique of all philosophy.

The basic ideas of the Mādhyamika system—the Absolute as devoid of empirical determinations, the falsity of appearance and the distinction between the ultimate and phenomena—were accepted. There was, however, a reaction against what appeared to some as its extreme and unqualified rejection of phenomena. The idealism of the Yogācāra (*vijñānavāda*) School is to be understood as a significant modification of the Mādhyamika negativism (*śūnyatā*).[2] It contends that the

1. See *Bodhicaryāvatāra*, IX, 7; *Viṁśatikā*, 10.
2. Founded by Maitreya-(nātha), Asaṅga and Vasubandhu (*c.* fourth century A. D.).

sole reality of *consciousness* cannot be denied, while the duality of subject and object with which it is apparently infected must be considered non-existent (*śūnya*); the duality is unreal; but that, where the negation of duality (*dvaya-śūnyatā*) obtains, *does exist*; it is nothing (*śūnya*).[1]

The critical philosophy of Kant led to the idealistic systems of Fichte, Schelling and Hegel in the West; here too the Yogācāra idealism follows as a direct outcome of the Mādhyamika. this is the third great phase of Buddhism.

Tāntricism (*Vajra-yāna*, *Mantra-yāna*, etc.) supervened on *Vijñāna-vāda*. *Tāntricism* is a unique combination of *mantra*, ritual and worship on an absolutistic basis; it is both religion and philosophy. It was especially this phase of Buddhism that was propagated in Tibet when it disappeared from India (eleventh to twelfth centuries). Some of the classical Schools of Buddhism find their continuation in China and Japan[2] even to this day.

This division of Buddhist thought into the realistic, absolutistic and idealistic phases is in full accord with its logical and chronological development. Buston[3] and other historians of Buddhism speak of these periods as the three swingings of the wheel of law (*Dharma-cakra-pravarttana*) The non-Buddhists invariably mention four Schools of Buddhism—the Vaibhāṣika, the sautrāntika, the Mādhyamika and the Yogācāra. The first two belong to the Hīnayāna and are pluralistic and realistic, and the last two to the Mahāyāna and are absolutistic. The Vaibhāṣika (Ābhidharmika) system occupies the same place in Buddhism as the Sāṅkhya on the orthodox side. Other systems have grown as modification and criticism of this. It is not to be supposed that with the rise of the Mādhyamika, the Ābhidharmika ceased to grow or that the Mādhyamika went out of vogue when the Yogācāra appeared. These Schools continued to develop side by side for centuries; the prior-

1. cf. the first verse of the *Madhyānta-vibhāga* (p. 9).
abhūta-parikalpo' sti dvayaṁ tatra na vidyate
śūnyatā vidyate tvatra tasyām api sa vidyate.

2. Sarvāsti-vāda (Kusha), Sautrāntika (Jojitsu), Yogācāra (Fa-hsiang or Hosso); Mādhyamika (Sanron). See Takakusu's *Essentials of Buddhist Philosophy*, Honolulu, 1947.

3. *History of Buddhism.*, Vol. II, pp. 52-4.

ity of the one to the other applies only to its first systematic formulation. Buddhism has remained in all the three periods, a *dharma* theory based on the cardinal doctrine of dependent origination (*pratitya-samutpāda*), which received different interpretations; every Buddhist system has claimed to be the *middle path*. The earlier Buddhism of the Ābhidharmika systems take the *dharma*-theory as denying *substance* (*ātman*), but establishing the reality of the separate *elements* (*dharmas*). *Pratītya-samutpāda* is the causal law regulating the rise and subsidence of discrete entities; the middle path is the steering clear of eternalism and nihilism. In the Mādhyamika, this principle is interpreted as the essential dependence of things, the unreality of separate elements; the middle path is the non-acceptance of the two basic views—affirmative (*sat*) and negative (*a-sat*). The *Vijñāna-vāda* avoids the dogmatism of realism (the reality of objects) and the scepticism of nihilism (the rejection of both object and consciousness).

2. The Basic Doctrines of Buddhism

Existence is declared *anicca* (impermanent), *anatta* (substanceless) and *dukkha* (pain) in the *Pāli* Canons. But this was arrived at rather through intuition and observation than by any rigorous *a priori* arguments. This was done later, especially by the Sautrāntika. The characteristic *nairātmya* standpoint of all Buddhism can be presented as a polemic against substance, the permanent and the universal taken as real in the systems of the *ātma*-tradition; it maintains the three connected theses—momentariness (*kṣaṇikatva*) substancelessness (*anātmatva*) and uniqueness (*sva-lakṣaṇa*) of entities.

The *real* is the efficient, i.e. that which causes some effect (*artha-kriyākārin*). The permanent as the non-efficient is unreal. Causal efficiency can be either simultaneous or successive. If simultaneous, all the effects being completed at once, it may be asked whether the permanent exists after the first moment or not? If it does, it should produce the same effects in the second and succeeding moments, thus giving rise to an interminable series of the same effect from one cause. This is an absurdity. If it does not produce this series, though continuing to exist in the succeeding moments, then it is evident that there is a manifest difference in its nature between the first and other moments: for in the first moment it is efficient (*samartha*) while in other moments it is not so (*a-samartha*) with regard to the same effect. That cannot be one (i.e. an identical thing) of which two or more opposed characteristics are predicated.[1] Nor is the permanent efficient successively, e.g. A first produces X, then Y, then Z. It might be asked whether A is capable of producing Y when it is producing X. If it were, A would produce all the effects at once, and the second alternative will be reduced to the first one of simultaneous production. If it is not capable, it will never produce the effect, as a piece of stone cannot produce the sprout given any length of time. If we still think that A is one and the same entity in two or more moments, then it is both efficient and inefficient at once with regard to the same effect.

It may be objected that a cause (e.g. the seed) is the same: only the efficiency is owing to the presence or absence of auxiliary conditions (*sahakārin*). But do these conditions mean anything to the permanent? The mere inoperative presence of them will not bring about any result. They must therefore first *modify* the seed before it can sprout. It is the seed as *changed* that produces the effect. If the modification were an integral part of the seed, it should have that always. If it is not, then the seed has two natures—one, what it is in itself and the other what it becomes in response to its auxiliary conditions. But accepting two natures of a thing is really to accept two things, according to the Buddhist dictum already mentioned. Thus things are different every moment; difference of time is difference of thing; at no two moments is a thing identical. Existence is momentary (*kṣaṇika*).

The same conclusion can be enforced by the consideration of decay and destruction. The vulgar notion is that a thing will continue to exist unless it is destroyed by opposite forces. But if a thing is not capable of destruction by itself, no amount of external influence can affect it, much less reduce it to nothing. The blow from a stick destroys the pitcher, it may be said. But if destruction were not inherent to the pitcher, the blow should mean nothing to it; it should continue to exist as before untouched, like empty space. If the destruction were inherent to the

1. This is the Buddhist dictum: *Yo viruddha-dharmādhyāsavān nāsāvekaḥ.*

pitcher, the blow of the stick is merely an occasion for its cessation; it does not bring it about. Consider for a moment what is meant by the ageing or decaying of a thing. It is not the case that a thing continues to exist unaffected for any stretch of time and then suddenly begins to change. It changes every moment, uniformly, unperceivedly, relentlessly. Can we not say, therefore, that change or even birth is death every moment; the thing must become different at every moment of its existence. Permanence of a thing is an illusion, like the oneness of the flame or of the stream. Existence is flux. A thing is a point-instant, having neither a "before" nor an "after"; it has no span temporally; there is no duration. Cessation is inherent to things and is entire (*a-hetuko nir-anvayo vināśaḥ*).

Precisely the same logic is applied to refute the reality of the *whole* (*avayavin*). What constitutes *one* thing? We might hold with common sense that the table is one entity, the tree is one, though they may consist of parts. But the table is partly seen and partly not, as it is impossible to see all the parts at once. Parts of the tree move and some other parts do not; a part of it is in shade and a part of it is sunlit. How can that be one entity of which two or more opposed characteristics (e.g. seen and unseen, moving and unmoving, dark and sunlit) are ascribed? It is not possible to escape this logic by stating that what is moving is one part and what is not moving is different from it. For both the parts belong to the *same* thing; the characteristics of the parts belong to the thing—the whole of which they are parts. Therefore there are as many things as there are distinguishable "parts" or aspects. An entity has no extensity or complexity of content. The oneness of many things ("parts" and aspects) is illusory as the oneness of a heap of corn.[1]

So a thing is not only an instant (*kṣaṇika*) lacking duration, but also a spatial point lacking all magnitude and diversity as well.

By the same logic we are led to the denial of the *universal* (*sāmānya*) or identical aspect of things. Each entity is discrete and unique (*sva-lakṣaṇa*). The existence of the universal, uniform and identical, in all the particulars is beset with insuper-

1. *arciṣāṁ santāne pradīpa iti upacaryate, eka iveti kṛtvā, AKV.*, p. 713; *rāśīvad dhārāvad iti. ibid.*, p. 705.

able difficulties. How can one entity exist in a number of particulars separated by distance of space and time, in entirety, untouched by what happens to the particulars? Moreover, in cognizing a thing, we do not certainly cognize it (the particular), and its duplicate (the universal). Wherefrom does a universal, say manhood, come into a newborn man? Where does it go when the man dies? Owing to such difficulties the Buddhist holds that all existence is particular; the *universal* is a thought-construct, a *vikalpa*.

The existence *of* a thing or *its* destruction are mere modes of expression, like the body of a statue or the head of "*Rāhu.*"[1] Existence and destruction are not attributes or accretions of a thing but the thing itself. Change, on the Buddhist conception, is replacement of one entity by another; it is a series of entities emerging and perishing in entirety; one entity does not become another. Movement is not the passage of an entity from one point to another; it is the emergence, at appropriate intervals, of a series of entities,[2] like the individual pictures of a "movie" show. There is neither flow nor movement in each entity nor in the series; it is the spectator who projects that into the several static entities.

As knowledge and object are not simultaneous, there is no grasping of or appropriation of one by the other; the relation is causal. And as there is no persistence of entities and they emerge and perish entire, causation really turns out to be a kind of occasionalism.[3] These inherent difficulties lead Buddhist thought towards subjectivism and idealism.

3. The Ābhidharmika Philosophy

The Thera-vāda and the Sarvāsti-vāda

The Ābhidharmika is the first systematic attempt to synthesize the Buddha's teachings. It is the realistic and dogmatic tendency that gets expressed first; the absolutist systems arise as a criticism of this. "*Abhidharma*" is defined in the *Abhidharma-kośa*[4] as pure intuitive knowledge of the *dharmas* (existents)

1. See *MKV.*, pp. 66-9.
2. *Na gatir nāśāt saṅskṛtaṁ kṣaṇikaṁ yataḥ*, *AK.*, IV. 2. *TS.*, pp. 231-2.
3. *PV.*, II, 416-20.
4. *Prajñā amalā sānucarā abhidharmaḥ*, *AKV.*, p. 18; see also *Mahāyāna-sūtrālaṅkāra*, XI, 3.

with its subsidiary discipline. It is an attempt to penetrate to the ultimate reality and define it.

Thera-vāda.—The seven *Abhidhamma* treatises[1] of the *Pāli* Canon, traditionally treated as the word of the Buddha, are really the *Thera-vāda* interpretation. *The Dhamma-saṅgaṇi* and its subsidiary works consist of interminable lists of *dhammas* (entities) from various standpoints, the ethical interest predominating. The statements are mostly headlines or mnemonic aids (*mātikās*) meant to be supplemented by oral exposition. Thcreis little attempt at argument, and the underlying metaphysical principles are seldom elicited. This dogmatism continued to cramp *Thera-vāda* down the ages. The first systematic treatise of this School—The *Visuddhi-magga* of Buddhaghosa (Vasubandhu's contemporary) compares rather unfavourably with the *Abhidharma-kośa* in metaphysical content; it is, however, valuable as an ethical treatise. Anuruddha's *Abhidhammattha-saṅgaha*[2] (eleventh century A.D.), widely used in Ceylon, Burma and Siam, is not a very illuminating compendium; it is one more compilation of lists.

It is doubtful if *Thera-vāda* was ever cultivated on the mainland of India; it is an almost exclusive product of the southern Buddhist countries. When the Mādhyamika or the Yogācāra refer to the *Abhidharma* system, it is invariably to the *Sarvāsti-vāda* and not to the *Pāli* or Ceylonese School.[3]

Sarvāsti-vāda.—The *Sarvāsti-vāda* can claim to be as old as the *Thera-vāda* with which it has close doctrinal affinity. Its ultra-realistic tendency evinced in taking the past and the future events as equally existent as the present has been criticized by other Schools. From this the School derives its name, *Sarva-(dā)sti-vāda* as the doctrine that affirms existence at all times.

The Sarvāsti-vādins kept their Canons in Sanskrit; fragments of these have been discovered in Central Asia and Gilgit. Though spread in the entire country, it had its principal seat at Kāśmīra and Gāndhāra. Its extensive *Abhidharma* literature,

1. These are: *Dhamma-saṅgaṇi*, *Vibhaṅga*, *Dhātu-kathā*, *Puggala-paññatti*, *Kathā-vatthu*, *Yamaka* and *Paṭṭhāna*.
2. Trans. by Aung and Mrs. Rhys Davids.
3. McGovern: *A Manual of Buddhist Philosophy*, Vol. I, pp. 16-17.

lost in Sanskrit, is preserved in entirety in Chinese[1] and partially in Tibetan. The basic work is the *Jñāna-prasthāna* of Kātyāyanīputra with the six subsidiary works[2] (*Ṣaṭ-pādāḥ*), three of which are attributed to the immediate disciples of the Buddha. These are : *Prakaraṇa-pāda* by Vasumitra, *Vijñāna-kāya* by Devaśarman, *Dharma-skandha* by Śāriputra, *Prajñapti-śāstra* by Maudgalāyana, *Dhātu-kāya* by Pūrṇa and *Saṅgiti-paryāya* by Mahākauṣṭhila.

A further stage in the development of the *Sarvāsti-vāda* is represented by the composition of commentaries of epic proportions, the *Mahā-vibhāṣā* and the shorter *Vibhāṣā* during or about the reign of Kaniṣka (*c*. A.D. 125). According to Takakusu, the former belongs to the Kāśmīra and the latter to the Gāndhāra section.[3] *Sarvāsti-vāda* is usually called the Vaibhāṣika[4] because it is a system based on the *Vibhāṣā*.

The *Abhidharma-hṛdaya* by Dharmottara and its commentary mark the beginnings of the third and systematic period of the School. The *Abhidharma-kośa*[5] of Vasubandhu (*c*. 350) is the acknowledged standard treatise (*śāstra*) of this system. *Nyāyānusāra* (Nanjio, 1265) and *Abhidharma-samaya-pradīpikā* (Nanjio, 1266) were written by his contemporary, Saṅgabhadra, to correct the Sautrāntika leanings of Vasubandhu. The *Sphuṭārthā* of Yaśomitra is a very valuable and extensive commentary extant in Sanskrit.

Dharma.—The Vaibhāṣika is a radical pluralism erected on the denial of substance and the acceptance of discrete momentary *dharmas*. "*Dharma*" is the ultimate factor or element of existence—a sense which the term has only in Buddhism. *Dharmas* are ultimate, as they are simple (*pṛthag*) and not compounded of simpler entities. A thing (e.g. chair, tree, man) is an aggregate (*skandha*) of these elements; the aggregate or the whole

1. Takakusu gives a comprehensive survey of the *Abhidharma Literature of the Sarvāsti-vādins*, pp. 67-146, *JPTS.*, 1905.

2. This is according to *AKV.*, pp. 9 and 11 and Buston, *History of Buddhism*, Vol. I, pp. 49-50. For a slight variation in authorship, see Takakusu's article on *Sarvāsti-vāda* literature, pp. 74-8.

3. See p. 60, *The Essentials of Buddhist Philosophy*. Honolulu, 1947.

4. *Vibhāṣayā dīvyanti, caranti vā, vibhāṣāṁ vidanti, Vaibhāṣikāḥ, AKV.*, p. 12.

5. The rare Sanskrit MS. of the *Abhidharma-kośa-bhāṣya* discovered in Tibet by Rahula Sankrityayana is still awaiting publication.

(*avayavin*) is not an additional reality as in the Vaiśeṣika. The elements are impermanent; they are momentary and durationless. "There is no inherence of one element in another, hence no substance apart from qualities; no matter beyond the separate sense-data, and no *soul* beyond the separate mental data (*dharma = anātman*)."[1]

The *dharmas* are classified and defined in the *Ābhidharma* treatises, notably in the *Kośa*. The *Sarvāsti-vāda* lists 75 *dharmas* in all, 72 conditioned phenomena (*saṁskṛta*, literally, the co-operating) and 3 unconditioned noumena (*a-saṁskṛta*, the non-co-operating). Conditioned by *ignorance* (*avidyā*) and its satellite passions (*kleśas*), the elements cooperate to flow as the defiled stream (*sāsrava*) of phenomenal life[2] (*saṁsāra, upādāna*); the *saṁskṛta* are thus pain (*duḥkha*) or cause of pain (*samudaya*). The same elements, separated and suppressed through spiritual discipline (*mārga*) culminating in intuitive knowledge (*prajñā*), are reduced to quiescence,[3] a state of blank (*nirvāṇa*). This is one of the three *unconditioned* realities. The second is the cessation (*a-pratisaṅkhyā-nirodha*)[4] produced, not by knowledge as in the case of *nirvāṇa*, but by lack of necessary conditions; for example, owing to attention being diverted elsewhere, smell, taste, etc., lapse away without being apprehended. The third unconditioned is space (*ākāśa*); it is defined as non-obstruction :[5] it neither obstructs as providing room for entities nor is obstructed, being empty.

Declaring them nominal, the Sautrāntikas rejected all the three *unconditioned*, including *nirvāṇa*. The Thera-vādins accepted *nirvāṇa* alone, while the Yogācāra increased them to six, adding *acalā* (stable), *sañjñāvedayitṛ-nirodha* (catalyptic ecstasy) and *tathatā* (thatness), the last of which alone is really the *noumenon*.

The classification of the *dharmas* into *skandha*, *āyatana* and *dhātu* is such a persistent and universal feature of the Canons that it can be attributed to the Buddha himself. These analyse the individual into a number of states without the residue of any soul or substance. The classifications may be called *subjective*,

1. *Central Conception of Buddhism*, p. 74.
2. *AKV.*, pp. 12, 13.
3. *AKV.*, p. 16.
4. *AKV.*, p. 17.
5. *AKV.*, p. 15.

as the interest is predominantly in sentient experience, in the individual and his components.

The *skandhas* (groups)[1] are five : *rūpa* (material or bodily factors), *vedanā* (feeling), *saṅjñā* (conception and generalizing), *saṁskāra* (will and other forces) and *vijñāna* (pure awareness). The *āyatana* is literally a "door" for the emergence of consciousness and its factors. The *āyatanas* are twelve—the six sense-organs (including the *manas*) with the corresponding six sense-data, including the objects of thought. The *dhātu* is a further elaboration of the *āyatana*; they make eighteen with the interpolation of the six resultant apprehensions, e.g. visual consciousness, etc., in between the sense-organs and the sense-data.

In the *objective* classification,[2] the *dharmas* are divided into 5 classes: *rūpa* (matter) (11), *citta* [consciousness (1),] *cetasika* [mental states and characteristics (46)], *Citta-viprayukta-saṁskāra* [forces which are neither mental nor material but common to both (14)] and the *a-saṁskṛta* [the unconditioned (3)]. The last category has already been considered.

Matter (*rūpa*) is impenetrable, hard (*sapratigha*). It is divided into the five sense-data (colour, etc.), five sense organs (*indriya*) which are conceived as a kind of translucent subtle matter (*rūpa-prasāda*) and unmanifest matter (*a-vijñapti-rūpa*)[3] which is the result, good or bad, of any act or resolution; this corresponds to the *adṛṣṭa* of the *brāhmaṇical* systems. Matter is either primary (*bhūta* or *mahā-bhūta*) or secondary (*bhautika*). The primary[4] are four—earth, water, fire and air; they are known by their characteristics—solidity, moisture, heat and motion; their functions are supporting, cohesion, ripening and expansion.

"The general elements of matter, like all Buddhist elements, are more forces than substances. These four elements appear always together, always in equal proportion. There is as much element of heat in a blazing flame as there is in wood or in water, and *vice versa*, the difference is only in their intensity."[5]

1. *AKV.*, p. 42.
2. *AKV.*, pp. 24 ff. See McGovern, *Manual of Buddhism*, pp. 103 ff.; Rosenberg, *Probleme die Buddhist Philosophie*, pp. 128-9.
3. *AKV.*, pp. 29 ff.
4. *AKV.*, p. 33.
5. *Central Cunception*, p. 13.

Citta or *vijñāna* is contentless consciousness and represents but one element, though it may be spoken of as admitting six modes depending on the sense-organs invoking it. The Theravādins elaborately classify this into 89 kinds according to the planes of existence and conditions.[1] The Yogācāra enumerates eight *vijñānas*, adding *ālaya* and *kliṣṭa-mano-vijñāna* to the six.

The "mentals" (*caittas, cetasikas*) are enumerated as 46[1] and are subdivided into those that are present in all states (*mahābhūmika*, 10), ten general properties associated with "good" (*kuśala*) states, 6 primary passions (*kleśas*), 2 evil mental properties (*a-kuśala*), 10 subsidiary passions (*upa-kleśa*) and 8 indeterminate elements (*a-niyata*).

Under the category non-mental forces (*citta-viprayukta-saṁskāra*) the *Sarvāsti-vāda* brings fourteen[2] functions, like attainment (*prāpti*), birth, continuation, decay, death, etc. The Yogācāras inflate this list to 24; all these are, however, phenomenal with them. The Sautrāntikas refused to accept these as separate entities, as they are but modes of conceiving the behaviour of elements.

Causal Law:—The ultimate elements of existence have been determined and defined. We have now to explain the modes of their combination to make phenomena (*saṁskṛta*); the question is about the dynamics of the World-process.

Buddhism has always insisted upon the universality and inexorability of the causal law. The Buddha, rejecting the opposite views of eternalism and nihilism, applied the principle especially in the context of moral responsibility. Things do not happen through chance, fate or God (*Īśvara*); nor are they immutable. It is *karman*—the deed that we did and do—that constitutes the world and accounts for its variety (*karmajaṁ lokavaicitryam*).[3] The causal law implies in Buddhism, as we have seen, momentariness, substancelessness and particularity (*sva-lakṣaṇa*). It is inexorably and incessantly operative in all the three planes of existence; only the unconditioned are beyond the pale of this. It is also a necessary implication of the conditioned that it cannot be produced from a single cause[4]

1. *Manual of Buddhism*, p. 136.
2. *Central Conception*, pp. 10 ff.
3. *AK.*, II. 35 ff.; *AKV.*, pp. 142 ff.
4. *AK.*, IV.

(*na hyekam ekasmāt*), but from a conglomeration of causes, and that the effect is different from the cause.

Causality is conceived both in a general and a special sense. The former is represented by the division into principal cause[1] (*hetu*, e.g. the seed in producing the sprout) and the three kinds of conditions (*pratyayas*), namely object condition (*ālambana*), immediate antecedence (*samanantara*) and dominant condition (*adhipati*).

The special application of the causal law in the case of the individual is the twelve-linked chain of *pratītya-samutpāda*. The *Abhidharma-kośa* interprets this thus : "The *ātman* (substance) exists not; the five groups progressing as a stream of momentary entities, conditioned by *karman* and passions, enter into the womb. And nourished by the appropriate *karman* and passions, the continuum of states passes from birth to birth. This incessantly rotating wheel of life is the *pratītya-samutpāda*—the twelve-link-chain with its three subdivisions. The first two members—ignorance and passions (*avidyā* and *saṁskāras*)—belong to the previous life, the eight in the middle to the present and the last two to the future birth."[2]

Phenomenal existence is pain. It is caused by attachment, aversion, greed and the other passions (*kleśas*). These have their origin in ignorance, the wrong view that there is a permanent, identical being (*ātman*); we cling to things taking them as permanent. The wrong belief in the *ātman* (*sat-kāya-dṛṣṭi*) is thus the root-cause of pain; it starts and keeps going the chain of existence (*pratītya-samutpāda*). Realizing this, the aspirant for *nirvāṇa* undertakes the spiritual discipline leading to the cessation of pain. As in all Buddhism, the discipline consists of three stages—practice of virtues (*śīla*), contemplation (*samādhi*) and intuitive insight (*prajñā*). The Abhidharma treatises speak of the four stages of attainment and the sixteen moments of realization of insight, four for each basic truth (*ārya-satya*).

According to the Abhidharma conception there is a real transformation of the conditioned (*saṁskṛta*) into the unconditioned noumenal state through the force of insight. *Nirvāṇa* is

1. *AK.*, II, 65; *AKV.*, p. 20.
2. *AK.*, II. 49; *AKV.*, pp. 231 ff., 41; *AK.*, III, 18 ff.

conceived almost as a state of negation or extinction of the phenomenal forces. All this implies that *nirvāṇa* and phenomena are totally different. The Mādhyamika controverts these.

4. The Sautrāntika School
(*Critical Realism*)

Criticism of Sarvāsti-vāda.—The dogmatism of the Ābhidharmika, its tendency to hypostatize subjective notions and words into objective realities and especially its doctrine of the existence of the elements at all times, evoked criticism from other Schools. The Sautrāntika, which discards the Abhidharma works and bases itself on the direct discourses (*sūtra*) of the Buddha, represents the systematic form of this criticism.[1]

The Sarvāsti-vādins assert the existence of all elements (*dharmas*) in the past, present and future, "(1) because this has been declared in Scripture, (2) because of the double (cause of perception), (3) because of the existence of the object of perception, (4) because of the production of a result (by previous deeds). Since we maintain that all this exists, we profess the theory that everything exists (*Sarvāsti-vāda*)."[2] The main argument is that as cognition is engendered by the appropriate sense-organ and the object, when we remember a past event or think of the future, these must be existent to function as objects. Past passions too are observed to influence our attitude in the present. Four alternative theories[3] were propounded to explain the nature of existence in the three times.

The Sautrāntika asks: "If the element in the future and in the past exists just in the same sense as in the present, why is it future and past?" All temporal distinctions would then get submerged. Nor can it be said that the *essence* of an element exists in the past and future and not its function; for a thing is

1. *Ye sūtra-prāmāṇikā na śāstra-prāmāṇikāḥ, te Sautrāntikāḥ, AKV.*, p. 11.
2. *AKV.*, p. 25; *AKV*, pp. 468 ff.; *Central Conception*, p. 77.
3. *AK.*, V, 26. There are four views inasmuch as they maintain (1) a change of existence (*bhāva-pariṇāma*, attributed to Dharmatrāta); (2) change of aspect (*lakṣaṇa-pariṇāma* ascribed to Ghoṣa); (3) a change of condition (*avasthā-pariṇāma*, advocated by Vasumitra) or contingency (*apekṣā-pariṇāma* by Buddhadeva). The third alternative is right. The difference in time rests on a difference of the functions (*kāritra-bheda*) of the elements. *Central Conception*, pp. 78-9.

nothing but the function. To accept the continued existence of elements is a species of eternalism. It is also not necessary that something must be actually present to be an object of thought. This would lead to absurd consequences : the remote future, the non-existent or the unattained *nirvāṇa* would exist when they are thought of. The naive realist that he is, the Sarvāsti-vādin fails to distinguish between the existent and the subsistent thought-forms.

Dharmas.—The Sautrāntikas cut down the inflated lists of *dharmas* drawn by the Vaibhāṣikas. Not only did they reject the past and the future phases, but also space (*ākāśa*), *nirvāṇa* and the non-mental forces (*citta-viprayukta*). In the final analysis, a list of 43 elements[1] under five heads was drawn up. This comprises:

(*a*) Matter (*rūpa*)—four primary forms (*upādāna*) and four derivative (*upādāya-rūpa*);

(*b*) Feelings (*vedanā*)—pleasure, pain and neutral;

(*c*) Signs, sense-organs (*sañjñā*) 6—five sense-organs and mind (*citta*);

(*d*) Consciousness (*vijñāna*) 6—corresponding to the six signs mentioned above;

(*e*) Forces (*saṁskāras*) 20—ten good and ten bad

Epistemology.—The real contribution of the Sautrāntika to the development of Indian thought is the discovery of the subjective—the transcendental function of the mind in constructing the empirical world. Diṅnāga (fifth century) and Dharmakīrtti[2] (seventh century) have formulated a rigorous and revolutionary logic and epistemology on Kantian lines.

1. This list is according to the commentary on *Śiva-jñāna-siddhi*, a Śaiva-siddhānta treatise by Aruṇandi (thirteenth century). Pt. Aiyaswami Sastri has been the first to draw our attention to this (see his Appendix to the *Ālambana-parīkṣā.*)

2. The *Magnum opus* of Diṅnāga is the *Pramāṇa-samuccaya* with his own commentary (*vṛtti*). Its place in Buddhist Logic is like that of the *Nyāya-sūtra.* Besides this, he has written numerous smaller works of which *Ālambana-parīkṣā*, *Tri-kāla-parīkṣā*, *Hetu-cakra-samarthana* and *Nyāya-mukha* are the important ones. *Ālambana-parīkṣā* and *Pramāṇa-samuccaya* (partially) have been restored from Tibetan into Sanskrit; all other works are available only in Tibetan. *Nyāya-praveśa*, attributed to Diṅnāga, is really the work of Saṅkarasvāmin.

Dharmakīrtti has written the celebrated *Pramāṇa-vārttika* (a sort of running commentary on Diṅnāga's *Pramāṇa-samuccaya*), *Pramāṇa-viniścaya*, *Hetubindu*,

Pramāṇa (valid avenues of knowledge) is the subject of enquiry. *Pramāṇa* is defined as knowledge[1] that is not at variance with the real; further, it is the cognition of the uncognized.[2] Four are the issues[3] with regard to the *pramāṇas*—their number, nature, object and result (*phala*). The entire Buddhist logic is based on the acceptance of two[4] modes of knowledge: immediate (*pratyakṣa*) and mediate (*anumāna*); they are mutually exclusive and exhaustive taken together. The function of the one is to *receive* (*grahaṇa*) or acquaint us with the given, of the other is to *think*[5] it (*adhyavasāya*) according to some pattern. There is a remarkable coincidence of this with Kant's position: ".... there are two stems of human knowledge, namely, *sensibility* and *understanding*, which perhaps spring from a common, but to us unknown, root. Through the former, objects are given to us; through the latter, they are thought."[6]

This does not mean that there are two co-ordinate realities—the particular and the universal. The particular alone is real (*meyaṁ tvekaṁ sva-lakṣaṇam*). But it is cognized in a two-fold[7] way: one as it is in itself (*sva-rūpa*) in perception and second through forms other to it (*para-rūpa*) in the understanding. Of the two sources, perception is the prius of which the understanding is a secondary and false elaboration. The particular alone is unconditionedly real (*paramārtha-sat*); the universal (*sāmānya-lakṣaṇa*) is ultimately unreal (*a-vastu*); inference is essentially misapprehension[8] (*bhrāntam anumānam*). Ultimately unreal, it is, however, empirically veridical. "Neither of the two rays, one emanating from the jewel and the other forming the lamp, is the jewel; but by mistaking the former for the jewel, it can be reached, not by the other."[9]

Sambandha-parikṣā, *Santānāntara-siddhi* and *Nyāya-bindu*. Only the first and the last of these are available in Sanskrit. The entire *Sambandha Parīkṣā* consisting of 22 Kārikās is given in the Jain work *Prameya Kamala Mārttaṇḍa* (pp. 504-511).

1. *PV.*, I, 3; *NBT.*, p. 3.
2. *PV.*, I, 7; *NBT.*, p. 3.
3. *PS.*, p. 4; *NBT.*, p. 5.
4. *PS.*, p. 4; PV., II, *NBT.*, pp. 5 ff.
5. *NBT.*, p. 12; *Buddhist Logic,* Vol. I, pp. 147 ff.
6. *Critique of Pure Reason* (Kemp Smith's Trans.), pp. 61-2. See also pp. 65, 93, etc.
7. *PV.*, II, 53-4.
8. *PV.*, II, 55-6; *NBT.*, p. 7, cf. Kant's doctrine about the empirical reality and transcendental ideality of space, time and the categories.
9. *PV.*, II. 57-8.

Indirect knowledge (*anumāna*) cannot be dispensed with. For, to assert that perception is the *only*[1] source involves distinction and relation as we speak *about* it. Besides, to have the sensation "blue" is not to know it *as* blue. To be aware of perception *as* perception is to define and distinguish it from others. And definition (*adhyavasāya*) can come only through conception (*vikalpa*). Moreover, an intra-subjective world wherein several percipients participate necessitates exposition of one's experience through the mediation of symbols and concepts. Inference (*anumāna*) has therefore to be accepted besides perception.

"*Pratyakṣa*" signifies, etymologically, "present to sense"; but the essential factor underlying such knowledge may be taken as immediacy,[2] pure acquaintance. Diṅnāga[3] defines *pratyakṣa* as (knowledge) free from construction (*kalpanā*), i.e. name and generality, etc. The definition is necessarily negative as excluding thought-construction; it only serves to distinguish perception from what it is not, from the nameable. It is not valid to urge that nothing is left over when the thought-forms are abstracted from a thing; for there must be in experience the irreducible core of the given, the *that* on which thought-forms are overlaid. If the *that* were not experienced, thought cannot be stimulated to begin its interpretation. That the subject in a judgment is not reducible to the predicate does not warrant its rejection. The real subject falls outside the judgment which is an ideal content predicated of it. "Thought would be empty without the percept," the given in intuition. Its presence or absence[4] marks all the difference to experience.

Intuition is essentially true, non-discrepant from its object. The possibility of error[5] is ruled out as there is no judgment, interpretation. Its object is the thing-in-itself (*paramārtha-sat*)

1. *PV.*, II, 65 ff.
2. *NBT.*, p. 6.
3. *PS.*, p. 8.
4. *NBT.*, p. 13.
5. Diṅnāga therefore does not find it necessary to define *pratyakṣa* so as to exclude the illusory. Dharmakīrtti, however, defines it as knowledge that is free from construction and error. This is done to exclude errors that are engendered not by thought-construction but by purely physical and physiological factors, e.g. swift motion, distance, injury and disease of the sense-organ, etc. See *NB.*, I, 6.

which the Sautrāntika, as a true Buddhist, takes as the unique point-instant (*sva-lakṣaṇa*).[1] Some Advaitins too assert that in perception we intuit the thing-in-itself; but here it is the universal differenceless Identity (*Brahman*).

Four are the varieties of intuition: (1) the sensuous (*indriya-nimittam*); (2) the mental[2] (*mānasa-pratyakṣa*) which is consequent on the preceding sensuous intuition, having for its object the point-instant immediately following that of the sensuous. The need for admitting this rather ghostly function is the same that prompted Kant to formulate his schematism of the categories, i.e. to find a *modus vivendi*[3] between perception and thought. (3) The direct intuition (self-awareness, *sva-saṁvedana*) of consciousness and the mental states as pleasure and pain etc. These are neither non-cognized as in the Bhāṭṭa view nor cognized by another state as in the Nyāya. (4) The *yogi-pratyakṣa*[4] is the non-sensuous intellectual intuition of the saint, who by the power of concentration (*bhāvanā*) perceives things as they are with the utmost clarity.

For the Buddhist, the determinate (*sa-vikalpa*) perception of the Nyāya and Mīmāṁsā is not perception, as it is complicated with thought (*vikalpa*). As synthesizing the thing with the one seen earlier, as in recognition, it is not confined to the immediately given. The baby's recognizing[5] its mother's breast as the same (*sa eveti*) and leaving off crying has all the ingredients of *vikalpa*, though words may not be used actually. *Vikalpa* is thus knowledge that is identified with verbal designations or[6] fit to be so. Diṅnāga defined it as the application of *name* and *universal*. This has been criticized[7] because the universal (substance, etc.) is nothing but a name.

As *kalpanā* is name, a classification of *kalpanā* is a classification of names. Diṅnāga[8] thus takes over the current categories of words

1. *NB.*, I, 12-14.
2. *PV.*, II, 243; *NB.*, I, 9.
3. See *Buddhist Logic*, Vol. II, p. 28 n.
4. *NB.*, I, II; *PV.*, II, 281 ff.
5. *NBT.*, p. 8.
6. *NB.*, I, 5.
7. *TS.*, pp. 372 ff.
8. *PS.*, p. 12; *Buddhist Logic*, Vol. I, p. 217.

as Kant does the table of judgments of formal logic. These are: *Individual* (proper) names, *universals*, *substance*, *attribute* and *action*.

If knowledge of generality (*nāma-jāti*) were the object of inference alone (*sāmānya-viṣayam anumānam*), and inference is impossible without the conscious use of the general (*hetu*, middle term), a vicious circle or a regress is unavoidable. Kumārila[1] pertinently raises this objection against the Buddhist doctrine of two acts of knowledge with two exclusive objects. The Buddhist, however, escapes this predicament by accepting two orders[2] of the *vikalpa*—one that is tied to the percept (*pratyakṣa-pṛṣṭha-bhāvi-vikalpa*) and the other freed from it and used consciously as a sign (*liṅga*, middle term) in inference (*anumāna-vikalpa*). The former is the judgment which is the ascription of an ideal content to the sense given; the latter is inference, the ascription of an idea through another idea.

The perceptual judgment—and this is judgment *par excellence*—is not a third[3] source of knowledge in either of its forms: affirmative (*vidhi-vikalpa*) and negative, i.e. differentiation (*niṣedha-vikalpa*). As entities are different by themselves, differentiation in thought does not state anything new; it is thus not a valid source of knowledge. Affirmation or glossing over differences of entities and their momentariness to present an identical generalized aspect is virtually a false ascription; hence this too is not a valid source.

Inference is two-fold, inference for oneself (*svārthānumāna*) and that meant for others (*parārthānumāna*). The first is primary and the second is but the verbal demonstration that convinces others. Inference is the cognition of the non-presented through the conscious use of a sign (*liṅga*, middle term), e.g. smoke, necessarily possessing the three[4] characteristics (*tri-rūpa*): the presence of the middle in the subject of inference (*pakṣa*, minor) wholly, its presence in similar instances (*sapakṣa*) only and its absence from all dissimilar instances (*vipakṣa*). The violation of these rules leads respectively

1. *Śloka-vārttika* (*Anumāna-pariccheda*, 149 ff.), quoted in *Hetu-bindu-ṭīkā* of Arcata, pp. 23-4. This is a commentary on Dharmakīrti's work (*Hetu-bindu*) published in the G. O. S., Baroda.

2. *Hetu-bindu-ṭīkā*, p. 24.

3. *ibid.*, pp. 25-8.

4. *NB.*, II, 3-7.

to the three fallacies, *a-siddha* (inconclusive), *anaikāntika* (discrepant) and the *viruddha* (contrary)

There are only three types of concomitance[1] (*a-vinā-bhāva*) or categories of relation between the middle and the major terms. The two primary modes are dichotomically two—one for affirming and the other for denying (*anupalabdhi*) the existence of the thing in question (*sādhya*). The first admits of two sub-classes—one in which two concepts have one identical[2] objective reference (*tādātmya* or *svabhāva-hetu*), e.g. this is a tree, because it is an oak; and the other in which the two, though different, are yet necessarily dependent[3] as cause and effect (*tad-utpatti* or *kārya-hetu*), e.g. there is fire, because of smoke. All these types of relation are established neither by observation nor by non-observation;[4] they are the *a priori* necessity of thought.

In both immediate and mediate knowledge, the resultant knowledge (*pramiti*) is identical[5] with the means which engenders it.

5. The Dialectical Absolutism of the Mādhyamika

Criticism of Sautrāntika.—The Sautrāntika epistemology is a two-level theory. It is based on the recognition of two classes of objects—the thing-in-itself given in intuition and its conceptual representation in thought (*vikalpa*). Experience is the synthesis or identification (*sārūpya*) of these two heterogeneous[6] factors. This relation of *sārūpya* has been taken to mean representationism. The essence of representationism is that we do not directly perceive objects, but are aware of our ideas only (the copies of things). The Sautrāntika, however, emphatically asserts that we are in direct contact with the real in perception. His doctrine only means that the subjective factor in our knowledge is mistaken for the objective, the thing-in-itself. The mistake, however, is not empirical in origin. The Sautrāntika theory has

1. *PV.*, III, 1; *NB.*, II, 11-12.
2. *NBT.*, p. 24.
3. *NB.*, II, 18 ff.
4. *PV.*, III, 30.
5. *PV.*, II, 306; *NB.*, I, 18 ff.
6. *atyanta-vilakṣaṇānāṁ sālakṣaṇyam. Tātparya-ṭīkā*, p. 340.

greater affinity with Kant's analysis of experience than with Locke's; it reveals, through criticism, the function of thought.

This devastating discovery of the Sautrāntika led to important developments in two directions—to the Mādhyamika absolutism and the Yogācāra idealism. The Mādhyamika urges that the Sautrāntika indeed alights on the subjective, but does not appreciate its greater depth; he hastily erects a speculative system by accepting the reality of momentary entities on which thought-forms are imposed. He is not critical enough. An equally plausible system can be and has been erected by the Vedānta, on the opposite theory of the real as permanent, universal and identical on which difference and change are superimposed. One is the *nairātmya-vāda* and the other is the *ātma-vāda*, and they are antinomical.[1] Both cannot be true, and the conflict cannot be resolved except by rejecting both as subjective. The real cannot be conceived either as momentary or permanent, particular or universal. Both are *vikalpa*—conceptual construction. To apprehend the real as it is, these viewpoints (*dṛṣṭis*) have to be negated (*śūnyatā* of *dṛṣṭis*). This is the Mādhyamika dialectic; it is criticism grown to maturity.

The Ygācāra was considerably exercised over the relation (*sārūpya*) between the thing and its subjective counterpart. That the one is falsely identified with the other presupposes a foundational reality. This can be no other than consciousness (*vijñapti-mātratā*). The Sautrāntika, while insisting on the ideality of the phenomenal object, accepts the independence of the thing in itself. The Yogācāra criticism, like the Hegelian criticism of Kant, is that the other in thought (objectivity) is itself a creation of *vijñāna*—consciousness; the dualism of subject and object (*grāha-dvaya*)—presupposes a non-dual consciousness. This alone is ultimately real.

The critical realism of the Sautrāntika thus leads on the one hand to the dialectical absolutism of the Mādhyamika and the idealism of the *Vijñānavāda* on the other.

Evolution of Mādhyamika Thought.—Dialectic is the soul of the

1. cf. *ātmeti, kāśyapa, ayam eko'ntaḥ; nairātmyam ityayaṁ dvitīyo'ntaḥ : yad ātma-nairātmyayor madhyaṁ tad arūpyam anidarśanam....iyam ucyate....madhyamā pratipad dharmāṇāṁ bhūta-pratyavekṣā—Kāśyapa-parivarta*, p. 87; quoted in *MKV.*, p. 358.

Mādhyamika philosophy. It is anticipated in essentials by the Buddha when he declined to answer the fourteen questions (the *avyākṛta*) regarding the world, the soul and the perfect being (*tathāgata*) and kept silent.[1] It has been suggested that the Buddha, practical-minded, was indifferent to metaphysics or that he was an agnostic or a nihilist. Professor Radhakrishnan states the correct solution of this silence: "If the Buddha declined to define the nature of the Absolute or if he contented himself with negative definitions, it is only to indicate that absolute being is above all determinations."[2] The Buddha sets himself above all dogmatism: "The Tathāgata is free from all theories."[3] To Kaccāyana he says: "That everything exists is one extreme; that it does not exist is another. The Tathāgata preaches the truth from the middle position[4] (*majjhena dhammam deseti*)." This is the essence of the Mādhyamika dialectic and Nāgārjuna[5] makes pointed reference to this passage.

The *Prajñā-pāram-itā* texts,[6] *Sad-dharma-puṇḍarika*, *Kāśyapa-parivarta* (*ratna-kūṭa*) and other Mahāyāna *sūtras* form the next stage in the development of the Mādhyamika. The one basic idea that is reiterated in these treatises is that there is no origination or cessation, no coming in or going out and that the real is neither *ātman* nor *anātman*, etc.; it is utterly devoid (*śūnya*) of empirical determinations. The doctrine of two truths and the non-distinction of the absolute and phenomena are also emphasized.

The Mādhyamika system seems to have been perfected at one stroke by the genius of its founder—Nāgārjuna (*c.* A.D. 150). There have not been many important changes in its philosophy after him. He has been ably helped by his brilliant disciple, Āryadeva. According to Buston, six are the main treatises by Nāgār-

1. See specially, Majjh. N. (Sutta 72,) Sam. N., III, pp. 257 ff, IV, pp. 374-403; *MK*, Chaps. XXII, XXV, XXVII, and *Aṣṭa-sāhasrikā*, pp. 269 ff.

2. *Gautama the Buddha*, p. 59; see also *Ind. Phil.*, Vol. I, pp. 682-3.

3. Majjh. N. (Sutta 72); Warren, *Buddhism in Translations*, p. 125.

4. Sam. N., II, 17.

5. *MK.*, XV, 7.

6. This is available in several recensions. The *Aṣṭa-sāhasrikā* (*c.* first century B.C.) appears to be the basic text of which the *Śata-sāhasrikā*, *Pañca-viṁśati*, etc., are elaborations and the *Vajra-cchedikā*, the *Adhyardha-śatikā* are abridgments.

juna: *Mūla-Madhyamaka-kārikā* (*Prajñāmūla*) which is *the Śāstra* of this School, *Śūnyatā-saptati*, *Yukti-ṣaṣṭikā*, *Vigraha-vyāvarttanī*, *Vaidalya-sūtra* and *Vyavahāra-siddhi*. Numerous other works are also attributed to Nāgārjuna, some (*Ratnāvalī*, *Catuḥstava*, etc.) with justification. Āryadeva's *Catuḥ-śatikā* is next in importance only to the *Madhyamaka-kārikā*. By his great dialectical skill and refutation of non-Buddhist systems as the Sāṅkhya and the Vaiśeṣika, he made the system strong and popular.

In the next stage there is the splitting up of the Mādhyamika into two Schools—the prāsaṅgika represented by Buddhapālita and the Svātantrika upheld by Bhāvaviveka,[1] who considers that the Mādhyamika should not rest content with *reductio ad absurdum* (*prasaṅga*) arguments but must advance counter-arguments of his own. Hence the name *Svatantra Mādhyamika*. Both were contemporaries and belonged to the fifth century A.D.

It is Candrakīrtti (sixth century) and Śāntideva (seventh century) that give to the Mādhyamika system its rigorous orthodox form. Candrakīrtti is a commentator and author of unequalled merit; his dialectical skill is of the highest order. Stcherbatsky describes him as "a mighty champion of the purely negative method of establishing monism." Against Bhāvaviveka he reaffirms the *reductio ad absurdum* (*prasaṅga*) as the correct Mādhyamika method. Besides his commentaries on the works of Nāgārjuna and Āryadeva, Candrakīrtti has written a valuable work on the system entitled the *Madhyamakāvatāra*.

Śāntideva's *Śikṣā-samuccaya* (a compendium of Mahāyāna texts) and *Bodhi-caryāvatāra* are the two most popular works in the entire Mahāyāna literature. A very high order of spiritual serenity and detachment pervades his works.

In Śāntarakṣita's (*c.* eighth century) *Tattva-saṅgraha* and his disciple Kamalaśīla's *Pañjikā*, we find a new phase—the syncreticism of the Yogācāra and the Mādhyamika. "It is they who culturally conquered Tibet and made it a land of Buddhism. The Mādhyamika remains to this day the official philosophy of the Tibetan Church."

1. *Madhyamaka-vṛtti* and *Prajñā-pradīpa* are the commentaries on the *Madhyamaka-kārikā* by Buddhapālita and Bhāvaviveka respectively. The latter is also the author of *Tarka-jvālā*, *Madhyamakārtha-saṅgraha*, etc., all preserved in Tibetan.

The Structure of the Mādhyamika Dialectic.—Dialectical consciousness is engendered by at least two viewpoings (*dṛṣṭis*) diametrically opposed to each other as thesis and antithesis. The opposition is total, as affecting every aspect of things and practically interminable as there is no appeal to experience. Philosophy, cultivated seriously and systematically, leads to this conflict in *reason*; dialectic is implicit in philosophy.

The substance-view (*ātma-vāda*) of the *brāhmaṇical* systems and the modal view (*nairārtmya-vāda*) of the earlier Buddhism are the two "moments" of the Mādhyamika dialectic. The primary alternatives are thus two: the affirmative (*sat*, "is") and the negative (*a-sat*, "not-is"). These are conjunctively affirmed and denied, yielding two derivative alternatives of the form, both is and not-is (*sadasat*) and neither is nor not-is (*na sat naivāsat*). This is the celebrated *catuṣ-koṭi* of the Mādhyamika. These four alternatives[1] represent all the possible standpoints from which every problem can be viewed; they also provide a schema under which all systems of philosophy can be classified.

The conflict is sought to be resolved in other dialectical systems, as in Hegel and Jainism, by synthesizing or combining the alternatives. In the Mādhyamika, the resolution is achieved by rejecting the alternatives taken singly or in combination and rising to a higher standpoint which is really no position. Every thesis is turned against itself; its implicit self-contradiction is laid bare by the dialectic through *reductio ad absurdum* (*prasaṅga*)[2] arguments. The Mādhyamika does not adduce arguments and examples of his own, as he has no thesis of his own to prove; his sole concern is to disprove others on principles and arguments acceptable to them.[3]

To illustrate the dialectical procedure in the case of causality. The Sāṅkhya advocates the theory of self-becoming or identity between cause and effect. The Madhyamika cogently urges[4] that there is no point in self-duplication, nor is there any conceivable limit to such duplication. The opposite theory of the effect

1. *Catasras tvetā dṛṣṭayaḥ. MKV.*, pp. 572-3; see also *Catuḥ-śatikā* XIV, 21.

2. *ācāryo bhūyasā prasaṅgāpatti-mukhenaiva para-pakṣaṁ nirākaroti sma*, *MKV.*, p. 24.

3. See *MKV.*, pp. 16, 18, 34.

4. *MKV.*, pp. 14., 22; *MK.*, XX, 20.

being an other to the cause does not fare better. As the two are different, the effect should be capable of emerging from everywhere,[1] nowhere. If on the former theory, there is really no emergence or production, in the second, there is emergence but it is uncaused. A synthesis of the two theories, like that of the Jaina, only exposes itself to the objections raised against either. The fourth alternative which denies both the views really denies causation and supports fortuitous origination.

The same devastating criticism is applied in turn against all categories—substance, quality, relation, etc. Like Bradley, Nāgārjuna comes to the conclusion that there is no entity which is not relative.[2] And the relative is unreal. Thought distorts reality and gives us appearance only.

It is held that criticism is not possible without holding a standpoint of one's own. The acceptance of a common or special standpoint by the disputants cannot obviously decide the issue in anyone's favour. A theory can be refuted not by advancing a rival theory but by bringing home to the holder of the theory its self-contradictions. This and only this the Mādhyamika does. Nor can it be urged that criticism of theories is one more theory, that the *śūnyatā* of views (*dṛṣṭis*) is itself a view. Criticism as awareness or analysis of views is not the advocacy of one other view, but the showing up of the constitution of views. *Prajñā* (*śūnyatā*) is thus the resolution[3] of viewpoints.

Absolute.—It might be thought that the Mādhyamika dialectic ends in utter negation and the system is a special pleading of elaborate nihilism. The criticism is misinformed and misses the nature of the system. The method is negative, and not the end. Denial of the competence of thought to cognize reality is not denial of the real. Thought is not the only form of knowledge. The Mādhyamika dialectic rises by three "moments" to an intuitive or non-dual knowledge of the real. There is first the clash of the views (*dṛṣṭi-vāda*) as indulged in by dogmatism. The second moment arises with the awareness of these views or thought-contructs as a falsification of the real. This is enforced

1. *MKV.*, p. 36; *MK.*, XX, 19.

2. *MK.*, XVIII, 10, XXIV, 19. For the principle of the dialectic, see *MK.*, II, 21, XIX, 6; *MKV.*, p. 200.

3. *MK.*, XIII, 8; XXIV, II; *MKV.*, pp. 247-8.

by *reductio ad absurdum* arguments. The utter negation of thought is at once the intuition of the *tattva* (Real) free from the duality of "is" and "not -is". It is *prajñā* (wisdom) or *jñānam*[1] *advayam*, and is identical with the Absolute.

Tattva[2] (Real) is accepted as basic to appearances, and is defined as "transcendent to thought, as non-relative, indeterminate, quiescent, non-discursive and non-dual." Affirmative as well as negative predicates are denied of it. The absolute is devoid (*śūnya*) of every kind of thought-determination. The transcendence of the absolute does not mean that it is an other and is outside phenomenon; it is their essential reality. Nāgārjuna therefore declares that there is not the least difference[3] between the Absolute (*nirvāṇa*) and the universe. The universe, viewed as a process in relation to causes and conditions, is the phenomenal world. The same when the causes and conditions are disregarded, i.e. the world as a whole, sub *specie aeternitatis*, is the Absolute."

As implying a difference between what is in itself and its appearance under conditions, Absolutism has necessarily to make the distinction between two orders of reality and truth. According to Nāgārjuna, "Those that are unaware of the two truths—*paramārtha* and *saṁvṛti*—are incapable of grasping the deep significance of the teachings[4] of the Buddha."

Paramārtha-satya (Absolute truth) is the knowledge of the real as it is (*a-kṛtrimaṁ vastu-rūpam*) without the mediation and distortion of thought-forms; it is really the unutterable (*anabhilāpya*), unthinkable, unteachable[5]. *Saṁvṛti-satya* is truth so-called, the appearance. Candrakīrtti defines it in three ways: :[6] "as that which covers up entirely the nature of the real and makes it appear otherwise; it is also the mutual dependence of things, the relativity of all phenomena; it is further the conventional order of things, empirically real" This doctrine does not mean that there

1. *Prajñāpāramitā jñānam advayaṁ sa tathāgataḥ. Prajñā-pāram-itā-piṇḍārtha-nirdeśa* by Diṅnāga.

2. *MK.*, XVIII, *Bodhi-caryāvatāra* IX. 2.

3. *MK.*, XXV, 19, 20, 9.

4. *MK.*, XXIV, 9.

5. *MKV.*, p. 493.

6. *MKV.*, p. 492.

are two reals and two co-ordinate truths. The *Paramārtha* is the only real or truth.

The Mādhyamika dialectic as culminating in intellectual intuition (*prajñā*) is not only the fruition of the theoretic consciousness; it is the fruition of the practical and religious consciousness as well. The root-cause of pain and imperfection is *avidyā*, the tendency to conceptualize the real and invest it with unreal forms. Mistaking it as permanent or impermanent, we get attached or evince aversion to it. Nāgārjuna says: "Freedom is the cessation of *karman* and evil; these have their origin in *vikalpa*—the tendency to misconstrue things. And this ceases with the knowledge of *śūnyatā*."[1] The dialectic as immediate knowledge (*nirvikalpa*) takes us beyond the possibility of pain. It is itself *freedom* (*nirvāṇa*).

The highest knowledge (*prajñā-pāram-itā*) is one with the Tathāgata in his aspect as the *essence* of all beings (*Dharma-kāya*). He is the *ens perfectissimum* which all beings are potentially and which they eventually become through spiritual discipline. "The Tathāgata is Bhagavān (personal God), endowed as he is with power and perfection. He has completely eliminated all passion and *karman* and the two obscurations (*kleśāvaraṇa* and *jñeyāvaraṇa*). He is omniscient (*sarva-jña* and *sarvākāra-jña*) having a full knowledge of the absolute truth (*prajñā-pāram-itā*) and the empirical world likewise." What makes the Buddha a loving God is his great compassion (*mahā-karuṇā*), his active, unceasing and disinterested help for all beings.

The Tathāgata is the free, phenomenalized (personal) aspect of the Absolute (*śūnya*, *prajñā*) which is the matrix from which the Tathāgatas manifest themselves from time to time according to the needs and circumstances. The Tathāgata, like the Iśvara or Brahman in the Advaita, is a *free person* but lower in status than the Absolute.

6. The Yogācāra (Vijñāna-vāda) Idealism

The trend of Buddhism has been subjective. It had from the very beginning denied the objective reality of many entities commonly taken as real, e.g. the whole, the permanent, and the universal, and had reduced them to mere ideas (*vikalpa*). The

1. *MK.*, XVIII, 5, XXIII.

Sautrāntika had already reached this position; but it still clung, as a realism, to the existence of the thing-in-itself. The Yogācāra denies the reality of this ghostly entity and makes it out as a creation of consciousness (*vijñāna*) Subscribing in the main to the *śūnyatā* of the Mādhyamika, the Yogācāra had its deviations from it, and modified it considerably.

Yogācāra.—The founder of the Yogācāra School is Maitreyanātha (*c.* A.D. 270-350) whose historicity[1] is now generally accepted. But he is represented by his illustrious disciple Asaṅga and his more renowned brother, Vasubandhu.[2] Five works are attributed to Asaṅga: *Mahāyāna-sūtrālaṅkāra*, *Madhyānta-vibhāga*, *Dharmādharmatā-vibhaṅga*, *Abhisamayālaṅkāra*, and *Uttara-tantra.* The first three are from the Yogācāra standpoint, while the fourth concerns itself with the spiritual path common to the Mādhyamika, and the last work is distinctly Mādhyamika in character. This presents a problem[3] about the philosophical affiliation of Asaṅga. Vasubhandhu's *Vijñapti-mātratā-siddhi* (*Viṁśatikā and Triṁśikā*) is the basic work of the system, and has been commented upon by Sthiramati, Dharmapāla and others. Vasubandhu has commented on the *Madhyānta-vibhāga* (the distinction between the middle and the extreme) and has written the *Trisvabhāva-nirdeśa* and a host of minor treatises. Sthiramati (*c.* fifth century A.D.) has written very illuminating commentaries on all the principal works of Vasubandhu.

The Yogācāra was continued by the *Vijñāna-vāda* of Diṅnāga, Īśvarasena, Dharmapāla and Dharmakīrtti. Diṅnāga and Dharmakīrtti paid great attention to logic and epistemology; they had strong Sautrāntika leanings. The earlier Yogācāra doctrine of *Ālaya-vijñāna* is dropped completely by them. It would be truer to speak of this later phase of this school as a syncretism of the Sautrāntika and the Yogācāra: Sautrāntika with regard to phenomena and Yogācāra with regard to the ultimate reality. Owing to the impact and influence of the Mādhyamika, there was probably a combination with that too. Śāntarakṣita

1. See Tucci, *Some Aspects of the Doctrines of Maitreyanātha*, pp. 2 ff.

2. There is difference of opinion with regard to the date of Vasubandhu, whether he lived between A.D. 280-360 or 420-500. The former is the one now generally accepted.

3. See Obermiller, *The Doctrine of Prajñāpāramitā*, pp. 99-100.

and Kamalaśīla represent this last phase as we can gather from their works and the testimony of Tibetan historians.

Idealistic arguments.—"The Vijñānavādin maintains two contentions[1]: *Vijñāna* is *real*, not apparent; *vijñāna alone* is real, not the object. The first is against the Mādhyamika for whom both the knowing consciousness and the object known are relative to each other, and are therefore nothing in themselves. The second is against the realist who uncritically accepts the object as real on a par with *vijñāna.*"

(1) The most effective argument of *Vijñānavāda* against the Mādhyamika is that everything may be dialectically analysed away and rejected as illusory; but the illusion itself implies the ground[2] (*vijñāna*) on which the illusory construction takes place. Accepting the *śūnyatā* of the *Prajñāpāramitās* and even protesting that they interpret it correctly,[3] they take it as meaning pure consciousness, which is devoid of the duality of subject and object (*dvaya-śūnyatā*). The object cannot stand by itself, but consciousness can. It alone undergoes modifications, is infected with passions (*saṅkliṣṭā*) and purifies[4] itself by getting rid of the superimposed duality.

The Vijñānavādin arrives at the unreality of the object on certain plausible grounds. It is supposed by the realist that the form of knowledge (*jñānākāra*) is engendered by the object-condition (*ālambana*) existing independently of consciousness. There are several insuperable difficulties on this hypothesis. (1) There is want of conformity between the form of knowledge (viz. "tree," "chair," etc.) and the supposed object-condition, which is the "atom," singly or in combination. The cognition is of the gross sizeable form (*sthūla-pratibhāsa*), but the atom cannot serve as the objective counterpart, as it lacks the gross form. What figures in knowledge has no counterpart outside, thus the knowledge form is uncaused, and what is supposedly outside does not[5] figure in knowledge. The whole (*avayavin*) or a real combination

1. *Triṁśikā-bhāṣya*, p. 15.
2. *Triṁśika-bhāṣya*, p. 66.
3. *Madhyānta-vibhāga-ṭīkā*, pp. 9, 13-14, 18.
4. *Saṅkliṣṭā ca viśuddhā ca samalā vimalā ca. Madhyānta*, pp. 42-3.
5. *Ālambana-parīkṣā* (of Diṅnāga), 1, 2; *Viṁśatikā* II; see also *TS.*, pp. 551 ff.

consisting of parts is not accepted, as the Nyāya-Vaiśeṣika does. The earlier Buddhism, specially the Sautrāntika, had already cogently refuted the reality of the whole[1] (*avayavin*).

(2) The manifest difficulties inherent in accounting for cognition on a dualistic basis, viz. knowledge here and object there with a supposed relation of identity (*sārūpya*) between them point to its unsoundness. All relation is within knowledge[2] and not between knowledge and an other outside it. For this relation can never be known or verified.

(3) The fact of cognition and its object being always inseparable, their being identical[3] (*sahopalambha-niyama*) or the inconceivability of an unknown object is the chief idealistic argument.

(4) The occurrence of illusion, dreams, etc., where admittedly there is knowledge-form without any assignable object[4] proves that consciousness creates its own content, it is self-contained and does not depend on the external object.

(5) The Vijñānavādin can and does plausibly explain all[5] facts of experience, viz. difference between true and false knowledge, a common intra-subjective world, duration of objects, etc., on his theory that *vijñāna* manifests the object content from time to time owing to its own internal modifications caused by primordial latent forces (*vāsanās*).

Strata of Consciousness.—*Vijñāna* is the sole reality; the object in its form as substance, e.g. (chair, table, man, etc.) and modes or attributes is a false superimposition[6] (*upacāra*) on the states of consciousness which alone are real. The states or strata of *vijñāna* are three; *ālaya-vijñāna*, *mano-vijñāna* and *pravṛtti* (or *viṣaya*) *vijñāna*.

The *ālaya* is the repository, the carrier, of all *vāsanās*, the potential state of things. The other *vijñānas* are connected with it as its consequences. The other two strata not only draw upon the *ālaya*, but also replenish it. The *ālaya* is not static; it is compared to a mighty stream. Our mental dispositions change every

1. See section II of this article.
2. *PV.*, II, 442-5.
3. *PV.*, II, 336, 389-91, pp. 571 ff.
4. *Viṁśatikā* 1, 9.
5. *Viṁśatika* 2 ff.
6. *Triṁśikā* 1.

moment; they get augmented or are enfeebled. The *ālaya* is coterminous with phenomenal existence.[1] If there were no *ālaya*, one particular modification of consciousness or even a series of them will come to a dead stop. It seems that we are drawing upon our capital only to add something more to it. Again, if there were no *ālaya*, the endeavour to achieve freedom from *saṁsāra* would be meaningless. As it is the nature of one state to last but for a moment, no effort is required to remove it. The *ālaya* is definitely taken as ceasing even in the *Arhat* stage, a stage corresponding to *Jivan-mukti*.[2]

The second modification of *vijñāna* is the process of intellection, *manovijñāna*. If the *ālaya* is a realm of possibilities, *manana* is the state of actualization, not the actualized state. We may conceive this as the categorizing or the synthesizing activity of the mind nourishing on the false notions of the "*I*" and the "*mine*." The third modification of *vijñāna* gives ust he six kinds of objectivity—namely, the five external sense-data and the datum of the inner sense.

The Absolute Consciousness.—These modifications of consciousness are projected outside, and there arises the apprehension of things as houses, trees, mountains, etc., existing independent of consciousness. But they do not so exist. They are therefore called *parikalpita*,[3] unreal by their very nature. What about the reality of the ideas ? The tree may not exist outside, but the "tree-idea" certainly exists as a subjective fact, it might be held. Berkeley and other subjective idealists take this view. The position of the Vijñāna vādin is totally different. Take away the object, and the idea, the subjective fact, also loses its distinctive character as this or that idea. The modifications of consciousness, including the *ālaya*, are called *para-tantra*,[4] the dependent. They are unreal insofar as they depend on the object for their determinate character. They are not, however, unreal in essence, as they are one with the *pariniṣpanna*, with pure consciousness, the Absolute. Hence the *para-tantra*—the subjective world of ideas—is said to be neither identical with nor

1. *evam ālaya-viiñāne sati saṁsāra-pravṛttir nivṛttiś ca.* *Triṁśikā*, p. 38.
2. *ibid., tasya vyāvṛttir arhatve.*
3. *Triṁśikā*, 20.
4. *ibid.*, 21.

different from the *parinișpanna*.[1] It is not identical with the Absolute (*parinișpanna*) as the *para-tantra* is infected with the duality of subject and object. Nor is it different; for the absolute is nothing else than the *para-tantra* without duality and without change and diversity. The *parinișpanna* is also called *dharmatā* or *tathatā*, the thatness of things. It is of one undifferentiated nature like space.[2] It is realized in transcendental consciousness (*jñānaṁ lokottaraṁ ca tat*). That state is beyond all trace of the duality of subject and object. One cannot even be said to have realized it as long as there is this apprehension of having realized it. For this smacks of duality still. Vasubandhu concludes: "So long as consciousness is not rooted in pure consciousness, the tendency to apprehend duality will not cease." "Even apprehending 'This is all pure consciousness' does one present something before oneself; and (so) does not remain in the state of pure consciousness." "When consciousness does not cognize any object, then it is pure consciousness: in the absence of the object, the subject as apprehending also ceases. How are we to describe that state of pure consciousness?" "It is not mind, not apprehension: but transcendental consciousness (*lokottaraṁ jñānam*); *ālaya* has ceased owing to the destruction of the two-fold delusion." "It is the undefiled *essence* (*dhātu*), unthinkable, benign, eternal, blessed—the *free dharma-kāya* of the Lord Buddha."[3]

7. Conclusion

Some Problems in Interpretation

Nirvāṇa.—"The history of Buddhism is the history of *nirvāṇa*." In the Hīnayāna Schools it is a real state of extinction engendered by spiritual discipline; a difference between *saṁsāra* and *nirvāṇa* is made. The Mādhyamika does not admit difference between the two; *nirvāṇa* is not the dissolution of phenomena, but of our wrong views only (*kalpanā-kṣayo hi nirvāṇam*). The Vijñānavādin, as an absolutist, rightly refuses to characterize it; but he identifies it with pure *vijñāna* which undergoes the double process of defilement and purification. For the Mādhyamika the

1. *ibid.*, 22.
2. *Triṁśikā-bhāṣya*, pp. 39-41.
3. *Triṁśikā*, 26-30.

identification of the absolute with *vijñāna* and the conception of a real transformation of it are dogmatic and unwarranted. In the Mahāyāna Schools, the *dharma-kāya* is the religious analogue of the Absolute.

Relation to other systems.—As the Buddhist Schools evolved alongside of Jain and *Brāhmaṇical* systems, mutual influence may reasonably be assumed. It is not, however, easy, owing to the vastness and complication of the problem, to estimate with any measure of precision the nature and extent of the influence. Influence may be expressed not necessarily by imitation and acceptance but by opposition and rejection. This is very true of Buddhist and non-Buddhist thought.

Despite great diversity, the Sāṅkhya provides the prototype and the point of departure for the Ābhidharmika system. The conception of *dharma* is closely modelled on that of *prakṛti*. The problem of change is central in both the systems. Buddhism, however, refused to exempt any existent (like the *puruṣa* of the Sāṅkhya) from the pale of universal change; and change itself is conceived as replacement, the emergence and cessation of durationless entities.

At a subsequent stage, we find direct and sustained conflict between Buddhism (the Sautrāntika especially) and the realistic systems, the Nyāya-Vaiśeṣika, the Mīmāṁsā and Jainism. We have ample evidence of this in the works of Akṣapāda (*Nyāya-sūtra*), Vātsyāyana, Uddyotakara, Vācaspati Miśra, Kumārila, Udayana, Jayanta, etc., on the *brāhmaṇical* side and Diṅnāga, Dharmakīrtti and Dharmottara on the other. The influence was felt on practically every important problem—perception, inference, *apoha* (nominalism), whole (*avayavin*), universal (*sāmānya*). The Nyāya and the Mīmāṁsā reformulated their realism with greater thoroughness and self-consciousness. The Buddhists stuck to their subjective and critical trends. Each system gained, owing to this impact, in clarity and depth. An interpretation of Indian philosophy in terms of this conflict should prove instructive.

The influence of the Vedānta on the development of Mahāyāna and *vice versa* presents us with another problem no less interesting. Earlier Buddhism is realistic and pluralistic. The *advaitic* turn that it took in the Mādhyamika and Yogācāra systems suggests the influence of the conception of Brahman as the unaffected reality underlying the appearances. Some scholars[1] hold that there has been direct borrowing.

Gauḍapāda and Śaṅkara revolutionized the Vedānta thought by establishing non-dualism dialectically; they characterize phenomena as false appearance (*māyā*) and formulate the doctrine of three truths and two texts (*para* and *a-para*). The non-*advaitic* Schools of the Vedānta have roundly taken all these as concealed Buddhism, and some modern scholars have fallen in line with this view.[2]

It must, however, be recognized that the *Ātmavāda* of the *Upaniṣads* was impelled by its inner dynamism, heading towards *advaitism* like the prior movement on the Buddhist side. The pre-Śaṅkara Vedānta establishes the reality of one substance by a criticism of the Sāṅkhya dualism; Śaṅkara himself arrives at his non-dualism by a criticism of the *bhedābheda* (unity-in-difference) view of Bharttṛprapañca and others. There is no evidence of direct borrowing in Śaṅkara. Gauḍapāda's *Māṇḍūkya-kārikā* does, however, show in diction and doctrines the influence[3] of the Mahāyāna. The different parts of it, however, are loosely connected; they may be the work of different authors;[4] and only in the III and IV books are there unmistakable Buddhist influences. It is also difficult to conceive how the philosophers belonging to the *ātman*-tradition could borrow doctrines from the *nairātmya* tradition. It can therefore be suggested that there has been borrowing of technique rather than of tenets. The dialectic of Nāgārjuna, the *Vijñānavāda* analysis of illusion and their doctrines of two truths might have suggested to Gauḍapāda and Śaṅkara the most consistent way of interpreting the *Upaniṣadic* tradition.

Different Absolutisms.—This leads us to the intrinsic problem about the correct interpretation of the different absolutisms, the *Śūnyatā*, *vijñaptimātratā* and Brahman. Do they differ merely in name ?

Thanks to the lead of Professor Radhakrishnan, the nihilistic

1. "That the Mahāyāna is indebted to some *Aupaniṣada* influence is probable," Stcherbatsky, *Buddhist Nirvāṇa*, pp. 51.
2. *Buddhist Nirvāṇa*, pp. 51, 62.
3. Professor V. Bhattacharya has established this with his characteristic thoroughness in his *Āgama Śāstra of Gauḍapāda*.
4. *Āgama Śāstra*, pp. cxliv, lv.

interpretation of *śūnyatā* is now discredited; perhaps it had relied on no better evidence than the awe-inspiring term *śūnya*. There is, however, the apprehension that the differences of these systems, at least in their method and approach, might be glossed over. The systems criticize each other and distinguish themselves sharply. Can we find any meaning in their polemic ?

It may be suggested that while agreeing with regard to the *form* of the Absolute, these systems differ in the mode of their approach and the entity with which they identify the Absolute. In all these systems, the Absolute is transcendent, as free from empirical determinations; it is at once immanent as being the essence of phenomena. Further, they all speak of it as realizable in a non-empirical mode of intuition. All of them have recourse to the complementary doctrine of appearance.

The differences should not be overlooked. The Vedānta starts with an extra-logical or theological revelation of the Vedāntas (*Upaniṣads*) about the sole reality of the *ātman*; this is sought to be realized through reason (*manana*) and contemplation. The Mādhyamika takes hold of the dialectical consciousness, which emerges logically in the conflict of viewpoints. The Yogācāra is convinced of the sole reality of consciousness on the experience of trance-states where it continues to exist even though the object may be absent. The Vedānta and *Vijñānavāda* begin with the analysis of an empirical illusion and they apply it analogically to the world. For the Vedānta, the real is the "*this*", the giveṇ or pure being; the "*silver*" as subsisting withiṇ consciousness only is apearance (*prātibhāsika*). The Vijñānavādin takes the opposite view; the given "*this*" is an unreal or free projection of consciousness which alone is real. *Vijñāna* is understood not as *pure being* (static), but as creating and projecting; it can be construed as Cosmic Will. Differing from both, the Mādhyamika addresses himself directly to the transcendental illusion created by the opposition of standpoints; he reaches the Absolute through this dialectical consciousness. If Brahman is *pure being* and *vijñāna* is creative force, *śūnyatā* is identified with nothing that we empirically experience; it is the critical or reflective awareness itself. All these present problems in higher philosophical interpretation.

ABBREVIATIONS

AKV. *Abhidharma-kośa-vyākhyā of* Yaśomitra. Ed. by Woghihara, Tokio.

MK. *Madhyamaka-kārikā of* Nāgārjuna. Ed. by de la V. Poussin (Bib. Budd. IV).

MKV. *Madhyamaka-kārikā-vṛtti* (*Prasanna-padā*), by Candrakīrtti (Bib. Budd. IV).

NB. *Nyāya-bindu* of Dharmakīrtti (Bib. Budd. VII).

NBT. *Nyāya-bindu-ṭikā of* Dharmottara (Bib. Budd. VII).

PS. *Pramāṇa-samuccaya of* Diṅnāga, Part I, Restored into Sanskrit by H. R. H. Iyengar, Mysore.

PV. *Pramāṇa-vārttika of* Dharmakīrtti with the *Manorathanandini*, *JBORS*, Patna.

TS. *Tattva-saṅgraha of* Sāntarakṣita, 2 vols. G. O. S., Baroda.

BIBLIOGRAPHY

YAŚOMITRA: *Abhidharma-kośa-vyākhyā.*

DHARMAKĪRTTI: *Pramāṇa-vārttika.*

,, *Nyāya-bindu.*

NĀGĀRJUNA: *Mūla-Madhyamaka-kārikā*, with the *Prasanna-padā* of Candrakīrtti.

ŚĀNTIDEVA: *Bodhi-caryāvatāra.*

VASUBANDHU: *Vijñapti-mātratā-siddhi.*

ŚĀNTARAKṢITA: *Tattva-saṅgraha.*

OBERMILLER: *Buston's History of Buddhism*, Vols. I and II (trans.).

RADHAKRISHNAN: *Indian Philosophy*, Vol. I, pp. 611 ff.

DASGUPTA: *History of Indian Philosophy*, Vols. I and II.

STCHERBATSKY: *The Central Conception of Buddhism.*

,, *The Buddhist Conception of Nirvāṇa.*

,, *Buddhist Logic*, 2 vols.

WINTERNITZ: *History of Indian Literature* (Eng. trans.) Vol. II.

MURTI, T. R. V. *The Central Philosophy of Buddhism.*

5.7 INDIAN REALISM OR VIJNĀNAVĀDA AND ITS REFUTATION*

Review of *Indian Realism* by Jadunath Sinha, M. A., Ph.D., Kegan Paul, Trench, Trubner & Co., Ltd. London; Pp. xiv—287; 1938; price 10/6d.

The title of the book under review is misleading. It is not a work on Indian Realism. It might be more aptly described as "Vijñānavāda and its Refutation by other Systems of Indian thought." The author first attempts an exposition of Vijñānavāda, an Indian School of Idealism, and then gives in several chapters criticism of the same by each one of the important systems of Indian thought, as the Jaina, Mīmāṁsā, Nyāya-Vaiśeṣika, Sāṅkhya-Yoga, Vedānta, etc. In fact, there is not one exposition but twelve or thirteen different expositions and the corresponding criticisms are more than a score. It cannot be contended that the several expositions and criticisms all bring out new arguments. Many of them are invariably repeated.** A more acceptable presentation would have been to give a main exposition and refutation, adding the necessary variations at the proper places. As it stands, the book appears very suspiciously like a free rendering of the various passages relating to Vijñānavāda scattered in the Sanskrit philosophical texts. Nevertheless, the work of Prof. Sinha is eminently useful as a source-book on an important but neglected branch of Indian thought. The parallel references that Prof. Sinha makes between Indian and Western thought are helpful and striking. The book is throughout very well documented.

*Reprinted from *The Philosophical Quarterly*, 1939.

**These arguments among others are repeated in the course of the exposition of Vijñānavāda: The "simultaneous perception of subject and object." pp. 6, 27, 48, 80 ff, 113, 149, 152, 228.

Self-awareness of knowledge : p. 12 ff, 112 ff.

Metaphysical arguments against the existence of the object: p. 4, 32, 61 ff, 227.

Comparison with dream-consciousness, pp. 49, 103, 229.

Relativity of sensa: pp. 92, 116.

For repetitions in the counter-arguments of the realists, see footnote elsewhere.

In Indian Philosophy the antithesis of Realism and Idealism is not so important as the antithesis between Pluralism and Absolutism. Prof. Sinha characterises Vijñānavāda as Subjective Idealism, sometimes calling it Sensationism even. "He (the Yogācāra) is a thoroughgoing subjectivist." (p. 9). "The Yogācāra doctrine may be compared with Hume's sensationism" (p. 10). "The Yogācāra holds that cognitions are many and non-eternal. But Śaṅkara holds that there is only one, eternal universal consciousness or *Brahman*. The former is a sensationist. The latter is a monist or absolute idealist. The discrete, momentary cognitions in individual streams of consciousness (santāna) constitute the reality of the Yogācāra .... He reduces the so-called external objects to mere cognitions of the individual minds or psychic continua. He is a sensationist like David Hume and J. S. Mill" (p. 225). "The Yogācāra's absolute reality is a plurality of momentary cognitions with no self abiding in them and with no external objects to produce them. He does not admit the reality of one, infinite, eternal, self-luminous consciousness or Brahman, but of a beginningless series of momentary cognitions which appear and disappear in individual minds or streams of consciousness" (*Indian Realism*, p. 227). I am led to doubt very seriously the correctness of the statements.

First and foremost, the Yogācāra is an absolutist and a transcendentalist. He urges the hollowness of the separate elements[1] by refuting the externality of the object and establishes the reality of one undifferentiated, Pure Consciousness variously called, *Dharmatā*, *Dharmakāya*, *Tathatā* and *Vijñaptimātratā*. The Vijñānavādin realises, unlike Berkeley and other subjectivists, that the negation of the outer object necessarily entails the negation of the inner circle of ideas. Prof. Sinha seems to be too much pre-occupied with the polemic on either side to notice the constructive side expounded in such works as *The Abhisamayālaṅkāra*, *Daśabhūmikā-Śāstra*, *Mahāyāna-Sūtrālaṅkāra*

1. Cf. Sthiramati's introduction to the *Triṁśikā*, Varanaseya Sanskrit Vishvavidyalaya edn. 1972, p. 91:
atha vā dharma-pudgalābhiniviṣṭāś cittamātraṁ yathābhūtaṁ na jānanti'tyato dharma-pudgalanairātmyapradarśanena saphale vijñaptimātre'nupūrveṇa praveśārthaḥ prakaraṇā'rambhaḥ.

and more systematically in the *Vijñaptimātratāsiddhi* of Vasubandhu.

The main argument for the sole reality of consciousness is the identity of subject and object, their distinction being illusory.[1] Consciousness is a unity of which subject and object are false abstractions. All distinction (relation) is within consciousness. Even the remotest object is equally within; the "known" and the "unknown" are conscious distinctions. There can be no relation between consciousness and something outside of it and co-ordinate with it. This is the most fundamental truth of Vijñānavāda. The realist theories, one and all, seek to account for knowledge by relating consciousness with the object by way of representation (sārūpya), parallelism, causation or a unique relation called *svarūpa sambandha* (the Nyāya position). Prof. Sinha gives a very good exposition of the detailed arguments by which the Idealist refutes the realist theories. The insuperable difficulty in all such attempted relations between consciousness and object is that one or the other end of the relation is unknown and unknowable. For consciousness has in that case to perform two functions at once : it has to appear as one of the terms related and as that which is conscious of the relation. On the representationist or causal hypothesis, knowledge has not only to be a copy or effect but at once to know itself as such. It has to assume two positions at once, that of a combatant in the arena and that of a spectator of the combat—an impossible feat. Consciousness is nothing if not all-comprehensive and universal. The object cannot be placed on an equal footing beside it. Hence the distinctions such as consciousness and object; which appear within the all-comprehensive reality, are false.

All these difficulties crop up, the realist would say, because of the illegitimate demand that the relation between consciousness and object must itself be known, if there is to be knowledge. They might urge that the relation between consciousness and object is factual like the relation obtaining between any two objects, there is nothing unique about this relation. If so, a

1. sahopalambhaniyamād abhedo nilataddhiyoḥ
bhedastu bhrāntivijñānair dṛśya indāvivādvaye.
Quoted in *Bhāmatī* on *Br. sūt.* II.ii. 28 *Śāṅkara-bhāṣya.*

map because it is a representation of the terrain of a country, should be conscious. The effect must be aware of the cause and so on. It might be said in answer that consciousness of a thing does not necessarily mean self-consciousness. As Moore would say, I look *through* consciousness but not *at it*. Kumārila says likewise, "When I *see*, I see the coloured surface, but not the eye which sees." "The typical realist position is that of the Nyāya: "When I know the object, I simply know it but do not know knowledge : later by a separate act of knowledge called introspection (*anuvyavasāya*) I make the previous knowledge an object and thus become self-conscious." Though such a view is universally held, it is far from the truth. In the first act there is knowledge of object but not self-consciousness; the second act (introspection) has a different object (the first knowledge presumably), but again there need not be any self-consciousness. The content of the two cognitions is different, and one may even closely follow the other in time; but the mode of knowing is the same. If the previous one is not self-conscious, the other shares the same fate. If it be said that self-consciousness is that mode of knowledge in which the first knowledge (the act or subject) is made an object subsequently, the identity between the two is an unprovable assumption.

If consciousness were not already implied in the first act, we should have no means of becoming aware of it subsequently by a separate act. The Vijñānavādin therefore says: "On the theory that consciousness is not self-evident, there cannot be knowledge of object even."[1] This is not to be understood to mean that we first become aware of consciousness and then we have the knowledge of object; but that Consciousness is the implicate of all content-knowledge much like space of spatial distinctions. Our awareness of the implicate of all knowledge is transcendental (*lokottara prajñā*), but the awareness of content-consciousness is empirical—a distinction which it suits the convenience of the realists to ignore. They make their task all too easy by taking both the awarenesses to be empirical, and triumphantly show that the distinction lacks experiential basis.[2]

1. "apratyakṣopalambhasya nārthadṛṣṭiḥ prasajyate" and the doctrine of *svasaṁvedana* of consciousness.

2. Cf. the criticism of this doctrine by the Realists, by the Mīmāṁsā (pp. 135 ff.), by the Nyāya (pp. 183 ff.) *Indian Realism*.

Consciousness on the realist hypothesis is at best considered as an impressionable entity which records the outside world by its plasticity, and there might be a secondary recording of the inside world. But a record is not awareness. Its unique nature must be recognised. Consciousness is nothing if not self-evident. It can be distinguished from object, but cannot be conceived in terms of the object.

Why have the realist systems failed to appreciate the unique nature of Consciousness ? Empiricists one and all, they have never tried to go beyond the commonly accepted notions of consciousness. They have even accommodated their philosophies to common sense. We never become aware of the unique character of consciousness so long as our unreflective objective attitude is not transcended. It is illusion that awakens us from our dogmatic slumber. The Yogācāra builds his system on an explicit recognition of this. As Vasubandhu states it : "*Vijñapti* is all (the sole reality), because of the apprehension of unreal objects." The object may well be unreal, but for the appearance of the unreal, for something to be mistaken for the real, Consciousness must be real. The Vijñānavāḍin cannot accept both consciousness and object as real—the realist position; nor can he hold both as unreal—the Mādhyamika position[1]

The realist may answer that illusion is impossible without the reality of the two—the thing mistaken and the thing mistaken for, corresponding respectively to the rope and the "snake" in the stock example. The "snake" may not be present here and now, but it is real elsewhere. Only the mistaking, the relation of the one with the other, is unreal. The object may not, as in dreams etc., be present there; nevertheless, illusion would be impossible but for the traces left by the previous experience of real objects. Thus even for the occurrence of illusion, for the suspicion of objectivity itself, the object must exist in reality. Śaṅkara himself raises this objection against the Idealist. He asks: If the Idealists had no experience of the externality of

1. Sthiramati's introduction to *Triṁśikā* p. 93: atha vā vijñānavad vijñeyam api dravyata eveti kecit manyante; vijñeyavad vjñānamapi saṁvṛtita eva, na paramārthata ityasya dviprakārasyā'pyekānta-vādasya pratiṣedhārthaḥ prakaraṇārambhaḥ.

the object, how then do they speak of consciousness as presenting objects *as if* they were external.[1]

Sthiramati anticipates such objections and answers them in his commentary on the *Triṁśikā* of Vasubandhu.[2] The reality of the object superimposed is in no way necessary for illusion. What is required is that we should have an idea, a *Vāsanā*, of the unreal. A pillar might be mistaken for a ghost. This need not mean that the ghost is somewhere real or that it has been experienced before. It may well be that all our notions of the ghost are mere imagination, fantastic descriptions lacking any experiential basis. If it be contended that such fantasies themselves are based upon fact, then nothing will be unreal. Some realists have clearly perceived the implication of this position. The Vijñānavādin says that we have only a false belief, a *Vāsanā*, of the object existing independently of consciousness. And a *Vāsanā* need not be the trace left by a previous experience, but it might be referred to another previous *vāsanā* and so on. It might be beginningless. However, the contention that the belief in objectivity is *vāsanā*, an illusion without any real basis, implies that consciousness as such in its pristine state is free from the false abstractions of subject and object.

This state is not only the prius and logical presupposition of the Yogācāra contention, but in the light of that alone does it derive all its significance. Such a consciousness is non-empirical; it is beyond all thought; and concepts cannot define it. There is no indication in the entire body of *Indian Realism* that Prof. Sinha appreciates the transcendental stand-point. He appears to think that the ultimate of the Yogācāra is the empirical series of states chasing one another. Vasubandhu, is quite clear in the matter.

He first describes the three stratifications of Consciousness—*ālaya*, *manovijñāna* and *pravṛttivijñāna*—which serve as the ground

1. Cf. the Realist Criticisms. pp. 123 ff. pp. 190 ff. *Indian Realism.* Śaṅkara's comment on *Br. Sūt.* II.ii.28.

2. Sthiramati's comment on *Triṁśikā* I, p. 118: anyaṣtv āha asatyātmani mukhye dharmeṣu copacāro na yujyate. upacāro hi triṣu bhavati nānyatamābhāve; mukhyapadārthe, tatsadṛśe cā'nyasmin viṣaye, tayoś ca sādṛśye.

for the illusion of things and essences existing outside.[1] The *ālaya* is the repository, the carrier, of all *vāsanās*, the potential state of things. This might correspond in a way with the *petites perceptions* of Leibniz or the *mūlāvidyā* of the Vedānta. The other Vijñānas are connected with it as its consequences. The other two strata not only draw upon the *ālaya*, but also replenish it. It must be understood that the *ālaya* is not static; it is compared to a mighty stream. Our mental dispositions change every moment; they get augmented or are enfeebled. The *ālaya* is co-terminus with phenomenal existence.[2] If there were no *ālaya*, one particular modification of consciousness or even a series of them will come to a dead stop. It seems that we are drawing upon our capital only to add something more to it. Again, if there were no *ālaya*, the endeavour to achieve freedom from *saṁsāra* is meaningless. As it is the nature of one state to last but for a moment, no effort is required to remove it. The past, even if it be accepted, is not a source of trouble, and there is no possibility of any new state emerging later. If possibilities are accepted, they will differ but in name from the *ālaya*. The *ālaya* is definitely taken as ceasing even in the Arhat stage, a stage corresponding to *jīvan-mukti*.[3]

The second modification of *vijñāna* is the process of intellection, *Manovijñāna*. If the *ālaya* is a realm of possibilities, Manana is the state of actualisation, not the actualised state. We may conceive this as the categorising or the synthesising activity of the mind. The third modification of vijñāna gives us the six kinds of objectivity,—namely the five external sense data and the datum of the inner sense.

These modifications of consciousness are projected outside, and there arises the apprehension of things as houses, trees, mountains, etc., existing independent of consciousness. But these do not in fact so exist, for reasons already urged. They are called

1. *Triṁśikā* I, 2 and 4:
ātma-dharmopacāro hi vividho yaḥ pravarttate
vijñāna-pariṇāme'sau pariṇāmaḥ sa ca tridhā.
vipāko mananākhyaś ca vijñaptir viṣayasya ca
tatrālayākhyaṁ vijñānaṁ vipākaḥ sarvabījakam.
.... tac ca varttate srotasaughavat.

2. Sthiramati's comment on *Triṁśikā* 19, p. 298: evam ālaya-vijñāne sati saṁsāra-pravṛttir nivṛttiś ca.

3. *Triṁśikā* 205 : tasya vyāvṛttir-arhattve.

parikalpita,[1] and are unreal by their very nature. They appear to be independent of consciousness but do not so exist. What about the reality of the ideas ? The tree may not exist outside, but the "tree-idea" certainly exists as a subjective fact, it might be held. Berkeley and other subjective idealists take this view. They are led to formulate a species of sensationism—a doctrine which Prof. Sinha has fathered upon the Yogācāra too. The real position of the Vijñānavādin is totally different. Take away the object, and the idea, the subjective fact, also loses its distinctive character as this or that idea. The modifications of consciousness, including the *ālaya*, are called *Paratantra*,[2] the dependent. They are unreal insofar as they depend on the object for their determinate character. They are not however unreal in essence, as they are one with the *parinispanna*, with Pure Consciousness, the Absolute. Hence the Paratantra—the subjective world of ideas—is said to be neither identical with nor different from the Parinispanna.[3] It is not identical with the Absolute (*parinispanna*) as the *paratantra* is infected with the duality of subject and object. Nor is it different; for the absolute is nothing else than the *paratantra* without duality and without change and diversity. The Parinispanna is also called *Dharmatā* or *Tathatā*, the thatness of things. It is of one undifferentiated nature like space (*"parnispannaś cākāśavad ekarasaṁ jñānaṁ ca yathoktaṁ nirvikalpena jñānenākāśa-samatāyāṁ sarvadharmān paśyatiti paratantra-dharmāṇāṁ tathatāmātradarśanāt". "sarvakālaṁ tathābhāvāt, saiva vijñaptirmātratā"—Vijñaptimātratāsiddhi*, pp. 39-41). It is realised in transcendental consciousness (*jñānaṁ lokottaraṁ ca tat*). That state is beyond all trace of the duality of subject and object. One cannot even be said to have realised it as long as there is

1. *Ibid* 20:
yena yena vikalpena yad yad vastu vikalpyate
parikalpita evāsau svabhāvo na sa vidyate.
Sthiramati's comment p. 30: yad yad vastu prakalpyate, ādhyātmikaṁ bāhyaṁ vā'ntaśo yāvad buddha-dharmā api.
2. *Triṁśikā* 21:
paratantra-svabhāvas tu vikalpaḥ pratyayodbhavaḥ.
Quoted in Sthiramati's comment, p. 30:
abhutaparikalpas tu citta-caittās traidhātukāḥ.
3. *Triṁśikā* 21-22:
niṣpannas tasya pūrveṇa sadā rahitatā tu yā.
ata eva sa naivānyo ṇānyaḥ paratantratah.

this apprehension of having realised it. For this smacks of duality still—Vasubandhu concludes: "So long as consciousness is not rooted in Pure Consciousness, the tendency to apprehend duality will not cease." Even apprehending "This is all Pure Consciousness" does one present something before oneself; and (so) does not remain in the state of Pure Consciousness. "When Consciousness does not cognise any object, then it is Pure Consciousness : in the absence of the object, the apprehending subject also ceases" (*grāhyābhāve grāhakābhāvam api pratipadyate*). How are we to describe that state, of Pure Consciousness ? "It is not mind, not apprehension : but Transcendental Consciousness (*lokottaraṁ jñānam*); ālaya has ceased owing to the destruction of the two-fold delusion." "It is the undefiled Essence (*Dhātu*), unthinkable, benign, eternal, blessed—the Free *Dharmakāya* of the Lord Buddha"[1] (*Vijñaptimātratāsiddhi*, Triṁśikā, 26-30).

II

Indian Realism, as already indicated falls into two unequal parts—the exposition of Vijñānavāda and the criticism of it by each one of the more well-known schools of Indian thought. The criticisms are not co-ordinated: there are ever so many arguments which are repeated *ad nauseam*.[2] No plan is evident beyond the one of separating the criticisms on the basis of authorship and origin. The refutation of Vijñānavāda by Malliṣeṇa gives

1. *Ibid.* 26-30:
yāvad vijñapti-mātratve vijñānaṁ nāvatiṣṭhate
grāhadvayasyānuśayas tāvan na vinivarttate.
vijñapti-mātram evedam-ityapi hyupalambhataḥ
sthāpayannagrataḥ kiñcit tanmātre nāvatiṣṭhate.
yadā tvālambanaṁ jñānaṁ naivopalabhate tadā
sthitaṁ vijñānamātratve grāhyābhāve tadagrahāt.
acitto'nupalambho'sau jñānaṁ lokottaraṁ ca tat
āśrayasya parāvṛttir dvidhā dauṣṭhulya-hānitaḥ.
sa evānāsravo dhātur acintyaḥ kuśalo dhruvaḥ
sukho vimukti-kāyo'sau dharmākhyo'yaṁ mahāmuneḥ.

2. Repetitions of criticisms against Vijñānavāda:
If cognition were its object then the form of consciousness should be "I am blue." 67, 77, 131, 182 etc. One and the same thing cannot be subject and object; 131, 135. Consciousness is not self-conscious; 184 ff.
Even illusions have real basis—119 ff, 170 ff, 221 ff.—*Indian Realism*.

the title, Jaina Realism[1] to the chapter; the refutation by Kumārila and others is called Mīmāṁsā Realism, etc. We would very much like to know from Prof. Sinha what is peculiarly Jaina about Malliṣeṇa's criticism, peculiarly Mīmāṁsā about Kumārila's criticism, etc. If he had let us know how, for instance, the Jaina or the Nyāya types of realism can be understood in the light of this key-problem of the nature of knowledge and object, he would have rendered a service to Indian realism.

The criticisms against Vijñānavāda easily fall into two or perhaps three classes : first those that emanate from the realist schools, Nyāya, Vaiśeṣika, Mīmāṁsā, Jaina, Vaibhāṣika and Sautrāntika; second, the criticims by the Absolutist schools, Vedānta and Mādhyamika.[2] The Sāṅkhya-Yoga position is peculiar, and may be said to constitute a third class.

The realist systems, in some sense or other, fail to appreciate the difference between the subject and the object. They reduce everything to the category of the object; they know no other. They consider knowledge as known, at least knowable in principle, much in the same way as the object is. With knowledge not enjoying any unique and all-comprehensive position, the independence of the object is assured.

All the realist systems are also pluralistic. And this raises the interesting problem whether realism as such is pluralistic, and its converse problem whether pluralism must necessarily be realist. The pluralistic position is arrived at differently in each system, Nyāya, Jaina, etc. Any exposition of this thesis is clearly beyond the scope of this review.

It is also significant to note that all realisms are necessarily empirical and dogmatic; they are not critical and reflective. Their doctrines follow from certain basic propositions, which are assumed, not questioned, much less justified. It is interesting to derive and expound all the chief doctrines of each system from their basic assumptions. Such an undertaking will have the merit of exhibiting each system as a well-knit and unified body

1. The chapter on Jaina Realism is drawn chiefly from *Syādvāda-mañjarī*. There are *other* equally important expositions and criticisms of Vijñānavāda in the Jaina texts: *Sammati Tarka* pp. 349, 366 ff, chap. VII.

2. There is no reference in prof. Sinha's book, to the Mādhyamika criticism of Vijñānavāda. Cf. *Bodhicaryāvatāra* pp. 389 ff. (B. Indica); *Mādhyamika kārikā*, Candrakīrti's Commentary: pp. 61 ff. (B. B.)

of doctrines. Incidentally, it would facilitate criticism, as we will not have to criticise a host of seemingly un-connected doctrines, but one basic principle.

The empiricism of the realist systems is inevitable, as their metaphysics is an extension of the common sense notions of knowledge, object, causality, etc. It is not an outcome of thorough questioning. Questioning follows in the wake of the consciousness of illusion. We never question anything unless it goes wrong. It is then that we grow self-conscious.

This criticism can otherwise be expressed by saying that the realist systems have no conception of the spirit and the spiritual. They take the spirit or the self as one among other things. Truly, spirit is the spirit of things, their very essence or soul. The inner soul is realised only as we crack the shell. Without the rejection of the object as false, there is not, truly speaking, a consciousness of the spirit. It is thus that all absolute systems, Vedānta, Vijñānavāda and Mādhyamika, are all explicitly based on such negation of appearance as false. Their ultimate is beyond the empirical plane.

The principles of Vijñānavāda and their refutation by the realist systems can thus be shown to move on two totally different planes. The arguments and counter-arguments never traverse each other. Prof. Sinha does not seem to be conscious of the disparity of the two positions. The Vijñānavādin, by his dictum of unity of consciousness (*sahopalambhaniyama*), implies that there can be no relation whatever between consciousness and something beside it. The realist arguments urge that without such relation commonly accepted distinctions between subject and object etc. will be lost. Again, the realist's criticism of the doctrine of Self-evidence of knowledge (*sva-saṁvedana*) misses the point; he understands it to mean that we first become aware of knowledge before becoming aware of a content. This puts consciousness and object on a par with each other which is clearly wrong. Nor is our awareness of the two successive and empirical. The true Vijñānavāda position is that all content-knowledge *implies* the all-comprehensive consciousness.

III

This brings us to the second set of objections against Vijñānavāda—those from Vedānta and the Mādhyamika. These are also absolutists, and yet they are far from accepting Vijñānavāda. We find them fiercely refuting each other. An easy way of explaining away this curious position is to say that the Vedāntin has misunderstood the Yogācāra: he does not discriminate between friend and foe. Still another explanation, casually suggested by Stcherbatsky, is that "Śaṅkara, in combating Buddhist idealism, resorts to arguments of which he himself does not believe a word, since they are arguments which the most genuine realist would use. He thus argues not *sva-matena*, but *paramatam āśritya*, a method very much in vogue among Indian pandits. Deussen's interpretation of this point as a vindication of *vyavahārasatya* is a misunderstanding since the Buddhists never denied the *vyavahāra* or *saṁvṛti*" (*The Conception of Buddhist Nirvāṇa*, p. 38).

Recourse should be had to such heroic explanations only if other modes of reconciling facts fail us. Possibly some other hypothesis may be hazarded to explain the difference in the three absolutisms. The Vedāntic Brahman may not be exactly the Dharmatā or Tathātā of the Vijñānavādin and the Śūnya of the Mādhyamika. The question may be mooted whether spirit can be conceived in more than one way. And as spirit is realised, in the absolutist systems, as we negate phenomena, the entire question would turn upon the alternative modes of interpreting illusion and cancellation. On the Vedāntic, view of the cancelling consciousness, "This is not silver," the "this" (the conchshell) is not *silver*; its supposed silver character is negated. The "this" is of course real, even though its reality was not known to us. The Vijñānavādin negates the "this-ness" alone of the silver; *this* is not silver; its externality and independence of consciousness is unreal. Its essential unity and identity with consciousness is reinstated through cancellation. The Mādhyamika takes illusion as the emergence of the unreal and its appearance as real—the real in his system being the Indeterminate, Śūnya. To the Mādhyamika both the *this* and the *silver* are equally false, for the one appeared inseparable from the other, and negation applies equally to both: *this* is not *silver*.

For the Vijñānavādin consciousness is an essential unity of which subject (*grāhaka*) and object (*grāhya*) are false abstractions. The type of consciousness comparable to this may, with some justification, be called Feeling. Vijñānavāda would, on this view, be taken as representing the Absolute of Feeling, rather than that of knowledge. The Vedāntic Brahman is Truth. Truth is so true that it need not be known to be true. Knownness (*dṛśyatva*) is declared illusory. This is eminently true of the cognitive type of consciousness. In knowledge we discover what is already there, not seeking to add to or to distort the thing known. If the object known as true were incapable of existing without its relation to the knowing subject, we would be creating or at least distorting it.[1] It will not be the truth at all. The Vedāntic Brahman is the Absolute of knowledge. The Mādhyamika conceives the absolute as *Śūnya*—the Indeterminate. The Indeterminate is the sole ground of all appearance; it is creative *par excellence*. This may be identified with the willing consciousness. Willing brings into being the object from itself, from nothing as it were.

The scheme suggested may at least have the merit of explaining why these three absolutisms criticise each other inspite of much common ground. It may explain how Śaṅkara adopts the so-called realistic view of the independence of the object. Committed as he is to the Absolutism of Truth, he could not have taken Being as existing only in relation to the knowing subject

IV

The position of the Sāṅkhya-Yoga is peculiar. It is realistic but not a realism. It cannot go the whole hog with realism in holding that the object is wholly independent of consciousness. Prakṛti does act and change by itself. It may be said to exist in itself and change *by itself*, but not *for itself*.. The term 'self' can be applied to it in respect of its existence and activity, but not in respect of its value. This is the significance of the argument for the existence of *Puruṣa* (*saṅghāta-parārthatvāt*) The Sāṅkhya-Yoga finds no contradiction in separating value from existence. The object is self-existent, but its value-function (its *raison d'etre*) is bound up with the *Puruṣa*.[2] Possibly, the Sāṅkhya would not go to the extent of admitting that *Prakṛti* and its modifications will continue to exist even if there were no *Puruṣa* to

1. Cf. *Br. Sūt. Bhāṣya* I. i. iv.
2. Y. Sūt. II. 18, bhogāpavargārthaṁ dṛśyam. Y. S. II, 21, Tadartha eva dṛśyasyātmā.

experience. The realists would not find much difficulty in accepting the total independence of the object. But not so the Sāṅkhya.

The Sāṅkhya manages to reconcile the dual aspect of *Prakṛti*—its existence and its value—by the admission of the plurality of *puruṣas*. The object may not exist for one who has dissociated himself from it; but it continues to exist as it is common to other individuals (*kṛtārthaṁ prati naṣṭam apy anaṣṭaṁ tad anyasādhāraṇatvāt. Yoga Sūtra* II.22). Will there ever come a time when all the Puruṣas shall have achieved salvation, thus terminating the world-process? The Sāṅkhya-Yoga fights shy of a straight answer.[1] It says that the number of *puruṣas* is infinite, and so there is no fear of the cessation of the world. But if the number of *puruṣas* were really infinite (not merely large), how can there be a real subtraction from it from time to time? The achievement of salvation by some Puruṣas is not a real achievement then. For even if after the release of some *puruṣas* the sum-total of *puruṣas* is infinite, we should say that there was no real release. However, this clearly shows that the plurality of puruṣas is not an after-thought in the Sāṅkhya. This doctrine is essential for the existence and duration of Prakṛti.

The Sāṅkhya *prakṛti* is not self-contained; it exists, but is no end to itself. This bifurcation of value and existence in the nature of Prakṛti is the direct outcome of what appears to the Sāṅkhya as axiomatic: that which changes cannot be conscious; and that which is consciousness cannot change. The position has a Vedāntic ring about it. Vedānta agrees with the Sāṅkhya that consciousness cannot change. There is all the world of difference between the two as the Vedānta holds change to be illusory. It denies *pariṇāma*. The Vedānta may thus be said to reduce the problem of change to that of illusion. The Sāṅkhya-Yoga does just the reverse. *Vidyā* and *avidyā* are conceived as real *pariṇāmas*; *Vidyā* does not destroy *avidyā*. It merely changes it and makes it harmless like the burnt seed (*dagdhabījabhāvāḥ kleśāḥ*). There is not absolute cancellation, but only a change of states. All this is due to the Sāṅkhya-Yoga standpoint of interpreting knowledge and ignorance in terms of change.

1. Cf. The Bhāṣya on the Y. Sūtra, IV. 33.

6.1 THE GĪTĀ-CONCEPTION OF PHILOSOPHY AND RELIGION*

After exhorting Arjuna on the true nature of the self, Lord Kṛṣṇa says: "This path has been told thee according to the Sāṅkhya; hear now the way of the Yoga following which thou shalt be freed from the bondage of Karma" (*Gītā*, II, 39).[1] The critical arguments regarding the true nature of the self and its distinction from the body are referred to as the Sāṅkhya (II, ff). And this is distinguished from the Yoga which follows. In fact almost the entire *Gītā* treats of Yoga. Sañjaya, who reported the whole discourse to the old King Dhṛtarāṣṭra, describes it as the "exalted Yoga heard directly from the Lord of the Yoga" (*Yogeśvara*; XVIII, 74-5).[2] The Lord himself names his teaching Yoga (IV, 1).[3] It is of the utmost importance, in understanding the *Gītā*, that we should have the proper interpretation of Sāṅkhya and Yoga.

The terms do not, as has been held by some, refer to the two allied classical systems of philosophy originated by Kapila and Patañjali. It is inconceivable that an academic disquisition on the relative merits of the two systems of thought should have formed a fit topic on the battle-field; Arjuna wanted advice on a point of practical conduct. Nor do the considerations regarding the self referred to as the Sāṅkhya show anything peculiar to the classical Sāṅkhya system. Besides, all the great commentators, Śaṅkara, Rāmānuja and others, construe 'Sāṅkhya' as discrimination (*Viveka*). It is suggested here that 'Sāṅkhya'

*Reprinted from the Journal of the Banaras Hindu University, July, 1938.

1. Gītā, ii, 39.
   eṣā te'bhihitā sāṅkhye buddhir yoge tvimāṁ śṛṇu,
   buddhyā yukto yayā Pārtha karma-bandhaṁ prahāsyasi.
2. *ibid.*, xviii, 74-75.
   ityaham vāsudevasya pārthasya ca mahātmanaḥ,
   saṁvādam idam aśrauṣam adbhutaṁ romaharṣaṇam.
   Vyāsa-prasādāc chrutavān etad guhyam ahaṁ param,
   yogaṁ yogeśvarāt kṛṣṇāt sākṣāt kathayataḥ svayam.
3. *ibid.*, iv, I.
   imaṁ Vivasvate yogaṁ proktavān aham avyayam.

and 'Yoga' stand for philosophy and religion respectively. An examination of the passages in which these terms occur indicates the view of the *Gītā* on the relation between philosophy and religion.

Scores of times the words, *Yoga*, *yukta*, *yoga-yukta* and the compounds, *buddhi-yoga* and *karma-yoga*, occur in the *Gītā*. Arjuna is enjoined to become a yogin. Luckily, we are not left in doubt about the meaning of Yoga. It is even formally defined as *samatva*, identity or union with the cosmic will (II, 48; VI, 29).[1] And again as excellence in action. Excellence consists in doing action without being bound by it (II, 50; V, 7 ff).[2] This is achieved, negatively, by the abandonment of egoity, as actions prompted by selfish ends lead to bondage (III, 9)[3] and positively by the synthetic union or identity with God (IX, 34).[4] The two definitions are thus inter-related.

Yoga or religious consciousness arises with the faith in the living presence of a supreme will creating and sustaining all

1. *ibid.*, ii, 48.
   siddhy asiddhyoḥ samo bhūtvā samatvaṁ yoga ucyate.
   ibid., vi, 29.
   sarvabhūtastham ātmānaṁ sarvabhūtāni cātmani,
   ikṣate yogayuktātmā sarvatra samadarśanaḥ.
   ibid., v, 18.
   śuni caiva śvapāke ca paṇḍitāḥ samadarśinaḥ.
   ibid., xviii, 54.
   samaḥ sarveṣu bhūteṣu.
2. *ibid.*, ii, 50.
   buddhi-yukto jahātiha ubhe sukṛtaduṣkṛte,
   tasmād yogāya yujyasva yogaḥ karmasu kauśalam.
   ibid., v, 7.
   sarvabhūtātma-bhūtātmā kurvann api na lipyate.
   ibid., v, 8.
   naiva kiñcit karomīti yukto manyeta tattvavit.
   ibid., v, 10 ff.
   Brahmaṇyādhāya karmāṇi saṅgaṁ tyaktvā karoti yaḥ,
   lipyate na sa pāpena padma-patram ivāmbhasā.
3. *ibid.*, iii, 9.
   yajñārthāt karmaṇo'nyatra loko'yam karma-bandhanaḥ,
   tadarthaṁ karma Kaunteya mukta-saṅgaḥ samācara.
4. *ibid.*, ix, 34.
   manmanā bhava madbhakto madyāji māṁ namaskuru,
   mām evaiṣyasi yuktvaivam ātmānaṁ matparāyaṇaḥ.

things (X, 8, 42; V, 29).[1] This faith grows to fullness and becomes a reality by the practice of Yoga—the union of the individual with the Cosmic Will through self-surrender. The *Gitā* indicates certain stages of the Yoga. There is first the renunciation of all desire for the results of one's action (V, 11ff; III, 19).[2] Positively, this is to offer the fruit of every action to the Lord (IX, 27).[3] In the next stage, the devotee consciously allies himself with the universal good (*yajña*), feeling that he is a spoke in the cosmic wheel (*lokasaṅgraha*). Though it is the universal and not the individual good that he is striving for, the devotee is still conscious of his separate personality and considers that he is fighting evil. The duality between good and evil is present. In the last stage, however, he loses all sense of his doing anything (V, 8),[4] and realizes that there is only one will, the Cosmic Will (XVIII, 61).[5] As the only will, God is not conscious of any opposition to overcome. He is Freedom beyond good and evil, beyond the three *guṇas*, *sattva* included. The Yogī, realizing his identity with the Cosmic Consciousness, is likewise incapable of likes and dislikes; he transcends the sway of the *guṇas* or

1. *ibid.*, x, 8.
aham̐ sarvasya prabhavo mattaḥ sarvam̐ pravarttate,
iti matvā bhajante mām̐ budhā bhāva-samanvitāḥ.
ibid., x, 42.
athavā bahunaitena kim̐ jñātena tavārjuna.
viṣṭabhyāham idam kṛtsnam ekām̐śena sthito jagat.
ibid., v, 29.
Bhoktāram yajña-tapasām̐ sarva-loka-maheśvaram,
suhṛdam sarvabhūtānām̐ jñātvā mām̐ śāntim ṛcchati.
2. *ibid.*, v, 11.
Kāyena manasā buddhyā kevalair indriyair api,
yoginaḥ karma kurvanti saṅgam̐ tyaktvā'tma-śuddhaye.
ibid., iii, 9.
tasmād asaktaḥ satatam̐ kāryam̐ karma samācara.
3. *ibid.*, ix, 27.
yat karoṣi yad aśnāsi yaj juhoṣi dadāsi yat,
yat tapasyasi kaunteya tat kuruṣva madarpaṇam.
4. *ibid.*, v, 8.
naiva kiñcit karomī'ti yukto manyeta tattvavit.
5. *ibid.*, xviii, 61.
īśvaraḥ sarva-bhūtānām̐ hṛddeśe'rjuna tiṣṭhati,
bhrāmayan sarva-bhūtāni yantrārūḍhāni māyayā.

phenomenal existence. This is the fruition of religious life; the ego-consciousness is lost for good (XIV, 19 ff).[1]

An examination of the considerations referred to as the Sāṅkhya shows that it is a "thinking criticism of things". The true and essential self is, through critical reflection, distinguished from what merely passes for it, from the not-self as the body and other objects. Experience is analysed and reflected upon. The false appearance is discriminated from the truth. Philosophical consciousness is a sustained process of abstraction or withdrawal into the innermost recess of oneself. In reflection, the interest is invariably shifted from the object to the knowing subject. To contemplate on the how and why of an action is not doing, the action, but only thinking it in relation to oneself. Being subjective and introspective, philosophical consciousness is, by its very nature, not conducive to action. Sāṅkhya is therefore characterized as *karma-sannyāsa* or even *sannyāsa* (V, 2, 6).[2] In Yoga, however, *karma* is not abandoned; only there is the realization that ultimately the Lord alone is the real doer and that one is but a tool in His hands. It is karma-yoga, doing *karma* with skill. It should also be noted that in philosophical consciousness there is no necessary appeal to any objective or cosmic spirit. For religion, on the other hand, this appeal is vital. If philosophy is analytic and subjective, religious consciousness is, as it seeks union with God, synthetic and objective in its attitude.

According to the *Gītā*, philosophy and religion (Sāṅkhya and Yoga) are two different approaches towards spiritual realization (*Dvidhā Niṣṭhā*; III, 3, V, 2).[3] Both are equally innate and primordial. There was never a time, in the history of mankind, when religious consciousness was absent. The Lord tells us that he taught the Yoga to Vivasvat in the beginning

1. *ibid.*, xiv, 19.
   nānyaṁ guṇebhyaḥ kartāraṁ yadā draṣṭā'nupaśyati,
   guṇebhyaśca paraṁ vetti madbhāvaṁ so'dhigacchati.
2. *ibid.*, v, 2.
   Sannyāsaḥ karma-yogaśca niḥśreyasakarāvubhau,
   tayostu karma-sannyāsāt karmayogo viśiṣyate.
3. *ibid.*, iii, 3.
   Loke'smin dvividhā niṣṭhā purā proktā mayā'nagha,
   jñāna-yogena sāṅkhyānāṁ karma-yogena yoginām.
   ibid., v, 2.
   Sannyāsaḥ karma-yogaś ca niḥśreyasakarāvubhau.

(IV, 1, 23).[1] And this teaching is re-inculcated and re-vivified from time to time. This holds good in the life of the individual too.

Religious consciousness has to be enlivened and deepened, having for its goal the realization of God-consciousness. But there is no appeal to anything external to justify religion. Nowhere in the *Gitā* are intellectual arguments adduced to prove the existence of God and his creativity. Any such appeal would mean the giving up of the innateness of religious consciousness.

Not only is religion innate, but, being less specialized, it is more universal and easy of attainment than philosophy. The Lord seems to imply this when he tells Arjuna that the path of *sannyāsa* (*Sāṅkhya*) is difficult to attain, whereas by following the Yoga realization is easier (V, 6).[2] Philosophy demands a special process of abstraction; but few have the particular inclination. Not all persons have a taste for mathematics; nor is it obligatory. So is it with philosophy. None, however, can afford to take a holiday from the practising of virtue. In this religion is like morality.

That philosophy and religion are two alternative paths of spiritual *sādhanā* necessarily implies that they lead to the same result. It is therefore asserted that they are identical because of this (V, 4, 5).[3] However, each path has to be followed in its purity (*āsthitaḥ samyag*, V, 4). When Arjuna refused to fight, fearing certain undesirable consequences of the battle, his inaction was motivated by a confusion of attitudes. It was neither

1. *ibid.*, iv, 1.
   Imaṁ Vivasvate yogaṁ proktavān aham avyayam.
   ibid., iv, 2.
   sa kāleneha mahatā yogo naṣṭaḥ parantapa.
   ibid., iv, 3.
   sa evāyaṁ mayā te'dya yogaḥ proktaḥ purātanaḥ.
2. *ibid.*, v, 6.
   saṅnyāsastu mahābāho duḥkham āptum ayogataḥ,
   yogayukto munir brahma na cireṇādhigacchati.
3. *ibid.*, v, 4.
   sāṅkhya-yogau pṛthag bālāḥ pravadanti na paṇḍitāḥ,
   ekam apyāsthitaḥ samyag ubhayor vindate phalam.
   ibid., v, 5.
   yat sāṅkhyaiḥ prāpyate sthānaṁ tad yogair api gamyate,
   ekaṁ sāṅkhyaṁ ca yogaṁ ca yaḥ paśyati sa paśyati.

philosophy nor religion: not philosophy,[1] for Arjuna falsely ascribes to the self characteristics, as birth, death and decay, true of the body only; he does not sufficiently discriminate between reality and its false appearance. He needed to be pointed out the distinction. The Lord thus indicates the Sāṅkhya or the path of philosophy. Arjuna's attitude in refusing to fight was not inspired by religion either. For he was all the while obsessed by his own ego, as if he was fighting to gain his private ends and as if he was free to do or not to do as he chose. The *Gītā* substitutes the cosmic for the ego-centric outlook. God is the only free and supreme will. Not even a sparrow can fall without Him. God-consciousness has to be realized by Yoga, self-surrender and identification with the Cosmic Spirit. By a rare vision the Lord actually shows to Arjuna that the wrong-doers, the Kauravas, are already slain by Him; Arjuna has but to ide. tify himself passively with the cosmic action (XI, 26-33).[2] Knowing Arjuna's devotional and active nature, the Lord suggests Yoga for him rather than philosophy (IV, 3, 42)[3] And thus it happens that the *Gītā* is, in the main, a discourse on universal religion.

1. *ibid.*, ii, II.
aśocyān anvaśocas tvaṁ prajñā-vādāṁś ca bhāṣase,
gatāsūn agatāsūṁś ca nānuśocanti paṇḍitāḥ.

2. *ibid.*, xi, 26.
ami ca tvām Dhṛtarāṣṭrasya putrāḥ sarve sahaivāvanipāla-saṅghaiḥ.
Bhīṣmo Droṇaḥ sūtaputras tathāsau sahāsmadīyair api yodha-mukhyaiḥ.
ibid., xi, 27
vaktrāṇi te tvaramāṇāḥ viśanti daṁṣṭrā-karālāni bhayānakāni.
ibid., xi, 38.
mayaivaite nihatāḥ pūrvam eva nimittamātraṁ bhava Savyasācin.

3. *ibid.*, iv, 3.
sa evāyam mayā te'dya yogaḥ proktaḥ purātanaḥ,
bhakto'si me sakhā ceti rahasyaṁ hyetad uttamam.
ibid., iv, 42.
chitvainaṁ saṁśayaṁ yogam ātiṣṭhottiṣṭha bhārata.
ibid., vi, 47.
śraddhāvān bhajate yo māṁ sa me yuktatamo mataḥ.

6.2 THE CONCEPT OF FREEDOM AS REDEMPTION*

In this paper, I am proposing to present the broad features of the Indian Conception of Redemption as Freedom from suffering and worldliness. The soteriological aspects of Hindu religious and philosophical systems are dealt with here. In the course of the paper, attempt is also made to bring out some of the differences obtaining in the different systems of philosophy as well as to point out the basic difference behind the Indian Conception of redemption and that of the Semitic religions.

I

All Indian religions and philosophical systems, except that of materialism (*Cārvāka*) take Mukti or Freedom from suffering and worldly life (*saṁsāra*) as the goal of spiritual endeavour. The present state of man is one of pain and suffering (*duḥkha*), a state of bondage conditioned by Ignorance (*avidyā, ajñāna*) from which release is sought. The means for achieving freedom is the cancellation of ignorance by knowledge of reality (*tattva-jñāna*). In some form or other, all Indian religious and philosophical systems therefore subscribe to the teaching of Freedom through knowledge (*jñānān mukti*).

Although in itself the state of mukti is positive, it is gained by the divestification and discarding of delusions and wrong identifications of the Self with the not-self (body, possessions). It is therefore expressed in negative terms and is said to be Inexpressible as in the case of Nirvāṇa. The state of Redemption is eternal and everlasting and absolute. This is to be sharply distinguished from Paradise or Heavenly Joy (*svarga*) or Enjoyment of pleasures. It is not a state of acquisition, but one of Self-Recovery or Self Realisation. It is not a Conferment or bestowal of some status by God on man to which he was not entitled as of right or by his own nature. Freedom differs from Salvation by God as in Judaism and Christianity.

The idea of Redemption of freedom from suffering may be practical or religious, but the means or the way leading to such

*Reprinted from *Numen*, Suppl. XVIII, Leiden : E. J. Brill, 1970

Redemption is philosophical. It is by the gaining of knowledge or insight into the nature of the real which dispels illusion and ignorance. In the Indian systems of thought, there is no conflict between Religion and Philosophy as it obtains in the West.

II

Corresponding to the Consciousness of Sin in the Semitic Religions, especially in Judaism and Christianity, we have in the Indian Religions the Consciousness of Suffering, Pain. There is no religious problem for man unless, in his reflective mood, he reviews his position and is conscious of his peril. No religious problem is involved in efforts to overcome the hardships imposed by adverse Nature or in making adjustments with fellow men. Both of these could be solved without recourse to any total or transcendental effort. The religious situation emerges only when man reviews his existence as a whole. It is an awareness of the deeper aspects of life, of the root problem, and extends over his entire existence. The religious solution, like the problem, aims at a final and total solution of all problems. It is man's ultimate concern (*parama-puruṣārtha*). This statement of the religious problem would be acceptable to Buddhism and Jainism and some forms of Hinduism which do not find a place for a personal God and, therefore, cannot consider the aim of religious endeavour as the establishment of an intimate relationship with God.

We are led to this review of our existence by a deep and sustained sense of frustration. This is suffering, and it takes the form principally of disease, decay, and death. The Buddha describes suffering graphically: "Birth is ill;decay is ill; sickness is ill; death is ill; to be conjoined to things which we dislike, to be separated from things which we like—that is also sorrow".[1] If all our desires were completely and instantaneously satisfied as they arose in our mind, or, in the alternative, if our nature were completely in accord with the environment, no frustration could arise, and no suffering would result. But the very nature of the individual, or the ego, engenders suffering. As an ego, its essence consists in self-centeredness, and its pursuits and impulses

1. *Saṁyutta-nikāya*, Part II (Nidāna-vagga), XV. 3 ("*Assu-sutta*") L. Feer, ed., (London: Pali Text Society edition, 1888), pp. 179-180.

are selfish. And yet, the ego has to depend on other selves and on the entire creation. A kind of implicit and inherent disharmony seems to be built into the very essence of the individual self.

Suffering, unlike enjoyment, which lulls us into a sense of security, engenders reflection. Man becomes aware of himself when he becomes aware of his deep involvement. To be conscious of suffering is to be conscious of an alternative to the present state in which we happen to find ourselves. Without the contrast between what is and what might have been, between the actual state and the possible, there could be no sense of grievance; hence no suffering. If everything that happens to us were thought to be completely inevitable and inexorable, there could be no grievance. We feel that things can be helped; they could have been otherwise; we could have done better. Thus, in all suffering, man is conscious, however, implicitly, of freedom, of the non-inevitability of the present situation and of his ability to help it.

If, on the other hand, we enjoyed freedom so completely as to dominate all situations and if our will could prevail absolutely over all and always, there would be no suffering. This, then, is the inherent dialectic of suffering. Man is free, but not completely free. Suffering discloses the inherent freedom of man. And, although it is freedom in involvement, it is pregnant with possibilities. There is a demand to realise freedom fully and in final form, as *mokṣa* or *nirvāṇa*.

The germ of spirituality is implicit in suffering (*duḥkha*). Buddhism and all the systems of Indian philosophy (excluding the *Cārvāka*) show their keen spiritual insight in beginning with the truth of suffering (*duḥkha-satya*). To all of them, not only the actual states of painful feeling, but phenomenal existence in its entirety (*saṁsāra*) is suffering. A state of unpleasant feeling is but a sample of what could befall us at all times. The awareness is not complete unless it is extended before and after this life. Its inexorability, given the causes and conditions which engender it, must be realized. Much of our pleasure is pain in the making; pleasures make us hanker after them and thus create anxiety. Frustration in this pursuit begets anger, bitterness, and conflict. Moreover, one's pleasures are by way of encroaching upon others. We seem to take for granted our right to happiness, even though it may be at the expense of others. Again, our short-sightedness and distraction in the immediate present prevent us from appraising our existence in all its comprehension and depth.

Excepting the materialist (*Cārvākas*), every section of Indian thought without question believes and accepts the Law of Karma—the exercise of free will and the responsibility for its consequence and the continuous chain of birth, death, and rebirth. The doctrine of rebirth seems to be a necessary implication of the more basic doctrine of the souls (*jivas*, individuals) as being uncreated, their existing beginninglessly and not perishing with the body. What was the mode of their existence before the actual physical birth and what will it be after the death of the body? What other more plausible explanation could we offer for the inequalities of beings than the doctrine of karma and rebirth, which is consistent with free will and the conservation of moral values? The Semitic religions, which assert the creation of finite souls by a personal God, not only do not seem to feel the need for the doctrine of rebirth, but are even opposed to it. They cannot satisfactorily explain the transmission of original sin committed by Adam to individual souls born here and now. The acceptance of the Law of Karma and rebirth means a more universal perspective. Unlike the Semitic religions, Indian religions are not necessarily committed to theism and to a personal deity. Absolute dependence on God, even for the existence of the soul, determines that the highest and perhaps the only form of spirituality is the loving personal relationship of trust of and surrender to God.

III

This is suffering; it is beginningless like the original sin, but it is caused and conditioned (*naisargikatve 'pi naimittikatvam*). If suffering were uncaused, if it were a brute fact of nature inevitable and inexorable, it could not be removed; we cannot attain freedom. If Suffering were imposed by God or by inscrutable Fate, then also it is not amenable to cessation. Suffering is caused, according to Indian philosophy, by Ignorance, by our wrong knowledge of the real state of things. This engenders wrong willing, sinful and immoral act and consequent involvement and suffering. In the Semitic religions, it is principally wrong willing or wilfulness or disobedience towards God that is the cause of suffering and estrangement from Him. And this estrangement is sought to be overcome, on the side of man by loving God with all his heart and soul, and by dutifully carrying out his commands; on the side of God it is by Grace and Love. The Love of God takes the form of Incarnation as man, as in Christianity, and his sacrifice on the Cross to redeem humanity.

In Indian religious thought, there is no dependence on such dramatic event or intervention by God. Although the Grace of God is accepted by most Indian religions for revelation of the real, and although self-surrender and devotion to God (*bhakti*) may help very intimately in attaining freedom, it is through knowledge or Insight that we could dispel ignorance and thus achieve freedom. The problem is principally cognitive.

There are two fundamental presuppositions underlying this position. One is that all our troubles are due to ignorance, primarily ignorance of oneself. This is not merely privation of right knowledge, but a positive wrong idea. I wrongly take myself as the body or the mental states or even the intellect, and, owing to this wrong identification, I gratuitously share the misfortunes of the body. With its injury or death I consider myself to be undergoing these misfortunes. This wrong identification is not a conscious, deliberate process. No one can consciously fall into illusion. One does not say, "Lo, I am falling into illusion" or "Let me commit this error". He may get out of it consciously and also know when he gets out of it. We can consciously disassociate or disavow our connection with the body, and not vice versa. Nor is it that the self (the "I") and the body started their career as separate and independent entities and at some particular time were joined together. The Indian view is that we can begin only with their togetherness, their fusion or confusion. All accounts depicting a point of time when they were apart, etc , are merely expressions to bring out the essential purity and uniqueness of the self. It is a demand to disassociate it from the body. Although we cannot assign any conceivable beginning to this incongruous relationship, it is not inseparable. We can undo this wrong identification. We can educate and correct ourselves. Any attempt to refute this position would itself presuppose correction, i.e. the removal of my wrong views by the opponent. In fact, only wrong views are removed.

It is common ground in all the Indian systems that ignorance (*avidyā, ajñāna*) is the cause of suffering. The nature of ignorance, or wrong knowledge, differs somewhat in the various systems, depending upon their different metaphysical standpoints. In the Sāṅkhya, it is wrong identification of the self (*puruṣa*) with the object (*prakṛti*) in its various modification beginning with the intellect; in the Advaita Vedānta, it is considering the self as finite and limited, whereas it is really the infinite Brahman. In Jainism, it is the intrusion of karmic matter into the soul (*jīva*). In earlier Buddhism, it is the substance-idea itself, wrongly taking things (which are really changing and perishing) as permanent and identical and clinging to them; in the Mādhyamika, it is indulging in philosophical speculation, in the setting forth of *views* of the real.

The second presupposition, which is almost a consequence of the first, is that in the make-up of the self there are several layers or aspects. To a superficial view, the individual is the "body-mind-I" complex, and in the ordinary course of life the distinction among these elements is seldom made. It is only when we become reflective and begin to raise questions about our true nature that the distinction can be made. Spiritual discipline has for its objective the progressive realization of the pure self as distinct from the body. The body itself is understood in a much wider sense, to include not only the physical body but also the sense-organs, the mental states, the intellect, the psychical dispositions, etc., which constitute the inner body, as it were. It is stripping the 'I' of all its external trappings and accidental accretions. The point to be reached is a foundational consciousness that is unconditional, self-evident, and immediate (*svayam-prakāśā*). It is that to which everything is presented, but is itself no presentation, that which knows all, but is itself no object. The self should not be confused with the contents and states which it enjoys and manipulates. If we have to give an account of it, we can describe it only as what it is not, for any positive description of it would be possible only if it could be made an object of observation, which from the nature of the case it is not. We "know" it only as we withdraw ourselves from the body with which we happen to be identified, in this transition.

That such a foundational self is there and can be reached by the right kind of discipline is taught by the Vedānta. The

Sāṅkhya view is not very different. Mahāyāna Buddhism implicitly affirms the existence of a deep underlying reality behind all empirical manifestations in the conception of *Śūnyatā* (the indeterminate, the void), or *Vijñapti-mātratā* (consciousness only), or *tathatā* (that-ness), or *dharmatā* (noumenal reality). Its spiritual discipline differs considerably from that of the Vedānta or the Sāṅkhya, but the ultimate goal is remarkably similar.

IV

Some account, or at least a general indication, of the lines of approach to the ultimate reality may be given. What strikes one in this regard is the diversity of the paths advocated, and some of them represent daring experiments with the psyche. There is an explicit recognition, not only of the obvious surface differences among individuals, but also of the diversity in their deeper psychical levels, or their spiritual temperaments. Individuality is not mere plurality, the colourless stereotyped repetition of entities, but the recognition of many distinct types. Within the basic types, there are sub-types, and these shade off into personal variations and versions. Indian religious thought is explicitly aware of the different modes of spiritual progression as depending upon basic types—*prasthāna-bheda* (differences in modes of practice) and *gotra-bheda* (differences of family relationships). Either they all lead to the same result or they meet at some penultimate point where the others are merged into one mode.

All would enjoin, as prerequisite of the spiritual life, the practice of moral virtues and concentrations of mind (*śīla* and *samādhi* in Buddhism). It is customary to speak of the three paths of knowledge (*jñāna*), of action (*karma*), and of devotion (*bhakti*), as leading to *mokṣa*. In actual practice, these three are not exclusive. It is not that in the path of knowledge there is no place for an active good life or for a feeling of devotion to God. These latter would be required in the preparatory stage, to purify the intellect of its passions and prejudices and to make it one-pointed. But it is the knowledge or the insight into the real that will engender freedom, or is freedom itself. The cognitive urge to know the ultimate truth is the spearhead behind which other psychic factors work. And this spearhead gives the predominant tone to the entire discipline, not that the other factors are absent. There is a psychological reason why this should be so and not otherwise. As spiritual attainment is the satisfaction of the entire man and not merely of a part of him, if the urge for active altruism or the feeling of surrender to God is repressed, there will result a split in the personality of the individual; there will be no integration of personality, which is distinctive mark of the spiritual. It is possible, however, to organize the various factors with different emphases. Each such organization would be a distinct and integrated unit, and not a medley of discordant notes. And this would be in conformity with the demand that the spiritual path chosen should be suited to the individual's particular spiritual temperament. One master idea or sentiment will so fully and utterly grip the mind as to bring about a catalytic reaction in the personality—for instance, in the Advaita Vedānta the knowledge "I am Brahman" (*ahaṁ brahmāsmi*) (i.e., I am not this body, or these mental states, or the puny creature that I have been taking myself to be) is of this nature. The thought or the conviction that I am Brahman makes for the individual's regeneration. This is not a mere idea or a reasoned conviction lacking metaphysical foundation, but we are not at the moment concerned with that aspect of it. When this conviction or realization sways the mind and possesses it, one no longer sorrows after the body or is drawn into the pettiness of secular life. Friendliness, charity, non-violence and other virtues follow easily, and are not laboured and restricted. The picture drawn here is *mutatis mutandis* true of other modes of religious thought also.

The religious or spiritual life in Indian thought is conceived in terms of self-control and self-regeneration. We may speak of it as a new dimension of being, much as St. Paul says, "I do not live, Christ liveth in me" This is a re-discovery or regaining of what one had lost unconsciously in ignorance. It is not a new acquisition; for if it were so, there could be no finality; the accumulation of merit could mount higher and higher, there being no conceivable limit to its amount. And, conditioned as it would be by certain specific circumstances, the state of freedom would be transitory; it might even cease to be. It would also admit of degrees. This is not how *mokṣa* is understood in the Indian religions. It is eternal, does not admit of gradation, and is unconditioned. In its attainment, there may be epistemic novelty or emergence, but ontologically nothing new is engendered. Therefore, Śaṅkara always speaks of *mokṣa* as no effect, as the nature of Brahman. Nāgārjuna says, "Nirvāṇa is what is not abandoned or acquired, what is not annihilation or eternality, what is not destroyed or created".[1]

Freedom is not a conferment of something which one did not possess; it is release from delusion and suffering. God does not confer freedom; he may and does show us the way to achieve freedom. That is his grace. Freedom is therefore not exactly the same as the salvation of the Semitic religions.

The solution of suffering offered by the Vedānta and Mahāyāna Buddhism, which understand freedom as the attainment of a positive state of fullness and complete identification with all beings is both a negative process and a positive attainment. It is negative insofar as the "I" is dissociated from its accidental limitations by the removal of ignorance; but this results in a positive and transcendent realization of one's true nature as the Absolute.

The theistic schools of Śaivism and Vaiṣṇavism conceive the highest goal of human attainment as an intimate and inalienable relationship with God and not as complete identity.

V

What is the state of final Redemption? Is it a kind of ineffable absorption into the abyss of the Absolute (*Brahman* or *Nirvāṇa*), or is it a form of God-realization? This is bound up with the question, as to whether there is a separate and individual salvation from time to time or universal salvation. The question is discussed in all seriousness and implication both in Mahāyāna Buddhism and the Advaita Vedānta, where it takes the pointed form of "freedom of one or of all" (*eka-mukti* or *sarva-mukti*).

Mahāyāna Buddhism has clearly given the answer in its doctrine of the Buddha and the *bodhi-sattva* (one whose essence is perfect wisdom). Even while entering the path of spiritual

1. *Mādhyamika-kārikā*, XXV. 5-6, Louis de la Vallee-Poussin, ed. Bibliotheca Buddhica, Vol. IV (St. Petersburgh, Bibliotheca Buddhica, 1913), pp. 521, 527.

discipline for enlightenment, the *bodhi-sattva* makes the Great Vows. The chief one of these is that the merit and the knowledge that he would acquire would be for all beings, high and low, and not for himself. "He shuns retiring into the final state of nirvāṇa, though fully entitled to it, preferring, by his own free choice, to toil for even the lowest of beings for ages. He is actuated by this motiveless altruism from the very start of his career. It is not that the *bodhi-sattva* cannot achieve his own freedom without achieving the freedom of all. For this would involve a vicious circle; he cannot free others without first freeing himself, and he cannot free himself without freeing others. No, his freedom is full and complete by itself; but he condescends to raise others to his level. This is a free phenomenalizing act of grace and compassion. A deeply religious element is introduced into Buddhism, which would have otherwise remained an exalted moral naturalism. The Buddha which the *bodhi-sattvas* follow, and eventually become, is a Person, the Highest Person. In the Buddha, we have the conception of a person without any trace of ego. There is activity without attachment".[1] In the *Mahā-vagga* of the *Vinaya-piṭaka* we have a very moving account of how Gautama the Buddha was sorely tempted, after his enlightenment, to pass away into the final release, but was persuaded by Brahmā, the Great God (actually, his innate religious consciousness), to accept the ministry. Free, egoless personality must be accepted. It is not that as one achieves freedom one is absorbed into the Absolute wholly and at once. Though free, one has still enough of the phenomenal in oneself to feel kinship with fellow beings and to help them out of worldly life. Freedom does not repel personality; nor does all personality mean bondage. There can be a free person, and the Buddha is such a person.

In the Advaita Vedānta, too, the position is not different. It is definitely accepted that, as long as other individuals remain to be liberated, the freed self-realizes his union, perhaps even his oneness, with God (īśvara), rather than become merged in the Absolute (*Brahman*). The reason for this is that, as long as other individual souls are struggling in this world, there will

1. Quoted from T. R. V. Murti, *The Central Philosophy of Buddhism* (London: George Allen & Unwin, 1960), pp. 263-264.

continue to be the distinction between God (*iśvara*) and the finite selves (*jīvas*); there is no Pure Being (*Brahman*) as such apart from its varied manifestations. God will continue to perform his function as long as there are any souls needing to realize their identity with *Brahman*. How and when will there be the state in which all the souls shall have been freed is an apocalyptic question that cannot be easily answered. The possibility of such a happy event as the total release of all souls is not ruled out. The question regarding the nature of the interim release of individual souls is fully discussed in the *Brahma-Sūtra* and by Śaṅkara in his Commentary thereon.[1] It is stated with cogent argument that identity with the Lord (*iśvara-bhāvā-patti*) is the nature of liberation of individual souls.

1. *Brahma-sūtra*, IV. iv. 5, 7, and the Commentary of Śaṅkara thereon; see also the *Siddhāntaleśa-saṅgraha*, (Benares: Chowkhamba end., 1916), pp. 512-542. Consult the Symposium on *eka-mukti* and *sarva-mukti* in the *Proceedings of the Indian Philosophical Congress*, Mysore, 1932.

6.3. THE WORLD AND THE INDIVIDUAL IN INDIAN RELIGIOUS THOUGHT*

Introduction

As a Preliminary Definition we may take the individual as a free being, exercising choice and doing actions purposefully, and as one who has attained some measure of awareness of his situation. Whether this person is ultimately free, whether his individuality or personality is real, and what his destiny is and whether it is bound up with that of other individuals are precisely the questions for which we seek an answer in this discussion. The human world may be understood as the community (reciprocity) of such "free" beings, or individuals. But among men there are different grades or types of spiritual temperament. Indian thought—especially the Vedānta and Mahāyāna Buddhism—expressly recognizes these empirical differences and provides for their spiritual needs.

I. *The Religious Problem*

There is no religious problem for man unless, in his reflective mood, he reviews his position and is conscious of his peril. No religious problem is involved in efforts to overcome the hardships imposed by adverse Nature or in making adjustments with fellow men. Both of these could be solved without recourse to any total or transcendental effort. The religious situation emerges only when man reviews his existence as a whole. It is an awareness of the deeper aspects of life, of the root problem, and extends over his entire existence. The religious solution, like the problem, aims at a final and total solution of all problems. It is man's ultimate concern (*parama-puruṣārtha*). This statement of the religious problem would be acceptable to Buddhism and Jainism and some forms of Hinduism which do not find a place for a personal God and, therefore, cannot

*Reprinted from *The Indian Mind*, edited by C. A. Moore. Honolulu : University of Hawaii Press, 1967. First published in *The Status of the Individual in East and West*, edited by C. A. Moore. Honolulu : University of Hawaii Press, 1968.

consider the aim of religious endeavor as the establishment of an intimate relationship with God.

We are led to this review of our existence by a deep and sustained sense of frustration. This is suffering, and it takes the form principally of disease, decay, and death. The Buddha describes suffering graphically: "Birth is ill; decay is ill; sickness is ill; death is ill; to be conjoined to things which we dislike, to be separated from things which we like—that is also sorrow."[1] If all our desires were completely and instantaneously satisfied as they arose in our mind, or, in the alternative, if our nature were completely in accord with the environment, no frustration could arise, and no suffering would result. But the very nature of the individual, or the ego, engenders suffering. As an ego, its essence consists in self-centeredness, and its pursuits and impulses are selfish. And yet, the ego has to depend on other selves and on the entire creation. A kind of implicit and inherent disharmony seems to be built into the very essence of the individual self.

Suffering, unlike enjoyment, which lulls us into a sense of security, engenders reflection. Man becomes aware of himself when he becomes aware of his deep involvement. To be conscious of suffering is to be conscious of an alternative to the present state in which we happen to find ourselves. Without the contrast between what is and what might have been, between the actual state and the possible, there could be no sense of grievance; hence no suffering. If everything that happens to us were thought to be completely inevitable and inexorable, there could be no grievance. We feel that things can be helped; they could have been otherwise; we could have done better. Thus, in all suffering, man is conscious, however implicitly, of freedom, of the non-inevitability of the present situation and of his ability to help it.

If, on the other hand, we enjoyed freedom so completely as to dominate all situations and if our will could prevail absolutely over all and always, there would be no suffering. This, then, is the inherent dialectic of suffering. Man is free, but not completely free. Suffering discloses the inherent freedom of

1. *Saṁyutta-nikāya*, Part II (*Nidāna-vagga*), XV.3 ("Assu-sutta"), L. Feer, ed. (London: Pali Text Society edition, 1888), pp. 179-180.

man. And, although it is freedom in involvement, it is pregnant with possibilities. There is a demand to realize freedom fully and in final form, as *mokṣa* or *nirvāṇa*.

The germ of spirituality is implicit in suffering (*duḥkha*). Buddhism and all the systems of Indian philosophy (excluding the Cārvāka) show their keen spiritual insight in beginning with the truth of suffering (*duḥkha-satya*). To all of them, not only the actual states of painful feeling, but phenomenal existence in its entirety (*saṁsāra*) is suffering.[1] A state of unpleasant feeling is but a sample of what could befall us at all times. The awareness is not complete unless it is extended before and after this life. Its inexorability, given the causes and conditions which engender it, must be realized. Much of our pleasure is pain in the making; pleasures make us hanker after them and thus create anxiety. Frustration in this pursuit brings anger, bitterness, and conflict. Moreover, one's pleasures are by way of encroaching upon others. We seem to take for granted our right to happiness, even though it may be at the expense of others. Again, our shortsightedness and distraction in the immediate present prevent us from appraising our existence in all its comprehension and depth.[2]

1. The Buddha gives a graphic description of this fact of suffering: "What do you think, O monks! Which may be more, the flow of tears you have shed on this long way, running again and again to new birth and new death, united to the disliked, separated from the liked, complaining and weeping, or the water of the four great oceans?....But how is this possible? Without beginning or end, O monks, is this round of rebirth. There cannot be discerned the first beginning of beings, who, sunk in ignorance and bound by thirst, are incessantly transmigrating and again and again run to a new birth. And thus, O monks, through a long time you have experienced suffering, pain and misery, and enlarged the burying ground; truly long enough to be disgusted with every kind of existence, long enough to turn away from every kind of existence, long enough to deliver yourself from it." *Saṁyutta-nikāya*, II.xv.13. Quoted in Grimm, *The Doctrine of the Buddha*, (Berlin: Akademie-Verlag, 1958), pp. 100-101.

Jaigīṣavya (*Yoga-sūtra-bhāṣya*, III.18) gives expression to *duḥkha-satya* in identical terms: *daśaṣu mahāsargeṣu bhāvyatvād anabhibhūtena buddhisattvena mayā naraka-tiryagbhavam duḥkham sampaśyatā devamanuṣyeṣu punaḥ punar utpadyamānena yat kiñcid anubhūtam tat sarvam duḥkham eva pratyavaimi.*

2. *Duḥkha* is usually considered in the threefold way: *duḥkha-duḥkhatā* (the actual pain); *tāpa-duḥkhatā* (longing, desire); and the *saṁskāra-duḥkhatā*—the root causes, *kleśas* (passions), e.g., attachment, aversion, etc. In short, phenomenal existence, or all the five *upādāna-skandhas*, are pain.

Excepting the materialists (Cārvākas), every section of Indian thought without question believes and accepts the Law of *Karma*—the exercise of free will and the responsibility for its consequence and the continuous chain of birth, death, and re-birth. The doctrine of rebirth seems to be a necessary implication of the more basic doctrine of the souls (*jivas*, individuals) as being uncreated, their existing beginninglessly and not perishing with the body. What was the mode of their existence before the actual physical birth and what will it be after the death of the body? What other more plausible explanation could we offer for the inequalities of beings than the doctrine of *karma* and rebirth, which is consistent with free will and the conservation of moral values? The Semitic religions, which assert the creation of finite souls by a personal God, not only do not seem to feel the need for the doctrine of rebirth, but are even opposed to it. The acceptance of the Law of *Karma* and rebirth means a more universal perspective. Unlike the Semitic religions, Indian religions are not necessarily committed to a theism and a personal deity. Absolute dependence on God, even for the existence of the soul, determines that the highest and perhaps the only form of spirituality is the loving personal relationship of trust of and surrender to God.

The existentialist philosophers of the present day pointedly bring out the predicament of man, his anxiety and deep distress, caused by the thought of the inevitability of passing away into nothingness. Many of their analyses and the phraseology used could be matched by passages from Buddhist and Hindu texts. What the existentialist philosophers fail to present, however, is a clear and sure way out of this anxiety and distress. Indian religious thought is most re-assuring in this respect. It definitely and most emphatically asserts that man can overcome his predicament and that he can attain freedom and the fullness of his being. It is also singularly rich in indicating some well-tried paths or types of spiritual life by which freedom can be attained.

It is common ground in Indian thought that the adoption of secular means and methods do not lead to freedom or salvation. It may be held that, if we could conquer Nature and fully exploit her resources, we might satisfy all our wants, and as soon as they arise. The modern man in the atomic age with his immense faith in technology is prone to think that the solution lies this way. But wants may still outstrip our ability to satisfy them; a leap-frog race may result. The root problem is left untouched. Technology cannot provide the wisdom and the good will necessary to make a wholesome use of our power. Control over Nature without control over oneself (self-restraint) can lead only to rivalry, domination, conflict, and suicidal warfare. The human problem is basically spiritual; it lies in self-control and self-education.

Still another ill-advised way out of the difficulty is that of succumbing to the existential situation and, in utter despair, to seek extinction of one's being. To succumb to instincts and to consider ourselves as sharing the destruction of the body are a species of spiritual suicide.

A third way to end suffering is what may be called purely ethical discipline by the practice of a strict regimen to control the passions calculated to stop the flow of phenomenal life. The Hīnayāna ideal of the *arhat* (Buddhist perfected man) and the self-mortification of the Jaina could be cited as instances of this. The ethical discipline in both of these is very impressive in vigor and intensity. The ego is disarmed, suppressed, and made inoperative; but it is not put to any active good use. Negatively, there is the cessation of suffering; this is not accompanied by any positive fulfilment. The *arhat* or the *kevalin* (one who has attained isolation from material adjuncts in Jainism) seems to be bent only upon achieving his own salvation. There is even a lurking fear that the world would enmesh him again if he tarried here too long. Does not the very insistence on getting away smack of selfishness, and is it not therefore unspiritual? An essential mark of the spiritual is the identification of one's good with the good of all. It may well be that the egoistic tendencies are not entirely eliminated. The Mahāyāna makes pointed criticism of this.

We have, finally, the solution of suffering offered by the Vedānta and Mahāyāna Buddhism, which understand freedom as the attainment of a positive state of fullness and complete identification with all beings. It is both a negative process and a positive attainment. It is negative insofar as the "I" is dissociated from its accidental limitations by the removal of ignorance; but this results in a positive and transcendent realization of one's true nature as the Absolute.

The theistic schools of Śaivism and Vaiṣṇavism conceive the highest goal of human attainment as an intimate and inalienable relationship with God and not as complete identity.

In the kindling of spiritual life and the way to the highest attainment, the guidance of God, or revelation, is considered necessary. Otherwise, as there are several possibilities, and, if man were to rely on his unaided reason, he might go astray. It is said in the Vedānta that the *Ātman* is attained by him to whom it chooses to reveal itself; even the inclination toward the Advaita is itself the grace of God. Śaivism explicitly states, "It is through God's grace that we adore his feet," and that is a descent of grace (*śakti-pāta*). It is the deity that chooses to reveal himself to man and takes possession of him. He comes to us in the form of the *guru* (spiritual preceptor and guide).

In the context of freedom and spiritual discipline, the entire range of Indian thought can be classified under three heads :

(1) There were those who did not accept freedom or autonomy of spirit in any form. The Cārvākas denied the existence of the individual self apart from the physical body and ridiculed the very notion of salvation. As a piece of Nature and constituted by a conglomeration of natural ingredients, consciousness or man can have no value other than gross bodily pleasures. The question of freedom does not arise. The Ājīvikas (materialists or naturalists), although they accepted the *jīvas*, conceived the world process and the entire progress of the soul as an automatic and inevitable process; they advocated a most rigorous form of determinism (*niyativāda*). Everyone is bound to reach his destiny in the fullness of time. They advocated, according to Buddhism and Jainism, a thoroughgoing fatalism and denied the Law of *Karma*. Both the Buddha and the Jaina Mahāvīra call this doctrine a species of non-activism and condemn it as pernicious and inimical to the spiritual life.[1]

(2) There were philosophers and religious men, such as the Buddha and Mahāvīra, who accepted what we might call immanent freedom as felt and exercised in human involvement. Every man's suffering is evidence of this freedom. The Buddha took his stand, like Kant, on the moral act, the immanent freedom

1. Madhva's doctrine of predestination comes perilously close to this point of view.

implicit in man's endeavor to better his condition. The emphasis is on self-effort and the right exercise of one's volition.

The fundament in Buddhism and Jainism is the autonomy of the Moral Law (*karma*)—the freedom which we feel and exercise in our actions, in our involvement, and which determines what we are and what we would be. The Moral Law is moral, i.e., it is not a natural or mechanistic operation of brute necessity. Nor is it the dictate of an inscrutable and capricious Person—God. The Moral Law is impersonal; it has absolute authority, no matter whether it is fulfilled frequently or seldom or not at all; its authority is innate and underived. The Moral Law is perfectly autonomous.

This was not an altogether new idea discovered by the Buddha or Mahāvīra. The Ṛg-vedic hymns speak of *Ṛta* and *Satya*, the Order and Truth of the universe; the deities Indra, Agni, and Varuṇa are invariably spoken of as upholders of the moral order (*dhṛta-vrata*, *satya-dharma*, *dharmasya-goptā*). It is not, as in the Semitic religions, God's fiat which makes anything moral or good. There is an innate propriety (*dharma*) in things, and the deities only reveal and uphold this order; they do not create the order. The impersonality of the Law of *Karma* was first developed as a cosmic principle by the Mīmāṁsakas, who were the first to deny a personal God. Unfortunately, the *karma* or *dharma* they understood and were interested in was ritualistic *karma*, the performance of what the *Bhagavad-gītā* would term "*dravya-yajña*" (sacrifice with substance-oblations) and not duty or moral *karma*. And it was with the latter that the Buddha and Mahāvīra were concerned.

Taking his stand on the autonomy of the Moral Law, the Buddha was led to deny two opposed standpoints: one was naturalism (*sva-bhāva-vāda*) or nihilism (*uccheda-vāda*), which totally denied, as is done by the Cārvāka and the Ājīvika, the Moral Law (free act and its result, *karma* and *karma-phala*), and reduced man to a fortuitous conglomeration of natural forces; the other opposed standpoint was that of eternalism (*śāśvata-vāda*), which stood for the transcendent freedom of God (and even of an unchanging soul or *ātman*), who is above the Moral Law (*karma*). The Buddha characterizes both *uccheda-vāda* and *śāśvata-vāda* as specimens of inactivism (*akriyā-vāda*).

Salvation or, rather, freedom is freedom from moral evil, from passions and their defilement (*saṁskāra*); spiritual discipline is the path of purification (*viśuddhi-mārga*; Pāli : *visuddhi-magga*), and this is achieved through self-effort and self-regeneration. There is no place for outside help or divine guidance. Salvation is strictly a sustained and heroic act on the part of the individual man himself. It is not an act of God or co-operation between man and God. Buddhism, at least early Buddhism, is a moral religion, a universal religion without God, a perfection of self-discipline and self-analysis. As the spiritual discipline is a catharsis or eradication of passions, the Ultimate is described negatively as *Nirvāṇa.*

The position of earlier Buddhism was considerably modified in the Mahāyāna. To all intents and purposes, the Buddha becomes a divine person—the free phenomenalization of the impersonal Absolute. The personality of the Buddha and the awareness of his unique position ushered in this revolution in Buddhism.

(3) The third class is represented by the Hindu (Brāhmaṇical) systems, which in some form or other accepted a free, transcendent Being (God) besides the finite selves. It is not that this free being achieved his freedom after destroying his previous bondage. He is eternally free (*sadaiva-muktaḥ*) and transcendent (*sadaiva-iśvaraḥ*).

If for Buddhism the fundament is the moral consciousness, and the spiritual urge is for purifying the mind of its passions, the fundament of Hinduism is God-consciousness; and the goal is exaltation or deification. The Vedas, which are the fountain source of all forms of Hinduism, are intoxicated with the idea of God, of a transcendent Being, ever free and ever the Lord. The Vedic seers had an unusually quick and open sensitiveness to the transcendent being. They try to grasp him now as Agni, now as Indra, now as Varuṇa, Viṣṇu, or Rudra, and in a hundred other ways. These are predicates or characteristics of the Godhead rather than substantive entities in their own right, as has been wrongly contended. The Vedic seers had an almost overwhelming sense of the infinite impinging on man. Religion, for them, was not the labored suppression of passions, of control and regimen, as in Buddhism, but a relationship with the transcendent through prayer and devotion. This *en rapport* relationship with God is what distinguishes Hinduism from earlier

Buddhism. And this consciousness has never left it at any stage of its long history. Newer deities emerge; rather, the old ones are given new names (e.g., Rudra is called Śiva; Viṣṇu is Nārāyaṇa or Vāsudeva) and are worshipped in newer forms; but the pattern remains the same. This may be theism, but it is not a theism of the Semitic type. The difference between God and man (creatures) is not absolute.

The deity is not discovered by man by his self-effort; it is the deity that freely chooses to reveal itself. Man just receives and realizes it. He is saved by this relationship, by his sense of kinship and identity with the transcendent spirit. Practice of moral virtues and concentration of mind have value as enabling one to perceive this inherent identity, just as a spotless mirror is able to entertain the image without distortion. The purity of the mirror is not, however, the source of the image; it is merely ancillary to the reflection. As realizing an already existing fact, spiritual attainment for Hinduism is symbolic, not labored and literal, as in earlier Buddhism.

It might be thought that the atheistic Mīmāṁsā and the Sāṅkhya do not conform to the pattern of a pure, transcendent Being. But, since in both of these the Veda (the Eternal Word) is accepted as the infallible and omniscient source of truth, the conformity is essentially present.

It is interesting to note, however, that in the Hindu and the non-Hindu (Buddhist and Jaina) traditions, both the impersonal spirit and a personal God find a place. This is the basic dialectic in Indian religious thought. There is no doubt that this obtains in other religions also. This problem will engage us toward the end of the paper.

II. Religious Life

The religious or spiritual life in Indian thought is conceived in terms of self-control and self-regeneration. We may speak of it as a new dimension of being, much as St. Paul said, "I do not live, Christ liveth in me." This is a re-discovery or regaining of what one had lost unconsciously in ignorance.[1] It is not a new acquisition; for, if it were so, there could be no finality;

1. The Christian doctrine of the Fall and Redemption may be taken in some sense as the religious counterpart of this conception.

the accumulation of merit could mount higher and higher, there being no conceivable limit to its amount. And, conditioned as it would be by certain specific circumstances, the state of freedom would be transitory; it might even cease to be. It would also admit of degrees. This is not how *mokṣa* is understood in the Indian religions. It is eternal, does not admit of gradation, and is unconditioned. In its attainment, there may be epistemic novelty or emergence, but ontologically nothing new is engendered. Therefore Śaṅkara always speaks of *mokṣa* as no effect and as the nature of *Brahman*.[1] Nāgārjuna says, "*Nirvāṇa* is what is not abandoned or acquired, what is not annihilation or eternality, what is not destroyed or created."[2]

Freedom is not a conferment of something which one did not possess; it is release from delusion and suffering. God does not confer freedom; he may and does show us the way to achieve freedom. That is his grace. Freedom is therefore not exactly the same as the salvation of the Semitic religions.

The essence of self-control is the bringing about of a change in oneself, in one's mentality, and not in the environment. To control the external world, including the world of fellow human beings, is the way of worldly men. This is bound, sooner or later, to raise antagonism and strife. And this is precisely what we wish to avoid. Philosophical knowledge or wisdom (*prajñā*) does not transform the world, but only our attitude. It certainly means a radical change in our mental make-up.

The path of freedom is one of purification and disassociation from the not-self, from the false or superficial aspects of the self. Cognitively, it is a case of enlightenment or insight into the nature of things. We may call it a negative process, since it is a case of divestification of the encumbrances with which we have cluttered ourselves on life's journey. It is not negative in result. For what we are left with is not nothing, but our real being in its innate immediacy. Also, the path's being characterized in negative phraseology does not mean that we are to be inactive or that it is easy of accomplishment.

1. Śaṅkara's *Bhāṣya* on *Brahma-sūtra*, I.i.4.

2. *Mādhyamika-kārikā*, XXV.5-6, Louise de la Vallee-Poussin, ed. Bibliotheca Buddhica, Vol. IV. (St. Petersburgh, Bibliotheca Buddhica, 1913), pp. 521, 527.

There are two fundamental presuppositions underlying this position. One is that all our troubles are due to ignorance, primarily ignorance of oneself. This is not merely privation of right knowledge, but a positive wrong idea. I wrongly take myself as the body or the mental states or even the intellect, and, owing to this wrong identification, I gratuitously share the misfortunes of the body. With its injury or death, I consider myself to be undergoing these misfortunes. This wrong identification is not a conscious, deliberate process. No one can consciously fall into illusion. One does not say, "Lo, I am falling into illusion" or "Let me commit this error." He may get out of it consciously and also know when he gets out of it. We can consciously disassociate or disavow our connection with the body, but not *vice versa* Nor is it that the self (the "I") and the body started their career as separate and independent entities and at some particular time were joined together. The Indian view is that we can begin only with their togetherness, their fusion or confusion. All accounts depicting a point of time when they were apart, etc., are merely expressions to bring out the essential purity and uniqueness of the self. It is a demand to disassociate it from the body. Although we cannot assign any conceivable beginning to this incongruous relationship, it is not inseparable. We can undo this wrong identification. We can educate and correct ourselves. Any attempt to refute this position would itself presuppose correction, i.e., the removal of my wrong views by the opponent. In fact, only wrong views are removed.

It is common ground in all the Indian systems that ignorance (*avidyā*, *ajñāna*) is the cause of suffering. The nature of ignorance, or wrong knowledge, differs somewhat in the various systems, depending upon their different metaphysical standpoints. In the Sāṅkhya, it is wrong identification of the self (*puruṣa*) with the object (*prakṛti*) in its various modifications beginning with the intellect; in the Advaita Vedānta, it is considering the self as finite and limited, whereas it is really the infinite *Brahman*; in Jainism, it is the intrusion of karmic matter into the soul (*jīva*); in earlier Buddhism, it is the substance-idea itself, wrongly taking things (which are really changing and perishing) as permanent and identical and clinging to them; in the Mādhyamika, it is indulging in philosophical speculation, in the setting forth of views of the real.

The second presupposition, which is almost a consequence of the first, is that in the make-up of the self there are several layers or aspects. To a superficial view, the individual is the "body-mind-I" complex, and in the ordinary course of life the distinction among these elements is seldom made. It is only when we become reflective and begin to raise questions about our true nature that the distinction can be made. Spiritual discipline has for its objective the progressive realization of the pure self as distinct from the body. The body itself is understood in a much wider sense, to include not only the physical body but also the sense-organs, the mental states, the intellect, the psychical dispositions, etc., which constitute the inner body, as it were. It is stripping the "I" of all its external trappings and accidental accretions. The point to be reached is a foundational consciousness that is unconditional, self-evident, and immediate (*svayaṁ-prakāśa*) It is that to which everything is presented, but is itself no presentation, that which knows all, but is itself no object. The self should not be confused with the contents and states which it enjoys and manipulates. If we have to give an account of it, we can describe it only as what it is not, for any positive description of it would be possible only if it could be made an object of observation, which from the nature of the case it is not. We "know" it only as we withdraw ourselves from the body with which we happen to be identified, in this transition.

That such a foundational self is there and can be reached by the right kind of discipline is taught by the Vedānta. The Sāṅkhya view is not very different. Mahāyāna Buddhism implicitly affirms the existence of a deep underlying reality[1] behind all empirical manifestations in its conception of *śūnyatā* (the indeterminate, the void), or *vijñapti-mātratā* (consciousness only), or *tathatā* (thatness), or *dharmatā* (noumenal reality). Its spiritual discipline differs considerably from that of the Vedānta or the Sāṅkhya, but the ultimate goal is remarkably similar.

We have been talking of the spirit and the spiritual; some definition of it may be attempted. In all religions, especially in the Indian religions, spirituality implies the giving up of narrow, selfish, ego-centeredness and the attainment of the universal. In its extreme form, this would take the form of

1. *Mādhyamika-kārikā*, XXV.5-6, Louis de La Vallée-Poussin, ed. Bibliotheca Buddhica, Vol. IV. (St. Petersburgh, Bibliotheca Buddhica 1913), pp. 521, 527.

complete identity with all beings, as in the case of the Advaita Vedānta and the Mahāyāna. The good of one is the good of all. The spiritual person does not divide himself from others. Nor is he divided in himself. His personality is integrated, as there is no conflict—or cross-purposes—in his inner make-up. The secular man does not react to a situation in a total way; in him, there are surface motives and deeper drives, often in disharmony. In the spiritual, the means and the end coincide. In the moral or social sphere, we do certain acts, e.g., acts of charity and kindness, for some other-worldly benefits or for social solidarity which may benefit us indirectly. Nor do moral acts carry with them their own sanctity. Their observance is commanded by external authority, fear of God, or the approval of society. The spiritual person is good, he is chaste or charitable, not because he desires to gain anything in this or the other world. It is his nature to be so; his goodness is motiveless. The spiritual act is not a means to an end; it is the end itself. It therefore carries within itself the criterion of its validity and efficacy.

Some account, or at least a general indication, of the lines of approach to the ultimate reality may be given. What strikes one in this regard is the diversity of the paths advocated, and some of them represent daring experiments with the psyche. There is an explicit recognition, not only of the obvious surface differences among individuals, but also of the diversity in their deeper psychical levels, or their spiritual temperaments. Individuality is not mere plurality, the colorless stereotyped repetition of entities, but the recognition of many distinct types. Within the basic types, there are sub-types, and these shade off into personal variations and versions. Indian religious thought is explicitly aware of the different modes of spiritual progression as depending upon basic types—*prasthāna-bheda* (differences in modes of practice) and *gotra-bheda* (differences of family relationships). Either they all lead to the same result or they meet at some penultimate point where the others are merged into one mode.

All would enjoin, as a prerequisite of the spiritual life, the practice of moral virtues and concentration of mind (*śīla* and *samādhi* in Buddhism).[1] It is customary to speak of the three

1. Śaṅkara (*Brahma-sūtra-bhāṣya*, I.i.i), for instance, lays down four conditions as necessary prerequisites for undertaking *Brahmajijñāsā* (Brahma-

paths of knowledge (*jñāna*), of action (*karma*), and of devotion (*bhakti*), as leading to *mokṣa*. In actual practice, these three are not exclusive. It is not that in the path of knowledge there is no place for an active good life or for a feeling of devotion to God. These latter would be required in the preparatory stage, to purify the intellect of its passions and prejudices and to make it one-pointed. But it is the knowledge or the insight into the real that will engender freedom, or is freedom itself. The cognitive urge to know the ultimate truth is the spearhead behind which other psychic factors work. And this spearhead gives the predominant tone to the entire discipline—not that the other factors are absent. There is a psychological reason why this should be so and not otherwise. As spiritual attainment is the satisfaction of the entire man and not merely of a part of him, if the urge for active altruism or the feeling of surrender to God is repressed, there will result a split in the personality of the individual; there will be no integration of personality, which is a distinctive mark of the spiritual. It is possible, however, to organize the various factors with differing emphases. Each such organization would be a distinct and integrated unit, and not a medley of discordant notes. And this would be in confornity with the demand that the spiritual path chosen should be suited to the individual's particular spiritual temperament. One master idea or sentiment will so fully and utterly grip the mind as to bring about a catalytic reaction in the entire personality—for instance, in the Advaita Vedānta the knowledge, "I am *Brahman*" (*aham brahmāsmi*) (i.e., I am not this body, or these mental states, or the puny creature that I have been taking myself to be) is of this nature. The thought or the conviction that I am *Brahman* makes for the individual's regeneration. This is not a mere idea or a reasoned conviction lacking metaphysical foundation, but we are not at the moment concerned with that aspect of it. When this conviction or

knowledge): discrimination between the true and the false (literally the eternal and the ephemeral), detachment from secular pursuits of this world and from heavenly pleasures; practice of the moral virtues of control and contentment, and an intense desire for freedom. The *Yoga-sūtra* enjoins the observance of restraints (*yama*)—non-violence, truthfulness, non-covetousness, continence, non-acquisition—and the practice of moral virtues (*niyama*)—contentment, purity, penance, reading of scriptures, and devotion to God—as the first steps to the higher reaches of *yoga* discipline.

realization sways the mind and possesses it, one no longer sorrows after the body or is drawn into the pettiness of secular life. Friendliness, charity, non-violence, and other virtues follow easily, and are not labored and restricted. The picture drawn here is *mutatis mutandis* true of other modes of religious thought also.

III. *Individual, God, and Absolute*

What is the state of final attainment, the goal? Is it a kind of ineffable absorption into the abyss of the Absolute (*Brahman* or *Nirvāṇa*), or is it a form of God-realization? This is bound up with the question, as to whether there is separate and individual salvation from time to time or universal salvation. The question is discussed in all seriousness and implication both in Mahāyāna Buddhism and the Advaita Vedānta, where it takes the pointed form of "freedom of one or of all" (*eka-mukti* or *sarva-mukti*).

Mahāyāna Buddhism has clearly given the answer in its doctrine of the Buddha and the *bodhi-sattva* (one whose essence is perfect wisdom) Even while entering the path of spiritual discipline for enlightenment, the *bodhi-sattva* makes the Great Vows. The chief one of these is that the merit and the knowledge that he would acquire would be for all beings, high and low, and not for himself.[1] "He shuns retiring into the final state of *nirvāṇa*, though fully entitled to it, preferring, by his own free choice, to toil for even the lowest of beings for ages. He is actuated by this motiveless altruism from the very start of his career. It is not that the *bodhisattva* cannot achieve his own freedom without achieving the freedom of all. This would involve a vicious circle: he cannot free others without first freeing himself, and he cannot free himself without freeing others. No, his freedom is full and complete by itself; but he condescends to raise others to his level. This is a free phenomenalizing act of grace and compassion. A deeply religious element is introduced into Buddhism, which would have otherwise remained

1. See *Aṣṭa-sāhasrikā-prajñā-pāramitā*, R. L. Mitra, ed. (Calcutta: Bibliotheca Indian edn., 1888), p. 293. See also *Śikṣā-samuccaya* (St. Petersburgh: Bibliotheca of Śantideva, Cecil Bendell, ed., Bibliotheca Buddhica, 1897-1902, MLBD Reprint Delhi, 1981), Vol. I, p. 14.

an exalted moral naturalism. The Buddha, which the *bodhisattvas* follow and eventually become, is a Person, the Highest Person. In the Buddha, we have the conception of a person without any trace of ego. There is activity without attachment."[1] In the *Mahā-vagga* of the *Vinaya-piṭaka* we have a very moving account of how Gautama the Buddha was sorely tempted, after his enlightenment, to pass away into final release, but was persuaded by Brahmā, the Great God (actually his innate religious consciousness), to accept the ministry.[2] Free, egoless personality must be accepted. It is not that as one achieves freedom one is absorbed into the Absolute wholly and at once. Though free, one has still enough of the phenomenal in oneself to feel kinship with fellow beings and to help them out of worldly life. Freedom does not repel personality; nor does all personality mean bondage. There can be a free person, and the Buddha is such a person.

In the Advaita Vedānta, too, the position is not different. It is definitely accepted that, as long as other individuals remain to be liberated, the freed self realizes his union, perhaps even his oneness, with God (Īśvara), rather than become merged in the Absolute (*Brahman*). The reason for this is that, as long as other individual souls are struggling in this world, there will continue to be the distinction between God (Īśvara) and the finite selves (*jivas*); there is no Pure Being (*Brahman*) as such apart from its varied manifestations. God will continue to perform his function as long as there are any souls needing to realize their identity with *Brahman*. How and when will there be the state in which all the souls shall have been freed is an apocalyptic question that cannot be easily answered. The possibility of such a happy event as the total release of all souls is not ruled out. The question regarding the nature of the interim release of individual souls is fully discussed in the *Brahma-sūtra* and by Śaṅkara in his Commentary thereon.[3] It is stated

1. Quoted from T. R. V. Murti, *The Central Philosophy of Buddhism* (London: George Allen & Unwin Ltd., 1960), pp. 263-264.

2. The *Mahā-vagga* of the *Vinaya-piṭaka*, Sec. I. Söderblom, in his *The Living God*, comments on this, saying that only the Buddha or Christ could be subjected to this unique kind of temptation. (Jesus is reported to have uttered: "Let this cup pass from me. Father, Thy will be done.")

3. *Brahma-sūtra*, IV.iv.5, 7, and the Commentary of Śaṅkara thereon;

with cogent arguments that identity with the Lord (*Īśvara-bhāvāpatti*) is the nature of liberation of individual souls.

In the state of union with God (Īśvara), the individual, for all practical purposes, is God; he is no longer an ego, having transcended his petty and private status. Like God, he is also an egoless personality. He freely identifies himself with others and enters into their being. Of this state it is said in the Upaniṣads, "He attains all his desires; he becomes one-, two-, threefold, aye, manifold." "He goes along disporting himself... [and so on]."[1] It is stated that even such freed souls are sent on cosmic errands (*ādhikārika-puruṣas*)[2] and actively participate in the maintenance of the cosmic order. From the nature of the case, these statements are not capable of rational explanation.

The factors which generally constitute the empirical individual and which mark him off from other individuals, e.g., the physical body, mental traits, and dispositions, aspirations and achievements, may not be present in this state. But it cannot be denied that some form of personality is present. The desire to help others and the capacity to participate actively in the cosmic good are present and may constitute the basis of personality.

It may well be asked: Why should we accept both the Absolute (*Brahman*) and God (Īśvara), impersonal and personal spirit? Could not either of them do as well? The basic dialectic in Indian religious thought, as stated earlier, is between personal God and Impersonal Spirit. This assertion is not made on *a priori* grounds but because we find it exemplified quite pointedly in the orthodox Hindu as well as in the Buddhist tradition. There is no doubt that this obtains in other religions also. Tillich speaks of the "tension between Being and God," or of "the God beyond God." Either the personal appears first, as in Hinduism, or the impersonal, as in Buddhism and Jainism. Very soon the other dialectical aspect discloses itself and has to be reckoned with. A synthesis is called for.

To explain. The personal God or gods of the Vedic hymns are the first intimations of the holy or the numinous in Hindu

see also the *Siddhāntaleśa-saṅgraha*, (Benares: Chowkhamba edn., 1916), pp. 512-542. Consult the Symposium on *eka-mukti* and *sarvamukti* in the *Proceedings of the Indian Philosophical Congress*, Mysore Session, 1932.

1. *Chāndogya Upaniṣad*, VII.xxvi.2; VIII.xii.3.
2. See *Brahma-sūtra*, IV.iv.17-18.

religious consciousness. From the personal God, there is the movement toward the unity underlying this, the Godhead behind these manifestations, *That One* (*tad ekam*), for which the gods really stand. This position is explicitly reached in the Upaniṣads and is formulated as the philosophy of the Vedānta. In Buddhism (and this is largely true of Jainism, too), the impersonal as the Moral Order (*Dharma*) and the ideal of *Nirvāṇa* is the prius; the personal is even repudiated and the stand is antitheistic. However, the inner dynamism of the spiritual life led, as explicitly admitted by the Mahāyāna, to God in the person of the Buddha. It is not that the Mahāyānists deified the human Buddha, but that the Buddha's divinity became clear to them as a new insight. In fact, the human form of the Buddha prevented his being recognized as divine. The Buddha performs the divine functions of grace and revelation, though not the cosmic functions of creation and sustenance of the world. *Dharma* or *Nirvāṇa*, being impersonal and completely transcendent, could not reveal or declare itself to man. It requires the appropriate organism, a teacher endowed with the necessary qualities; just as geometrical truths cannot reveal themselves—they require to be taught by a teacher. If *Nirvāṇa* itself could come down, as it were, and disclose itself, then we could be persuaded of its authenticity. And yet, only a person can perform this function. Paradoxically, the Buddha had therefore to be at once identical with *Nirvāṇa* (so as to enable him to have direct and intimate knowledge of *Nirvāṇa*) and also be different from it, as only a person (accepting and operating under human conditions and using human forms of communication) could reveal and declare the truth of *Nirvāṇa*. Impelled by this dialectic of religious consciousness, "the Buddhas were subjected to a six-fold process: they were multiplied, immortalised, deified, spiritualised, universalized, and unified," as Dr. Har Dayal so happily states.[1]

The problem of Absolute and God is really the problem of ultimacy and concreteness, their relation and balance. How to preserve both without reducing one or the other to insignificance ? God's nature is not exhausted in his relationship to man or in the performance of cosmic functions; he has a non-relational,

1. Har Dayal *The Bodhisattva Doctrine in Buddhist Sanskrit Literature* (MLBD Reprint, Delhi 1975), p. 28.

transcendent nature of his own; he is something *in himself.* This is the Absolute. The theistic religions generally slur over this distinction. God as the "Wholly Other" has to be sharply distinguished from the creatures over whom he dominates. Here God is one term of the relation of difference. But God is also the being of all things, that in which they move and have their being. In the latter sense, as the foundational and only Being, God cannot be distinguished from anything, as there is no other besides him. The Advaita Vedānta rightly understands God in this aspect as the "*Great It,*" as *Brahman*, the Great Being without a second. Even the relation of "I and Thou" is itself possible because of the Being underlying the opposites; it is the common platform on which both of them stand equally. Therefore, the Absolute cannot be denied. It stands for the principle of ultimacy, the original and inexhaustible source of being and power. It is Being without any touch or threat of non-being. As Being without any other facing it, it is the whole or universal being. Not lacking anything, as full being, it is termed bliss on that account. As the only being without divisions, without even the division of subject and object, it does not stand in need of being evidenced. Although not evidenced, it is immediate and self-evident.

There are two prevalent misconceptions regarding Being (*Brahman*). One is to take it as a particular existent, conditioned and limited. The other, which is more pernicious, is to understand Being as a conception, as a generalized idea or abstraction. Hegel is guilty of this. He created a phantom so that he could the more easily knock it down. He used what might be called the de-ontological argument, the ontological argument in reverse. For he reduces the Ontic Being to an idea or a descriptive character. It is less of a mistake to identify Being with any particular existent (God or man), for here at least we have a concrete experience of Being. This is why the Upaniṣads speak of it as "*neti, neti,*" and Śaṅkara understands *Brahman* as *nirguṇa* (without qualities), because it is the fullness of Being, and not a system or bundle of ideas.

If the Absolute cannot be denied, God also cannot be denied. For it is he who reveals to us the nature of *Brahman.* The truth, being impersonal, needs to be declared and proclaimed as truth by a person. *Tathatā* (the thatness of things) requires a *tathāgata* (one who has realized thatness) to reveal it to us. The two facets, then, are present in Hinduism and Buddhism, in any mature religion. They cannot be left unrelated; nor can they be related co-ordinately, as this would make for opposition. As they have to be synthesized or related in a whole, the only alternative left is to take one as higher, the other as lower—higher in the sense of providing the ground or sustenance for the other. If I may venture to coin a term for this situation, I would call it "Synthesis in Depth", to distinguish it from synthesis in comprehension, in extensity and inclusiveness. The Hegelian synthesis is of the latter kind. Depth-synthesis is the acceptance of two levels of Being, the impersonal and the personal spirit. No doubt, these are spatial metaphors, but they may help to bring out more picturesquely the relationship between the two.

Depth-synthesis also implies a mechanism or device by which the impersonal spirit can become the personal God, without loss, without being transformed or diminished. It is the logic of a one-sided relation. It may well be that all relation is one-sided. It is a connection between two terms, one and only one of which has a transcendent existence (i.e., is not exhausted in the relational context), while the other is confined to the relational context[1]. *Māyā,* or *avidyā,* is the principle of this mediation. It is a device to reconcile God's transcendence with his immanence—what he is in himself and the manner in which he chooses to reveal himself to finite beings. It is not the principle of utter rejection or negation of God or the world in the Absolute, but the insistence on the transcendence of the Godhead and the inapplicability of empirical characteristics to it. *Māyā* is not an explanation, much less a derivation of the lower from the higher (we may leave this jugglery to Hegel). The mystery remains. In fact, "*māyā*" is the most expressive term for the mystery of such so-called derivation. It affirms, however, that they are not unrelated or independent entities. The correct formula is that the lower is neither identical with nor different from the higher, the absolute (*tattvānyatvābhyām-anirvacaniya*). A sort of

1. For a somewhat fuller discussion of the concept of relation in the Advaita Vedānta, reference may be made to the writer's paper, "The Two Definitions of Brahman in the Advaita," in the *Professor K. C. Bhattacharyya Memorial Volume* (Amalner: Indian Institute of Philosophy, 1958), pp. 136ff.

hierarchy is implied between *Brahman* and Iśvara (as between *Dharmatā* or *Śūnyatā* and the Buddha), without either of them being unreal or redundant.

In a way, *Brahman* and Īśvara (*Dharmatā* and the Buddha) typify the two ways in which we can understand freedom—freedom as "free *from*" and freedom as "free to do." Free Being (*Brahman* or *Śūnyatā* or *Dharmatā*) is free from empirical determination and limitations. Īśvara or the Buddha is a free agent, free to act ; his will or act, being always in accord with the truth (*satya-kāma* and *satya-saṅkalpa*), is never impeded (*apratihata-śaktiḥ*). In both the traditions, it is well-understood that it is only through the mediation of Īśvara or the Buddha that we can realize our free nature as *Brahman* or *Dharmatā*, and that the liberated individual first realizes his identity or union with Iśvara or the Buddha.

Question : You observe, almost in the beginning of your paper, that "there is no religious problem unless man is conscious of his peril." I have also been saying that every religion is a kind of answer to the problem of evil. But, conceivably, religion could arise in some way other than from suffering; as, for instance, in a feeling of ecstatic wonder or sublimity with regard to the world. Perhaps, we make too much of sin-consciousness. You make the observation that "the Vedic seers had an unusually quick and open sensitiveness to the transcendent being and that religion was not the labored suppression of passions, of regimen and control, but the *en rapport* relationship with the transcendent through prayer and devotion." Would you agree that we could have religion without suffering and sin-consciousness ?

Answer : I largely agree with you. In Buddhism and Jainism the fundament is the moral consciousness and suffering is emphasized. In the Vedic religion, the religious attitude as kinship with God is prominent. Even in this *en rapport* relation there is the consciousness of a lack or imperfection in the background. The distinction eventually turns out to be one of relative emphasis on one or the other—on exaltedness or suffering.

Question : Regarding freedom, you say that in "the state of union with God, the individual for all practical purposes is God; he is no more an ego." What sort of personality does an individual have in that state ?

Answer : Although no longer self-centered and egoistic in his pursuits and outlook, the freed individual still has a personality insofar as he unceasingly and intelligently strives for the good of others and participates in the cosmic order. He is not a mere principle. The term "ego-less personality" is not an inconsistent expression, nor is that state an incongruous one. All enlightened sages, like the Buddha, freed of their ignorance and selfishness, are concrete examples of this. They are actively free And this freedom may be distinguished from the freedom of Pure Being (*Brahman*), which is a state of absorption and a self-completeness. Personality could significantly be attributed to one who is actively free.

6.4 SUFFERING AND ITS CONQUEST

I take it that the purpose underlying the Conference is to discuss and to suggest, by exchange of views, certain practical proposals for overcoming suffering rather than to investigate the theoretic or philosophical foundations of the concept of suffering and its removal. As we proceed, it will, however, become apparent that philosophical considerations cannot be ruled out completely, though we may agree to imply them and not to discuss them. I shall try to keep the problem at the empirical level, as far as possible.

It may also be surmised that the intention of the sponsoring bodies in bringing together philosophers belonging to two different traditions is to seek a sort of representative consideration of the issues involved. Without making explicit and elaborate statements of the standpoints held by our systems of thought, I shall be concened to present a viewpoint in consonance with the spirit of Indian thought. I should not, however, be supposed to imply that the East and the West hold or have held in the past incommensurable attitudes all along the line. I am convinced that all patterns of thought are available in both the traditions; some features are emphasised more in one tradition than in the other.

The entire range of Indian philosophical and religious thought swings between the two poles of suffering (*duḥkha*—equated with phenomenal existence) and freedom (*Mokṣa* or *Nirvāṇa*). Buddhism is an extreme example of the great concern with this basic problem. To the modern man this attitude to life may appear morbid. It is no longer fashionable to speak of human suffering. No doubt theological studies produced at the present day continue to discuss this problem. But it is not a live issue. Concerned far too much with physical suffering (wants, disease and old age) and only secondarily with its individual and social manifestations (e.g., tension and conflict), the modern man does not appraise the question in all its intensity and universality, as a moral and spiritual problem. He even nurses the fond hope that with the advance of science and technology suffering would be reduced to negligible proportions, if not eliminated altogether, in the not too distant future.

Are we to understand that humanity is very near banishing suffering from the world? "The contrast between the success of modern European minds in controlling almost any situation in which the elements are physical bodies and the forces physical forces, and their inability to control situations in which the elements are human beings and the forces mental forces" is too evident to need any elaboration. Our control of ourselves and our relations with fellow beings and groups has grown in inverse proportion to our phenomenal control of nature. Rivalry, tension and conflict have become more complex and widespread. Man finds himself the unhappy victim of the forces which he has released, but which he is unable to control. There is suffering. Only we are not sufficiently sensitive to it, dazzled as we are by the achievements of technology.

The notion that suffering is physical pain or even social evil appears to me to be an over-simplification. Suffering is not merely an objective fact. A situation which is acutely painful to one may not be so felt by another or at least not to the same extent. Nor for the same person is that situation painful always. Loss of property, poverty or bereavement are not suffering *per se*; some persons may even be heartened by them. Suffering depends primarily on the attitude of the person who suffers. When our desires and expectations are not fulfilled or not done in the expected measure there is suffering. The hiatus or want of conformity between desires and their satisfaction is suffering. This is almost a commonplace and need not be argued.

When we think of desires we actually mean the volitions engendered by them. For, a desire generally leads to the will to realise and enjoy it as an accomplished fact. That many of our desires do not lead to volition is because they are inhibited by the knowledge that they stood no chance of realisation. An unfulfilled desire is a case of arrested willing and is an unpleasant state. Suffering itself may be understood as frustrated will; it is the feeling of helplessness. If our desires could be satisfied as they arose or soon after, there would not be any suffering. There is nothing inherently incongruous in supposing that one's power of actualising the desires could be equal to the desires themselves. God is conceived as such a being. But this does not apply to us. Our desires far outstrip our capacity to satisfy them. We know, as a well-established psychological fact, that the satisfaction of some desires whets our appetite, and the desires multiply in number and intensity. A leapfrog race is started, and satisfaction can never prove even remotely adequate to the desires. As an oft-quoted Indian saying points out: "Not by the enjoyment of desires do they subside; they flare up increasingly even as the fire fed by oblations of butter." An abiding unrest of the mind is the inevitable result of such unfettered indulgence. This itself is suffering, for it leads to hankering, disappointment, dissipation and other attendant unpleasant situations.

Quite an opposite remedy is the well-known Buddhist recipe to eradicate desire (*tṛṣṇā*) as such, because it is suffering itself and is the source of all other suffering. This may not be impracticable, but it may not be very desirable, as with the extinction of all desire, personality itself shall have been extinguished as in the void of Nirvāṇa or the fathomless depth of Brahman. The remedy may prove worse than the disease. The discipline may well be beyond the competence of but a few. This poses for us a pertinent question: Are we, in our quest to overcome suffering, left with these two alternatives only—full indulgence of desires or total elimination of them?

The matter is not so simple as this. Desires are not satisfied in a vacuum. If we had Nature alone to contend against, the human will should prevail absolutely; for, except figuratively, nature does not resist or withhold anything. Our lack of the proper knowledge and the technical means would be the only impediments in satisfying what we desire to do. But as human beings live and develop their personality only in a society of fellow beings, our desires and wills are helped or hindered by other wills. We encounter here a new dimension which, unlike nature, is resistant to our will and is as fully autonomous as our own will. In fact, suffering is brought home to us in this human context. Impelled by what we consider as our good and as our due, we encroach upon others and are rebuffed or *vice versa*. We are either active agents in inflicting suffering on others or patients thereof. This man-made suffering is more intolerable, as it is infinitely varied and greatly entangled. It generally proves recalcitrant to our efforts.

There is one more factor which induces suffering. Things happen to us either through the agency of Nature (e.g. extremes of climate, natural calamities) or through the agency of fellow beings (e.g. rivalries, conflicts and war). We cannot obviously help them. But all of us can, to a greater or lesser extent, help feeling aggrieved about it and from fretting and fuming. I may call this kind of suffering secondary involvement, and I should think that the amount of suffering on this score is more considerable than is realised. As we are completely free to eliminate or reduce the secondary involvement, the problem of suffering may profitably be attacked from this angle. To accept resignedly that things happen as part of a cosmic order or divine disposition becomes a spiritual virtue. Stoicism and Spinozism are good examples of this attitude.

One good feature of suffering is that it is not taken as a desirable state *per se*. No one desires to do any act which might result in suffering to himself. Everyone desires his good always. To this extent the Socratic maxim that no man does evil knowingly may be accepted, with some modification however. In many cases, our acts which prove injurious to others and even to ourselves are done through ignorance of their consequences. Quite often we consider our good as paramount and pursue it regardless of the good of others and even knowing that it may bring suffering on others. Not only evil which is motivated by self-interest, but also unmotivated evil (the diabolical element) is perhaps present with us to a greater extent than we suspect or are prepared to own. It is not plausible to say that the evil or unjust man is intensely unhappy in his soul, as Plato makes out in the *Republic* and that if he knew this he would not be wicked. It may also be held that evil man will be subject to suffering sooner or later owing to the operation of the Moral Law or Divine Dispensation.

The first is a matter for psychological analysis. Looking from outside, the wicked man does not seem to suffer from the pangs of conscience; he has successfully managed to smother it. It is also within the limits of possibility that a class of human beings may be nurtured in a severely conditioned environment without the moral sense, but doing actions based on the animal reactions to hunger and fear. As for the contention that the wicked man would be properly punished in this life or the next by the operation of the moral law, it is a wish, quite just and reasonable but unprovable. It is either religion or philosophy that can at all deal with this problem. A nest of problems regarding afterlife, survival, the nature of the soul, the cosmic order, God etc., is involved in this question. This shows that we are not able to demonstrate the relation between evil (vice and wickedness) and suffering. The problem of suffering cannot adequately be treated purely on the empirical level. Any suggestion that we may make would be a rough guess, something that may be practicable and serviceable in some measure in lessening conflict and bitterness.

It may be questioned whether we should seek any connection between suffering and evil (pursuit of egotistic interests as vice and wickedness). It may be pointed out that suffering, though painful, may not be evil in itself or caused by it, for it may chasten and ennoble a man; it may even be the sole means to moral and spiritual regeneration of man. This seems plausible, because suffering is taken as a situation or a set of conditions. I have argued against this manner of understanding suffering. The essence of it is really our wrong attitude to a situation, the feeling of helplessness and frustration. When we have corrected ourselves to look upon the situation as a help rather than as a hindrance, it ceases to be suffering. We have robbed it of its barbs and fangs.

To say that suffering is not caused by evil is really to say that suffering is a brute fact, that is, is uncaused. It would then be unmerited. Because it is not caused or merited, it cannot be removed. Denying causal relation between evil and suffering is really as much a dogmatic philosophical position as its opposite.

A knowledge of the nature of suffering and how it arises can have value only on the assumptions that desires, motives and will can be reformed by the understanding. If we could perceive clearly that our inordinate desires, our insistence upon the claims of our ego are the real cause of our suffering, we shall have taken a sure step towards a solution of this problem. The ego manifests itself in many and varied forms, as personal ego (individuality), as a class, racial or national ego. Even in the sphere of religion, it may take the form that my religion is the only true religion, others are false. In a more positive way we should realise that our real good cannot be different from the good of all. Only then can suffering be subdued and eliminated.

In the foregoing analysis, I have tried to emphasise two considerations : First, although we cannot prove it, there seems to be some intimate relation between suffering and evil. Suffering may not always be the consequence of evil, but evil (vice and wickedness) cannot go unpunished and uncorrected. It would be repugnant to the moral governance of the world, if it were otherwise. A perception of this connection should have a sobering influence on selfish traits of our make-up. The second consideration is that there are features of suffering that are remediable, because they are amenable to reason. Take for instance what I have termed secondary involvement which consists in feeling aggrieved at things and happenings. When a misfortune has happened or some person has wronged us, we do not certainly lessen our suffering by worrying or being bitter; on the contrary, we shall considerably be adding to it. The worry and bitterness are also likely to befog our mind and hinder it from functioning efficiently. This is common sense and does not need any metaphysical investigation. With the lessening of the secondary involvement, we are on the way to lessen the primary one also. An attitude of composure or holding ourselves in hand may be cultivated.

It is also equally easy to see that immoderateness in satisfying desires is not conducive to mental health. We may strike a mean between complete desirelessness and full indulgence. We may voluntarily restrict them to the necessary ones. We cannot obviously draw up a list of the desires allowable, for this is essentially a matter of personal requirement and inclination.

We are still at the periphery of the problem. The real core of suffering is the Ego. Inordinate desire is itself a form of selfishness, the way our ego desires to grasp and possess all things to itself. Secondary involvement also is the result of looking at things from the egocentric standpoint instead of from the universal and the cosmic. The 'I' is absolute; its demands are imperative and relentless; it knows no moderation or satiety. One ego is kept in check by other egos which also claim equal absoluteness in their own right. Clashes occur and are inevitable. Each individual pursues what he thinks is good for him, sometimes in conformity with the collective good and often without it. If our good could be identical or at least taken to be identical with that of all others, the chances of conflict would be less. We do sometimes achieve this as in the family or within select groups. But this identity of interests is neither complete nor permanent. Differences break out, resulting in the pursuit of a separate or divided good. For the complete elimination of suffering therefore the identification of the individual good with the good of all seems necessary.

I am convinced that this identification of the individual with the universal good cannot be enforced by compulsion, as is being done by certain forms of state organisations. Such external compulsion could only drive the ego underground and result in creating greater and permanent bitterness. The ego must surrender its egoity freely and with conviction, as is conceived in the Bodhisattva ideal. Nothing less than a spiritual education or regeneration can achieve this end. The conviction that ultimately my good is identical with that of all is not also a matter of dogmatic belief or religious faith. If our understanding or reason were left out of this process, it would prove antagonistic. The individual would stand permanently divided in himself and suffer from the disease of split personality. Suffering can be completely resolved only by the inner spiritual regeneration of man through religion or religious philosophy.

7.1. THE PHILOSOPHY OF LANGUAGE IN THE INDIAN CONTEXT*

I must first express my grateful thanks to the members of the Indian Philosophical Congress for electing me General President of the 37th Session. I am not aware of any special merit or distinction in me to deserve this choice. Probably, as one who has been a teacher of Philosophy for quite a number of years and a devoted student of Indian Thought, the choice may not altogether be undeserved. By way of Address as General President of the Session, I propose to share with you some thoughts on the philosophy of language. It is not intended, nor is it possible for me, to attempt any systematic consideration of this interesting and important subject. What I propose to do is to touch upon those aspects of the subject which have close bearing on the Indian approach to it. My intention is to draw pointed attention to the Indian views and contributions which are by no means inconsiderable or insignificant.

A good deal of present day philosophising in the West, at least the more vocal part of it, is linguistic philosophy. Although Comparative Philology, Semantics and Study of Structural Analysis had been cultivated since the beginning of the nineteenth century, philosophical interest in language began with the attempts of logician-mathematicians like Frege, Russell, Whitehead and Wittgenstein to formulate a rigorous and precise language as a reform in logic—a new symbolism. Soon it became clear that the issue was not that simple. It became evident that these innovations were based upon metaphysical implications. What consequences this new symbolism had upon mathematics and the methodology of sciences is difficult for a layman like me to assess, but its influence upon philosophy and the philosophical disciplines has been well-nigh revolutionary. An Indian proverb has it : "While digging a well, emerged a demon." A prescriptive use has been made of this new and striking trend. Linguistic philosophy has, however, succeeded in making us aware of the nature

*Reprinted from the Proceedings of the 37th Session, Indian Philosophical Congress, 1963.

of the universal tool of expression—language which we have been taking for granted. Positivists and linguistic philosophers are not the only ones concerning themselves with language. Phenomenologists and Existentialists and even theologians have investigated this field. More fundamental, though less spectacular, strides have been made by Ernst Cassirer in his three volumes on the *Philosophy of Symbolic Forms*. His analysis about the three stages of language, the mimetic (or imitative), analogical and the symbolical, the last being its highest expression, has found wide acceptance. What is amply borne upon us by linguistic philosophers and others is that the philosophy of language is not one aspect or branch of philosophy, but is all philosophy. The problem of Meaning is basic. Philosophy may be re-defined as Critique of Language. The problem of what we can know is closely bound up with the question of what we can say. It is only thought as expressed in words that can be understood, communicated and criticised. Language is not an accidental, dispensable garb which could be put on and put off. It grows with thought, or rather thought grows with it. In the ultimate analysis they may be identical. Bhartṛhari in his *Vākyapadiya* (I,124) asserts this basic truth : "There is no cognition without the operation of the word; shot through and through is cognition by the word, as it were. All knowledge is illumined by the word."[1] It is not that we have a thought, well-formed and complete, and then we seek a word to express it; or that we have a lonely word which we seek to connect with a thought. Word and thought develop together, or rather they are the expressions of one deep spiritual impulse to know and to communicate. Sapir "is strongly of the opinion that the feeling entertained by so many that they can think or even reason without language is an illusion. A still more fruitful source of the illusive feeling that language may be dispensed within thought is the common failure to realise that language is not identical with its auditory synthesis." (*Language, p.* 15-6). It is an old and established doctrine that Consciousness (*Caitanya*) is identical with Speech (*Vāk*).

1. *Vākyapadīya*, 1.123
Na so'sti pratyayo loke yaḥ śabdānugamād ṛte,
anuviddham iva jñānaṁ sarvaṁ śabdena bhāsate.

Indian philosophy has rightly considered language and thought as intimately related. The Nyāya-Vaiśeṣika is essentially a philosophy of *padārtha*, the meaning of words. As in Aristotle, here also categories of language are categories of Being. For most of its ontological entities, e.g., *dik*, *kāla*, *sāmānya*, *samavāya*, etc., the Nyāya adduces only linguistic usage (*Vyavahāra*). Both the Pūrva and Uttara Mīmāṁsā (the Vedānta) do not profess to be anything more than an Exegesis of the Revealed Word (the Veda). With rare insight, Professor K. C. Bhattacharyya, in expounding the concept of philosophy, expounds the different grades of the Speakable, thereby implicitly identifying thought and language.

As Urban points out in his *Language and Reality* (p. 331), the Kantian problem of the possibility of transcendental knowledge of God, Freedom and Immortality may be re-stated in this new key: "Is discourse about such objects intelligible discourse or is it meaningless. It is for this reason that, as Mauthner says, Kant's *Critique of Pure Reason* is really a *Kritik der Sprache*."

Any philosophical discussion, sooner or later, turns upon definition and clarification of the basic terms employed by the disputants. It is a demand to distinguish and make explicit the metaphysical pre-suppositions implicit in the discourse. It is not also unusual that questions regarding the competence of language to grasp and express reality should be raised. Does language reveal reality or hide or distort it ? Is it adequate to express all our scientific and other needs and should it not be re-designed, as for instance Whitehead asks? This is to raise questions about the function of language and its relation to reality. We are thus led from logical questions of definition and clarification to metalogical questions. This is almost inevitable, for our logical differences are but implicit metaphysical differences, and they are brought to the fore when any serious discussion is carried on.

I may also venture to make this point that differing evaluations of language are the necessary reflexes of different philosophies or metaphysical stands. There is no neutral or agreed philosophy of language. To quote a recent criticism of linguistic philosophy : "Linguistic philosophy is, amongst other things, a theory of language. In essence, it consists in seeing language naturalistically......This view denies that language is, in fact or in principle or in some hidden way, a mirror of reality, a mirror such that from the nature of the basic constituents of *language* one could infer the basic constituents of *reality*." It views language as a game, or as a multiplicity of language-games, according to the varieties of usage. So Wittgenstein says in his *Philosophical Investigations* (§ 23). This, however, has not always been the European tradition with regard to language, nor even an important attitude. With the Greeks and the Mediaeval Christian Philosophers the Logos or the Word was divine; it reveals and expresses the ontological being. Wilhelm von Humboldt, who in the early years of the nineteenth century gave the impetus to the discipline of the philosophy of language, follows the idealistic tradition of Kant and Herder. He considers language "not as a mere work but as an activity, that the 'facts' of language become fully comprehensible only if we trace them back to the spiritual actions from which they arise." Heidegger in some of his utterances in his *Sein und Zeit* comes very close to the Indian conception of language. He regards "language not so much as a manifestation of Dasein as the locus and vehicle of the self-revelation of being itself. Language is the house of Being, a house in which man, too, has his dwelling. It is here that Being is to be sought for and found through the patient creative effort of raising in words a temple in which Being may shine forth in its truth. Language is 'brought to pass' by Being, a house put together by Being, existing within which man is aware of Being and his relationship with it." Heidegger attaches great significance to the elucidation of category-words enshrined in tradition and quite often this is taken by him as insight into the nature of Being.

Indian speculations on language began with the Veda and have continued till recently without any break. In the *Ṛg Veda* several hymns are devoted to *Vāk* (Speech) and the same spiritual trends are continued in the *Brāhmaṇas* and the *Upaniṣads*. Patañjali in his *Mahābhāṣya* quotes some of these striking utterances and comments on them. It can truly be said that the philosophy of language as cultivated by the School of Grammar and the Mīmāṁsā is the elaboration of the suggestions found in the Veda. The divine nature of speech, rather its being the great God himself, the creative and illuminative power of the word, and the different levels of speech—these doctrines which formed the main plank of the philosophy of language in Indian thought all stem from the Veda. The ancillary disciplines of the Veda, phonetics, grammar (linguistic analysis) and Nirukta (Definitions of Terms) were directly connected with the Veda. The Mīmāṁsā is basically a systematic exegesis. On this arena of language the different philosophical systems met and clashed. It is no exaggeration to state that Indian philosophy is repeated twice over—once in the accredited metaphysical systems as we know them and once again in their stand-point with regard to language. Almost all types of metaphysics—Absolutism and Pluralism, Empiricism and Transcendentalism, Realism and Nominalism and their shades and sub-shades are found here. Every system of philosophy had to consider language at some stage or other; and each one had to ponder over ultimate questions concerning the relation of the word to Reality, of the modes of meaning and the validity of verbal knowledge. Their metaphysical bias determined their answers to these questions. It should be an interesting and almost an engrossing study to view and to expound Indian philosophy from this angle.

Two principal schools—the Mīmāṁsā and the philosophy of Grammar made massive and the most significant contributions to the philosophy of language, with the Nyāya playing an important role on the empirical level. The *Ālaṅkārikas* (Rhetoricians) also made very acute analyses of linguistic and literary meaning. We may re-interpret Indian philosophy as stemming from two principal traditions based on their different evaluation of language. The Brāhmaṇical tradition stemming from the Veda takes language as of Divine origin (Daivī Vāk), as Spirit descending and embodying itself in phenomena, assuming various guises and disclosing its real nature to the sensitive soul. The well-known Ṛg Veda verse, '*catvāri śṛṅgāḥ*' expresses this truth in poetic form.[1] It symbolises speech as the Bellowing Bull of abundant fecundity, as the Great God descending into the sphere of the mortals (*maho devo martyāṁ āviveśa*). Patañjali asks: Who is this Great God and answers—Speech itself (*mahān devaḥ, śabdaḥ*). Another verse of the Ṛg Veda tells us that the

1. *Ṛg Veda,* iv. 58, 3.
Catvāri śṛṅgā trayo asya pādā dve śirṣe sapta hastāso asya,
tridhā baddho vṛṣabho roraviti maho devo martyāṁ ā viveśa.

ignorant man seeing and hearing speech in its overt manifest forms does not know its real nature. To the wise, Speech reveals her intrinsic nature, even as the loving wife does to her lord.[1] Lost in appearances we fail to penetrate to the deeper reality. The Vedānta, Mīmāṁsā, the Sāṅkhya-Yoga and the school of Grammar and Kashmir Śaivism, among others, are loyal to this tradition.

In opposition to this high evaluation of language we have the naturalistic conception of language, as an arbitrary and conventional tool. This stand denied the validity of testimony as a source of knowledge. It was nominalistic, positivistic and sceptical in this regard. The Cārvāka and earlier Buddhism are representatives of this tradition. Empiricists as they are, the Jaina and the Nyāya occupy a somewhat intermediary position.

A philosophy of language is a reflective awareness of language, a review of its function. We are led to this self-examination because of a breakdown or frustration in its working, when it fails to convey the intended meaning. As long as a mechanism is working smoothly, our attention is not directed to its inner working or structure. It cannot be said that to use language and to be proficient in it, we must have a prior knowledge of its inner working. Probably, the opposite is the case. Frustration or breakdown occurs, when there is confusion of different levels and modes of language; when for instance, what is symbolic is construed literally. The positivist's summary rejection of religion and metaphysics is based on this demand for literal or factual meaning in these spheres as it obtains in science. Therefore, the primary concern of the philosophy of language is to set forth clearly the different levels or grades of language and meaning. Failure to distinguish and appraise the different levels of speech results in confusion, and quite often leads to positivism and scepticism.

Philosophy of language is an end in itself. It is not cultivated as a means to acquire greater proficiency in the use of language. Through philosophy, Speech becomes conscious of itself. It awakens to its role as the creator and matrix of Word and Meaning which encompass the entire universe of things.

1. *ibid.*, x. I, 4.
Uta tvaḥ paśyan na dadarśa vācam uta tvaḥ śṛṇvan na śṛṇotyenāṃ. uto tvasmai tanvaṁ visasre jāyeva patya uśati suvāsāh.

Western thinkers generally take "language as a purely human and non-instinctive method of communicating ideas, emotions, desires, by means of a system of voluntarily produced symbols." Or as we may state briefly, it is a system of articulate sounds which have acquired meaning. A particular sound or a combination of sounds becomes the bearer or vehicle of meaning; it represents or stands for something not present. The essence of language consists in this representative function (Darstellung) and the intention, on the part of the speaker, to communicate something to the hearer through the vehicle of words. Language then has to be understood as participation in a speech-community, in communication. Not only the speaker and the hearer—the two poles of communication—but probably a neutral witness or judge to whom appeals could be made in case of doubt or dispute are implied in communication. There can be no solipsism in language; its very life is communication. The term 'speech' rather than language brings out this aspect more clearly. For the Indian thinkers, language was primarily the spoken word or speaking itself (*Vāk*). Patañjali defines the word as That on the utterance of which there is common understanding regarding objects (*Sampratyaya*).[1]

This definition of language (the word) does not identify it with the overt sounds produced and propagated physiologically. In fact, the distinction between *śabda* (Word) and *dhvani* (Sound) is basic to the Indian philosophy of language. To identify them, to take the physical sound as the word, is a *category mistake*. It is to confound entities of two different orders, like the confusion of the soul with the body. The word, like the soul, has a physical embodiment in the sound and is made manifest through the latter, but the conveyance of meaning is the function of the word; the sound only invokes the word.

Attempts have been made both in Western and Indian philosophy to derive language from non-linguistic ingredients, from bodily gestures, from expletives, interjectional sounds, from imitative sounds, etc. It is further believed that language has been evolved generally through convention. Eighteenth century

1. *Mahābhāṣya, Āhnika* I.
Yenoccāritena sāsnā-lāṅgūla-kakuda-khura-viṣāṇināṁ sampratyayo bhavati sa śabdaḥ.

speculations on language were largely concerned with *the origin of language and the original language of man.* Although each theory contains some particle of truth, they are unable, either singly or in combination, to explain the symbolising activity which is the essence of language. We also do not start with separate words and then combine them into sentences. The true position is that sentences and larger units come first. Language is an *Urphenomen*, as Cassirer so incisively urges. It is underived and is *sui generis*. Urban sums up the consensus of present-day appraisal thus:—"The idea that language is an *Urphenomen* neither reducible to nor explainable in terms of non-linguistic fact, seems to be a common assumption of linguistic study". (*Language and Reality*, p. 62).

That language is underived and that the word is a form and is thus distinct from its material embodiment, sound, are established by the Mīmāṁsā theory of the Eternality of the Word (*śabda-nityatva-vāda*).[1] Words and their relation with meaning are eternal, underived and impersonal.[2] It may be thought that we give names to persons and things and thus initiate new conventions, and that the same logic should be applied to the other words also. They too were the result of convention (*saṅketa*), and where human convention is not available, recourse may be had to divine convention. Against this view the Mīmāṁsā argues rightly that the relation between the word and the meaning is not an arbitrary convention, established by man or even by God either now or in the past. We do not *have record of any such convention.* Convention itself presupposes language, which is sought to be derived from convention. To make conventions, words have to be used and understood by persons participating in the convention. This is clearly circular. Invoking God does not help either. How could God make known his intentions, his conventions between words and their respective meanings, to persons who did not use language already ? And if they had been already using language, God's convention does not obviously

1. *Mahābhāṣya*, *Āhnika* I.
siddhe śabdārtha-sambandhe....nitya-paryāya-vāci siddhaśabdaḥ.
2. *Mīmāṁsā Sūtra*, I.I, 5.
autpattikas tu śabdasyārthena sambandhas tasya jñānam upadeśo'vyatirekaś cārthe'nupalabdhe tat pramāṇaṁ Bādarāyaṇasyānapekṣatvāt. *Śabara* on the above. autpattika iti nityaṁ brūmaḥ.

initiate language. However far back we might push the beginning of convention, we would still find language preceding it. An absolute beginning of language is untenable. Lingusitic usage is continuous.

The attempt to assign a temporal beginning of language probably arises from a confusion of the word with the sound. Is the Word to be taken as the complex of sounds produced by the speaker through his vocal and other physiological organs and received by the hearer as auditory sensations? It is natural to take it this way. But a little reflection would show that this natural and easy way is beset with difficulties. In that case, there would be as many and different versions of each word 'cow', 'man', 'tree', etc., as there are instances of pronouncing them. Each single utterance of the word would be so unique that there would be no *common* word that passes around. It might be said that they are not utterly different or identical, but are similar. But similarity itself presuposes a norm of recognisability with degrees of tolerance. Without identity there is no intelligibility, and *identity implies independence of place, time and personal effort.* Although the word cow may be pronounced in many different ways, slowly, quickly, softly, harshly and at different places and times and by different persons, it is recognised as *the same* word cow, *inspite* of the differences. The Platonic arguments for the universality, identity and eternality of the Idea apply to the Word. In fact, the eternality of Words as propounded by the schools of Mīmāṁsā and Grammar is the Indian counterpart of the doctrine of Ideas. The Word Cow is a form, identical and immutable, although the instances of its utterance may differ. The nerve of the argument, as in Plato, is that verbal communication and intelligibility necessitate the acceptance of the Word-Forms. The Word (*śabda*) is manifested, not constituted, by the vocal sounds. As in Plato, the problem of the relation of the Idea to the 'Copies' appears here as the relation of the immutable word to its several physical manifestations, which instance it.

Another set of problems clusters round the conception of meaning. Does the word signify the particular (*vyakti*) primarily and acquire general application by mental construction and repeated usage? Or, does the word connote the Universal (*jāti*) primarily and is applied to the particular objects by implication? Or, does the word connote the Universal and denote the particulars equally as part of its meaning? This is the same old problem of the Universals. An entire range of views from the extreme nominalism of Buddhism (*apohavāda*) and the realism of the Mīmāṁsā and the Nyāya-Vaiśeṣika with several interesting intermediary positions is to be found in Indian thought. This topic is treated in the accredited scholastic style with a wealth of arguments and plenty of polemic. I do not propose to enter into this subject, for even a summary statement would take us long. I shall content myself with indicating, in the briefest manner, the characteristic views of the School of Grammar on the subject.

In the *Vākyapadiya*, Bhartṛhari states and expounds, two principal views on the question of meaning of words. It must be understood that the real unit of language is the sentence, and words are, for pedagogical purposes, *abstracted* from the sentence and *ascribed* a meaning. The division of words into several syllables and of a sentence into several words is a convenient fiction. According to one view, associated with Vājapyāyana, connotation is the principal meaning and this is necessarily the universal (*jāti*). The universal is primarily a Word-Form and by way of transference this is applied to the Idea-Universal. The particulars are the appearances of the universal. In all things there is the duality of Real and Appearance which are related by way of identification or one-sided dependence. Although in common parlance we speak of several universals, such as man, cow, horse, etc., and this is valid for all practical purposes, there is really one ultimate universal—Being, uniformly and invariably present in the several universals; all words mean this alone. That is the meaning of all Names and Verbs. That is the great Self (*Vākyapadiya*, III 33-4).[1] The school of Grammar is an *Advaitavāda* (Absolutism) and shares in the virtues and difficulties of all absolutism.

1. *Vākyapadīya*, III, 33-34.
sambandhi-bhedāt sattaiva bhidyamānagavādiṣu.
jātir ityucyate tasyāṁ sarve śabdā vyavasthitāḥ.
tāṁ prātipadikārthaṁ ca dhātvarthaṁ ca pracakṣate,
sā nityā sā mahānātmā tām āhus tva-talādayaḥ.

On the other view, attributed to Vyāḍi, the substantive or substance as the Individual (*dravya*) is the meaning of words. Substance is the permanent being persistent amidst the changes of its modifications. It retains its identity in spite of changing vicissitudes. Meaning on this view is denotation—the *That* of things. There is ultimately one indivisible Being which is the meaning of all words, all the other individuals—men, cows, horses, etc., are so many appearances, through limitation (*upādhi*) of that Being.

What constitutes the unit of language ? Does each letter of a word or each word in a sentence have a separate meaning by itself or do they have meaning as combined together. Obviously, not the first alternative, for each letter of any particular word does not convey either a part or the whole meaning. Nor the second; for, combination of syllables which make up the word or the several words which make up the sentence are not present in consciousness as one whole. Notoriously, the syllables of a word of a sentence are never together; they die out as they are pronounced; and when we arrive at the last letter of a word or the last word of a sentence, the previous elements have already dropped out. How then is a combination possible ? It may be surmised that we have the last word or rather the last syllable of a sentence actually present in our ken and this combined with the memory of the other letters and words engenders the meaning. But order or sequence of letters and words should also be taken into account, otherwise the words Lamp and Palm would have the same meaning. But what would determine the order of words in the absence of an awareness of the whole ? Again, as the meaning is a whole, a unit, the generating verbal condition must likewise be a whole. The Grammar School is led, from such considerations, to advance the Doctrine of Sphoṭa—the Unitary Word—particularly the *Akhaṇḍa-Vākya-Sphoṭa*—that the sentence is an indivisible unit whole. And this engenders meaning. The separate letters or the words serve merely to manifest and bring the *Akhaṇḍa-Vākya-Sphoṭa* into play. It may be rebutted, as is done by the Mīmāṁsaka that the manifestation or invoking of the *Sphoṭa* does not escape the objections raised against the theory of individual letters or separate words generating meaning. Is the *Sphoṭa* manifested by a few letters or by all the letters taken together and in what order ? In any case, the letters or the words of a sentence are indispensable. In addition, the Grammar School makes a gratuitous assumption of a mythical entity like the *Sphoṭa*.

This criticism misses the deeper significance of the *Sphoṭa* conception. In linguistic apprehension, as in other cognitions, there is the interplay of two factors of different levels—the empirical manifold of sense-data (the separate letters or words in this case) and the transcendental or *a priori* synthesis of the manifold which alone imparts a unity to those elements which would otherwise have remained a mere manifold. I have interpreted the doctrine of *Sphoṭa* in terms of Kant's doctrine: that all knowledge is a synthesis of the manifold of sense-data because the *Sphoṭa* functions exactly like a transcendental category of the Whole or Unity. That is why the Grammar school brings in what might appear to many as a superfluous entity. Through the *Sphoṭa*, which is activated by the pronunciation or hearing of the separate letters or words, the meaning of the Sentence is engendered as a whole. The *Sphoṭa* is the Real sentence or Word-Unit which operates behind the facade of the overt sensuous syllables and words. Against the empiricism of the Mīmāṁsā and the Nyāya, the Grammar School is a form of Transcendentalism. Epistemologically, it is a two-level theory as applied to linguistic cognition. The Sphoṭa is a necessary intermediary and is called the *Madhyamā vāk* as distinct from the overt empirical speech called *vaikhari*. These two belong to different orders—one is empirical and the other is submerged and hidden and has, therefore, to be excited and manifested by the overt sounds (*nādābhivyaṅgyaḥ sphoṭaḥ*). The relation between them, like that of the Soul and Body, is one of identification or super-imposition. They act and behave as one and are ordinarily indistinguishable. Only a subtle analysis can reveal their distinction.

We have so far been considering Word and Meaning as two separate entities, somehow related. The truth of the matter is somewhat different. That they stand related and are even generally identified implies that they both spring from some common source which is the ground of their being. Linguistic speculations in the West do not reach out beyond the phenomenological sphere—the realm of ideational, linguistic discourse. Ontological questions are not considered, and are even studiously avoided. Cassirer, who has done so much for the autonomy of the philosophy of language, is himself a notable example of the purely phenomenological attitude. Indian philosophers of language are not content to stop with any duality, the duality of Word and Meaning or the duality of Thought and Reality. As Bhartṛhari states it: "All difference presupposes a unity" (*abheda-pūrvako bhedaḥ*); where there is a duality, there is an identity pervading it. Otherwise, one cannot be related to the other; each would constitute a world by itself. The very assertion of duality is not possible. *The alternative to absolutism* is *monadism and solipsism.*

The dependence of the differents on their ground is not to be understood as one of being contained as in a passive encompassing receptum, for this would still smack of duality; their relation would be an external juxtaposition of two entities. The ground is therefore conceived as generative or creative of the differences through its inner dynamism or Power (*śakti*). The generation should not again be understood as that the ground is transformed to any extent or as in any manner entangled or involved in this modification. The Ultimate Ground is Transcendent, and generation of differences should be taken as a sort of emanation (*vivarta*) which does not affect the Ultimate Cause. Bhartṛhari sees the entire world as a non-transforming emanation of the Non-Dual *Brahman*, the WORD. "*Brahman*, without beginning or end, the indestructible Essence of Speech, manifests Itself in the form of things; the world-process thus proceeds." (*Vākyapadīya*, I.1.).[1] This is quite in keeping with the accepted doctrine that creation is out of the words of the Veda.[2] It may be questioned: Why should the non-dual Brahman, in which the distinction of Word and Meaning has not emerged, be identified with the Essence of Speech (*śabda-tattva*) ? Because it is the Causal Ground of the Word and because it is so realised, in the order of our discovery, through analysis of the Word-Symbolism.

1. *ibid.*, I. 1.
anādinidhanaṁ brahma śabdatattvaṁ yadakṣaram vivartatértha-bhāvena prakriyā jagato yataḥ.

2. *Manusmṛti*, I. 21.
sarveṣāṁ tu sa nāmāni karmāṇi ca pṛthak pṛthak.
vedaśabdebhya evādau pṛthak-saṁsthaśca nirmame.

II

In the Introduction to the *Tractatus Logico-Philosophicus*, Russell says : "Everything, therefore, which is involved in the very idea of the expressiveness of language must remain incapable of being expressed in language and is, therefore inexpressible in a perfectly precise manner. This inexpressible contains, according to Mr. Wittgenstein, the whole of logic and philosophy."........"that every language has a structure concerning which, *in the language*, nothing can be said, but that there may be another language dealing with the structure of the first language, and having itself a new structure, and that to this hierarchy of languages there may be no limit." (*Tractatus*, p. 21, p. 23).

Whether this is held by Wittgenstein himself in his later *Philosophical Investigations* or not, the statement contains a very important truth. A statement about language as such, e.g., "Language is symbolic", "All meaningful propositions have empirical usage", "All philosophical views are dogmatic", raises a curious paradox. That language is symbolic is not itself symbolic, as it makes a plain and precise statement about the nature of language. If it were itself symbolic, it could not show up the symbolic character of language. And yet as this statement is itself expressed in language, it should be symbolic. Instances of such paradoxes may be multiplied. 'The world is illusory'—Is not this statement, as part of the world, itself illusory, and yet it is put forth as an absolute and true statement.

To escape this paradox, we may have recourse to a hierarchy of languages. We can make out a case for at least two language levels, if not more. A position and its review, a linguistic puzzle and its clarification, an imperfectly understood theme and its explanation are examples of this. The review or criticism of a position is not a different and one more position; it is turning the original position inside out. And even if this review turns out to be another position, this can be known only at a third level. To use language and to be aware of that use of language, are not identical, although they are connected.

It may be argued that this would lead to an unending series of hierarchy of languages. For example, it is not uncommon to have explanations of explanations and still further explanations of those explanations and so on. I may know that I know that I know..........endlessly. Although such a series is theoretically possible and plausible, it is legitimate to hold that such is not and should not be the case. At some stage, the criticism or clarification becomes so thoroughly transparent and self-evident that no further clarification is called for. Otherwise, the dictum that 'there is an unending series of clarification and criticism' would itself be in a flux and be relative. This consideration of the hierarchy of languages gives us a clue to the range of language. At the bottom of the scale, we start with something which is indefinite and untouched by any process of interpretation, selection or discrimination; it is the pre-logical as it were. We end up with some language which cannot be further clarified—being self-evident. Language will range between these two poles of absolute potentiality, indefiniteness and absolute clarity or self-evidence.

The first grade is common-sense language, which has not attained any pronounced bias in favour of a particular view or stand. It is the matrix or the datum of all specific investigations. It does not rule out any sphere of interest or standpoint. For to rule out and reject certain spheres, we must have entertained them at first. Nor do we consciously acquire it; for to acquire consciously, we must desire to possess it and exercise a choice. There is accretion, but no conscious acquisition. Common-sense may also be considered as the given or factual language. We start with it and return to it time and again, and all appeals are made to it.

If we were to continue in the state of pure common sense, the underived state of indefiniteness, there is the possibility of our becoming dull and unintelligible. Without conscious effort at control, regulation and organisation, the uncontrolled differences would be so great that persons or groups of persons using language would become isolated and unintelligible to each other. Setting up norms of correct or acceptable speech, Grammar, and the norms of discourse (Logic) and of conduct (Ethics) makes communication possible. The grammarian or the logician does not manufacture words or thoughts; they only regulate and canalise them; otherwise, there would be no objectivity and intelligibility. Intelligible discourse means the acceptance of certain identical principles or norms. Only through them, because of them, communication and progress in our scientific and literary enterprises are possible. This is the universe of meaning which is cultivated and maintained by thinking consistently. This is the world of *śāstra*—disciplined discourse. In this sense, logic is co-pervasive with thought or discourse. Nothing can be logical which does not have a *structural* make up; it means that there are parts of discourse which conform to certain accepted relationships. Anything that is not structured, e.g. the indefinite *par excellence* or the absolutely unitary, which for aught we may intuit and feel, cannot be communicated. In linguistic terms, any sentence or larger units must be syntactical.

The logical forms and norms employed in other disciplines could be disengaged from their exploitary usage in probing the object and contemplated as Ideas or Forms, as Plato did.

Both the factual language and logic which develops meaning by structuring it are within the empirical sphere, one as overt, and literal, the other as providing the structural frame-work for understanding it.

But we are also aware in logic and in the syntax of language of certain differences which are not logical. The existence of different logics and different interpretations of crucial situations and especially of value-judgments serves to draw our attention to a transcendental sphere. The seemingly syntactical difference obtaining in Indian Semantics, whether the substantive or the verb is the principal part of the sentence is really the reflex of the metaphysical view whether Being or Act is ultimately real. Common language is full of myths and legends, metaphors and allegories and references to gods and demons. These have no reference to sensuous objects. Above all, what about the act of speaking, the 'I' to which the objects are presented. We are likely to forget this, as it cannot be presented as an object or even as a meanable self-subsistent essence. We are conscious in these cases of linguistic usage of *a non-sensuous or transcendent sphere*. They give intimations of a reality or being behind the observable phenomena and in some sense as generating them. Such language which discovers or discloses the being of a different order, different from the sensuous, is the language of Religion. The question of its validity need not concern us now. We are interested in showing its distinctive features.

How does religious language manage to disclose or awake in us an awareness of a super-sensuous order ? Not by inventing a new language or by coining a different set of words, as these would fail to convey meaning to persons not acquainted with that language; but by using the terms current in common usage in an uncommon way. It uses words analogically and metaphorically and also profusely employs myths and legends. Religious language is symbolic to the core. Whatever in his natural experience appeared to man as valuable, majestic, life-giving, illuminating, gracious and benevolent was used, by a flexible use of the same terms, to describe or at least indicate the transcendent. As Höffding states it: "Symbols are taken from all accessible spheres of human experience, but it is chiefly from the great fundamental relations of nature and of human life—light and darkness, power and weakness, life and death, spirit and matter—that the material for symbol-making is drawn. A particular element of existence is promoted to be the most characteristic mark of the whole of existence; it is treated as though it entirely summed the relation between value and reality given in experience". (*Philosophy of Religion*, pp. 207-8.)

"Images or Patterns are taken from the narrow and more intuitable relations and used as expression for more universal and ideal relations which, because of their pervasiveness or ideality, cannot be directly expressed or perceived". It is a human predicament that we have to express the more universal and valuable in terms of the less with which we are acquainted more intimately. Thus we use the terms, Father, Mother, Master, Teacher, Friend, etc., of God. We also use symbols of non-human origin—Light, Strength, Power, Life, etc. But the great majority of symbols are drawn from human relationships; for man is the highest form of phenomenal existence, and we naturally use the very best we have at our disposal. Our first and most intimate acquaintance with super-sensuous reality is in our own Person, in the 'I' and its relationship with other persons. This accounts for the fact that religious language is predominantly, if not exclusively, anthropomorphic. God is conceived as a Person, as a Supreme Person (*Puruṣottama*).

Every religious symbol, e.g., Father, Love, Light, Life, etc., negates itself in its literal meaning and affirms its self-transcending meaning. There is enough indication in such expressions and the accompanying qualifications that the literal meaning is not intended. The *Puruṣa Sūkta* of the Ṛg Veda describes God as a Person but with thousands of Heads, thousands of Eyes, thousands of Feet, encompassing the universe and standing high above it. It is made amply clear that no earthly person is described here.

Although in the order of discovery we advance from human situations to the transcendent being, every religious symbol has a reflexive action. The Fatherhood of God, his Love or his Grace serves as a standard of measurement by which we assess finite things and actions. We expect the earthly father to approximate to the divine father. The reverence I feel for my father or teacher is a shadow of the reverence that I feel towards God. In this way religious language serves as a system of evaluation-categories.

This aspect of religious language may also serve to distinguish it from Poetry. The language of Poetry, like that of Religion, is metaphorical and imaginative. The Ṛg Veda is good poetry also. On this ground, Santayana closely identifies the two. To quote his words: "Religion and Poetry are identical in essence, and differ merely in the way in which they are attached to practical affairs. Poetry is called religion when it intervenes in life, and religion, when it merely supervenes upon life, is seen to be nothing but poetry." The vital question to ask is how and why religion could intervene in life as to transform it, whereas Poetry merely supervenes upon life, and is a luxury. In religion, the accent is upon the insight that the symbol gives as of a super-sensuous reality. The religious symbol leads and relates us in some way to the numinous reality. In Poetry, the accent is on the evoking of emotions of joy or elation. The Rasa theory makes the claim that the joy of poetic appreciation is spiritual. The cognitive element is secondary. Poetry, unlike Religion, is no ultimate concern of life.

The passage from the sensuous visible world to the numinous is made possible by the religious symbol. This passage is not 'inference' or even a necessary postulation to explain phenomena. It involves a 'leap', as there is no logical continuity between the two. Kant is eminently right in showing that there is no legitimate rational passing from the given to the First Cause or God. Śaṅkara, therefore, says that the definition of Brahman as the cause of the world is not a piece of inference, but a re-statement of the truth revealed by the Scriptures.

The validity of religious language is not questionable. It is not open to the Rationalist or the Positivist to deny the validity of the insight given by the religious symbol, simply on the score that it is through metaphor, symbol and myth. All such attempts betray an unpardonable assumption that Sense-Perception or logical inference is the only way to Truth and that the sensuous is the only reality. If this were granted, then religious language is a mere play of words without any cognitive significance. This is, however, question-begging. Such arguments can be legitimately used to distinguish and differentiate religious knowledge from the scientific or the sensuous and not to deny it.

From the nature of religious knowledge that it is symbolic and involves a 'leap', it follows that the symbols may be many and different. There is not one road to the Numinous. There is scope for many Religions and the number cannot theoretically be fixed or anticipated. The adoption of a particular key-symbol or set of symbols is not so much a matter of individual temperament as of the tradition to which a person belongs.

Religious language being essentially symbolic presents at *once a danger and demand.* The danger is that the language of religion is prone, time and again, to be taken literally. Positivism is always knocking at its door Certain spurious symbols which are not based on revelation and insight provide a convenient handle in this regard. The demand is to know God or ultimate reality, not in relation to the world or even in relation to human beings as Father, Master, Saviour, etc., but in its intrinsic form, free from the accidental trappings or symbols and metaphors. With this demand we pass on to the fourth and last grade of language.

That the demand is legitimate and is already conceded flows from the characterisation of religious language as symbolic. To know a symbol *as* symbol is already to have de-symbolised it, to have analysed and understood what the symbol stands for. In the relgious attitude itself, the symbol has to be taken almost literally. Religion can express the Truth only through symbols or myth and never without it. Rudolph Bultmann's demand for de-mythologisation within the religious consciousness itself is not legitimate, and Karl Jaspers is right in resisting the demand and pointing out that such de-mythologisation would lead to the loss of religious quality. It is, however, *quite legitimate to demand a non-symbolic knowledge of God.* This is philosophy. Philosophy would retain the insight gained by religion, but would clip away the symbolic and accidental trappings with which it is garbed. Its work is thus necessarily negative. It removes, by dialectic and criticism, the accidental and extraneous forms of our knowledge of God. The Upaniṣads, therefore, say boldly, "that is not *Brahman* which you contemplate. It is different equally from the known and from the unknown." Religious insight, riding on the wings of symbols, gives only a Relational knowledge of Brahman (its Taṭastha Lakṣaṇa), in relation to the world. There is the demand to know Brahman intrinsically as what It is (*svarūpa lakṣaṇa*). From the nature of the case, this knowledge has to be negative; we have to negate by criticism the anthropomorphic character of religious knowledge. What remains after this negation cannot be expressed discursively through concepts. It is not knowledge through representation and symbol, but knowledge by being the Real. One who knows *Brahman* becomes *Brahman* (*brahma veda, brahmaiva bhavati*). Reality is expressed as what cannot be expressed, by an eloquent silence.

Religion is the language of adventure and discovery. The establishing of intimate and inalienable personal relationship with God is the sole purpose of religion. In this venturing forth from the known to the unknown, religious consciousness uses symbols, metaphor and myth. The understanding of God as the Other is itself a symbol. In the ultimate analysis, God is really the Ultimate Self of Man As Professor Radhakrishnan has insisted in his numerous writings 'the personal God of Religion (*Īśvara*) is the Absolute of Philosophy'. Philosophy does not and cannot make the discovery of the numinous; that is the function of religion and needs not to be repeated by philosophy. Philosophical activity is an appraisal and a self-conscious awareness of its ultimacy. Without the discovery of the numinous made by religion, philosophy would remain empty, a vacuous play of the dialectic. It cannot then successfully resist positivism or being reduced to the logic of sciences. Without philosophical appraisal and critical alertness, religion would be blind, like the proverbial cock which had picked up a diamond but did not know its worth. It would degenerate into Dogma and Fanaticism.

8.1. THE PHILOSOPHY OF SPIRIT*

Personal Statement

I am grateful to the Editor, Professor Radhakrishnan, for asking me to contribute to this volume. I make no claim to formulate a system of philosophy. Certain convictions have been growing in me, largely as a study of philosophy and religion as cultivated in the East and the West. I am conscious that I approach philosophy from a standpoint that is essentially traditional. I accept many things which a western mind would find difficult to accept. As a Hindu, I have always believed in the Law of Karma. Reflection on it has induced in me a kind of conviction that it is quite a plausible explanation of the governance of the universe. The conception of the hierarchy of Values (*puruṣārtha*) with Freedom as the highest value has been no less a conviction. That Philosophy is not an affair of intellectual curiosity or theoretic analysis but a serious spiritual discipline (*sādhanā*) directed towards the attainment of Freedom is basic to Indian Philosophy, and I subscribe to it without reservation. It is difficult for me, as one brought up in the traditional Hindu atmosphere, to understand that there could be irreconcilable antagonism between Science and Philosophy or Religion. A proper appraisal of Values should, I believe, remove the conflict. These are some of the back-ground beliefs or presuppositions with which I approach philosophy.

In the following pages I have tried to present a Philosophy of Spirit, for I consider this as the basic quest in all philosophy. I have had to content myself, in an article of this limited size, with a statement of the main features without much attempt at argument or elaboration. My exposition is generally based on the Advaita Vedānta and the Mādhyamika systems—the two finest expressions of Indian Absolutism. Among contemporary Indian Absolutist thinkers I have learnt a great deal from Professor Radhakrishnan and the late Professor Krishnachandra Bhattacharyya. Apart from their writings, I have had the inestimable advantage of receiving their personal instruction and guidance.

*Reprinted from *The Contemporary Indian Philosophy*, 2nd Edn., (Library of Philosophy). London: George Allen and Unwin Ltd., 1952.

I. The Origin of Philosophical Consciousness

Philosophy is the discovery of Spirit (*adhyātmavidyā*). The actual progression towards this goal as well as its symbolic formulation may be comprised in the concept of philosophy. In all the strivings and speculations broadly taken as philosophy (metaphysics) and exemplified in the several systems of thought, the search for the Spirit is the underlying theme. Very often this objective is obscured by the dust of conflicts raised by different philosophies. The confusion with other pursuits, notably with science and culture, also clouds the issue. Criticism and positivism are protests against this tendency, and are valuable as guarding against this confusion.

The realisation of Spirit is not necessarily by philosophy alone. Religion, too, has the same aim. The Spiritual is the genus of which the philosophical and the religious consciousnesses are the species. On a different view, religion may be subordinated to philosophy and *vice versa*: philosophy could be understood as universal and ultimate and religion as regional and preparatory.

Science investigates the sensible world in a strictly objective way; it attempts to relate and describe objects in terms of other objects. It is a one-level knowledge. There is no occasion for raising such questions as whether the world is real or apparent, whether it is valuable or worthless. Such questions are unintelligible at the scientific level, and no conceivable scientific purpose would be affected by the kind of answer we give to these and similar questions. There is, however, no philosophy without evaluation, without reference to an attitude of the experiencing subject. Philosophy, as belonging to a different dimension is not an extension of science; nor is it a substitute for the latter. The two just do not intercept each other.

Logical Positivism has done a service to philosophy in drawing our attention to the difference between philosophical statements and scientific propositions. The latter refer to empirical existents and are verifiable, to a certain extent, by appeal to sense-experience. Thoughtful Positivists are realising that the criterion of verifiability is not strictly true even in science. No universal proposition, and science deals only with the universal, is verifiable in principle. Knowledge of future events and of other minds present formidable difficulties.

Logical Positivism is clearly fallacious when it claims to

legislate out of existence not only metaphysics but ethics and religion too. "All significant propositions are verifiable", what sort of statement is this ? It is neither empirical, for there is no fact corresponding to this; nor is it tautological, for its denial does not involve contradiction. It is metaphysical in the accepted sense. What the statement really does is that it takes over the criterion of significance presumed in science and declares that this is the only criterion of meaning available. This is an arbitrary restriction of meaning. If at all, it should be stated hypothetically: if the criterion of meaning presumed in science is the exemplar of all meaning, then metaphysics is non-significant. But insofar as it makes a downright universal statement, Positivism is not positivistic enough: it is metaphysical. It should simply say that the proposition as used in science and commonsense is *different from* statements in metaphysics. It should not make this difference a ground for preference; for, one might as well condemn science for not being significant like metaphysics.

Language contains words and expressions that do not signify the material or the physical realm. From words like God, Soul, Spirit, etc., we cannot directly prove the existence of these entities, as this would be a species of the ontological argument. They are, however, indications of a different realm. "Language is the actuality of culture"; it is the mirror of all our attainments.

Even the logical positivist has some acquaintance with the non-factual realm. For, he accepts, besides propositions concerning empirical matters of fact which are probable and verifiable, some others belonging to logic and pure mathematics. The function of the latter is merely to clarify, analyse and simplify complex propositions; they are tautologies. Are they propositions in any accepted sense ? They make no reference to actual or possible facts. They are not even statements, but are symbols of thought-operations. They need no verification being analytic and axiomatic. As completely containing their content within themselves and subject to their own laws of consistency, Logic and Mathematics constitute a self-subsistent realm in contrast to the factual world of empirical existence investigated by science.

The self-subsistent is by no means confined to logic and mathematics. Art and Literature belong to this autonomous universe. The difference between them is that while the former is regulative, the latter is creative. The poet or the artist creates his world of imagination, very often as an other to the real physical world. The canons of the aesthetic world are certainly not arbitrary, but they are totally different from natural laws. There is no natural necessity why the cultural should supervene on the physical. It is, however, a fact exemplified in all civilisations that the beautiful is superimposed on the merely useful. Shelter and dress must not only protect us from the rigours of the weather, but must look fine and artistic. The same tendency is observed in every detail about food, sex, etc.

Though not spirit or spiritual, the emergence of the cultural order facilitates the consciousness of the spirit. Spirit is the pervasive underlying reality. The apprehension of the universal is not possible without perceiving two or more particulars. The universal is not one more particular set side by side with other particulars. Nor does it exist separately in a different sphere by itself. Spirit is hidden because of its unobtrusive universality and non-utilitarian character. As all things, it is nothing in particular: as everywhere, it is nowhere specially. How then do we know it ? The universal is disengaged from the particulars, as what is common and continuous in the differents. Both the physical and the cultural are *to a consciousness*, to the "I" which experiences and enjoys them, though in diverse ways.

The two realms—natural and cultural—stand in thoroughgoing contrast: the first is alien to us, the other is created and sustained by our effort; the former is the world of empirical matter, the latter is a world of *a priori* self-sufficient forms. The greatest difference obtains in our mode of enjoying them. Material things have to be appropriated and their substance consumed to derive pleasure from them. Exclusiveness and rivalry are inseparable from pleasures. In this we do not differ from the animal. On the other hand, cultural pursuits, e.g. music, painting, literature, etc., elevate us; they give us joy, the joy of creation or at least sympathetic participation. There are no proprietary rights in them; they can be shared without diminution of content or quality. Such joys are not subject to limitations of time, "a thing of beauty is a joy for ever." While an animal would consume the flower to derive satisfaction from it, the deity will contemplate its beauty. Man is the meeting-point of the animal and the divine. He thus feels in himself the conflict of the "lower" and the "higher."

The existence of the natural and the cultural orders is not essential for the existence of Spirit. They are, however, necessary as a step in our *discovery* of Spirit. If our experience had been confined to one order for all time, we could not differentiate it from the spiritual. If we had only one mental state or even one phase of experience (e.g. the waking), we could not distinguish the self as different from its states. It is because the self is continuous and identical amidst change and difference that we are conscious of a self behind the states.

The existence and apprehension of the two orders provides only the background for the discovery of Spirit; one may, however, wander from one state to another without realising the significance of this alternation. Our attention must be drawn to it. This happens when our normal objective attitude is reversed, as we become subjective, reflective. Empirical illusions are occasions, in natures that are sensitive, for this inwardisation. What I have been taking as real turns out to be false. This throws a challenge and presents a problem. Painful experiences act in a similar way on the practical side. Our normal appraisal of values receives a rude shock. Such experiences are not exceptions; in fact, they now reveal themselves as quite the norm. The withdrawal or even suspicion of our dogmatic belief in the reality and value of the world is the dawning of philosophical consciousness.

II. The Different Approaches to the Real

It is commonly held that we start with a formal criterion of the Real as Non-Contradiction, Coherence or Correspondence, etc., and then apply the criterion to things, sit in judgment over them, accept them as real if they measure up to this criterion of ours or condemn them as false if they do not. There are some fatal objections to this procedure. It is not revealed how we have so secretly and securely alighted on this criterion at the very outset of our quest. The entire procedure would in that case be hypothetical: if we accept criterion A as the standard, then c, d, e are the consequences; but if B were accepted.... x, y, z, would be the consequences. Why should one accept criterion A rather than B? After having accepted one or the other, however, the argument can get under way. The logic of a system is posterior to its criterion, and so cannot justify it.

Our initial choice would remain arbitrary in the extreme. Besides, we have no means of deciding in favour of one criterion as against another, every criterion being equally formal. The suggested origin of the philosophical consciousness in a mere play of the imagination is artificial; it does not arise in the natural evolution of experience. There is no challenging problem before us the solution of which is provided here. The problem must be present to us in all its intensity and universality; we must be conscious of a mystery behind the entire range of things.

The most important reason for rejecting the formal mode of progression in philosophy is that we do not start with a mere idea or concept of spirit and then ask to be supplied with a concrete entity answering to it. We shall not then be able to escape the Kantian criticism. A concept can never acquire being; nor can any concept, however exalted, be identified with being. Spirit, as Pure Being, is apprehended in all experience : we are in intimate and inalienable contact with it. Philosophical analysis only serves *to disengage* it from things with which it is usually confused and to reveal its transcendence. There could also be no question of producing the consciousness of the spiritual *de novo*. Such consciousness having risen in the manner suggested before, philosophy or religion can direct and deepen it.

The real order of our discovery is that we reach the real by removing the imputed character with which it is clothed; only by breaking the outer shell of appearance do we penetrate to the kernel of reality within. Philosophy starts with the negative judgment or with the consciousness of the false. Only as a contrast is felt between what *appeared* at first to uncritical attention, but which later on turns out to be something else on close scrutiny, can the notion of the real or a quest for the truth arise.

We are here faced with a dilemma : can we negate the false without first being in possession of the knowledge of the real? For, only when we know what the thing in question really is can we be in a position to negate its imputed aspect. On the other hand, if we are already in possession of the truth, negation becomes a gratuitous procedure; it is not an indispensable instrument, a necessary movement, in our discovery of the real.

It is not always the case that we have first known what a thing really is before we negated its imputed character. The "snake" that I misperceive may be realised to be no snake at all from my shouts and cautious proddings, from a safe distance of course, not evoking any aggressive response from the "snake". In fact, my conviction that the presentation before me is not a snake at all, i.e. the negation itself, may lead me, by dissipating fear and ignorance, to the knowledge that the mistaken object is a rope. To take another instance. The extravagant claims and inconsistencies of one or several systems of philosophy may be sufficient ground to condemn them as false. No thesis can be accepted as true simply on the ground that another or a better one is not produced. The weakness of one view cannot by itself be the strength of another view. The very rejection of wrong views, on the score of their inherent flaws, may lead me, by clearing the ground of all undergrowth, to a true knowledge of the Real.

This mode of approach to the Real may be termed *dialectical.* The Mādhyamika system is a representative example of this. Speculative systems, because of their dogmatism, come into inevitable and interminable conflict with each other. If one system conceives reality on one pattern, a second system explains it on a different and opposed pattern. Such antinomical attempts of dogmatic metaphysics engender the Transcendental Illusion. Criticism is the awareness of this illusion, as it analyses and exhibits the inherent flaws infecting every system of thought. It is at once their resolution. It is not relevant to our purpose to examine whether criticism is possible without a position or whether criticism itself is not a position. A correct understanding of the function of criticism, which is the *reflective awareness* of a position, rules out its being another position; and on that very consideration, as being an impartial tribunal, criticism cannot presuppose a position. What the various systems of philosophy *say* with regard to the real may be false, for, they are mutually contradictory. But the philosophical consciousness of which they are the concrete expression cannot be questioned; what can be questioned is their *mis*direction. There are two important features in the dialectical approach to the real: one is its faith in the inner dynamism of the philosophical consciousness to take us to the real, through opposition and resolution of the opposition through criticism; the second is the purely negative function it assigns to criticism. What prevents us from having an intimate and immediate knowledge of the real is our views, thought-patterns, which obscure and obstruct our vision.

Intuitive knowledge of the Real (*prajñā*) is the total negation of all views (*dṛṣṭi*).

A different analysis of the context of illusion may be made; and this would of necessity mean a correspondingly different approach to the real. In the previous analysis we depended upon the situation discovering itself, by revealing the inherent flaws through its own inner dynamism. We can, however, conceive of that illusion-situation in which a reliable passerby tells us that the thing lying before us is a rope. With this assurance, we go near and directly perceive it to be just as it was described to us. Such knowledge may further provide the ground for the negative judgement, "This is not snake."

In the Vedānta approach to the real, we start our spiritual journey with a chart or true knowledge of the real already in our possession. The Upaniṣads reveal and declare to us, through words, that the *Ātman* (Spirit) alone is real. Such knowledge is even stated as possible only through revelation (aupaniṣada). If we already have knowledge of the real through revelation, extra-philosophically, what is the function of philosophy, it might be asked? Two answers are possible. It might be held that the initial knowledge that sets us on our journey and guides our path is knowledge through description, verbal and therefore mediate (*parokṣa*); it would be necessary to convert this knowledge into a direct experience of the real by our contemplation and meditation. More properly, it may be held that there is no qualitative difference in the two stages of our knowledge of the Real; for even from the outset, the knowledge pertaining to the Self (*Ātman, Brahman*) is direct and immediate (*aparokṣa*). Our later effort does not bring about any qualitative change, but merely removes certain misconceptions and doubts, thereby deepening and intensifying our initial knowledge. The function of negation or dialectic is secondary : it does not reveal the truth, but only serves to strengthen and complete it. The Vedānta approach may be termed theological, as it depends on extra-philosophical revelation that sets philosophy on its feet. It would however, be wrong to take it as dogmatic or as subordinating philosophy to theology. The cue may be received from revelation, but the ultimate knowledge of the Real is one's intimate and intuitive realisation of it. Our attention to an innate eternal truth, like principles and axioms, may be drawn by a teacher who propounds it to us; but it is realised by us and becomes an integral possession of our self.

What is common to both the approaches is the conception of Spirit as the reality of all things, its transcendence and our non-discursive intuitive apprehension of it.

III. The Transcendence of Spirit

There are two main stages in the discovery of Spirit. The first is the transition from things to Spirit, from appearances to their reality. The procedure is essentially negative : we literally uncover and divest things of their apparent character to reach their inner core. This is knowledge of Spirit as what it is not. And having gained access to the real, we know what it is by penetrating to its essential nature. The first is definition of Spirit *per accidens* (*taṭastha-lakṣaṇa*); the second is the intrinsic, intuitional apprehension of it (*svarūpa-lakṣaṇa*).

Spirit is the spirit of things, their inner essence or reality. It is not spirit and things : spirit on one side and things on the other. Conversely, the world can be conceived as the appearance of Spirit, as what it is mistaken for. The soul is apprehended as *not* the body with which it is ordinarily identified. We regain it only as we withdraw ourselves from the objects of sense and from our own body.

Though in the world of phenomena, Spirit is not of it. It is Transcendent Being. The appearance, however, is not without it. The relation between them is one-sided, not reciprocal : it is like the one obtaining between the ground and its appearance. This relation, which may be called transcendent identity, is *sui generis*. Other relational modes, e.g. substance-attribute, cause and effect, universal and particular, have to be conceived on this pattern.

The proof for the existence of Spirit as Transcendent Being (Absolute) is axiological. Without transcendence no evaluation is possible. The distinctions we make between truth and falsity and the dissatisfaction we feel with the objects of the world and our unceasing quest for something far transcending empirical things imply an absolute norm, it presupposes two orders, the higher and the lower. These are not spatial positions, nor can they be conceived as the more or the less extensive. The distinction is qualitative. The true and the false are not merely different like red and blue; there is preference or evaluation. The false is what is rejected or dispensable, and the true is the indispensable. The real and its appearance are not, therefore, mutually implicatory. To call anything appearance is to be aware of two aspects of a thing, the essential and the accidental : what a thing is in itself, absolutely, unrelatedly and what it appears to percipients under certain conditions. Again, what appears always appears *as* another; it is understandable only in the context of illusion or mistake.

All these implications follow, it might be urged, if we employed the notion of appearance. But are we necessitated to employ that notion at all? If all our perceptions were veridical and absolute without any subjective (accidental) element in them or if they were utterly subjective without a suggestion of the independently given, there would be no need to make the distinction of the real and the apparent. Such however is not the case. The ever-present problem in all experience is the sifting of the real from mere appearance.

A proper interpretation of relation would also lead to the same result. The logic is that the two terms sustaining a relation are not of the same order, one is *higher* and the other *lower* : the two terms are neither mutually dependent nor mutually independent, i.e. relation is neither "internal" nor "external". If mutually dependent, we cannot distinguish between the two terms; as they so necessarily imply each other that one cannot exist without the other any time and in any manner. We cannot even say that there are two terms, for the basis of distinction is lacking; distinction implies difference and separability. If mutually independent, there is no basis of connection : each term is a self, a self-contained universe as it were; the two terms could not be brought together. To escape this predicament we have to conceive one term as basic and thus capable of existing apart from the other; while the other is incapable of so doing and therefore dependent. One term, the higher, is not exhausted in the relationship; it has a transcendent or non-implicatory existence which is its intrinsic nature : and this makes for its distinction from the other term. The latter, however, is entirely exhausted within the relation and has no non-relative existence; this aspect provides for the relatedness or connection of the two terms.

To illustrate this logic *in concreto*. The attribute is not anything without substance; the latter is something by itself, self-existent and self-evident. Substance is not a mere name for the cluster of qualities; for, it must be already existent in its own right for the cluster to form. Spirit may be understood as the ultimate or only Substance, the prius of all things. The cause is free from and superior to the effect; the two are not on a par. In the ultimate analysis, only the Free can be the cause. If the cause transformed itself and were exhausted in the process, there would be annihilation and replacement, but no causation. The causal sequence has to be conceived as an emanation (*vivarta*), production without diminution of power. Spirit is the ultimate Free Cause. The Universal is not a mere name for the totality of particulars, nor is it dependent on them. Without the universal the different particulars cannot be related; they cannot even be compared or contrasted. The differences appear and have their being on a common platform. Differences presuppose unity and identity and not *vice versa*. The particulars depend on the universal without dividing it.

Spirit is free to manifest itself in numberless ways, and the manifestations are in and through Spirit. They are not integral parts of it. They indicate Spirit without constituting it. If they constituted it, Spirit would be nothing apart from finite things that are subject to decay and dissolution; it would not be transcendent. If, however, appearances did not indicate Spirit, we could not even be aware of its reality, much less reach it. It need not be feared that what does not constitute an entity cannot also indicate it or that only the differentia can distinguish a thing. Even an assumed mark can serve the purpose of definition. The bough of the tree may well indicate the location of the moon without belonging to it. The eagle perching on the chimney does serve to mark off and single out the particular house from among several, without forming a permanent fixture therein. What is essential is that the mark should not belong to any other, though it need not belong to this entity essentially. Likewise, the world of appearance may be indicative of Spirit without constituting it; the appearance may even be said to belong to Spirit in the sense of not belonging to any other.

Appearances are not different from the Absolute Spirit, though they are not one with it. The relation is neither reciprocal identity nor utter difference. It is what we have called Transcendent Identity. If not identical, Spirit and phenomenal things would fall asunder: Spirit would not be spirit of things, their reality. If there were no transcendence, things would be all, there would be no reality behind the appearances. The distinction between the real and appearance should not then arise. The Transcendence of Spirit is not to be mistaken for the illegitimate transcendent use of the Categories of thought, substance, causality, etc., beyond phenomena. It is the freeing of Being of the empirical accretions wrongly ascribed to it; it is not investing a concept with existence. We are already in intimate and inalienable contact with Spirit as Being.

IV. The Essential Nature of Spirit

The first stage in the discovery of Spirit is the transition from the world of appearance to its reality. The analysis of relation and the axiological argument based on value-judgments can but indicate the presence of the Spirit. We know that it is; we still do not have any definite apprehension of what it is. A cue to the nature of Spirit could be obtained if we analysed the nature of philosophical consciousness. And this, as I have stated before, is an attitude of the experiencing subject to the object or of a content to a consciousness that enjoys and evaluates it.

We could think of three, and possibly only three, attitudes of the experiencing subject to the content: one, in which the content determines the mode of attention : attention is, as it were, lost in the object, but not *vice versa*; or second, in which consciousness determines the content and not *vice versa*; or third, that in which the determination is either way, mutual. It might be thought that a fourth alternative is possible in a situation where neither determines the other. But this is clearly tantamount to denying all relation : the two things fall asunder, and we cannot even speak of them as two. Our a *priori* scheme thus yields only three modes of relation between consciousness and content. And these may be identified with Knowing, Willing and Feeling.

These three spirit-functions may be formulated thus. In knowing the Truth, our attitude is one of discovery or revelation of what is already present; the given is all. The object of knowledge, as in Truth, is unconstituted by the subjective act of knowing. There may arise a demand, as the goal of spiritual discipline, to realise the Truth as what is not, and need not be, known. The Thing-in-itself, the given, must be known without the mediation of the Categories of thought, without any trace of subjectivity—empirical and transcendental. The latter usually condition experience; and while from a practical point of view the object known through them may be valid, yet for a lover of the Truth, Pure Being must be known in its undistorted form. It is not a necessary part of the Truth that it should be known and declared as the truth. Nor does it suffer either by being known and declared. It may freely condescend to reveal itself. In Willing, the willed content is *wholly through* the act of willing not having any being without the latter. This is best exemplified in moral endeavour and in conscious imagination. The spiritual demand here will be to realise the *Pure Act* without any trace of the given, the other. In Feeling, content and consciousness, object and subject form an indistinguishable whole or unity; the separation of the one from the other would mean abstraction or hollowness and consequent loss of the feeling tone. As no empirical emotion, physical pleasures or even aesthetic joys can come up to this ideal, the spiritual demand would be to realise a state of perfect amplitude or Fullness of Feeling as Bliss (*paripūrṇatā* or *ānanda*).

The justification for holding that the nature of philosophical consciousness defines the nature of Spirit is that philosophy is the most significant expression of the human spirit. And Spirit is not another entity but essentially identical with the human : Man shorn of his adventitious and apparent characteristics is indeed Spirit. If this were not accepted, we shall have been left with no means of understanding and appreciating Spirit. It would be utterly foreign to us.

As a point of confirmation, it may be noted that all the great philosophies and religions of the world speak of the Triune Nature of Godhead. In spite of the admitted difficulty in giving a rational (conceptual) explanation of it, the doctrine of Trinity has been held as a vital definition of Godhead in deeper Christianity. In Buddhism we have the *Trikāya* conception of the Buddha. And the Vedānta conception of Brahman as *Sat*, *Cit* and *Ānanda* stands, I venture to suggest, for the three functions of Knowledge, Willing and Feeling. Spirit is Truth or

Knowledge; Spirit is Freedom or Will; Spirit is Bliss or Feeling. Each is *sui generis*, a Self : each is identical with Spirit (*Brahman*) wholly, and not a part or a predicate of it. It would indeed be less of a mistake to take them denotatively as things or substances. The three are not synonymous; their difference is not verbal. Pure Being, Act (Freedom) and Bliss are equally and fully Brahman. This does not mean a plurality of Absolutes, as there is no conceptual distinction; all these denote one entity, though in different ways. Brahman is their inexpressible substantial unity.

V. Spirit as the Basic Value and Basis of all Values

The Philosophy of Spirit is no speculative luxury. It is not for the satisfaction of a theoretic curiosity. Philosophy is not practical in any narrow sense; it would not solve any one problem in particular. But it is at the basis of every human activity, and it would solve not one but all problems. Realisation of Spirit is the realisation of all Values, as it is Truth, Freedom and Bliss. It is not only a vision of reality, but a consummation of life as well.

Even in the empirical sphere, the philosophy of spirit has great value. It is necessary to realise that our empirical differences exhibited in the political, social and cultural modes of life are but the outward expression of different ideologies or metaphysical premises. Any attempt to eliminate or stifle these basic and genuine differences succeeds in creating bitterness and competition. The cultural differences have not only to be tolerated but accepted in humility of spirit and fostered.

Owing to the phenomenal discoveries in science and their practical application, the peoples of the world have been brought together; the geographical and physical oneness of the world has been brought home to us. But our divergences and rivalries have also increased tremendously; war has become chronic and global in its proportions. The present-day world lacks unity and good will; it has no soul or spirit to animate and unify it.

A vicious materialistic philosophy produces unrest, strife and bitterness among men, as it is based on egoistic premises—appropriation and domination. Only a spiritual philosophy can serve as the basis of a world-culture. The essence of this consists in the utter negation of all egoity and the realisation of the unity of all being. It is only Absolutism of Spirit that can make for the fundamental unity of existence and at the same time allow for the differences that are exhibited in the great cultural groups of the world. The transcendence of Spirit means its freedom from every empirical standpoint and universality. Different ways of realising the Spirit are quite compatible with its universality.

8.2 THE CONCEPT OF PHILOSOPHY*

It must indeed appear odd to non-philosophers that we should be discussing, after indulging in philosophical activity for some thousands of years, what must appear as a preliminary question, the nature of Philosophy. The lack of agreement among philosophers on fundamentals is another source of vexation. There does not seem to be, in principle, any solid basis for agreement. I may make a preliminary observation that not only there are different philosophical systems, but different concepts of philosophy underlying them. It is not the case that all or some of them subscribe to a common concept of philosophy and only differ in their doctrinal content, in the way they elaborate and develop the common concept. If that were so, the differences would be traceable solely to defective logic or clumsy deductions. And being a procedural defect, this should be amenable to correction by closer attention to rules of logic and by discussion. Curiously, debate and discussions do not remove the philosophical differences; they only serve to highlight them. Nothing is more common in philosophical discussions than to find the disputants emerging at the end of the discussion with their differences more accentuated. If a neutral logic acceptable to all had been available to us, the differences would have been composed long ago. Deficiency of disinterestedness or of logical skill does not appear to be sufficient to explain lack of unanimity. It would be truer to say that our logical and empirical differences are themselves the necessary expressions of our metaphysical differences, ultimate standpoints. The concept of philosophy at the back of each philosophy is like the seed of which the philosophical system is the grown-up plant. It could be demonstrated, without calling for excessive ingenuity, that historically several conceptions of philosophy have been entertained by philosophers. The differing and conflicting answers given to this question in this seminar would but confirm this contention.

*Reprinted from BHU Darśana Series, *The Concept of Philosophy*, Banaras Hindu University, 1968.

This consideration should prove of help in understanding why the elucidation of the concept of philosophy is more difficult than the exposition of a philosophical system. For, the former is a question of the second order, of a deeper layer underlying the overt and avowed one In a sense, therefore, the question regarding the concept of philosophy is a philosophy of the history of philosophy or a philosophy of philosophy. It stands on a deeper level of reflective consciousness. Not only do we philosophise (or take note of the historical systems) but we are further led to the principle or pattern behind this.

Instances of philosophy occur first, and this enables us to raise a general question regarding its nature. Metaphysics as a natural disposition is cultivated or indulged in, almost inevitably, irresistibly. The history of philosophy, whether Indian or Greek or Chinese, would tell us that as soon as man had attained a reasonable command over nature to allow him some leisure and had cultivated the arts, especially poetry, philosophy dawned. Man began asking questions about the world around him, about his own origin and destiny. The philosophising was natural, not deliberately or artificially simulated. In a game or in mathematics, one starts with precise definitions, postulates and operational rules and develops the subject. The "postulation pattern" is totally foreign to philosophy as it is to any genuine and serious concern of man. The poet does not ask "what is poetry" before breaking out into poetry. One does not ask what is language and what are the rules of syntax before using language. It is indeed a misfortune for philosophy that the mathematical or natural science mode of knowledge was held before it as a norm to emulate. Metaphysics as a natural disposition has always been with man. We do not deliberately go about manufacturing it. We can only become explicitly self-conscious of this. Philosophy which begins as a speculative and interpretative activity grows to maturity through self-reflection and self-awareness. This I think is a unique feature of philosophy. And only from this maturity of self-reflection can we understand philosophy.

In explication of the nature of philosophical consciousness, I pose two questions principally :

1. What features distinguish an admittedly philosophical investigation from others ? Can we find any common

ground, either some basic tenet or method or attitude which marks off philosophy from other disciplines ? That is, what makes any enquiry philosophical ?

2. Why do philosophies differ ? Are their differences resolvable or are they ultimate and incommensurable ?

The two questions almost run into each other, and I shall not make any serious attempt to keep them separate.

In answering these questions, I naturally rely on the history of philosophy. This supplies samples or instances of philosophical consciousness, its exercise *in concreto*. But my method is not historical. I do not think that the question "what is Philosophy" is answered by tracing the genetic development of philosophy from its crude beginnings and by piecing together the different stages. For one thing, it can rightly be contended that this process is a continuing one and is not yet completed. The whole picture is not present before us. The piecing together of different stages and processes is itself possible because of a pattern or a whole into which we fit the various stages and steps. A philosophy is presupposed in the historical construction, which, however, is offered as an explanation of that philosophy.

The phenomenological or eidetic method of analysing the content or structure of each idea or sphere of ideas from within, from its authentic and autonomous standpoint, promises more fruitful results. But there does not seem to be a philosophy idea, a general and abstract notion. Each philosophy is a unique activity of interpretation through pre-suppositions in its speculative (or metaphysical) phase, and the explicit awareness of these pre-suppositions in its fuller and mature reflective phase.

Throughout this paper I am maintaining that the concept of philosophy is nothing but the exposition of the philosophical consciousness as concretely exemplified in all the historical systems of philosophy. My approach is more existentialist than phenomenological. Any one who has not practised philosophy himself or has not closely associated himself with it would find it empty and elusive. My concern is with the philosophy situation, and not with an idea. The concept of philosophy, if it is taken to mean a logical idea with a dictionary meaning or an accepted differentia, is misleading. I believe that although a positive definition of philosophy is not possible, it is, however, feasible to indicate some of the features which distinguish philosophy from other investigations.

Attempts have been made and will be made to deny philosophy, or to assimilate it, by reduction, to the logic of sciences or the elucidation of the usage of words. The nature of philosophy "provokes" these attempts, very much like the innocence of the lamb which 'incites' assaults on itself. Philosophy claims to convey knowledge of things terribly important and is meant as a discourse much in the same way as science or literature or religion. It uses the forms of knowledge and is clothed in the same linguistic garb as the other disciplines. This may explain why philosophy has been identified with these and some of them in turn mistaken for philosophy.

Such attempts to deny philosophy or assimilate it to other investigations are question-begging and inconsistent. Although they fail conspicuously in their avowed objective of eliminating metaphysics, they, however, perform one singular service. They serve to disengage genuine philosophy from disciplines with which it is generally confused. They serve to extricate philosophy and help it to regain its authenticity.

II

What strikes me as the most conspicuous characteristic of philosophical investigation is that it is a reflective awareness. By reflection I mean the act of turning upon oneself and one's doings. It may also be described as criticism or sitting on judgment over things—a kind of regressive movement.

We can imagine a world in which people said or did things without, at any time, being explicitly aware of what they said or did, steeped in stupor and dullness, like the lotos-eaters. If all our perceptions were completely in accord with existent things, there would be no occasion for reflection, no need for examination of oneself. On the practical side, if all our desires were satisfied as they arose in us, i.e. if there were no frustration, there would be no disappointment. Hence no need to ponder and to take stock of the situation. If a machine or contraption were running smoothly without hitch, we would not care to know how it works and what is the economy of its parts. Because our perceptions are not always veridical, and only few of our desires are satisfied and even they not wholly we become reflective.

Our attention is deflected from the objective to the subjective.

Unlike Poetry or Art which have their origin in wonder and ecstasy, Philosophy begins with doubt and disappointment. The basic keys with which philosophy operates are the "the Real" and "the False". In the history of Philosophy, this duality takes various forms—

Being and Non-Being (Becoming);
Archetypes and Copies;
Form and Matter;
God and Finite Self;
Noumenon and Phenomena.

Even the positivist who denies metaphysics uses such terms as true and pseudo-propositions.

Philosophy is essentially evaluative, not organisational or descriptive. It may be doubted whether even in organising (stringing together) some data or in describing them we are not importing into them our slants and bias. Is any neutral description or statement possible, although this may be held out as desirable? Criticism would show, as Kant has shown conclusively, that we cannot organise unorganised materials, if we were not already armed with some categories or patterns under which to organise them. This seems fairly obvious.

Though innocently stated as a description of facts, every philosophical system is an evaluation of things or a prescription to view them in a particular way. We do not acquire this prescription out of empirical data by abstraction or generalisation. The empirical data are far too neutral and pointless to yeild a standpoint or bias. Nor do we deliberately set about formulating them by postulation in a sportive way like the rules of a game. Philosophers are not conscious of their presuppositions and standpoints, and believe them to be objective and real, until they are forced in the open by other equally plausible but conflicting points of view. In Science, a dispute regarding rival hypotheses can, at least in principle, be settled by an appeal to sense-experience in the last resort. In Philosophy, hypotheses cannot be proved or disproved by any such appeal. Disputes become interminable conflicts. Dialectic is endemic to philosophy. There is no possibility of alighting upon an empirical fact which will upset any philosophy. For every fact is interpreted by it and is itself thus conditoned. Every philosophy is an elaboration, with the help of logic and language, of a basic stand or pattern, which validates other things and is not itself validated or subjected to proof. Kant would call this an Idea of Reason. Of this he says: "No actual experience has ever been completely adequate to an Idea of Reason, yet to it every actual experience belongs."

The intricacy and skill with which a particular metaphysical stand is elaborated and set forth cannot be offered as proof or justification of the premise on which it stands. A fine superstructure cannot be a proof of the title to the ground on which the edifice is erected. The elaboration and rigour of a philosophy only show that the parts of the system are consistent and coherent; it only proves that the consequences and implications are correctly drawn, and not that the basic principle or premise is rationally justified. I suspect that Hegel makes much of this implicatory elaboration and takes it as proof or validation of the unproved original stand. It is as if a clever witness or advocate took up an arbitrary stand and consistently stuck to it throughout the cross-examination and trial.

There is some merit in this, as many of the philosophical systems suffer from the blemish of not being internally coherent. Indian systems of philosophy are remarkably free from looseness and internal inconsistency, as each system has been cultivated for centuries by some of the best minds of the time. It can be shown that each philosophy, Indian and Western, is the self-expression of a specific metaphysical stand. If we are able to grasp the specific stand to which it is committed it should be possible to spell out all its tenets in a systematic manner. I have attempted this deduction with reference to many systems of Indian Thought. It should also be a fascinating study to give deduction of all the possible types of philosophical stands or viewpoints. A schematic conspectus is not implausible or even insignificant.

Coherence within a closed system is not proof or justification of the basic stand; at best, the elaboration is a self-expression and self-justification; and we become aware of the stand itself only through its unfoldment, in its empirical exposition and application. It is clear, then, that all philosophy moves on two planes or levels—the specific metaphysical stand and its empirical elaboration through logic and language. It is this amphibious nature of philosophy that makes for its evaluating and self-expressive function. It also distinguishes it from science in which it is possible to make propositions without explicit reference to the specific standpoint or subjective attitude, from which the proposition is made. Even in science, a completely empirical or a purely descriptive statement cannot be made; but the direction is towards such an ideal.

III

It must now be sufficiently clear that the key terms, Knowledge, Proof, Reasoning, Evidence, etc., used in philosophy and science are not of the same meaning. They are differently oriented. I wholly accept this part of modern linguistic analysis, but draw a different conclusion. My interest is not to deny philosophy, but to disentangle it from its close embrace with other disciplines—science, art and religion.

Although philosophy is a species of theoretic consciousness and we speak of it as giving us knowledge and we also attempt to reason and establish certain propositions and these are couched in the usual logical and linguistic forms, they should, however, be sharply distinguished from the procedure of science or mathematics. In the previous section, I dwelt at some length on the nature of philosophical knowledge. Scientific knowledge and investigation is definitely of a different genre. The confusion between them is inexcusable and should not have occurred at all. Not only laymen but philosophers themselves have been guilty of this confusion.

Logically, there should not have been the confusion. Factually and historically, however, the confusion is there and is a pervasive feature. It appears to be natural, unpremeditated and inevitable, unpreventable. This happens because we use the same language (verbal forms) and logical modes of expression, although in uncommon ways. We get over this confusion, as we grow circumspect, as we become aware of the true nature of philosophy.

But for this misadventure and its termination we would have remained ignorant of the nature of Philosophy. Only in this process of transition, in its being realised as *not* science, or mathematics or art does philosophy attain its maturity. In annulling its self-alienation, does it become aware of itself as philosophy.

The second consideration is that as each philosophy is the conceptual elaboration of an ultimate metaphysical standpoint and as argumentation or discourse is applicable within it and not outside it, every philosophical system is a metaphysical monad. This leads to certain very embarrassing paradoxes. If each metaphysical system, is monadic and incommensurable with every other system, how is discourse possible? How can we argue and convince others? Should we give it up as futile? We say : "Tastes differ and there is no arguing about them." Should we say likewise with regard to philosophy that it is a matter of spiritual taste and temperament?

This situation certainly obtains in religion. There could practically be no conversion or significant dialogue among religions which are authentically rooted, each in its basic stand.

'That philosophical systems differ basically and remain incommensurate' is in manifest conflict with our knowledge that they are not so. For, if each person is committed to one system and has no traffic with others, how does he know that there are other systems and that they are incommensurable. At least there is one person who has been able to go beyond the monadic shackles and he is addressing others to do likewise. Hence, the incommensurability and monadicism of metaphysical systems cannot be the last word. Besides the unique features which mark off each philosophy from the others, there should be some inexpressible common ground on which they stand.

We may here profitably consider two or three attempts to reach a stage higher than metaphysics as a natural disposition. One would be the obvious attempt to get rid of all metaphysics and pretence of knowing the supersensuous altogether. I have in view the stupendous and most consistent attempt of the Mādhyamika to abjure all speculative metaphysics, *dṛṣṭis* or philosophical stand-points by realising their futility. The relentless Mādhyamika dialectic assails each theory and through *reductio ad absurdum* arguments shows that it is a *cul de sac*; its conclusion is right provided you grant its premise, which, however, is the thing in dispute. Both positive and negative views or a combination or a denial of them, all possible modes of speculative metaphysics, are dialectically refuted. What is left over is the *Śūnya*. But what is *Śūnyatā*? Is it Being or Knowledge? Neither the one nor the other; for this would be to get into the same rut of metaphysics. The only safe answer is that *Śūnyatā* is the contentless dialectical awareness itself. Dialectic or criticism is true philosophy. The Mādhyamika claims to be the high tribunal before which all metaphysical systems without exception are arraigned and condemned. The Mādhyamika dialectic is a philosophy of philosophies.

The Kantian answer, though not so consistent, is on similar lines. We have and can have no legitimate ground to stretch the categories of the understanding beyond their meaningful application in the field of phenomena; nor do we have any non-sensuous (intellectual) intuition of the noumenon. Despairing of any *theoretic knowledge* of the noumenal entities, Kant has recourse to practical reason. The exercise of moral will vouchsafes for him this freedom from mechanical necessity and all empiricality.

The Christian Theologian has inherited a mistrust of philosophy, for which even otherwise he has not much use. Karl Barth is an extreme instance of this. Scriptural revelation provides the nexus to the existence of super-sensuous entities, and faith sustains the validity of these truths. Philosophy, when availed of, performs the useful function of rational justification and filling up of gaps.

These attempts are not only anti-metaphysical, but also anti-intellectual. For, do they not have recourse to practical reason or faith for access to the ultimate truths

The Vedānta has an initial theological bias. It is aware that on purely rational considerations it is not possible to decide among rival metaphysical theories; for each theory claims to give the correct and only explanation of things, and yet they are in mutual conflict. Though the Vedānta avails of revelation to break through the barrier of dogmatic metaphysics, it is not anti-metaphysical, nor anti-intellectual.

We do possess, according to the Vedānta, an unconditionally immediate, non-conceptual knowledge of Pure Being. It is Knowledge *through being* the thing known, knowledge from 'within' and not knowledge by representation through the medium of categories and concepts. Pure Being (Brahman) is the ultimate ground of all particular beings. It is implied in every cognition.

Could this awareness of ontic being be called knowledge? There is no valid reason for denying its cognitive character, simply because it is not arrived through essence and hence is not mediate and formal. This bias in favour of the circumstantial and indirect mode of knowledge is itself question-begging. The opposite may well be the case. Only direct Knowledge, without the use of conceptual representation, guarantees the absolute truth of our cognition. In all other cases there is scope for deviation and distortion. As thought cannot hang in the air and is thought of something given, direct acquaintance provides the basis for knowledge by description. The Advaita Vedānta is an attempt to break through metaphysical theories to capture the direct immensity of the ontic being. Dialectical criticism, by showing the inadequacy or conceptual constructions, leads to the ground—Pure Being—on which these constructions are made. Unlike the Mādhyamika Śūnya, here we have a positive and primordial awareness of Being and not Nothingness.

Regarding the value of philosophical investigation, it needs to be stated that being an autonomous activity it is not subservient to any other pursuit or interest. It is not a means, but an end in itself. Philosophical knowledge is liberation of the human mind from every kind of narrowness and prejudice. It is freedom itself.

9. COMPLETE BIBLIOGRAPHY OF THE WRITINGS OF PROFESSOR T. R. V. MURTI

Books

Ajñāna: Co-author with G. R. Malkani with R. Das (Murti's Contribution pp. 115 to 226). London: Luzac and Co., 1933.

The Central Philosophy of Buddhism. London: George Allen and Unwin Ltd. 1st Edn. 1955, 2nd Edn. 1960; Reprinted 1966, 1970, 1974. Paper Back Edition, 1980.

Papers and Articles

"The Rational Basis of Advaitism," *The Philosophical Quarterly* (shortened henceforward as *P. Q.*), Indian Institute of Philosophy, Amalner, India, 1930.

"The Neutral Monism of Bertrand Russell," *Banaras Hindu University Magazine*, 1931.

"Logic and Internal Relations," *P. Q.*, 1931.

"George Santayana's Doctrine of Essence," (2 Articles), *B.H.U. Magazine*, (Two Issues), 1932.

"Are Difference and Identity Relations ?," *P. Q.*, 1932.

"Nāgārjuna's Refutation of Motion and Rest," *P.Q.*, October, 1933.

"The Theory of Judgment in the Indian Systems" (1), *P. Q.*, 1933.

"*The Vibhrama Viveka of Maṇḍana Miśra*," (A Review), *P. Q.*, 1933.

"*The Six Ways of Knowing*" of Dr. D. M. Datta (Review Article), *P. Q.*, 1933.

"The Universal and the Particular," *P. Q.*, 1933.

"Knowing, Feeling and Willing as Functions of Consciousness," *P. Q.*, January 1934.

"Perception and its Object," *P. Q.*, vol. 5. 1, April, 1934.

"Types of Indian Realism" (1), *P. Q.*, 1934.

"Types of Indian Realism" (2), *P. Q.*, 1935.

"Illusion as Confusion of Subjective Functions," *P. Q.*, 1935.

"The Development of the Philosophy of Spinoza," (Review Article), *P. Q.*, vol. 11. 1, July, 1935.

"The Concept of Philosophy," *P. Q.*, April, 1936.

"The Place of Feeling in Conduct in the Vedānta," *P. Q.*, 1937.
"The Gita Conception of Philosophy and Religion," in the *Journal of the Banaras Hindu University*, July, 1938.
"The Conception of Body", *P. Q.*, vol. 15. 1, April, 1939.
"*Indian Realism* of Dr. Jadunath Sinha," (Review Article), *P. Q.*, 1940.
"The Nature and Value of Metaphysics," *P. Q.*, 1942.
"*A Study of Hindu Doctrines* of Rene Guénon," (Review Article) in the *Journal of the Banaras Hindu University*, Vol. 9, October, 1943.
"The Two Traditions in Indian Philosophy," in *The University of Ceylon Review*, vol. 10. 3, July, 1952.
"The Metaphysical Schools of Buddhism," in *The History of Philosophy, Eastern and Western*, vol. 1, London: George Allen and Unwin Ltd., 1952.
"Radhakrishnan and Buddhism," in *The Philosophy of Sarvepalli Radhakrishnan* (Library of Living Philosophers), New York: Tudor Publishing Company, 1952.
"The Philosophy of Spirit," in *The Contemporary Indian Philosophy*, 2nd Edn., (Library of Philosophy). London : George Allen and Unwin Ltd., 1952.
"The Rise of the Philosophical Schools" in the *Cultural Heritage of India*, vol. 3, Calcutta: Ramakrishna Mission, 1953.
"Buddhism and Contemporary Indian Thought," *Revue Internatinale de Philosophie*, No. 37, Fasc. 3, 1956.
"The Contribution of Buddhism to Philosophy," in the *Symposium on Buddhism's Contribution to Art, Letters and Philosophy*, 2500 Buddha Jayanti Celebrations, Govt. of India, 1956.
"Hinduism and Buddhism," in *The Traditional Cultures of South-East Asia* (pp. 210-271). Sponsored by the UNESCO, Madras : Orient Longmans, 1958.
"The Two Definitions of Brahman in the Advaita," in the *K. C. Bhattacharyya Memorial Volume*, Indian Institute of Philosophy, Amalner, India, 1958.
"Some Thoughts on the Indian Philosophy of Language." Presidential Address, Indian Philosophical Congress, 37th Session. Chandigarh, 1963.
"The Concept of Philosophy," in *The Concept of Philosophy*, (Seminar Papers), The Centre of Advanced Study in Philosophy, B.H.U., Varanasi, 1968.

"Vedanta and Buddhism," (Seminar Papers), The Centre of Advanced Study in Philosophy, B.H.U., 1968.

"The World and the Individual in Indian Religious Thought", in *The Status of the Individual in East and West*, University of Hawaii, Honolulu, 1968, p. 199-216.

"The Concept of Freedom as Redemption," in the *Types of Redemption*, *Numen*, Suppl. 18, Amsterdam: E. J. Brill, 1970.

"Nature and Function of Reason" (Inaugural Address), A Summary in the *Ānvikṣikī*, Centre of Advanced Study in Philosophy, B. H. U., Varanasi, 1973.

"Samvṛti and Paramārtha in Mādhyamika and Advaita Vedānta," in the *Two Truths of Buddhism and Vedānta*, Holland, Dodrecht: Reidel Publishing Company, 1973.

"Some Comments on the Philosophy of Language in the Indian Context," in the *Journal of Indian Philosophy*, No. 2, Dodrecht: Reidel Publishing Company, 1974.

"Knowledge and Truth," Presidential Address, Golden Jubilee Session of the Indian Philosophical Congress, Delhi, 1975. Pd. in *Knowledge, Culture and Value*, Part I. Delhi: Motilal Banarsidass.

"Conquest of Suffering," unpublished Paper. Read at a Seminar in Canberra, Australia, 1957.

"Reason and Revelation in Vedānta," *Journal of the Madras University*, January 1980.

"The Concept of Appearance," *Journal of the Madras University*, January 1980.

"Self-Luminosity," *Journal of the University of Madras*, Vol. LIII, Nos. 1 & 2, June & July 1981.

INDEX